Slavery

STANLEY M. ELKINS

Slavery

A Problem in American Institutional and Intellectual Life

Third Edition, Revised

THE UNIVERSITY OF CHICAGO PRESS

CHICAGO AND LONDON

To

DOROTHY

The University of Chicago Press, Chicago 60637
The University of Chicago Press, Ltd., London

© 1959, 1968, 1976 by The University of Chicago
All rights reserved. Third Edition Published 1976
Printed in the United States of America
80 79 78 77 76 987654321

Library of Congress Cataloging in Publication Data

Elkins, Stanley M.
　Slavery: a problem in American institutional and
intellectual life.

　Includes bibliographical references and index.
　1.　Slavery in the United States.　2.　Slavery in the
United States—Condition of slaves.　I.　Title.
E441.E44　1976　　　301.44'93'0973　　　76–615
ISBN 0–226–20476–6
ISBN 0–226–20477–4 pbk.

Contents

[v]

Preface to the Third Edition

The original edition of this work has not been altered here, in that its text remains as it was when first published in 1959. But two new parts have been added to the original four, thus extending the text by some forty per cent, in recognition that the subject itself has grown immensely during the intervening years. A word or two on these additions may be called for.

By the late 1960's a substantial body of critical commentary on my book had accumulated, and Professor Ann J. Lane undertook at that time to assemble some leading examples of it in a collection to which she invited me to contribute. I did so, and the resulting volume, under her editorship, was published in 1971 as *The Debate over Slavery: Stanley Elkins and his Critics* by the University of Illinois Press. The essay I prepared for that occasion, "Slavery and Ideology," reappears as Part V of the present edition.

In that essay I had two objects. One was to give due recognition to what had been written about my own work, and to amplify at certain points some of my original intentions. The other was to attempt a prediction on the form which future discussion of the subject might take. Work by such scholars as David Brion Davis, George Fredrickson, Winthrop Jordan, and Eric Foner has given substance to my guess that at least one major realm of interest would be that of ideology. But as things turned out, it was hardly the only one. By the end of 1974 it was apparent that another area—black culture—had come to predominate over all other concerns in the study of American slavery.

This absorption with culture, and my belief that it was approaching a kind of climax, provided the occasion for the other addition to this book. It seemed to me that the work published on slavery in the 1970's was of sufficient importance and impact, and had so modified the shape of the subject since I myself first wrote about it, that some attempt on my part to assess what had happened was imperative. The resulting essay, "The Two Arguments on Slavery," prepared during the summer of 1975 and published in the December 1975 issue of *Commentary,* appears herein as Part VI.

The entire subject of slavery, judging from the intense interest of scholars and public alike, is presently in a state of extraordinary vitality. I am aware that there are aspects of it which I have left largely untouched here. The American abolition movement, for example, is almost certain to receive some penetrating new scrutiny in the time just ahead. Although I have given some attention to abolitionism in Part V, others will soon be giving it far more, and at some point a major consideration of their work will certainly be in order.

The Appendixes that were added to the Second Edition (1968) have been dropped from the present one, as has Appendix B ("The 'Profitability' of Slavery"), which appeared in the First. Only the "Essay on Materials and Method" has been retained from the Appendixes of the original edition. A new Index has been compiled to accommodate the material in Parts V and VI.

Northampton, Massachusetts
November 1975

I

An Introduction: Slavery as a Problem in Historiography

Despite the vast amount of writing on American Negro slavery and the great variety of temperaments and talents that have been brought to the work, the very spiritual agony inherent in the subject itself imposes on the result a certain simplicity of organization and a kind of persistent rhythm. The primary categories of organization for over a century have continued to be those of right and wrong. To the present day, the rhythm of "right" and "wrong" which characterized ante-bellum discourse on the subject of slavery has retained much of its original simplicity and vigor. Certain inhibitions, moreover, have stood guard throughout. There is a painful touchiness in all aspects of the subject; the discourse contains almost too much immediacy, it makes too many connections with present problems. How a person thinks about Negro slavery historically makes a great deal of difference here and now; it tends to locate him morally in relation to a whole range of very immediate political, social, and philosophical issues which in some way refer back to slavery. It may be just as well that one does not move capriciously in matters of conscience. But that is what makes it so difficult to recognize the point of diminishing returns in a discourse which has been carried on for so long by so many distinguished advocates. The urgency, beyond any doubt, is still there. But is there anything more to say that has not been said already?

There is a coerciveness about the debate over slavery: it continues to be the same debate. The same tests for the rightness or wrongness of slavery remain in use year in and year out. Although few inquiries, from the viewpoint of sheer research, have

[1]

been conducted with greater energy, the sources have now been mined and remined; it is hard to imagine major veins of primary material lying still untapped. Has a settlement on this debate been reached? Are other debates, on the same subject but on different grounds, still possible? For light on these questions, we should examine more closely the grounds upon which men have considered the subject in the past.

I

THE OLD DEBATE

In ante-bellum times, the polemical works on slavery—the proslavery and antislavery arguments—clearly predominated. They set the tone for everything else.[1] There was almost nothing that could be called "objective" in the very strictest sense. Still, there was material produced in this period which contained a great

---

[1] The bulk of the polemical literature is overwhelming. The most widely circulated of such material, on the antislavery side, included the following: Albert Barnes, *An Inquiry into the Scriptural Views of Slavery* (Philadelphia: Perkins & Purves, 1846); James G. Birney, *A Collection of Valuable Documents, Being Birney's Vindication of Abolitionists* . . . (Boston, 1836); George Bourne, *A Condensed Anti-Slavery Bible Argument* (New York: S. W. Benedict, 1845); William Ellery Channing, *Emancipation* (New York: American Anti-Slavery Society, 1841); George B. Cheever, *The Guilt of Slavery and the Crime of Slaveholding* . . . (Boston: J. P. Jewett, 1860); Lydia Maria Child, *An Appeal in Favor of That Class of Americans Called Africans* (Boston: Allen & Ticknor, 1833); Charles Elliott, *Sinfulness of American Slavery* (2 vols.; Cincinnati, 1850); William Lloyd Garrison, *Selections from* . . . *Writings and Speeches* . . . (Boston: R. F. Wallcut, 1852); Joshua R. Giddings, *Speeches in Congress* (Cleveland: O. Jewett, Proctor & Worthington, 1853); William Goodell, *Slavery and Anti-Slavery* (New York: W. Harned, 1852); William Jay, *Miscellaneous Writings on Slavery* (Boston: J. P. Jewett, 1853); Theodore Parker, *Discourses on Slavery* (2 vols.; Boston, 1863); Wendell Phillips, *Speeches, Lectures, Letters* (Boston: Lee & Shepard, 1863); Parker Pillsbury, *The Church as It Is, or the Forlorn Hope of Slavery* (Concord, N.H.: Republican Press Assoc., 1885); Charles Sumner, *Works* (15 vols.; Boston: Lee & Shepard, 1870 ff.); LaRoy Sunderland, *Anti-Slavery Manual, Containing a Collection of Facts and Arguments on American Slavery* (New York: S. W. Benedict, 1837); Theodore Dwight Weld, *American Slavery as It Is: Testimony of a Thousand Witnesses* (New York: American Anti-Slavery Society, 1839). (Parker, Phillips, and Sumner are compilations of material earlier circulated in pamphlet form.) For the proslavery side, see below, Part IV, section 7.

deal of specific information and which is therefore suitable for historical uses. One type of effort in this line had to do with treatises on, and compilations of, the legal codes embracing slavery. "History" as a specific art was not very well developed then, and the discipline most likely to impose some kind of objective standards on work dealing with slavery was the discipline of the law. A fairly good and dependable tradition existed for this purpose. Although the writers and compilers were themselves by no means free from polemical intentions (indeed, they were for the most part inspired by them) the requirements of fact operated upon them in such a way that they left a number of works which are still of great value. The two leading examples were produced by men whose commitments to the subject itself were at opposite poles. Thomas R. R. Cobb's *Inquiry into the Law of Slavery* was the work of a Georgia jurist, and John Codman Hurd's *Law of Freedom and Bondage* that of a New Englander of strong abolitionist leanings. They are equally useful and equally dependable today.[2] The other line of effort in some way qualifying as historical evidence was that which produced the eyewitness accounts of ante-bellum slavery. Such accounts were both hostile and sympathetic in nature. It is perhaps best that each kind be given equal weight, as evidence in the judicial sense must always be, and the best presumption probably is that none of these observers was lying about the facts as he saw them. Different facts impressed different people, of course. But Fanny Kemble, Nehemiah Adams, Sir Charles Lyell, Susan Dabney, and Frederick Law Olmsted were men and women of character, and the things they wrote had character also; much is gained and not much lost on the provisional operating principle that they were all telling the truth.[3]

[2] Works based on legal compilations include Thomas R. R. Cobb, *An Inquiry into the Law of Negro Slavery in the United States of America* (Philadelphia: T. & J. W. Johnson, 1858); John Codman Hurd, *The Law of Freedom and Bondage in the United States* (Boston: Little, Brown, 1858); George M. Stroud, *A Sketch of the Laws Relating to Slavery in the Several States* . . . (Philadelphia: H. Longstreth, 1856); Jacob D. Wheeler, *Practical Treatise on the Law of Slavery* (New York: A. Pollock, Jr., 1837); William Goodell, *The American Slave Code* (New York: American & Foreign Anti-Slavery Society, 1853); Richard Hildreth, *Despotism in America* (Boston: O. Jewett, Proctor & Worthington, 1854).

[3] Kenneth Stampp made one side of this point in an article published in 1952. "The traveler in the South who viewed slavery with an entirely

Again, however, it was the polemic—or at least the heavy moral judgment—never very far below the surface, that ran through all of this. A strong moral bias, one way or the other, set the direction for just about anything that would be written on the subject in ante-bellum times.

---

open mind was rare indeed," he said, "but it does not necessarily follow that the only accurate reporters among them were those who viewed it sympathetically." "The Historian and Southern Negro Slavery," *American Historical Review,* LVII (April, 1952), 615. One must not only fully indorse this proposition but also reverse it; it does not follow that the only accurate reporters were the unsympathetic ones either.

Among the most useful of the travelers' and other eyewitness accounts are Nehemiah Adams, *A South-Side View of Slavery* (Boston: T. R. Marvin, and Sanborn, Carter, and Brazin, 1855); Frederika Bremer, *The Homes of the New World* (2 vols.; New York: Harper, 1853); J. S. Buckingham, *Slave States of America* (2 vols.; London: Fisher, Son & Co., 1842); William Chambers, *Things as They Are in America* (London: W. & R. Chambers, 1854) and *American Slavery and Colour* (London: W. & R. Chambers, 1857); George W. Featherstonhaugh, *Excursion through the Slave States* (New York: Harper, 1844); Basil Hall, *Travels in North America in the Years 1827 and 1828* (Edinburgh: Cadell, 1829); Joseph H. Ingraham, *The South-West, by a Yankee* (2 vols.; New York: Harper, 1835); Frances Anne Kemble, *Journal of a Residence on a Georgian Plantation in 1838–1839* (New York: Harper, 1863); Sir Charles Lyell, *A Second Visit to the United States of North America* (New York: Harper, 1849); Harriet Martineau, *Society in America* (2 vols.; London: Saunders & Otley, 1837); Frederick Law Olmsted, *A Journey in the Seaboard Slave States, with Remarks on Their Economy* (New York: Putnam, 1904), *A Journey through Texas* (New York: Edwards, 1857), *A Journey in the Back Country* (New York: Mason, 1860), and *The Cotton Kingdom: A Traveller's Observations on Cotton and Slavery in the American Slave States* (2 vols.; New York: Mason, 1861); James K. Paulding, *Slavery in the United States* (New York: Harper, 1836); William H. Russell, *My Diary North and South* (Boston: T. O. H. P. Burnham, 1863); Susan Dabney Smedes, *Memorials of a Southern Planter* (Baltimore: Cushings & Bailey, 1888).

To this material should be added whatever is dependable from the reminiscences and narratives of slaves themselves. Two such narratives are particularly convincing: David Wilson (ed.), *Narrative of Solomon Northrup* (Buffalo: Derby, Orton & Mulligan, 1853); and Kate E. R. Pickard, *The Kidnapped and the Ransomed, Being the Personal Recollections of Peter Still and His Wife Vina after Forty Years of Slavery* (Syracuse: W. T. Hamilton, 1856). Charles Stearns's *Narrative of Henry Box Brown* (1849) and *Life of J. Henson, Formerly a Slave* (Boston: A. D. Phelps, 1849) are heavily edited by abolitionists, though not entirely undepend-

Something of the sharpness and urgency of slavery as an issue was cut short by the termination of slavery as a fact. Throughout a good part of the postwar generation a moratorium on that subject was observed everywhere with surprising unanimity. The problem had in a practical sense been settled by the war and was superseded for the time being by the problems of reunion and reconciliation. The kind of moral ruthlessness in the North that had carried the antislavery standard into battle received a certain chastening afterward through the disillusioning experience of Reconstruction—an experience which, whatever else could be said of it, hardly had the moral simplicity of the crusade against slavery. The South had at least a reciprocal claim on the Northern conscience for the first time in many years. One of the results was that much literary energy during this period went into the staking-out of neutral ground upon which fraternal sentiments might again mingle: intersectional romance, the magnolia theme, antebellum chivalry, and the faithful retainer. By the 1880's the old-time abolitionist who had wept over *Uncle Tom's Cabin* in his youth could sit shedding furtive tears over "Marse Chan."[4]

Something else, meanwhile, had begun to develop and emerge: a tradition of historical scholarship, along with what has been called "nationalist" thinking and writing on problems of American history. "Nationalist" is a fairly accurate term for this thinking, if one considers it in the setting of the late eighties and nineties. For one thing, scholarship in itself, with the postwar development of historical seminars and graduate schools, had emerged as a value recognized and accepted to an extent wholly

---

able. Frederick Douglass' *My Bondage and My Freedom* (New York: Miller, Orton & Mulligan, 1855) is obviously not the work of an ordinary slave, but some of the author's insights into the slave system are very valuable. Two latter-day efforts to tell the story of slavery through interviews with former slaves are John B. Cade, "Out of the Mouths of Slaves," *Journal of Negro History*, XX (July, 1935), 294–337, and B. A. Botkin (ed.), *Lay My Burden Down* (Chicago: University of Chicago Press, 1945).

[4] Edward Channing related this story about Thomas Wentworth Higginson to Paul H. Buck. It is cited in Buck's *Road to Reunion* (Boston: Little, Brown, 1937), p. 235. Chapters viii and ix in that same book ("The South Begins To Write" and "The North Feels the Power of the Pen") contain much interesting material on the literary diplomacy, as it were, of the post-bellum rapproachment of North and South.

unknown in prewar times.[5] In addition, enough time had elapsed
by about the middle eighties that for the first time in decades (in
some ways, the first time ever) it became possible for the idea of
"American" history to operate on men's minds as something more
than an abstraction, as something comparable to the former concreteness of "North" and "South."

But with the full emergence of this tradition, in what spirit
would slavery be taken up once more? With the moral ground
having lain fallow for a generation and the subject now formally
protected behind the bulwarks of scholarship, how would slavery
be treated by the new "multivolume" historians—such writers as
Schouler, Von Holst, Rhodes, McMaster? Once more there
would be overtones very reminiscent of the abolitionists. With
some of the immediacy gone, it was possible to get at least a provisional consensus: with all the detachment in the world, no
scholar of principle could be expected in a new and enlightened
age to countenance human-chattel slavery.

The outstanding case is that of James Ford Rhodes. Despite
standards of scholarship which make his work still very useful,
Rhodes found it practically impossible not to take up the subject
once more on the terms set by the old-time polemics. Seeing slavery through the eyes of New England and the Middle West,
Rhodes began his treatment of it—in his *History,* the first two

[5] The seminar method had its beginnings in the 1870's at the University
of Michigan and at Harvard, though it was at Johns Hopkins in the
1880's that true graduate work first reached full development. The three
men most responsible for these beginnings, though not related, were all
named Adams. C. K. Adams at Michigan began an undergraduate seminar
in 1870–71, and by the 1880's had expanded it for graduate research in
source materials. When Adams went to Cornell as its president, he in-
stituted similar work there under Moses Coit Tyler. Henry Adams' students
at Harvard in the seventies included Henry Cabot Lodge, Henry Osborn
Taylor, J. Lawrence Laughlin, and Edward Channing. The key figure,
however, in pioneering American graduate study in history was the remarkable Herbert Baxter Adams. The products of his work, begun at
Johns Hopkins in the early eighties, included the famous "Johns Hopkins
University Studies" series, and a coterie of students who later made distinguished names for themselves as historians. They included Woodrow
Wilson, Frederick Jackson Turner, John Franklin Jameson, Charles M.
Andrews, and numerous others. See H. Hale Bellot, *American History
and American Historians* (London: University of London Press, 1952),
pp. 9–19.

volumes of which appeared in 1893—with a clear statement of moral position: slavery was fundamentally evil. He warned his readers that although his wish was "to describe the institution as it may have appeared before the war to a fair-minded man," his description could do no more than elaborate on the words of Henry Clay: "Slavery is a curse to the master and a wrong to the slave."[6]

Rhodes made a detailed indictment of the system. He attacked as an old heresy the assertion that ante-bellum slaves were on the whole "better fed, better clothed, and better lodged" than laborers in Northern cities and cited evidence that they were frequently overtasked to the point of physical breakdown. He showed their utter lack of protection in the matter of legal rights; he showed how the domestic slave trade, which separated husbands from wives and parents from children, made steady and pitiless assaults on whatever family life the slave might have; and he pictured the slave's helplessness against the aggressions of a brutal master. Rhodes pointed to numerous transactions in mulatto and quadroon girls for wanton purposes and to the corruption of plantation morals effected by the dalliance of the master and his sons with their female slaves—a fact which occasioned untold anguish to many Southern women. He emphasized the slave's degraded lot and his constant longing for freedom. And finally, in allocating responsibility for the system and its many immoralities, Rhodes did not restrict it to the planter class alone; he insisted that an entire society, North and South, must share the guilt. James Ford Rhodes thus did much to establish the pattern for whatever would subsequently be written on the subject of American Negro slavery.[7]

[6] James Ford Rhodes, *History of the United States from the Compromise of 1850 to the Final Restoration of Home Rule at the South in 1877* (New York: Macmillan, 1893), I, 303.

[7] *Ibid.*, pp. 303–83. There were other multivolume histories produced during the period, reflecting attitudes on slavery quite similar to those of Rhodes: e.g., James Schouler, *History of the United States of America under the Constitution* (7 vols.; Washington: W. H. & O. H. Morrison, 1880–1913); Hermann Eduard Von Holst, *The Constitutional and Political History of the United States* (8 vols.; Chicago: Callaghan, 1876–92); John Bach McMaster, *A History of the People of the United States from the Revolution to the Civil War* (8 vols.; New York: D. Appleton, 1883–1913). Neither Holst nor Schouler, both concerned with political and constitution-

By his own generation, Rhodes's work was accepted with surprising equanimity. His account of the years leading to the Civil War was praised by both North and South as impartial and fair, and his attack on slavery aroused remarkably little hostility even in the South. One reason for this was the growing conviction among a younger generation of Southerners that the future of the New South lay in industrial progress rather than in the rural conservatism of the old plantation regime. A number of rising young historians of the South—such men as William P. Trent, Woodrow Wilson, and William E. Dodd—were quite willing to write off the institution their fathers had fought for as hopelessly reactionary. Rhodes's treatment of the postwar period, moreover, pictured Southern affairs in a light that seemed to the South most reasonable. He deplored carpetbag reconstruction and the imposition of Negro suffrage by Federal power and was willing to recognize the South's right to deal with the "race question" in its own way. Rhodes's version of slavery, accordingly, remained more or less the standard one for nearly two decades.

Meanwhile, however, research at Johns Hopkins during the 1890's had taken the form of a series of restricted monographs on slavery set up on the model of "institutional" history promoted by Herbert Baxter Adams. They differed in a significant respect from the approach of Rhodes. The emphasis was genetic, with an ef-

---

al problems, takes up slavery specifically as a social institution. McMaster, who does, is so completely dominated by the Rhodes conception that his treatment is an actual plagiarization of Rhodes's. Compare Rhodes, I, 303–83, with McMaster, VII, 237–39. Edward Channing does not belong with this earlier group; it was not until 1921 that Channing would reach the point of dealing with slavery in his six-volume *History of the United States* (New York: Macmillan, 1905–25). By that time he had come under the influence of the newer viewpoint represented by the Southerner Ulrich Phillips (see below, pp. 9–15). Channing could not go the length Phillips did in characterizing the plantation as a beneficent patriarchal unit, but he was not unsympathetic to the many cares of a slaveholding planter. "It is by no means improbable," he wrote, "as a Southern writer [Phillips] has intimated, that the slaves were often happier than their masters." Channing recognized by that time, moreover, that a debate parallel to the sectional debate of earlier days had by then assumed its place in the realm of scholarship; he described the work of Rhodes and his Harvard colleague Hart as "the results of prolonged studies by Northern men." This acute consciousness of *two* defensible points of view on the subject was something neither Rhodes nor Hart could possibly have had.

fort toward total objectivity; the question was not so much whether the institution was good or bad, or how it worked, but simply, How did it get started? The result was that these studies —by Jeffrey R. Brackett, John S. Bassett, John H. T. McPherson, and others[8]—having no polemical, moral direction, appeared to have no direction at all. The price of detachment, ironically, was that the work—much of it admirably detailed—had little positive impact on other scholars; it could not really become part of the conversation on slavery. The Johns Hopkins monographs were widely used, though principally as stepping-stones for more polemics rather than as models of method. When Albert Bushnell Hart's *Slavery and Abolition* appeared in 1906, there was little evidence in it of the Johns Hopkins methodological influence; it followed, in all its major organizing categories, the pattern laid down by Rhodes a dozen years before.[9]

The appearance of Ulrich B. Phillips signified a profound change of phase. The Progressive Era, truly a new age in all things, brought to American history Dunning on Reconstruction and Phillips on slavery. Phillips, who showed the institution through Southern eyes for the first time in more than half a century and was at the same time guided by scholarly standards, made an inestimable contribution: he made it possible for the subject to be debated on scholarly grounds. No debate is worth much without a vigorous, knowledgeable, and principled opposition, and the vitality which this debate was to retain for so

[8] The "Johns Hopkins University Studies" which dealt with slavery were: Vol. VIII, Jeffrey R. Brackett, *The Negro in Maryland* (1890); Vol. IX, John H. T. McPherson, *History of Liberia* (1891); Vol. XI, Edward Ingle, *The Negro in the District of Columbia,* and Bernard C. Steiner, *History of Slavery in Connecticut* (1893); Vol. XIII, James B. Ballagh, *White Servitude in the Colony of Virginia,* and Edson L. Whitney, *Government in the Colony of South Carolina* (1895); Vol. XIV, Henry S. Cooley, *Slavery in New Jersey* (1896); Vol. XVII, John S. Bassett, *History of Slavery in North Carolina* (1899); Vol. XXII, Eugene I. McCormac, *White Servitude in Maryland* (1904); Extra Vol. XXIV, J. C. Ballagh, *A History of Slavery in Virginia* (1902).

[9] Albert Bushnell Hart, *Slavery and Abolition, 1831–1841* (New York: Harper, 1906). This book (which was dedicated to Rhodes) was Volume XVI in the "American Nation" series, of which Hart himself was the editor. It still remains one of the best works on the subject and contains excellent bibliographies. Hart was the son and grandson of abolitionists.

many years would be due in overwhelming measure to Ulrich Phillips and his followers.

Born in 1877 as the son of a Georgia merchant, Phillips was reared in an atmosphere of reverence for the values and standards of the old planter class. He found it impossible to believe that a society which had produced such values and such standards could have rested on a corrupt and immoral institution. Northerners, in the last analysis, could not really be expected to understand slavery. At the turn of the century Phillips was studying under Dunning at Columbia; he began very early on an intensive study of slavery that would not only challenge the deepest assumptions of Rhodes and Hart but would also make drastic alterations in the views held on that subject by thousands and thousands of American readers. A torrent of articles began flowing from Phillips' pen, and when his major work, *American Negro Slavery,* finally appeared in 1918, it was not a beginning but a grand culmination of nearly fifteen years of steadily growing influence.[10]

The basic assumption in *American Negro Slavery* was that of innate and inherited racial inferiority. There is no malice toward the Negro in Phillips' work. Phillips was deeply fond of the Negroes as a people; it was just that he could not take them seriously as men and women: they were children. His approach to the subject involved the most painstaking and responsible scholarship; it was necessary, he thought, to go to the sources. He gave small weight to legal codes, for they gave little indication of what ante-bellum slavery was actually like; he paid little attention to travelers' accounts, since those accounts were in-

[10] Ulrich B. Phillips, *American Negro Slavery: A Survey of the Supply, Employment and Control of Negro Labor as Determined by the Plantation Regime* (New York: D. Appleton, 1918). Phillips began publishing articles and essays on the subject in 1903 and by 1918 had 28 of them to his credit, as well as having edited the first two volumes of the *Documentary History of American Industrial Society* ("Plantation and Frontier Documents," Vols. I and II [Cleveland: A. H. Clark, 1909]). See David M. Potter, Jr., "A Bibliography of the Printed Writings of Ulrich Bonnell Phillips," *Georgia Historical Quarterly,* XVIII (September, 1934), 270–82; also Everett E. Edwards, "A Bibliography of the Writings of Professor Ulrich Bonnell Phillips," *Agricultural History,* VIII (October, 1934), 196–218. There is an essay on Phillips' life and work by Wood Gray in William T. Hutchinson (ed.), *The Marcus W. Jernegan Essays in American Historiography* (Chicago: University of Chicago Press, 1937), pp. 354–73.

tolerably distorted by antislavery bias. The true sources for the subject—the sources from which the full flavor of plantation life might be evoked—were the actual plantation records. The result was a sympathetic account of the old regime which succeeded (though not in the most obvious polemical sense) in neutralizing almost every assumption of the antislavery tradition.

Phillips found that, in the light of what he saw as the inherent character of the Negro race, plantation slavery was not by any means a cruel and inhuman system. Evidence drawn directly from the records did much to dispose of prior generalizations about inadequate food, clothing, and housing. He showed that earlier stories of cruelty and overwork had been wildly over-drawn. Everywhere in Phillips' pages the emphasis is on the genial side of the regime, on cheerfulness and contentment, on the profoundly human relationships between the paternal master and his faithful and childlike blacks. While there may have been "injustice, oppression, brutality and heartburning," as any-where in the world, there were also "gentleness, kind-hearted friendship and mutual loyalty to a degree hard for him to believe who regards the system with a theorist's eye and a partisan squint."[11] Not only did the institution of plantation slavery maintain a stable labor force for Southern agriculture; it functioned as a school. "On the whole the plantations were the best schools yet invented for the mass training of that sort of inert and backward people which the bulk of the American negroes represented."[12] On scholarly grounds alone—scope, depth of research, and use of original sources—*American Negro Slavery* far surpassed anything yet done, and Phillips was easily and beyond question established as the foremost authority on the subject.

The setting in which Phillips worked—and in which his ideas were so well received long before his book actually appeared—was the setting of the Progressive Era. "Progressivism" in the early years of the twentieth century had strong reformist over-tones, but the form which the progressive attitude took in this period on matters of race was quite different from that which it would take for later reform generations. Certain streams were by then coming together, making possible a wide acceptance

[11] *American Negro Slavery*, p. 514.   [12] *Ibid.*, p. 343.

[11]

North and South of the essentially tolerant view of Negro slavery which Ulrich Phillips represented.

In the South the muddy and anomalous (so far as the whites were concerned) post-Reconstruction position of the Negro was being systematically liquidated by the turn of the century. (The withdrawal of Federal troops in the 1870's had by no means been followed by the wholesale removal of Negro political and social rights; many of those rights had been maintained until well into the nineties.) But the Populists' organized though abortive efforts to make common political cause with the Negro had precipitated an all but unanimous determination, already coalescing throughout Southern white society, to eliminate Negroes from politics altogether. The tool whereby liberal white elements, in combination with Populist remnants, might then gain ascendancy in the Democratic party was the formula of a white man's government: the Negro must go. The Negro's by then precarious political status, together with the lukewarm conservatism of the old post-Reconstruction Bourbon element, constituted nothing further in the way of obstacles to the complete triumph of Jim Crow and thoroughgoing Negro disfranchisement. Negro leadership itself—dominated by Booker T. Washington—was quick to see the coming state of things and urged what amounted to full capitulation. This meant not only that the Negro had nothing more in the way of a political future but also that social survival would henceforth require a new form of the old ante-bellum dependency relationship between Negroes and white patrons. The meaning of political Progressivism in the South, therefore, was that civic purity and racial purity would be synonymous.[13]

[13] This thesis on the connection between Jim Crow and Progressivism has been developed by C. Vann Woodward. While the post–Civil War suppression of Negro rights did begin with the "Bourbon Restoration" of the 1870's, Professor Woodward emphasizes the not so widely appreciated fact that a new, systematic, and final phase of the Negro's relegation to second-class citizenship was not fully launched until the 1890's, precipitated by the Populist agitation of that decade and completed in a blaze of "reformist" fervor in the early 1900's. See particularly C. Vann Woodward, *The Strange Career of Jim Crow* (New York: Oxford University Press, 1955), pp. 13–95. Varied aspects of the process are treated at greater length in the same author's *Origins of the New South, 1877–1913* (Baton Rouge: Louisiana State University Press, 1951), pp. 321–68.

Progressivism in this sense was not limited to the South; it had its Northern counterpart. Imperialism and the white man's burden, ominous hordes of swarthy immigrants in the Northern cities, corrupting the bygone simplicity of municipal government and civic life—these things could contribute to, and combine very easily with, the nationwide surge for civic regeneration. In *The Passing of the Great Race* Madison Grant, an old-stock New Yorker and amateur anthropologist, warned that Nordic excellence was being smothered beneath the faster-spawning Mediterranean and eastern European masses. The response to these and related horrors was a tremendous reassertion of Anglo-Saxon vigor in communities everywhere: the strenuous life, the old-time virtues, assaults on civic degeneration. Here too, as with the South, civic purity and racial purity were to a great extent interchangeable, and the Southern case in all such matters had virtually ceased to be contested anywhere in the North. Side by side with the muckraking stories in *McClure's* might be found articles by Thomas Nelson Page, giving the "reasonable" version of Negro inferiority.[14]

So far as the writing of history was concerned, these things, together with the fact that Ulrich Phillips had established undisputed and superior claims on the level of scholarship, meant the triumph, North and South, of a view on slavery whose basic premise was racial inferiority. At no time in American history were Southern race dogmas so widely accepted throughout the entire nation as in the early years of the twentieth century; and for at least two decades after Phillips left college this was the intellectual climate in which he worked. Phillips' example, moreover, meant the establishment of a school; the intellectual status which he had secured for the Southern side of slavery was of

[14] Thomas Nelson Page, "The Negro: The South's Problem," *McClure's Magazine,* XXII (March, April, 1904), 548–54, 619–26; XXIII (May, 1904), 96–102. In the issue which carried the first of Page's three instalments there was an article on corruption by Lincoln Steffens, "Enemies of the Republic"; the second instalment was accompanied by a chapter of Ida Tarbell's "History of the Standard Oil Company"; and the third by "The Reign of Lawlessness," one of Ray Stannard Baker's exposés of conditions in the Colorado mining districts. These three months of 1904 in *McClure's* give a perfectly consistent index of the enlightened Progressive taste; each of these articles points to a particular form of moral degeneration that must be resisted through a combination of exposure and firm resolve.

untold value as a morale factor in the development of twentieth-century Southern historical scholarship. Not only would a number of Southern scholars, in special state studies on slavery, be sustained in their work by Phillips' genial view of the institution; Southern historians in general could now reach with assurance for an authoritative position on slavery to bulwark the most Southern of Southern positions on almost any problem of nineteenth-century American history.

The very pervasiveness of Phillips' influence makes that influence virtually impossible to "trace." The coincidence of impressive scholarship and popular ideology gave Phillips' work a special authority for those who followed him, an authority quite noticeable in the state studies on slavery that appeared at intervals for many years after the publication of Phillips' masterpiece. This is not to say that the authors of these monographs were intellectual puppets of the master, for none of them could ever quite match the intensity of Phillips' own conviction of the slave system's essential humanity; this in itself made a great deal of difference. Their reservations, on the one hand, and the reassurance of Phillips' example, on the other, create a fascinating balance which varies this way and that, depending on the individual writer. Charles Sydnor, the most distinguished of the group, concedes in his *Slavery in Mississippi* that "being a slave was not for the average negro a dreadful lot" but lets his story end on a somber note:

Generally, the chief difference between a slave and a free agricultural laborer lay outside the realm of food, clothing, shelter and work. The difference was that the slave was ordered to do his work; his food and clothing were allowanced; his movements were restricted; his every act was watched; he was sometimes punished and he might be sold. How distasteful life was under these conditions depended on two very variable factors: the character of the masters and the desire for freedom in the hearts of the slaves.[15]

In Ralph Flanders' *Plantation Slavery in Georgia* the balance is reversed; Flanders found more cruelty and violence in the system than Phillips had, but his concluding comment is most Phillips-like:

[15] Charles S. Sydnor, *Slavery in Mississippi* (New York: D. Appleton, 1933), p. 253.

As a means of social control slavery during the ante-bellum period was invaluable; as a profitable industrial system it was . . . profitable in proportion to the progressive spirit and ability of the individual planter; as a training school for the untutored savage it served to a large degree as a civilizing agency.[16]

The moral balance in the work of Phillips' successors, difficult enough to maintain on such a subject anyway and especially through changing times, is thus never quite so firm as the master's own. But the authority of the master's scholarship resolves many a doubt. Moreover, the specific categories of organization—work, food, clothing, shelter, care, police, profitability, and so on—were invariably the same as those Phillips had used, categories which he in turn had taken from Rhodes.[17]

[16] Ralph B. Flanders, *Plantation Slavery in Georgia* (Chapel Hill: University of North Carolina Press, 1933), pp. 299–300.

[17] Phillips' work, representing as it did a major turning point in attitude on slavery and the ante-bellum way of life, had an impact which is as difficult to trace as that of Frederick Jackson Turner. His emphasis on the social and economic life of the plantation appears in early monographs such as V. Alton Moody, *Slavery on Louisiana Sugar Plantations* (*Louisiana Historical Quarterly* reprint, April, 1924) and Rosser H. Taylor, *Slaveholding in North Carolina: An Economic View* (Chapel Hill: University of North Carolina Press, 1926), and unmistakably in the Flanders and Sydnor studies noted above. One might also include Charles S. Davis, *The Cotton Kingdom in Alabama* (Montgomery: Alabama State Department of Archives and History, 1939), and, with somewhat less assurance, James B. Sellers, *Slavery in Alabama* (University, Ala.: University of Alabama Press, 1950). The list of writers whose thinking was affected by Phillips could be extended indefinitely—to the point where it would begin to lose its meaning. It could include such diverse figures as Edward Channing and Avery Craven. Phillips would have been in excellent company with the "Twelve Southerners" of *I'll Take My Stand* (New York: Harper, 1930)—for instance, with the poet John Crowe Ransom, who in that symposium referred to slavery as "a feature monstrous enough in theory, but more often than not, humane in practice." Philip Newman, asking around in 1939 for opinions about the contributions and influence of Ulrich Phillips, wrote to the Georgia agricultural expert Fred Landon, who replied: "His general conclusions have not as yet been questioned and his influence is seen in the work of his former students and in the constant reference to his writings in the current productions of those working in the same field." See Philip Newman, "Ulrich Bonnell Phillips—the South's Foremost Historian," *Georgia Historical Quarterly*, XXV (September, 1941), 244–61. In short, when an entire attitude on slavery was finally challenged head-on by the revisionism of the 1940's it was just and proper

Even as the influence of Phillips diffused itself throughout Southern thought, a pivotal era in the intellectual life of the nation as a whole was already under way in the decade of the 1920's. Much of the period's intellectual vitality was based on the premise of popular ignorance—a premise which was itself made immensely "popular" by H. L. Mencken—and the popular position on the Negro continued to be a kind of racial fundamentalism. But in elite circles, on the other hand, that position underwent a good deal of erosion with the enhanced prestige of psychology and the social sciences. The environmentalism of Boas, Dewey, and Thomas (even of William Graham Sumner),[18] launched well over a decade before, was coming to be the accepted avant-garde position on race. "It would seem," Franz Boas wrote, "that, in different races, the organization of the mind is on the whole alike, and that the varieties of mind found in different races do not exceed, perhaps do not even reach, the amount of normal individual variation in each race." The basic thing was culture: ". . . the development of *culture* must not be confounded with the development of *mind*." And William I. Thomas: "The real variable is the individual, not the race." Such statements, abstract to the point of incomprehensibility in 1909, found much readier acceptance by the illuminati of the 1920's.[19]

---

that Ulrich Phillips should be the target. He, more than any other one historian, had been responsible for that attitude, and for the challenge to Rhodes which had kept the debate alive for so many years.

[18] Sumner's "folkways" concept can be, and has been, put to more than one kind of use. But in the sense that it emphasizes both the formative and limiting functions of culture and environment upon character and social behavior, it is a pioneering concept for modern sociology. In the case of race relations, the "folkways" concept could be used to justify the "organic" evolution of a new set of arrangements (segregation) required by the removal of slavery and to repel any outside interference with those arrangements. But it is still a cultural concept; there is no justification in it for racism. "We are forced to believe," Sumner wrote, "that, if a baby born in New England was taken to China and given to a Chinese family to rear and educate, he would become a Chinaman in all that belongs to the mores, that is to say, in his character, conduct, and code of life." William Graham Sumner, *Folkways* (Boston: Ginn, 1902), p. 108. Such a formulation may seem a bit pale now, but it is the fatal wedge for cracking any doctrine which tries to make character a product of race.

[19] These quotations are from a remarkable compilation of papers published under the editorship of William Isaac Thomas, *Source Book for*

Carl Brigham, a noted psychologist, published in 1923 a series of findings on intelligence tests which did seem to imply a connection between intelligence and race. But by 1930 Brigham had repudiated his work of seven years earlier.[20] By 1929, even Ulrich Phillips himself had somewhat altered his previous position on the Negro slave. In *Life and Labor in the Old South* he still assumed Negro inferiority, but he was no longer quite so ready to attribute this flatly to race. The emphasis by now was on the encumbrances of a primitive background.[21]

With the late 1930's and early 1940's came the full tide of reaction against the attitudes to which Ulrich Phillips' authority had given sanction. The egalitarian liberalism of the thirties had little place in it for racist bigotry, and that reaction would inexorably force its way into the debate on slavery. And yet in this period of change it was not the debate itself that changed; it was just that a reverse moral tone was making its way back into historical thinking on the subject. It was a tone much reminiscent of the earlier polemics, as indicated in Frederic Bancroft's *Slave Trading in the Old South,* Henrietta Buckmaster's *Let My People Go,* and especially Herbert Aptheker's *American Negro Slave Revolts,* all vibrant with the indignation of old times.[22] The debate had by no means adjourned; the

Social Origins: Ethnological Materials, Psychological Standpoint, Classified and Annotated Bibliographies for the Interpretation of Savage Society (Chicago: University of Chicago Press, 1909), pp. 155, 173. The volume went through a number of editions.

[20] Gunnar Myrdal, *An American Dilemma: The Negro Problem and Modern Democracy* (New York: Harper, 1944), pp. 96, 1190.

[21] Ulrich B. Phillips, *Life and Labor in the Old South* (Boston: Little, Brown, 1929). Actually, Phillips' tone throughout this work is much subdued in comparison to that of a decade before. The closest he comes to an outright statement on race is the following, in a mitigating passage on the ante-bellum law codes: "Fresh Africans were manifestly not to be incorporated in the body politic; and Negroes to the third and fourth generations were still in the main as distinctive in experience, habit, outlook, social discipline and civilian capacity as in the color of their skins or the contours of their faces. 'Twere better, it was thought, for them to suffer the ills they had than for all to fly to those they knew not of." *Ibid.,* p. 163.

[22] The clearest and most interesting evidence, however, of a developing challenge to the still-reigning scholarly attitude on slavery is to be found

other side was simply resuming the stand. There remained no further question of this when a flat challenge to the pieties of the Phillips school was issued in 1944 by Richard Hofstadter. Hofstadter had little patience with the proslavery sympathies of that school, but his strategy was ingenious, being executed on ostensibly neutral ground. Phillips' moral biases were challenged, but not head-on; nor was there any basic impeachment of Phillips' scholarly claims. Instead, Hofstadter challenged Phillips' technique of sampling: he urged that the evidence be extended to cover wider classes of cases. The implication was that, by enlarging the sample, fundamental errors of interpretation might be corrected.[23] Willy-nilly, the moral center of gravity was shifting once more to a strong antislavery position.

---

in the up-and-coming *Journal of Negro History* during the late thirties and early forties. The titles of the following articles in that journal, for example, tell their own story: Harvey Wish, "American Slave Insurrections before 1861," XXII (July, 1937), 299–320, and "Slave Disloyalty under the Confederacy," XXIII (October, 1938), 435–50; Herbert Aptheker, "Maroons within the Present Limits of the United States," XXIV (April, 1939), 167–84; Raymond A. Bauer and Alice H. Bauer, "Day to Day Resistance to Slavery," XXVII (October, 1942), 388–419; Kenneth W. Porter, "Three Fighters for Freedom," XXVIII (January, 1943), 51–72, and "Florida Slaves and Free Negroes in the Seminole War, 1835–1842," XXVIII (October, 1943), 390–421; Herbert Aptheker, "Notes on Slave Conspiracies in Confederate Mississippi," XXIX (January, 1944), 75–79. It was thus appropriate that the first fully deliberate anti-Phillips manifesto (see n. 23) should have been published in this journal.

[23] Richard Hofstadter, "U. B. Phillips and the Plantation Legend," *Journal of Negro History*, XXIX (April, 1944), 109–24. Actually, however, the most telling feature of Professor Hofstadter's critique of Phillips was not so much his claim that the plantation records which Phillips had used so heavily were unrepresentative, and therefore in a methodological sense biased, but rather his conclusion that Phillips himself was biased; he concluded that a "materially different version of the slave system" would emerge if scholars not sharing Phillips' biases were to subject the system to as intense a study as had Phillips. The final paragraph of the Hofstadter essay contains challenges to other scholars, certain of which have been accepted as incentives for the present study (see esp. below, Part III): "Let the study of the Old South be undertaken by other scholars who have absorbed the viewpoint of modern cultural anthropology, who have a feeling for social psychology . . . , who will concentrate upon the neglected rural elements that formed the great majority of the Southern population, who will not rule out the testimony of more critical observers, and who will realize that any history of slavery must be written in large

Meanwhile "science," in an all but fully popularized form, had come to dominate the argument and had in many ways taken charge of it. The Carnegie Foundation had decided by 1937 to sponsor a full-scale study of the "Negro problem" in the United States, an inquiry into the "American dilemma" between white democracy and second-class citizenship for Negroes. The Swedish scholar Gunnar Myrdal was engaged to conduct it, and it was imagined that the "neutral" and "non-imperialist" character of Myrdal's national background would eliminate any biases that might creep into the work of a more "committed" person. As it turned out, this was not much of a guaranty for or against anything, since what really set Myrdal's standards (and limits) was the contemporary academic and intellectual setting within which he would have to work while in this country and from which he would draw whatever advice and assistance were available to him. Among the men and women who advised and assisted him were Franz Boas, W. I. Thomas, Ruth Benedict, Ralph Bunche, W. E. B. DuBois, E. Franklin Frazier, John Dollard, Melville Herskovits, Otto Klineberg, Louis Wirth, Charles S. Johnson, and Donald Young. The result was a detailed inquiry into the numerous phases of the Negro situation, touching at any number of points upon the experience and consequences of slavery, with all the lore and techniques of the social sciences—anthropology, sociology, and social psychology—at the service of this mammoth project.

Myrdal's own book, *An American Dilemma* (1944), was only one of five that came out of the enterprise, and all five strongly reflected the state which the debate on slavery had by then reached. The basic theme of Myrdal's study, and of those that followed it, is inequality and its impact on every phase of Negro life and Negro personality. In this sense it bears a resemblance to the abolitionist literature of ante-bellum times that is more than coincidental, despite its modern dress. The reader can hardly avoid feeling some measure of guilt for the burdens that American society has heaped upon the Negro; implicit throughout, moreover, is the assumption (similar to abolitionist assump-

---

part from the standpoint of the slave—and then the possibilities of the Old South as a field of research and historical experience will loom larger than ever."

tions on the nature of slavery) that if only these burdens were lifted, full equality on every level would be swift and sure. *An American Dilemma,* a general survey (the rest were more specialized), did retain a somewhat more dispassionate tone than the others, and a certain vein of European sophistication runs all through it. But the others, for all the protections of "science," were bound by the very dedication of the investigators, and by the very nature of what they were investigating, to tremble constantly on the verge of the polemic. There were in these studies numerous *obiter dicta* on the functional interchangeability of the human race (already proved many times over by then), and even the purely descriptive basis upon which the work rested was full of implications which the sensitive reader could not but take in their normative rather than their descriptive character.[24]

The culmination and quintessence of the entire anti-Phillips reaction in historical writing came with Kenneth Stampp, whose own work was conceived at the flood tide of that reaction. *The Peculiar Institution,* which finally appeared in 1956 after many years of labor among source materials that exceeded in scope and volume those used by Phillips, has in the eyes of many students replaced *American Negro Slavery* as the authoritative statement on a long-mooted subject. There is now very little that Phillips did with the plantation regime that has not been done with greater thoroughness by his Northern successor. Not only has Phillips' moral position been overwhelmingly reversed, but even his scholarship—though nearly forty years would have to elapse

[24] Myrdal's study was designed to survey every aspect of America's Negro "dilemma." He began by indicating the fundamental clash between America's most cherished values and America's treatment of the Negro, and he carried this theme through a consideration of the Negro's economic and political life, his treatment by the courts and by government, his caste position, his leadership, and the nature of his community. The other works in the Myrdal series were Melville Herskovits, *The Myth of the Negro Past* (New York: Harper, 1941); Charles S. Johnson, *Patterns of Negro Segregation* (New York: Harper, 1943); Richard Sterner, *The Negro's Share* (New York: Harper, 1943); and Otto Klineberg (ed.), *Characteristics of the American Negro* (New York: Harper, 1944). Very much in the same line is Abram Kardiner and Lionel Ovesey, *The Mark of Oppression: A Psychosocial Study of the American Negro* (New York: Norton, 1951). Certain "scientific" assumptions of some of this work are questioned in Part III below.

before anyone finally accomplished it—has been left in the shade by scholarship more painstaking still.[25] Not only has the challenge been successful; the victory is devastating. What is more, to carry the echoes back yet another quarter-century beyond Phillips, a further vindication has been achieved. The view of American Negro slavery presented by James Ford Rhodes in 1893 has acquired a new legitimacy which a generation and more of Southern-dominated writing had denied it.

And yet what is even more striking than Professor Stampp's triumph is the fact that the coercions of a century-old debate remain irresistible: he has joined the debate; he may even have won it, but it is still very much the same debate. In spite of its outcome, the strategy of *The Peculiar Institution* was still dictated by Ulrich Phillips. The predominance of Phillips' work represented the ascendancy of a moral attitude toward the subject, and no basic changes could be made in a view long established as "classic" without first demolishing the picture of the kindly and paternal planter presiding over his family of submissive, irresponsible, and carefree blacks—the picture which Phillips had so carefully constructed and with which his work was so inextricably associated.

Stampp was convinced at the outset, for two general reasons, that such a major revision as he contemplated was entirely possible. For one thing, Phillips had been extremely selective in his choice of evidence, having depended primarily on the records of large plantations and having made only limited use of unfavorable travelers' accounts.[26] But the other stimulus seems to have been the really basic one: Phillips' work was grounded upon assumptions of inherent Negro inferiority which had been fully discredited by modern science. There was an implicit announcement of intention, as well as a statement of what the subject needed, in the opening paragraph of an essay Stampp wrote four years before he brought out his book: ". . . so far as Negro slavery is concerned we are still waiting for the first scientific and

[25] I am referring primarily to overlapping areas; I do not mean to say that Stampp's work has at every point superseded Phillips'. Phillips during his long career made a number of special investigations of phases which Stampp has not dealt with in this book and which, consequently, remain indispensable and as yet unsupplemented.

[26] Stampp, "The Historian and Southern Negro Slavery," p. 615.

completely objective study of the institution which is based upon no assumptions whose validity cannot be thoroughly proved."[27] With the "proved assumptions" of the social sciences at his disposal, plus his own willingness to use a much wider selection of source material, Stampp prepared to banish Phillips into full retirement and to produce the "objective study." In short, "objectivity" and the discrediting of Phillips were assumed to be not only fully compatible but inseparable.

Some of the results, judging from the earlier essay, were not foreseen by the author himself. He had once questioned the possibility of "loose and glib generalizing" about the living conditions and treatment of slaves. "The only generalization that can be made with relative confidence is that some masters were harsh and frugal, others were mild and generous, and the rest ran the whole gamut in between. . . . In short, the human factor introduced a variable that defied generalization."[28] And yet the very requirements of countering Phillips' mellow view of the plantation forced Stampp to abrogate his self-denying ordinance and engage in the same kind of generalizing. The categories he adopted for organizing his own work (food, shelter, police, medical care, etc.) had a very familiar look: they were the same that Phillips had used, Phillips in his turn having accepted them from Rhodes. As he discovered, Stampp could not avoid this and still remain in the argument. The aspects of the evidence which most impressed him, moreover, were those which showed the harshness and cruelty of the system as a whole.[29]

To challenge Phillips' assumptions of racial inferiority, Stampp made use of the extensive Myrdal material, whose scientific le-

[27] *Ibid.,* p. 613.   [28] *Ibid.,* p. 616.

[29] There are interesting correspondences, in some of the chapter titles, between *Slavery in Mississippi* by Charles Sydnor (the major influence upon whom was Phillips) and *The Peculiar Institution: Slavery in the Ante-Bellum South* (New York: Knopf, 1956) by Kenneth Stampp (whose line descends from Rhodes):

Sydnor	Stampp
"The Working Day of the Slave"	"From Day Clean to First Dark"
"Police and Discipline"	"To Make Them Stand in Fear"
"The Law of Slavery"	"Chattels Personal"
"Slave Trading"	"Slavemongering"
"Health, Shelter, Clothing"	"Maintenance, Morbidity, Mortality"

gitimacy had been unimpeachably established. But he did so without making much distinction between what was clearly "scientific" in it and what was earnestly and animatedly normative. Since the Myrdal studies themselves crackled with moral electricity, Stampp, by adopting their attitude (his own pages similarly crackle), was returning to a long-familiar moral position through the back door. Thus the simplest anthropological formulation of race, that Negroes and whites have all the same capacities, has been used as a scientific warrant (actually a moral one) for numerous other assumptions which seem not only unscientific but morally a little callous. The picture of the ideal Negro slave is that of a man who has fully resisted all the effects on personality of a social system as coercive as any yet known. Special attention is called to examples of Negro courage, Negro rebelliousness, Negro hatred for the slave system, and so on—all the characteristics one might expect of white men who knew nothing of what it meant to be reared in slavery.

Numerous "scientific" possibilities, it might be said, were ignored in *The Peculiar Institution*. Whatever submissiveness, cheerfulness, and childishness could be observed among the antebellum plantation Negroes was automatically discredited; these features could not be accepted as typical and normal—not for a white man, and therefore not for anyone: "Negroes *are,* after all, only white men with black skins, nothing more, nothing less."[30] The existence of a social system whose coercions were so pervasive as to induce those very characteristics, not dissembled but real, in men of whatever color seems not to have been given much speculative leeway. That the social system represented by American plantation slavery might have developed a sociology and social psychology of its own has apparently been ruled out in advance. Stampp, locked in his struggle with Ulrich Phillips, has seen no good reason to disengage his mind from the debate of which he, Phillips, and Rhodes were all a part and which they had taken over from the proslavery and antislavery debaters of ante-bellum times. Professor Stampp, like his abolitionist forbears, is still as much concerned as they to prove slavery an abomination and to prove master and slave equal before their Maker.[31]

30 *Peculiar Institution,* p. vii.

31 David Donald, reviewing Stampp's book in *Commentary* (XXII [December, 1956], 584–85), notices this feature, though his explanation for

The function of Allan Nevins' treatment of slavery, in his *Ordeal of the Union* (1947), was something very useful, something for which the author has not been duly credited. It involved a recognition that the debate had little future, had come to a stalemate, and that probably very little more would be said on either side that had not been said in some form already. Passion may have had its uses once (we can almost hear Professor Nevins saying), but the time has finally arrived when we can be fair and reasonable. All can, and at last do, agree that slavery was a corrupt institution which had to be eliminated, so it would do no harm now to try casting up the balance. It is as though the ledger were open and as though, for every entry on one side, there were a corresponding entry on the other. The degradations of slavery were sickening, though the genial view of plantation life emphasized by Phillips need not be denied its place. In *Ordeal of the Union,* Nevins really does what Rhodes in 1893 imagined he was doing but could not possibly do: close the accounts objectively.[32]

The assumption, then, in Nevins' work, is that the thing is settled: let there be peace. It is in many ways a decent and humane attitude, and decidedly not, as some have claimed, an evasive one.[33] And yet there is one thing that it does not anticipate: the possibility of a different line of argument entirely, conducted on grounds quite other than those of the old debate. If we still think *that* is possible, then of course the book-balancing technique will have to be supplemented by something else.

There remains the by no means easy question of how a break-

---

it—"ancestor worship"—sounds a little fanciful. It would be fairer and more accurate simply to recognize that the very necessities of such a debate require joining hands with one's more distant predecessors in order to rout one's immediate predecessors. There is many a problem in American history—even though slavery no longer seems to be one of them—that would profit greatly from just such a strategy.

[32] Allan Nevins, *Ordeal of the Union* (New York: Scribner, 1947), I, 423–61.

[33] There is a summary of the reactions to Nevins' book in Thomas J. Pressly, *Americans Interpret Their Civil War* (Princeton: Princeton University Press, 1954), pp. 317–20.

through should be recognized, if one should actually occur. The chances are that it would not make much of a splash; no one would pay a great deal of attention. The reason would be inherent in the setting amid which any new thing makes its appearance: uncertainty as to just where it fits in prior debates on the subject. The difficulty, which may or may not be a good sign, is that in most cases it will *not* fit. Frank Tannenbaum's *Slave and Citizen,* which made its appearance in 1948, seems to meet all these inauspicious qualifications.

Tannenbaum's book, in its format and proportions, was an excessively modest and unpretentious affair. There was no room, for instance, in the compendious Stampp work (eight years later) for taking any notice of it—not even in a footnote. But what would happen if the sort of thinking which Tannenbaum represents were simply moved out to the center of the stage? The technique of *Slave and Citizen* is one which has remained practically unexploited in the work done in American history—the technique of comparison—and there are conceivably problems in which one judicious and intelligent comparative statement can be worth an entire attic full of plantation records. Such a statement seems to have been made here. What Tannenbaum compares is the institution of slavery in two very distinct types of culture. Slavery as an evil is simply taken for granted; what interested the author were the resources of two cultures, Hispano-Portuguese and British-American, for sustaining and dealing with evil in their midst. He finds staggering contrasts and leaves us with a problem: the problem of *why*. Here is something that seems well worth picking up.

Another breakthrough, earlier and more widely recognized but still difficult to categorize, was Gilbert Barnes's *Anti-Slavery Impulse* (1933). Barnes also took for granted the evils of slavery and concentrated instead upon the organizational and stylistic features of the antislavery movement. He discovered baffling paradoxes. There was more than one kind of abolitionism; some techniques worked and others did not; Garrison, for example, was less effective in making converts than in breaking down the organizational structure of abolitionism itself. Abolition as an organized movement had been pretty well scattered by the 1840's, yet antislavery sentiment gained and gained until the result was war. Again, why? Barnes left problems whose challenge has never been fully accepted. About all that his work is remembered for is the discovery that Theodore Dwight Weld was really a more acceptable abolitionist than Garrison.[34] But why?

One substitute for "originality" (a virtue perhaps overrated in historical writing) might consist in letting ourselves be guided to new problems within a subject by the paradoxes and vicissitudes of past writing and thinking on the same subject, permitting that in itself to become part of the problem. Letting past thought be of assistance in formulating new questions need not come to the same thing as being coerced by that thought and seems much preferable to ignoring it. Such, at any rate, is to be the strategy of the present work. Certain positive challenges have been left by such writers as Tannenbaum and Barnes—and certain negative ones by the "scientific" writers of the 1930's and 1940's—challenges which do not seem to have had great impact on the main debate. An effort will be made to take up some of them here. Their nature is implied in the titles of the three remaining sections.

[34] Numerous bibliographies on the subject make a point of this, noting Barnes's shift of emphasis from Garrison's work to that of Weld. What appears to be less appreciated, however, is Weld's actual place in the movement and the reasons for his success.

II

Institutions and the Law of Slavery

I

INSTITUTIONAL BREAKDOWN IN AN AGE OF EXPANSION

It was inherent in the state of sensibility which Western civilization had attained by the nineteenth century that slavery, involving the most basic values of humanity, should at that time become morally absorbing to both Europeans and Americans. Englishmen, Frenchmen, Spaniards, and Portuguese each responded to the oppressive subject at various levels of intensity in thought and action; out of their complex experience each could focus upon slavery a variety of resources in order that they might judge its evils, mitigate its abuses, and finally abolish it altogether.[1] There is a certain sense in which the same might be said of the Americans. Yet the simple and harsh moral purity of our own antislavery movement, from the 1830's on, gave it a quality which set it apart from the others. The theory of society which was its backdrop, the intellectual expressions upon which it drew, the slogans which it sent to the market place, the schemes for practical action which it evolved—every phase of the movement combined to produce in our abolitionists that peculiar quality of abstraction

[1] The nineteenth century saw the steady collapse of slavery as an institution. The determined efforts of Wilberforce and Clarkson to end the slave trade were internationally successful by 1823 when Portugal joined Spain, France, and England in outlawing it. In the Spanish-speaking countries of Central and South America slavery itself was gradually eliminated during the first half of the century. It had already been abolished in the British West Indies by 1834 and in the colonies of France by 1848. When in 1858 Portugal proclaimed a status of peonage with eventual freedom for all its slaves, the future of slavery had become very dim.

which was, and has remained, uniquely American. For them, the question was *all* moral; it must be contemplated in terms untouched by expediency, untarnished by society's organic compromises, uncorrupted even by society itself. It was a problem of conscience which by mid-century would fasten itself in one form or another, and in varying degrees, upon men's feelings everywhere.

But while our thinkers and reformers considered the issue in such abstract purity, in such simple grandeur, there was, in principle if not in fact, an alternative philosophical mode. Slavery might have been approached not as a problem in pure morality but as a question of institutional arrangements—a question of those institutions which make the crucial difference in men's relationships with one another, of those arrangements whereby even so theoretically simple a connection as that between master and slave might take any of a dozen forms among which the sharpest and finest of moral distinctions might be made. This approach was of course never taken, and to expect it of nineteenth-century Americans would be to make impossible demands upon their experience. It is, however, still of interest to ask why this should be so. Why should the American of, say, 1830 have been so insensitive to institutions and their function?

Consider the seeming paradox of how by that time, in the very bright morning of American success, the power of so many American institutions had one by one melted away. The church had fallen into a thousand parts. The shadow of an Anglican church, disestablished in the wake of the Revolution and its doom forever sealed by the yearly anarchy of the camp meeting, was all that remained in the South of vested ecclesiastical authority; and in New England the Congregational church, which had once functioned as a powerful state establishment, was deprived of its last secular supports early in the century. It was not that religion itself was challenged—quite the contrary—but that as a source both of organized social power and internal discipline the church had undergone a relentless process of fragmentation. Religious vitality everywhere was overwhelming, but that vitality lay primarily in demands for individual satisfaction which took inevitable and repeated priority over institutional needs. The very ease with which the great evangelical sects could divide, by a sort of cellular fission, into myriads of tiny independent units, showed that the institutional balance between official coercion and individual self-expression had completely broken down.[2]

As for the bar, the very profusion of lawyers on the American scene, their numbers daily increasing, made a central focus of traditional and vested power among them out of the question; no such continuing structure as the English bar, with its institutional self-awareness, its standards of competence and discipline, its stabilized recruitment, its Temples and Inns of Court, could exist in America. There was a brief period, in the later eighteenth century, when organizations of the bar in our eastern cities did appear capable of providing such a nucleus of stability. But here too, as with the church and the ministry, the great expansion get-

---

[2] A positive distinction must be made between religious enthusiasm and organized ecclesiastical power. The great religious revival that followed the War of 1812 did not renew the strength and vitality of the older religious establishments in their *institutional* character. What actually tended to happen was that, with new churches springing up everywhere, both the ideal of a learned ministry and the role of the individual minister as a powerful leader in the community could hardly avoid being drastically undermined. See Richard Hildreth, *The History of the United States of America* (New York: Harper, 1858), VI, 597. Moreover, the new democratic sects, by their very nature, could have only the most limited kind of success in creating national organizations of their own, capable of wielding centralized power and discipline. William W. Sweet, *The Story of Religion in America* (New York: Harper, 1930), p. 258. The Methodists, with their episcopal form of organization, might at first glance appear to have been an exception. And yet even the Methodists made their greatest strides in growth not so much through perfecting their institutional structure as by their energy in sending out circuit riders and promoting camp meetings in the trans-Allegheny frontier regions. The kind of religion appropriate to such an operation was necessarily simple, direct, and emotional, and its power depended to an exceptional degree simply on the persuasive powers of the preachers in holding their audiences, without the many alternative sanctions of a long-rooted establishment. In short, Methodism, like most other forms of religion on the frontier, had many aspects of the promotional campaign whose success requires never losing touch with day-to-day consumer demand. As for discipline over the clergy, a preacher could of course be expelled from the Methodist organization, but this was hardly an "unfrocking"; he could make his transition to another sect with great ease. See William W. Sweet, *Methodism in American History* (New York: Methodist Book Concern, 1933), pp. 143–85. On this "promotional," competitive aspect see Sidney E. Mead, "Denominationalism: The Shape of Protestantism in America," *Church History*, XXIII (December, 1954), 3–32.

ting under way after the War of 1812, bringing so widespread a demand for services of whatever quality, soon made it clear that individual drives rather than institutional needs would prevail. With the democratization of the bar and its inevitable decline in standards, came a deterioration of whatever institutional bulwarks the bar might have developed.[3]

In our politics, as elsewhere, the old organizational balance was dissolving; something new and unprecedented was emerging in the shape of mass parties. In a way, of course, the sheer formlessness of the new system would cloak an inscrutable logic; its very innocence of principle would foster a special conservatism; its apparent lack of focus would be its own protection, enabling it to act as a kind of super-institution absorbing the functions of a dozen institutions which no longer existed. Yet in its very birth it was necessary that an older, a more stable and traditional conception of political responsibility should disappear. The Federalist party, even in New England, was by 1830 utterly dead. The Federalists, though in actual policy hardly different from their successors, had assumed and embodied certain traditional attributes of political life which later establishments did not and could not provide. They took their impulse and *esprit* from the Fathers themselves, and their very aura of exclusiveness made possible a certain sharpness of focus. They took for granted the tradition that politics was an occupation for men of affairs, prop-

[3] By the eve of the Revolution the power of the bar, especially in New York and Massachusetts, had come to be such that it could not only maintain rigid controls over its own standards of admission and professional conduct but also function as a potent force in society at large—"the judges and principal lawyers," according to Lieutenant-Governor Cadwallader Colden in 1764, being "proprietors of extravagant grants of land or strongly connected with them in interest or family alliances. . . ." Quoted in Charles Warren, *A History of the American Bar* (Boston: Little, Brown, 1911), p. 99. However, by 1830 all this had changed: "The tide of early nineteenth-century democracy carried before it almost all previously existing standards of admission to the profession: Every man was as good as every other, and everyone should find open the gate to self-advancement in any field." The bar ceased to have any meaning as a conservative institution, and in 1851 Indiana recognized this fact by providing in its constitution that "every person of good moral character, being a voter, shall be entitled to admission to practice law in all courts of justice." James Willard Hurst, *The Growth of American Law: The Law Makers* (Boston: Little, Brown, 1950), p. 250; see also pp. 278, 285.

erty, and learning. The Federalist party, by its very air of vested interest, came closer than any of its successors to providing a clear institutional nucleus for the loyalty and commitment of other vested interests in society—the intelligentsia, the ministry, the bar, the propertied classes.[4] But the wide democratization of politics in the 1820's ordained that political life in the United States should assume a completely new tone, one quite different from that imagined by the Fathers. Even the Jeffersonians, following the Federalists, had moved more or less instinctively to establish institutional safeguards for political leadership, discipline, and power; yet they too, in the 1820's, saw their special creation, the congressional caucus, swept away and damned as an engine of aristocracy and privilege.[5]

Even in the country's economic activity this breakdown of structural equilibrium was quite as evident as it was in other sectors of public life. The reasonably stable economic organizations maintained by the great trading families of the East were being challenged by a rising class of petty industrialists everywhere. It need not be supposed that these mercantile and banking structures were in a state of decline; yet in a relative sense their power and leadership, amid the proliferation of the small enterprise, no longer carried the decisive weight of former times.[6]

[4] By 1820, writes Ostrogorski, the "alliance between the magistracy, the clergy, property, and culture, was collapsing. The eclipse of the Federalists, who were the living image of government by leaders, robbed it of one of its strongest supports. The influence of the clergy, which had been one of the main props of the Federalists, was being thrust out of lay society." M. Ostrogorski, *Democracy and the Organization of Political Parties,* trans. Frederick Clarke (New York: Macmillan, 1908), II, 26–27.

[5] *Ibid.,* pp. 28–29, 39.

[6] In the Revolutionary and post-Revolutionary period there was little question but that an overwhelming share of the social and economic leadership rested with the eastern mercantile upper crust—a group which, far from being "destroyed" by the Revolution, was actually reconstituted by infusions of new blood. Robert A. East, *Business Enterprise in the American Revolutionary Era* (New York: Columbia University Press, 1938), pp. 13–14, 237–38, 261–62. In New York, according to Dixon Ryan Fox, "There was still a merchants' party just as there had been before the Revolutionary War," and this class—flanked by the bar, the Episcopal church, and the trustees of Columbia College—formed the strength and support of the Federalist party well into the nineteenth century. D. R. Fox, *The Decline of Aristocracy in the Politics of New*

The very tone of business life assumed a character peculiarly indicative of what was happening. Its keynote was the individual confronted with boundless opportunity; a veritable new culture-hero was being fashioned on the frontier of the Old Northwest: the young man on the make, in whose folklore the eastern banker, bulwarked by privilege and monopoly, would become a tarnished symbol.[7] The one really effective economic institution that did exist—the second Bank of the United States—was consigned to oblivion amid the cheers of the populace. Capitalism was burgeoning indeed, but in anything but a conservative way; its very dynamism was breaking old molds. Whatever institutional stability American capitalism could conceivably develop was at its lowest possible ebb in 1830.

And yet it was a society whose very energy and resources had themselves become a kind of stability. For such a society, traditional guaranties of order had become superfluous. Its religion was so dynamic that it needed no church; its wealth and opportunity were so boundless that a center of financial power could lose its meaning; and in its need for politicians and lawyers by the thousands it could do without a governing class and ignore

---

York (New York: Longmans, Green, 1919), pp. v, 11-12, 17-18, 28-29, and *passim*. Yet by 1830 this too had changed: "In a country such as ours, where the touch of energy could turn resources into wealth, prescriptive rights could not long remain unchallenged. In no colony had the lines of old caste been more clearly drawn than in New York; in no state were they more completely rubbed away." *Ibid.*, p. v. Economically the key to this fact was to be found in the sheer diffusion of power implicit in the growth of petty manufactures which, owing to "economies peculiar to small enterprises, the impossibility of engrossing either the redundant natural resources of the country or its rapidly expanding markets, and the manufacturing opportunities offered in the West," could not possibly be dominated by the older establishments, no matter how large. See Victor S. Clark, *History of Manufactures in the United States* (1929 ed.; reprinted New York: Peter Smith, 1949), I, 457. In no decade did such enterprises grow more rapidly in numbers than in that of the 1830's. Ernest L. Bogart, *Economic History of the American People* (New York: Longmans, Green, 1936), p. 385.

[7] "Originally a fight against political privilege, the Jacksonian movement [of the 1830's] had broadened into a fight against economic privilege, rallying to its support a host of 'rural capitalists and village entrepreneurs.'" Richard Hofstadter, *The American Political Tradition* (New York: Knopf, 1949), p. 66.

many an ancient tradition of bench and bar. Thus for the American of that day it was the very success of his society—of capitalism, of religious liberalism and political democracy—that made it unnecessary for him to be concerned with institutions. Had he a "past"? Yes; it was already two hundred years old, but he could afford to forget it. Had he once known "institutions"? Yes, of a sort, but he could now ignore their meaning; *his* style of life did not depend upon them.[8] His new system of values could now question "society" itself, that very society which had made success possible and which offered him his future. Because he no longer seemed to need it, it became an abstraction which even bore certain allusions to the sinister. He was able to imagine that "stability" resided not in social organization but in "human nature." He no longer appeared to draw from society his traditions, his culture, and all his aspirations; indeed he, the transcendent individual—the new symbol of virtue—now "confronted" society; he challenged it as something of a conspiracy to rob him of his birthright. Miraculously, all society then sprang to his aid in the celebration of that conceit.

We may suppose that such was not merely the general sense but one shared by those men who in other societies would be called "intellectuals"—those men whose traditional preoccupation is to reflect and express in various ways the state of society at large, its tensions, its ills, its well-being. So we should also ask about the consequences which such a happy state of things might have had for intellectual activity. Might there not have been (in spite of everything) a price? Where, for instance, in such a setting were art and learning to find their occupation? "No author, without a trial," wrote the lonely Hawthorne in his preface to *The Marble Faun,* "can conceive the difficulty of writing a romance about a country where there is no shadow, no antiquity, no mystery, no picturesque and gloomy wrong, nor anything but a commonplace prosperity, in broad and simple daylight, as is happily the case with my dear native land." This society with few problems and few visible institutions set the American intel-

[8] One or two contrasts with European society make this significant: take, for example, the life of the British aristocracy, with its close relationship to the church, army, and government, or that of the Prussian Junker, who depended on a strong state and an army for the very meaning of his personality.

lectual, such as he was, peculiarly on his own and made him as susceptible as anyone else to the philosophy of self-help. In the America of the 1830's and 1840's there was no other symbol of vitality to be found than the individual, and it was to the individual, with all his promise, that the thinker, like everyone else, would inexorably orient himself. Every reward which the age offered seemed pointed out by the way of self-reliance. But the thinker, thus oriented, left himself without a specific and concrete sense of society as such and without even a strong sense of himself as belonging to a community of other men of intellect. He was involuntarily cut off from the sources of power (the political, ecclesiastical, and financial power had become more and more diffuse), so that he could no longer operate, as it were, in the midst of things. For Americans of this generation the very concept of power—its meaning, its responsibilities, its uses—was something quite outside their experience. This intellectual disengagement from problems of power had a great deal to do with the peculiar abstractness of our thought on the subject of slavery.

Such was the state of mind in which Americans faced the gravest social problem that had yet confronted them as an established nation. Theirs had been, considering the bulk of their achievement, a mild existence in which the stimuli of chronic and complex institutional tensions had been absent; it was in such a setting that their habits of thought had been shaped; such was the experience with which they might approach the ills of society and deal with serious questions of morality.

By the 1830's slavery had come to offend the sensibilities of all Christendom. It was a problem partaking of the Christian conception of sin. Mortal sin lay in the path of all who dealt in slaves, and it was so defined and given meaning by the Christian church in countries where the church had power. Slavery, by its very age, had almost assumed the character of original sin, entailed as it was upon living generations by their predecessors. In America, slavery was unique among the other institutions of society. In one section of the country it had existed for over two centuries, having become interwoven with the means of production, the basic social arrangements, and the very tone of Southern culture. Slavery in the South, instead of diminishing, had spread. Though it had been a source of discomfort there a generation before, men could now see it, under pressure, as the keystone of a style of life in a sense that was not true of any other institution in American society. Conversely, it was at this very time that Americans of the North found themselves suddenly confronted, as it were, with slavery's full enormity.[9]

"No picturesque and gloomy wrong"—Hawthorne here referred to a society which, distinguished from the civilizations of Europe, was not concretely acquainted with sin. The innocence of America and the wickedness of Europe would form one of the great themes of nineteenth-century literature, but of all the writers who used it, perhaps it was Hawthorne's most distinguished biographer, Henry James, who best understood how even "sin," in European culture, had been institutionalized. There, an actual place had been made for it in life's crucial experience. It had been classified from time out of mind and given specific names; the reality of "lust," "avarice," and "oppression" had given rise to the most intricate of social arrangements, not for eliminating them, but for softening their impact and limiting their scope—for protecting the weak and defining the responsibilities of the strong. One powerful social agency in particular had made of iniquity its special province and had dealt with it in a thousand forms for centuries. All this may well have been in James's mind when he exclaimed of America: *"no church."*

What, then, might be expected to happen if sin *should* suddenly become apparent, in a nation whose every individual was, at least symbolically, expected to stand on his own two feet? The reaction was altogether destructive. The sense of outrage was personal; the sense of *personal* guilt was crushing. The gentle American of mild vices was transformed into the bloody avenger. It would seem that the reaction of a society to sin (as well as to any other problem) depends on the prior experience of that soci-

[9] By Jefferson's time, slavery in the older planting states, especially in Virginia, had become considerably less profitable than had been the case earlier in the eighteenth century, and Virginians of the post-Revolutionary era had begun to examine slavery from the point of view of their consciences, as well as economically. Yet the opening of the southwest frontier in the late 1790's, followed by the Louisiana Purchase, together with the spread of cotton culture to those regions and the perfecting of mechanical aids to large-scale production, had given slavery a new lease on life. By the 1830's the full implications of this resurgence were becoming visible.

ety; whether the wrong shall be torn out root and branch, or whether terms are to be made with it, depends on how intimate that society is with evil in all its forms. The outraged innocent can be a thousand times more terrible than the worldly temporizer. By 1830 the spread of slavery had begun to force upon Americans a catalogue of unsuspected revelations. And accordingly, their guilt and outrage were harassed and quickened from the days of Garrison's first blasts in 1831—"harsh as truth, uncompromising as justice"—until the upheaval of 1861 in which slavery was destroyed with fire and sword.

The sharpest spokesmen of North and South, more and more inclining to stand at polar opposites on all questions touching slavery in the thirty years before the Civil War, had at least a feature of style in common: each expressed himself with a simple moral severity. Each in his way thought of slavery as though it were a gross fact with certain universal, immutable, abstract features unalloyed by considerations of time and place. To the Northern reformer, every other concrete fact concerning slavery was dwarfed by its character as a moral evil—as an obscenity condemned of God and universally offensive to humanity. The Southerner replied in kind; slavery was a positive moral good— a necessary arrangement sanctioned in Scripture and thus by God Himself, in which an inferior race must live under the domination of a superior. "Slavery, authorized by God, permitted by Jesus Christ, sanctioned by the apostles, maintained by good men of all ages, is still existing in a portion of our beloved country."[10] "As a man, a Christian, and a citizen, we believe that slavery is right; that the condition of the slave, as it now exists in slaveholding states, is the best existing organization of civil society."[11] These were characteristic replies to sentiments such as those of the abolitionist George Bourne, who in 1834 had written, "The Mosaic law declares every slaveholder a THIEF; Paul the Apostle classes them among the vilest criminals. . . . To tolerate slavery, or to join in its practice is an insufferable crime, which tarnishes every other good quality. *For whosoever shall keep the law and*

[10] Mary H. Eastman, *Aunt Phillis's Cabin, or Southern Life as It Is* (Philadelphia: Lippincott, Grambo, 1862), p. 24.

[11] From the Washington *Telegraph,* quoted in LaRoy Sunderland, *Anti-Slavery Manual* (New York: S. W. Benedict, 1837), p. 52.

yet offend in one point, he is guilty of all."[12] Neither antagonist, in short—burning with guilt or moral righteousness, as the case may have been—could quite conceive of slavery as a social institution, functioning, for better or worse, by laws and logic like other institutions, mutable like others, a product of human custom, fashioned by the culture in which it flourished, and capable of infinite variation from one culture to another.

There is, in justice, little reason to expect that the question should have been argued otherwise than it was, in view of the intellectual setting available to the pre–Civil War generation. Yet we ourselves might see how slavery could in fact assume greatly differing institutional forms, were we to make a series of comparisons having to do with slavery as it existed in two very different types of culture. The two most obvious ones available for such a purpose are the liberal, Protestant, secularized, capitalist culture of America, and the conservative, paternalistic, Catholic, quasi-medieval culture of Spain and Portugal and their New World colonies.

2

THE DYNAMICS OF UNOPPOSED
CAPITALISM

How had Negro slavery in the United States come into being? There was nothing "natural" about it; it had no necessary connection with either tropical climate or tropical crops: in Virginia and Maryland, where the institution first appeared and flourished, the climate was hardly tropical, and the staple crop—tobacco—might have been grown as far north as Canada. It had nothing to do with characteristics which might have made the Negro peculiarly suited either to slavery or to the labor of tobacco culture. Slavery in past ages had been limited to no particular race, and the earliest planters of colonial Virginia appear to have preferred a laboring force of white servants from England, Scotland, and Ireland, rather than of blacks from Africa. Nor was it a matter of common-law precedent, for the British colonists who settled the areas eventually to be included in the United States brought with them no legal categories comparable to that of "slave," as

[12] George Bourne, *Picture of Slavery in the United States of America* (Middletown, Conn.: Edwin Hunt, 1834), pp. 11–12. Italics in original.

[37]

the term would be understood by the end of the seventeenth century. "Slavery," considered in the abstract as servile bondage, had existed elsewhere for centuries; indeed, the natives of Africa had known it intimately. Yet nothing was inherent, even in the fact of *Negro* slavery, which should compel it to take the form that it took in North America. Negro slavery flourished in Latin America at that same period, but there the system was strikingly different. In certain altogether crucial respects slavery as we know it was not imported from elsewhere but was created in America —fashioned on the spot by Englishmen in whose traditions such an institution had no part. American slavery was unique, in the sense that, for symmetry and precision of outline, nothing like it had ever previously been seen.

An important essay by Oscar and Mary Handlin has focused new attention upon these facts.[13] Although the first shipload of twenty Negroes had arrived in Virginia in 1619, it was not until the 1660's that the key item in the definition of their status—term of servitude—was clearly fixed in law. It was apparently possible for the earliest Negroes to fall into the various servant categories long familiar to the common law of England, none of which in a practical sense included perpetual and inherited chattel bondage.[14] The bulk of agricultural laborers coming into the colonies at this period were white servants whose terms, as time went on, were to become more and more definitely fixed by indenture, and the Negroes, so far as the law was concerned, could be regarded as "servants" like the rest; there was no articulated legal structure in the colonies to impede their becoming free after a term of service and entering society as artisans and holders of property. Indeed, it was still assumed that the profession of Christianity should itself make a difference in status.[15] Manumission, more-

[13] See Oscar and Mary F. Handlin, "Origins of the Southern Labor System," *William and Mary Quarterly,* 3d Series, VII (April, 1950), 199–222.

[14] The state of villeinage, which had once flourished in England during the Middle Ages, had many of the attributes which later characterized plantation slavery. Yet one crucial aspect of slavery—the legal suppression of the personality—was never present in villeinage. The status of villein, moreover, had by the seventeenth century become virtually extinct in England.

[15] This assumption, having its roots in tradition, was still persistent enough throughout most of the seventeenth century that, as late as the

over, for whatever reason, was a practice common enough to be taken for granted and was attended by no special legal restrictions.[16]

1690's, colonial assemblies felt the necessity to declare, in legal enactments, that baptism did not confer on the slave the right to be manumitted. See John Codman Hurd, *The Law of Freedom and Bondage in the United States* (Boston: Little, Brown, 1858), I, 232, 250, 297, 300–301.

[16] The implications of the Handlin thesis are sufficient for the limited purposes for which it is being used here. To the extent that the Handlins appear to argue that an indentured status was automatically assumed in this period, in the absence of automatic legal guaranties of slavery, to that extent is their essay quite misleading. Insofar as they point, on the other hand, to a condition legally indeterminate—with practice still sufficiently blurred as to allow a number of exceptions, unthinkable a generation later, to automatic slavery—they do no violence to what is known about the period.

This very indeterminancy has sustained a minor debate going back more than fifty years. James C. Ballagh in 1902 first challenged the accepted notion that slavery in Virginia dated from 1619. The parcel of twenty Negroes sold in that year to the Virginians from a Dutch ship were not held as slaves, Ballagh insisted, but rather as servants, and Virginia law did not recognize out-and-out slavery until more than forty years later. John H. Russell, writing in 1913, accepted Ballagh's position. While admitting that lifetime servitude in Virginia existed long before it was given statutory recognition, he agreed that without a prior system of slavery or a slave code it was "plausible that the Africans became servants who, after a term of service varying from two to eight years, were entitled to freedom." Russell cited examples of Negroes who sued for their freedom or who became independent landowners. The Ballagh-Russell thesis—accepted by Ulrich Phillips—was not questioned until Susie Ames's *Studies of the Virginia Eastern Shore* appeared in 1940. Miss Ames held that there was not enough evidence to support Ballagh and Russell, and that Russell's examples may simply have been of manumitted slaves (in other words, if Negroes were not automatically considered as indentured servants—which she thought doubtful—then they must have been automatically considered as slaves: it had to be one thing or the other). Wesley Frank Craven in 1949 gave further support to Miss Ames's position; in his opinion it was likely that "the trend from the first was toward a sharp distinction between . . . [the Negro] and the white servant." The Handlins, taking issue with Miss Ames, in effect brought the argument back to Ballagh and Russell—not asserting flatly (for Miss Ames and Mr. Craven were at least right about the scarcity of evidence) but calling it "much more logical to assume with Russell that these were servants who had completed their terms." And there the argument rests. See James C. Ballagh, *History of Slavery in Virginia* (Baltimore: Johns Hopkins, 1902), pp. 9–10, 27–31; John H. Russell, *The Free Negro in Virginia, 1619–1865* (Baltimore: Johns Hopkins, 1913), pp. 23–31; Ulrich

Yet all this began changing drastically with the 1660's. The very need for new colonists to people the country, and the very preference of planters for English-speaking whites rather than African savages as laborers, had already set into motion a trend to define in law the rights of white servants. To encourage the immigration of such servants and to counteract homeward-drifting rumors of indefinite servitude under desperate conditions, it was becoming more and more the practice to fix definite and limited terms of indenture—five or six years—as a guaranty that a clear future awaited the white man who would cast his lot with the colonies. The Negro, as the Handlins put it, "never profited from these enactments. Farthest removed from the English, least desired, he communicated with no friends who might be deterred from following. Since his coming was involuntary, nothing that happened to him would increase or decrease his numbers."[17] In short, every improvement in the status of the white servant, in widening the gulf between his condition and that of the Negro, served to dramatize the deepening significance of color and in effect to depress the black ever closer to a state of perpetual slavery. This tendency was ultimately recognized by the legislatures of Maryland and Virginia, and they were led to embody in law what had already become fact. "All negroes or other slaves within the province [according to a Maryland law of 1663], and all negroes and other slaves to be hereafter imported into the province, shall serve *durante vita;* and all children born of any negro or other slave, shall be slaves as their fathers were for the term of their lives."[18] Such was the first legal step whereby a black skin would itself ultimately be equatable with "slave."

B. Phillips, *American Negro Slavery* (New York: D. Appleton & Co., 1918), p. 75; Susie M. Ames, *Studies of the Virginia Eastern Shore in the Seventeenth Century* (Richmond, Va.: Dietz, 1940), pp. 100–106; Wesley Frank Craven, *The Southern Colonies in the Seventeenth Century, 1607–1689* (Baton Rouge: Louisiana State University, 1949), pp. 218–19. See also n. 19 below.

[17] Handlin and Handlin, "Origins of the Southern Labor System," p. 211.

[18] Quoted in Hurd, *Law of Freedom and Bondage,* I, 249. A Virginia act of the year before had assumed and implied lifetime slavery. It provided special punishments for servants who ran away in the company of "negroes who are incapable of making satisfaction by addition of a time." Helen T. Catterall, *Judicial Cases concerning American Slavery*

Now there is not much doubt that in actual practice the Negro in Virginia and Maryland had become a slave long before this time. There were precedents in English colonial practice—if not quite in law—that might have been drawn from Barbados any time after the 1630's.[19] In all likelihood the delay in defining Negro status may be ascribed to the fact that their numbers prior to the 1660's were never very great and hardly warranted special legislation.[20] But there is much significance simply in the fact that a state of legal indeterminacy existed for some forty years. During that period there are just enough examples of Negro suits for freedom, Negro ownership of property (with the legal incidents thereof), and so on, to convince one that even so small a margin between automatic lifetime slavery and something else made all the difference—considering what plantation slavery, both

---

and the Negro (Washington: Carnegie Institution, 1926 ff.), I, 59. The matter was made explicit when in 1670 it was enacted that "all servants not being Christians, imported into this colony by shipping, shall be slaves for their lives. . . ." Hurd, *Law of Freedom and Bondage,* I, 233.

[19] It should be noted that the Handlins do rule out rather too hastily the possibility of the Virginians' adapting the status of slavery from the West Indies, claiming as they do that Negroes there were still regarded as "servants" as late as 1663. Their assertion is not entirely correct. There were, indeed, few Negroes in the West Indies prior to the 1630's, and there was no slave code there until 1663. But by 1636, Negroes were already coming into Barbados in great enough numbers that the governor's council felt it necessary in that year, law or no law, to issue a regulation declaring that all Negroes or Indians landed on the island would be considered as slaves, bound to work there for the rest of their lives. See Sir Harry Johnston, *The Negro in the New World* (London: Methuen & Co., 1910), p. 211; Vincent Harlow, *A History of Barbados* (Oxford: Clarendon, 1926), pp. 309–10. Even in the Spanish colonies, lifetime servitude had been familiar for nearly a century.

Some kind of statutory recognition of slavery in the American colonies occurred as follows: Massachusetts, 1641; Connecticut, 1650; Virginia, 1661; Maryland, 1663; New York and New Jersey, 1664; South Carolina, 1684; and Rhode Island, 1700. The apparent significance of this chronology diminishes, however, when it is noted that although enactments in the Northern colonies recognized the legality of lifetime servitude, no effort was made to require all Negroes to be placed in that condition. The number of Negroes, moreover, was so small that in Massachusetts it was not until 1698 that any effort was made to consider the important problem of slave children's status. See Ballagh, *Slavery in Virginia,* pp. 35, 39.

[20] See n. 26 below.

in law and in fact, would be a generation later.[21] It meant a precious margin of space, not to be discounted, for the conservation of traditional human rights. However, once the initial step had been taken, and once Negroes began arriving in appreciable numbers—as they did in the years following the Restoration—there was, as it turned out, little to impede the restless inclination of the law to remove ambiguities. A further course of legislation in the colonies—to which by then had been added the Carolinas—was inaugurated in the period roughly centering upon the turn of the seventeenth century; this legislation began suppressing, with a certain methodical insistence, whatever rights of personality still remained to the Negro slave. It was thus that most of the features marking the system of American slavery, as the nineteenth century knew it, had been stamped upon it by about the middle of the eighteenth.

Yet before reviewing in greater detail the legal aspects of this servitude, we should note that the most vital facts about its inception remain quite unaccounted for. The reasons for its delay have been satisfactorily explained—but why did it occur at all? Why should the drive to establish such a status have got under way when it did? What was the force behind it, especially in view of the prior absence of any sort of laws defining slavery? We may on the one hand point out the lack of any legal structure automatically compelling the Negro to become a slave, but it is only fair, on the other, to note that there was equally little in the form of such a structure to prevent him from becoming one. It is not enough to indicate the simple process whereby the interests of white servants and black were systematically driven apart: what was its dynamic? Why should the status of "slave" have been elaborated, in little more than two generations following its initial definition, with such utter logic and completeness to make American slavery unique among all such systems known to civilization?[22]

---

[21] Russell, *Free Negro in Virginia,* pp. 24–39.

[22] The common-law tradition actually worked in more than one direction to help perfect the legal arrangements of slavery. Not only was there little in the common law, simply as law, to prevent the Negro from being compelled into a state of slavery, but the very philosophy of the common law would encourage the colonial courts to develop whatever laws appeared necessary to deal with unprecedented conditions.

Was it the "motive of gain"? Yes, but with a difference. The motive of gain, as a psychic "fact," can tell us little about what makes men behave as they do; the medieval peasant himself, with his virtually marketless economy, was hardly free from it. But in the emergent agricultural capitalism of colonial Virginia we may already make out a mode of economic organization which was taking on a purity of form never yet seen, and the difference lay in the fact that here a growing system of large-scale staple production for profit was free to develop in a society where no prior traditional institutions, with competing claims of their own, might interpose at any of a dozen points with sufficient power to retard or modify its progress. What happens when such energy meets no limits?[23]

Here, even in its embryonic stages, it is possible to see the process whereby capitalism would emerge as the principal dynamic force in American society. The New World had been discovered and exploited by a European civilization which had always, in contrast with other world cultures, placed a particularly high premium on personal achievement, and it was to be the special genius of Englishmen, from Elizabeth's time onward, to transform this career concept from its earlier chivalric form into one of economic fulfilment—from "glory" to "success." Virginia was settled during the very key period in which the English middle class forcibly reduced, by revolution, the power of those standing institutions—the church and the crown—which most directly symbolized society's traditional limitations upon personal success and

[23] Ever since the time of Marx and Engels (and indeed, before), the idea of "Capitalism" has been a standard tool in the analysis of social behavior. Up to a point this tool is useful; it can throw light on changes in behavior patterns at the point where capitalistic methods and habits in a society begin to supersede feudal ones. In Europe it made some sense. Here is how Engels argued: "According to this conception," he wrote in *Anti-Dühring,* "the ultimate causes of all social changes and political revolutions are to be sought, not in the minds of men, in their increasing insight into eternal truth and justice, but in changes in the mode of production and exchange; they are to be sought not in the *philosophy* but in the *economics* of the epoch concerned." But then this idea cannot tell us much about the differences between two societies, *both* capitalist, but in one of which the "means of production" have changed into capitalistic ones and in the other of which the means of production were never anything *but* capitalistic and in which no other forces were present to resist their development.

mobility. What the return of the crown betokened in 1660 was not so much "reaction" as the fact that all society had by then somehow made terms with the Puritan Revolution. Virginia had proven a uniquely appropriate theater for the acting-out of this narrower, essentially modern ideal of personal, of *economic,* success. Land in the early days was cheap and plentiful; a ready market for tobacco existed; even the yeoman farmer could rise rapidly if he could make the transition to staple production; and above all there was a quick recognition of accomplishment, by a standard which was not available in England but which was the only one available in Virginia: success in creating a plantation.[24]

The decade of the 1660's, inaugurated by the restoration of the Stuart monarchy, marked something of a turning point in the fortunes of the colony not unrelated to the movement there and in Maryland to fix irrevocably upon the Negro a lifetime of slavery. It was during this decade that certain factors bearing upon the colony's economic future were precipitated. One such factor was a serious drop in tobacco prices, brought on not only by overproduction but also by the Navigation Acts of 1660 and 1661,[25]

[24] Despite the relative mobility of English society since Tudor times, personal achievement and status still inhered in any number of preferable alternatives to trade and production. But the openness of Virginia lay in the fact that purely capitalistic incentives were being used to get people to come there. No nobles, with their retinues of peasants, migrated to the colony; indeed, there was little reason why the ideal of "making good" should in itself hold many attractions for an aristocracy already established. But for others there were rewards for risk-taking which were simply not available in England. True, Virginia did develop its own aristocracy, but it had to be a created one, based on terms peculiar to the new country, and—at least as a basis for aspirations—theoretically open to everyone. At any rate, the standards for joining it were not primarily chivalric: to be a "gentleman" one must first have been a successful planter.

[25] These acts embodied the Puritan mercantilist policy which Cromwell had never been able to enforce but which had been taken over by the Restoration government. Their general purpose was that of redirecting colonial trade (much of which had been engrossed by the Dutch during the Civil War) through the hands of English merchants. Their immediate effects on tobacco, before the market could readjust itself, was, from the viewpoint of colonial planters, most unfavorable. By limiting the sale of Virginia tobacco to England and requiring that it be transported in English ships, the Navigation Acts cut off Virginia's profitable trade with

and the market was not to be fully restored for another twenty years. This meant, with rising costs and a disappearing margin of profit, that commercial production on a small-scale basis was placed under serious disabilities. Another factor was the rise in the slave population. Whereas there had been only about 300 in 1650, by 1670 there were, according to Governor Berkeley, 2,000 slaves in a servant population of 8,000. This was already 25 per cent of the servants, and the figure was even more significant for the future, since the total white servant population in any given period could never be counted on to exceed their average annual immigration multiplied by five or six (the usual term in years, of their indenture), while the increase of slaves over the same period would be cumulative.[26] Such a development would by now be quite enough to stimulate the leaders of the colony—virtually all planters—to clarify in law once and for all the status of lifetime Negro servitude. The formation in 1662 of a Royal Company of Adventurers for the importation of Negroes symbolized

the Dutch and temporarily crippled its profitable foreign markets. This, according to Thomas J. Wertenbaker, was the basic cause for the serious drop in tobacco prices. See *Planters of Colonial Virginia* (Princeton: Princeton University Press, 1922), pp. 85–87, 90.

[26] "40,000 persons, men, women, and children, of which 2,000 are black slaves, 6,000 Christian servants for a short time. Gov. Berkeley." Evarts B. Greene and Virginia D. Harrington, *American Population before the Federal Census of 1790* (New York: Columbia University Press, 1932), p. 36. This figure may be looked at two ways. From the standpoint of *later* populations, one may call attention to its smallness. But consider how it must have appeared to the man looking back to a time only two decades before, when the number of Negroes was negligible. Now, in 1670, with Negroes constituting a full quarter of the servant population (a proportion which gave every promise of increasing), they become a force to be dealt with. By now, men would take them into account as a basis for future calculations in a way which previously they had never needed to do. The very laws demonstrate this. Moreover, Negroes had accumulated in large enough parcels in the hands of the colony's most powerful men to develop in these men deep vested interests in the Negroes' presence and a strong concern with the legal aspects of their future. Among the land patents of the sixties, for example, may already be seen Richard Lee with eighty Negroes, Carter of Corotoman with twenty, the Scarboroughs with thirty-nine, and numerous patents listing fifteen or more. Philip Alexander Bruce, *Economic History of Virginia in the Seventeenth Century* (New York: Macmillan, 1907), II, 78.

the crown's expectation that a labor force of slaves would be the coming thing in the colonies.[27]

It was thus in a period of relatively hard times that it became clear, if the colony of Virginia were to prosper, that capitalism would be the dynamic force in its economic life. "Success" could no longer be visualized as a rise from small beginnings, as it once could, but must now be conceived as a matter of substantial initial investments in land, equipment, and labor, plus the ability to undertake large annual commitments on credit. With the fall in tobacco prices, and with the tiny margin of profit that remained, the yeoman farmer found it difficult enough to eke out a bare living, let alone think of competing with the large planter or of purchasing slaves' or servants' indentures.[28] Success was still possible, but now its terms were clearer, and those who achieved it would be fewer in numbers. The man who managed it would be the man with the large holdings—the man who

[27] The subsequent increase of slaves in Virginia was not largely the work of this company. But its formation under royal protection, coming at the time it did, appears to form part of a general pattern of expectations regarding the future state of labor in the plantation colonies. This, taken together with the drop in tobacco prices and coincident with the Navigation Acts and the first general laws on perpetual servitude, all coming at once, seem to add up to something: profitable enterprise, when possible at all, would henceforth as never before have to be conceived in terms of heavily capitalized investment, and more and more men were recognizing this.

[28] This had not always been so; the aspirations of a farmer in, say, 1649, with prices at 3 pence a pound, could include a wide range of possibilities. But now, with the price at one-fourth of that figure and costs proportionately much greater than formerly, he could hardly think of the future realistically in terms of becoming a planter. See Lewis Cecil Gray, *History of Agriculture in the Southern States to 1860* (Washington: Carnegie Institution, 1933), I, 263. Now this does not mean that after 1660 the yeoman farmer invariably faced destitution. A great deal depended on how such a farmer conceived his future. The man who made his living from diversified subsistence farming and who planted tobacco as an extra-money crop would undoubtedly suffer less from a drop in prices than the heavily capitalized planter. However if this same farmer hoped to emulate "his predecessors of the earlier period in saving money, purchasing land . . . and becoming a substantial citizen, the task was well nigh impossible of accomplishment." Wertenbaker, *Planters of Colonial Virginia,* p. 97. See also *ibid.,* pp. 96–100, for an extended discussion of the effects of this depression on the yeomanry as a class.

could command a substantial force of laborers, white or black—who could afford a sizable yearly investment in the handling of his crop: in short, the capitalist planter.

The period beginning in the 1680's and ending about 1710 marked still a new phase. It saw, now under conditions of comparative prosperity, the full emergence of the plantation as the basic unit of capitalist agriculture. By about 1680 the market for Virginia and Maryland tobacco had been restored, though it is important to note that this was accompanied by no great rise in prices. It was rather a matter of having recaptured the European market by flooding it with cheap tobacco and underselling competitors. Returning prosperity, therefore, meant something far more concrete to the man with resources, who could produce tobacco in large enough amounts to make a slim profit margin worthwhile, than to the one whose productivity was limited by the acreage which he and his family could work. These years also witnessed the initial exploitation of the Carolinas, a process which moved much more directly toward large agricultural units than had been the case in Virginia.[29] The acceleration of this development toward clarifying the terms of commercial production—large plantations and substantial investments—had a direct connection with the widening of the market for slaves during this same period. Hand in hand with large holdings went slaves—an assumption which was now being taken more or less for granted. "A rational man," wrote a

[29] The Carolina proprietors had a far clearer notion of the terms on which money was to be made from their colony than had been true of the London Company of sixty years before with regard to Virginia. They appear at the very outset to have fostered the establishment of large estates, and a number of such estates set up in the 1670's and 1680's were organized by Barbados men with first-hand plantation experience. See Gray, *History of Agriculture,* I, 324–25; also J. P. Thomas, "Barbadians in Early South Carolina," *South Carolina Historical Magazine,* XXXI (April, 1930), 89. Although a dominant staple was not to emerge until some time later, with rice and indigo, it seems to have been conceived in terms of large units to a degree never envisaged at a comparable stage in the development of Virginia. One index of this is quickly seen in the composition of the laboring population there; a little over a generation after the first settlements the ratio of Negro slaves to whites in the total population could be safely estimated at about one to one, whereas the same ratio would not be attained in Virginia until late in the eighteenth century. Greene and Harrington, *American Population,* pp. 124, 137.

South Carolina colonist in 1682, "will certainly inquire, 'when I have Land, what shall I doe with it? What commoditys shall I be able to produce, that will yield me money in other countrys, that I may be inabled to buy Negro-slaves, (without which a planter can never doe any great matter)?'"[30] The point had clearly passed when white servants could realistically, on any long-term appraisal, be considered preferable to Negro slaves. Such appraisals were now being made in terms of capitalized earning power, a concept appropriate to large operations rather than small, to long-term rather than short-term planning.

It was, of course, only the man of means who could afford to think in this way. But then he is the one who most concerns us—the man responsible for Negro slavery. Determined in the sixties and seventies to make money despite hard times and low prices, and willing to undertake the investments which that required, he could now in the eighties reap the fruits of his foresight. His slaves were more valuable than ever—a monument to his patience and planning. What had made them so? For one thing he, unlike the yeoman farmer, had a large establishment for training them and was not pressed by the need, as he would have been with white servants on limited indenture, to exploit their *immediate* labor. The labor was his permanently. And for another thing, the system was by now just old enough to make clear for the first time the full meaning of a second generation of native-born American Negroes. These were the dividends: slaves born to the work and using English as their native tongue.[31] By the 1690's the demand for slaves in the British colonies had become so great, and the Royal African Company so inefficient in supplying them, that in 1698 Parliament revoked the company's monopoly on the African coast and threw open

[30] Quoted in Gray, *History of Agriculture,* I, 352.

[31] This is another point of view from which to consider the 1671 figure (cited in n. 25 above) on the Virginia slave population. The difference between the 300 Negroes of 1650 and the 2,000 of 1670 is substantial—nearly a sevenfold increase. According to Berkeley's testimony the importations over the previous seven years had not been more than two or three cargoes. If this were true, it would be safe to estimate that a significant number of that 2,000 must already have been native-born American Negroes. As for the period to which the above paragraph has reference—fifteen or twenty years later—the number of native-born must by then have increased considerably.

the traffic to independent merchants and traders. The stream of incoming slaves, already of some consequence, now became enormous, and at the same time the annual flow of white servants to Virginia and the Carolinas dropped sharply. By 1710 it had become virtually negligible.[32]

What meaning might all this have had for the legal status of the Negro? The connection was intimate and direct; with the full development of the plantation there was nothing, so far as his interests were concerned, to prevent unmitigated capitalism from becoming unmitigated slavery. The planter was now engaged in capitalistic agriculture with a labor force entirely under his control. The personal relationship between master and slave—in any case less likely to exist on large agricultural units than on smaller ones—now became far less important than the economic necessities which had forced the slave into this "unnatural" organization in the first place. For the plantation to operate efficiently and profitably, and with a force of laborers not all of whom may have been fully broken to plantation discipline, the necessity of training them to work long hours and to give unquestioning obedience to their masters and overseers superseded every other consideration. The master must have absolute power over the slave's body, and the law was developing in such a way as to give it to him at every crucial point. Physical discipline was made virtually unlimited[33] and

[32] Greene and Harrington, *American Population,* pp. 136–37; Gray, *History of Agriculture,* I, 349–50.

[33] As early as 1669 a Virginia law had declared it no felony if a master or overseer killed a slave who resisted punishment. According to the South Carolina code of 1712, the punishment for offering "any violence to any christian or white person, by striking, or the like" was a severe whipping for the first offense, branding for the second, and death for the third. Should the white man attacked be injured or maimed, the punishment was automatically death. The same act provided that a runaway slave be severely whipped for his first offense, branded for his second, his ears cut off for the third, and castrated for the fourth. It is doubtful whether such punishments were often used, but their very existence served to symbolize the relationship of absolute power over the slave's body. Hurd, *Law of Freedom and Bondage,* I, 232; Thomas Cooper and D. J. McCord (eds.), *Statutes at Large of South Carolina* (Columbia, S.C., 1836–41), VII, 357–59.

the slave's chattel status unalterably fixed.[34] It was in such a setting that those rights of personality traditionally regarded between men as private and inherent, quite apart from the matter of lifetime servitude, were left virtually without defense. The integrity of the family was ignored, and slave marriage was deprived of any legal or moral standing.[35] The condition of a bondsman's soul—a matter of much concern to church and civil authority in the Spanish colonies—was here very quickly dropped from consideration. A series of laws enacted between 1667 and 1671 had systematically removed any lingering doubts whether conversion to Christianity should make a difference in status: henceforth it made none.[36] The balance, therefore, involved on the one side the constant pressure of costs, prices, and the problems of management, and on the other the personal interests of the slave. Here, there were no counterweights: those interests were unsupported by any social pressures from the outside; they were cherished by no customary feudal immunities; they were no concern of the government (the king's main interest was in

[34] Slaves in seventeenth-century Virginia had become, as a matter of actual practice, classed on the same footing as household goods and other personal property. The code of 1705 made them a qualified form of real estate, but that law was in 1726 amended by another which declared that slaves were "to pass as chattels." Bruce, *Economic History,* II, 99; Hurd, *Law of Freedom and Bondage,* I, 242. The South Carolina code of 1740 made them "chattels personal, in the hands of their owners and possessors and their executors, administrators and assigns, to all intents, constructions and purposes whatsoever. . . ." *Ibid.,* I, 303.

[35] Bruce (*Economic History,* II, 108) describes a will, written about 1680, in which a woman "bequeathed to one daughter, . . . a negress and the third child to be born of her; to a second daughter, . . . the first and second child to be born of the same woman."

[36] See Handlin and Handlin, "Origins of the Southern Labor System," p. 212. The Maryland law of 1671 could leave no possible doubt in this matter, declaring that any Christianized slave "is, are and shall att all tymes hereafter be adjudged Reputed deemed and taken to be and Remayne in Servitude and Bondage and subject to the same Servitude and Bondage to all intents and purposes as if hee shee they every or any of them was or were in and Subject vnto before such his her or their Becomeing Christian or Christians or Receiving of the Sacrament of Baptizme any opinion or other matter or thing to the Contrary in any wise Notwithstanding." William Hand Browne (ed.), *Archives of Maryland* (Baltimore, 1884), II, 272. See also n. 15 above.

tobacco revenue); they could not be sustained by the church, for the church had little enough power and influence among its own white constituencies, to say nothing of the suspicion its ministers aroused at every proposal to enlarge the church's work among the blacks.[37] The local planter class controlled all those public concerns which most affected the daily life of the colony, and it was thus only in matters of the broadest and most general policy that this planter domination was in any way touched by

[37] What this meant to the Negro is admirably reflected in a book by Morgan Godwyn, an Anglican minister who served in the 1670's both in Barbados and in Virginia. Godwyn's book, *The Negro's and Indian's Advocate,* was a plea for the care of the Negro's soul. He attacked the planters for keeping religion from the slaves, for "not allowing their children *Baptism;* nor suffering them upon better terms than direct *Fornication,* to live with their Women, (for Wives, I may not call them, being never married). And accounting it Foppish; when Dead, to think of giving them *Christian,* or even decent Burial; that so their pretence for Brutifying them, might find no Contradiction" (p. 37). In Godwyn's eyes the planters were men "who for the most part do know no other God but money, nor Religion but Profit" (Preface). He quotes one Barbadian who "openly maintained . . . that Negroes were beasts, and had no more souls than beasts, and that religion did not concern them. Adding that they [his fellow Barbadians] went *not* to those parts to save souls, or propagate religion, but to get Money" (p. 39). Even the care of white souls in the colonies appears to have occupied a rather low order of concern. The Attorney-General of England in 1693 objected strenuously to the erection of a college in Virginia, though he was reminded of the need to educate young men for the ministry and was begged to consider the souls of the colonists. "Souls! Damn your souls," he replied, "make tobacco." Quoted in Wertenbaker, *Planters of Colonial Virginia,* p. 138. It is doubtful that the planters of Virginia were quite so brutal as the Barbadians in their attitude toward the Negro or in the management of their plantations, but even in Virginia Godwyn found that the idea of teaching religion to the Negro slave was thought "so idle and ridiculous, so utterly needless and unnecessary, that no Man can forfeit his Judgement more, than by any proposal looking or tending that way" (p. 172). That such an attitude had not changed by the eighteenth century is suggested by a piece in the *Athenian Oracle* of Boston in 1707 in which the writer declared, "Talk to a *Planter* of the *Soul* of a *Negro,* and he'll be apt to tell ye (or at least his actions speak it loudly) that the Body of one of them may be worth twenty pounds; but the Souls of an Hundred of them would not yield him one Farthing." Quoted in Marcus W. Jernegan, "Slavery and Conversion in the American Colonies," *American Historical Review,* XXI (April, 1916), 516.

bureaucratic decisions made in London. The emergent institution of slavery was in effect unchallenged by any other institutions.[38]

The result was that the slave, utterly powerless, would at every critical point see his interests further depressed. At those very points the drive of the law—unembarrassed by the perplexities of competing interests—was to clarify beyond all question, to rationalize, to simplify, and to make more logical and symmetrical the slave's status in society. So little impeded was this pressure to define and clarify that all the major categories in law which bore upon such status were very early established with great thoroughness and completeness. The unthinking aggressions upon the slave's personality which such a situation made possible becomes apparent upon an examination, in greater detail, of these legal categories.

3

SLAVERY IN CAPITALIST AND
NON-CAPITALIST CULTURES

The four major legal categories which defined the status of the American slave may be roughly classified as "term of servitude," "marriage and the family," "police and disciplinary powers over the slave" and "property and other civil rights." The first of these, from which somehow all the others flowed, had in effect been established during the latter half of the seventeenth century; a slave was a slave for the duration of his life, and slavery was a status which he transmitted by inheritance to his children and his children's children.

It would be fairest, for several reasons, to view the remaining three categories in terms of the jurisprudence of the nineteenth century. By that time the most savage aspects of slavery from the standpoint of Southern practice (and thus, to a certain extent, of law) had become greatly softened. We may accordingly see

[38] For the control exercised over colonial institutional life by this planter elite, see Craven, *Southern Colonies,* pp. 153, 159, 170–72, 274–78; Philip A. Bruce, *Institutional History of Virginia in the Seventeenth Century* (New York: Putnam, 1910), I, 468; and George M. Brydon, *Virginia's Mother Church, and the Political Conditions under Which It Grew* (Richmond: Virginia Historical Society, 1947), I, 94–96, 232.

it in its most humane light and at the same time note the clarity with which its basic outlines remained fixed and embodied in law, much as they had been laid down before the middle of the eighteenth century.[39]

That most ancient and intimate of institutional arrangements, marriage and the family, had long since been destroyed by the law, and the law never showed any inclination to rehabilitate it. Here was the area in which considerations of humanity might be expected most widely to prevail, and, indeed, there is every reason to suppose that on an informal daily basis they did: the contempt in which respectable society held the slave trader, who separated mother from child and husband from wife, is proverbial in Southern lore.[40] On the face of things, it ought to have been simple enough to translate this strong social sentiment into the appropriate legal enactments, which might systematically have guaranteed the inviolability of the family and the sanctity of the marriage bond, such as governed Christian polity everywhere. Yet the very nature of the plantation economy and the way in which the basic arrangements of Southern life radiated from it, made it inconceivable that the law should tolerate any ambiguity, should the painful clash between humanity and property interest ever occur. Any restrictions on the separate sale of slaves would have been reflected immediately in the market;

[39] We have a further advantage in regarding the law of slavery in the light of the nineteenth century. Two general developments of that period inspired a great wealth of writing on the subject in the form of commentaries by jurists and *obiter dicta* by judges, as well as a fresh course of marginal legislation bearing on some of slavery's social implications. These developments were the expansion of slavery into the Gulf states and, much more important, the moral pressures being exerted on Southerners both from the North and from abroad. The bulk of the Southern response to this latter fact took the form of various kinds of defenses of slavery, but for Southern jurists it naturally stimulated a re-examination of the legal aspects of their "peculiar institution."

[40] "In all the category of disreputable callings, there were none so despised as the slave-trader. The odium descended upon his children and his children's children. Against the legal right to buy and sell slaves for profit, this public sentiment lifted a strong arm, and rendered forever odious the name of 'Negro-trader.'" Beverly B. Munford, *Virginia's Attitude toward Slavery and Secession* (New York: Longmans, Green, 1909), pp. 101-2.

their price would have dropped considerably.[41] Thus the law could permit no aspect of the slave's conjugal state to have an independent legal existence outside the power of the man who owned him: "The relation of master and slave is wholly incompatible with even the qualified relation of husband and wife, as it is supposed to exist among slaves. . . ."[42] Marriage, for them, was denied any standing in law. Accordingly, as T. R. R. Cobb of Georgia admitted, "The contract of marriage not being recognized among slaves, none of its consequences follow. . . ."[43] "The relation between slaves," wrote a North Carolina judge in 1858, "is essentially different from that of man and wife joined in lawful wedlock . . . [for] with slaves it may be dissolved at the pleasure of either party, or by the sale of one or both, depending on the caprice or necessity of the owners."[44]

It would thus go without saying that the offspring of such "contubernial relationships," as they were called, had next to no guaranties against indiscriminate separation from their parents.[45]

[41] This may be tested against what did typically happen in cases where restrictions were placed by the seller himself upon the separation of slaves with whom he was obliged, for whatever reason, to part. "In proportion as these restrictions put important limitations on the purchaser's rights and were safeguarded, they lessened the slave's salability." Frederic Bancroft, *Slave-trading in the Old South* (Baltimore: J. H. Furst, 1931), p. 214.

[42] *Howard* v. *Howard*, 6 Jones N.C. 235 (December, 1858), quoted in Helen T. Catterall, *Judicial Cases concerning American Slavery and the Negro* (Washington: Carnegie Institution, 1926 ff.), II, 221.

[43] Thomas R. R. Cobb, *An Inquiry into the Law of Slavery in the United States of America* (Philadelphia: T. & J. W. Johnson, 1858), p. 246.

[44] Quoted in Catterall, *Judicial Cases*, II, 221.

[45] The few exceptions—none of which meant very much in practice, except perhaps the law of Louisiana—are discussed in Bancroft, *Slave-trading*, pp. 197–221. "Louisiana, least American of the Southern States," writes Mr. Bancroft, "was least inhuman. In becoming Americanized it lost many a liberal feature of the old French *code noir,* but it forbade sale of mothers from their children less than ten years of age (and *vice versa*) and bringing into the State any slave child under ten years of age without its mother, if living. The penalty for violating either prohibition was from $1,000 to $2,000 and the forfeiture of the slave. That would have meant much if it had been strictly enforced" (p. 197). Louisiana's Spanish and French background, plus the fact that in both the

Of additional interest is the fact that children derived their condition from that of their mother. This was not unique to American slavery, but it should be noted that especially in a system
conceived and evolved exclusively on grounds of property there
could be little doubt about how such a question would be
resolved. Had status been defined according to the father's condition—as was briefly the case in seventeenth-century Maryland,
following the ancient common law—there would instantly have
arisen the irksome question of what to do with the numerous
mulatto children born every year of white planter-fathers and
slave mothers. It would have meant the creation of a free mulatto
class, automatically relieving the master of so many slaves on
the one hand, while burdening him on the other with that many
colored children whom he could not own. Such equivocal relationships were never permitted to vex the law. That "the
father of a slave is unknown to our law" was the universal
understanding of Southern jurists.[46] It was thus that a father,
among slaves, was legally "unknown," a husband without the
rights of his bed,[47] the state of marriage defined as "only that
concubinage . . . with which alone, perhaps, their condition is
compatible,"[48] and motherhood clothed in the scant dignity of the
breeding function.[49]

---

legal and social senses slavery in Latin America generally was very different from slavery in North America, may furnish significant clues to
some of the idiosyncrasies in the Louisiana code. See below.

[46] *Frazier* v. *Spear,* 2 Bibb (Ken.), 385 (Fall, 1811), quoted in Catterall, *Judicial Cases,* I, 287.

[47] "A slave has never maintained an action against the violator of his
bed. A slave is not admonished for incontinence, or punished for fornication or adultery; never prosecuted for bigamy, or petty treason for killing
a husband being a slave, any more than admitted to an appeal for murder." Opinion of Daniel Dulany, Esq., Attorney-General of Maryland,
quoted in William Goodell, *The American Slave Code in Theory and
Practice* (New York: American and Foreign Anti-Slavery Society, 1853),
pp. 106-7.

[48] *State* v. *Samuel (a slave),* 2 Dev. and Bat. (N.C.), 177 (December,
1836), quoted in Catterall, *Judicial Cases,* II, 77.

[49] The picturesque charge that planters deliberately "bred" their slave
women has never been substantiated, and Avery Craven's point that
white women bred about as young and as often as their black sisters is a
sensible one. But with no law to prevent the separation of parents and

Regarding matters of police and discipline, it is hardly necessary to view the typical slave's lot in the nineteenth century as one of stripes and torture. Indeed, we should probably not stretch the truth greatly were we to concede Ulrich Phillips' sympathetic picture of a just regime tempered with paternal indulgence on the majority of well-run plantations. Among decent Southerners the remark, "I have been told that he does not use his people well," was a pronouncement of deep social censure.[50] Yet here again what impresses us is not the laxity with which much of the daily discipline was undoubtedly handled, but rather the completeness with which such questions, even extending to life and limb, were in fact under the master's dominion. "On our estates," wrote the Southern publicist J. D. B. DeBow in 1853, "we dispense with the whole machinery of public police and public courts of justice. Thus we try, decide, and execute the sentences in thousands of cases, which in other countries would go into the courts."[51] The law deplored "cruel and unusual punishment." But wherever protection was on the one hand theoretically extended,[52] it was practically canceled on

---

children, and with the value of a slave being much in excess of what it cost to rear him, the temptation to think and talk about a prolific Negro woman as a "rattlin' good breeder" was very strong. See Avery Craven, *The Coming of the Civil War* (New York: Scribner, 1942; 2d ed.; Chicago: University of Chicago Press, 1957), p. 84; Stampp, *Peculiar Institution*, p. 249. Frederic Bancroft gives numerous examples of advertisements describing Negro women in just this way. *Slave-trading,* pp. 68–79.

[50] "There is a public sentiment to which they are amenable; a cruel, neglectful master is marked and despised; and if cruel and neglectful by proxy, he does not escape reprobation." Nehemiah Adams, *A South-Side View of Slavery* (1855), p. 97. Such a man, according to Frederick Law Olmsted, was known as a "nigger-killer." *Journey in the Seaboard Slave States* (New York: Putnam, 1904), I, 120–21.

[51] DeBow, *Industrial Resources* (1852–53), II, 249.

[52] There was, for example, a South Carolina law of 1740 which provided that, "In case any person shall wilfully cut out the tongue, put out the eye, castrate, or cruelly scald, burn, or deprive any slave of any limb or member, or shall inflict any other cruel punishment, other than whipping, or beating with a horsewhip, cowskin, switch, or small stick, or by putting irons on, or confining or imprisoning such slave, every such person shall, for every such offense, forfeit the sum of one hundred pounds current money." Goodell, *American Slave Code,* pp. 159–60.

the other by the universal prohibition in Southern law against permitting slaves to testify in court, except against each other, and in any case the courts generally accepted the principle that the line between correction and cruelty was impossible to determine. Thus a Virginia judge in 1827, faced with an indictment against a master "for cruelly beating his own slave," felt bound to decline jurisdiction with the rhetorical demand: "Without any proofs that the common law did ever protect the slave against minor injuries from the hand of the master . . . where are we to look for the power which is now claimed for us?"[53] To the jurist Cobb it seemed clear on principle that "the battery of a slave, without special enactment, could not be prosecuted criminally."[54] Public opinion itself should, it was generally held, deter wanton brutalities. But the final argument was that of self-interest. "Where the battery was committed by the master himself, there would be no redress whatever, for the reason given in Exodus 21:21, 'for he is his money.' The powerful protection of the master's private interest would of itself go far to remedy this evil."[55]

Even the murder of a slave found the law straining all its

---

[53] *Commonwealth* v. *Turner,* 5 Randolph 678 (November, 1827), quoted in Catterall, *Judicial Cases,* I, 150. It was in the same spirit that Judge Ruffin of North Carolina expressed himself in the case of *State* v. *Mann* in 1829. "But upon the general question whether the owner is answerable, *criminalter,* for a battery upon his own slave . . . the Court entertains but little doubt. That he is so liable has never been decided, nor, as far as is known, been hitherto contended. There has been no prosecutions of the sort. The established and uniform practice of the country in this respect is the best evidence of the portion of the power deemed by the whole community requisite to the preservation of the master's dominion. . . . The power of the master must be absolute to render the submission of the slave perfect. I most freely confess my sense of the harshness of the proposition. I feel it as deeply as any man can. . . . But it is inherent in the relation of master and slave. . . . We cannot allow the right of the master to be brought into discussion in the Courts of justice. The slave, to remain a slave, must be made sensible that there is no appeal from his master. . . ." Quoted in Goodell, *American Slave Code,* pp. 171–73.

[54] Cobb, *Inquiry,* p. 90. "This [the Negro's helplessness] is one of the most vulnerable points in the system of negro slavery," Cobb admitted, "and should be further guarded by legislation." *Ibid.,* p. 98.

[55] *Ibid.,* p. 98.

resources to avoid jurisdiction.[56] Murder was indeed punishable, but under circumstances peculiar to the state of slavery, not in ways applying to white society, and always under the disabilities which barred the testimony of Negroes in the courts. An act of North Carolina in 1798 provided that the punishment for "maliciously killing a slave" should be the same as for the murder of a free person—but it did not apply to an outlawed slave or to a slave "in the act of resistance to his lawful owner" or to a slave "dying under moderate correction."[57] The law in South Carolina allowed that in the absence of competent witnesses to the homicide of a slave, the affidavit of the accused was admissible in his favor before a jury.[58] The criminal jurisprudence of Virginia had never known, before 1851, a case of "more atrocious and wicked cruelty" than that of a man named Souther who had killed his slave, Sam, under the most lurid circumstances.[59] Yet the conviction was for murder in the second degree, and Souther escaped with five years in the penitentiary. In general, the court's primary care—not only in the killing of slaves by persons other than the master but also in cases where the slave himself had committed murder and was executed by the state—was for the pecuniary interest of the owner. Numerous

[56] "It would seem that from the very nature of slavery, and the necessarily degraded social position of the slave, many acts would extenuate the homicide of a slave, and reduce the offence to a lower grade, which would not constitute a legal provocation if done by a white person." *Ibid.*, p. 92.

[57] Goodell, *American Slave Code*, p. 180. There was a law in Tennessee to the same effect and in virtually the same words. See Hurd, *Law of Freedom and Bondage*, II, 90.

[58] Cobb, *Inquiry*, p. 96.

[59] "The negro was tied to a tree and whipped with switches. When Souther became fatigued with the labour of whipping, he called upon a negro man of his, and made him cob Sam with a shingle. He also made a negro woman of his help to cob him. And after cobbing and whipping, he applied fire to the body of the slave; about his back, belly and private parts. He then caused him to be washed down with hot water, in which pods of red pepper had been steeped. The negro was also tied to a log and to the bed post with ropes, which choked him, and he was kicked and stamped by Souther. This sort of punishment was continued and repeated until the negro died under its infliction." *Souther v. Commonwealth*, 7 Grattan 673 (June, 1851), quoted in Catterall, *Judicial Cases*, I, 224.

enactments provided for compensation in either event.[60] It was precisely this pecuniary interest which was at the very heart of legal logic on all such questions. Just as it was presumed to operate against "cruel and unusual punishment," so it became virtually a *non sequitur* that a man should kill his own slave. The principle had been enunciated very early: "It cannot be presumed that prepensed malice (which alone makes murder felony) should induce any man to destroy his own estate."[61]

The rights of property, and all other civil and legal "rights," were everywhere denied the slave with a clarity that left no doubt of his utter dependency upon his master. "A slave is in absolute bondage; he has no civil right, and can hold no property, except at the will and pleasure of his master."[62] He could neither give nor receive gifts; he could make no will, nor could he, by will, inherit anything. He could not hire himself out or make contracts for any purpose—even including, as we have seen, that of matrimony—and thus neither his word nor his bond had any standing in law. He could buy or sell nothing at all, except as his master's agent, could keep no cattle, horses, hogs, or sheep and, in Mississippi at least, could raise no cotton. Even masters who permitted such transactions, except under express arrangement, were uniformly liable to fines.[63] It was obvious, then, that the case of a slave who should presume to buy his own freedom—he being unable to possess money—would involve a legal absurdity. "Slaves have no legal rights in things, real or personal; but whatever they may acquire, belongs, in point of law, to their masters."[64]

[60] See Hurd, *Law of Freedom and Bondage,* I, 253, 296–97, 300.

[61] "An act about the casual killing of slaves" (Virginia, 1669), *ibid.,* I, 232.

[62] Opinion of Judge Crenshaw in *Brandon et al.* v. *Planters' and Merchants' Bank of Huntsville,* 1 Stewart's Ala. Report, 320 (January, 1838), quoted in Goodell, *American Slave Code,* p. 92.

[63] *Ibid.,* pp. 89–104.

[64] *Ibid.,* p. 88. A substantial number of Negroes did in fact buy their freedom in the ante-bellum South, but this required the full co-operation of their masters. Legally the slave had no claim to the money he may have collected for his own purchase. This highly precarious customary sanction, if such it may be called, should be compared to the fully articulated legal sanction embodied in the Cuban *coartación* (see n. 109 below). For a discussion of hiring-out arrangements which, although

Such proscriptions were extended not only over all civil rights but even to the civic privileges of education and worship. Every Southern state except Maryland and Kentucky had stringent laws forbidding anyone to teach slaves reading and writing, and in some states the penalties applied to the educating of free Negroes and mulattoes as well. It was thought that "teaching slaves to read and write tends to dissatisfaction in their minds, and to produce insurrection and rebellion";[65] in North Carolina it was a crime to distribute among them any pamphlet or book, not excluding the Bible. The same apprehensions applied to instruction in religion. Southern society was not disposed to withhold the consolations of divine worship from its slaves, but the conditions would have to be laid down not by the church as an institution, not even by the planters as laity, but by planters simply as masters. The conscientious master no doubt welcomed having the gospel preached to his slaves, provided that they should hear it, as J. W. Fowler of Coahoma County, Mississippi, specified, "in its original purity and simplicity." Fowler wrote to his overseer that "in view of the fanaticism of the age it behooves the Master or Overseer to be present on all such occasions."[66] Alexander Telfair, of Savannah, instructed his overseer that there should be "no night-meeting or preaching . . . allowed on the place, except on Saturday night & Sunday morn."[67] Similar restrictions found their way into the law itself. Typical were the acts of South Carolina forbidding religious meetings of slaves or free Negroes "either before the rising of the sun or after the setting of the same," and of Mississippi permitting slaves, if authorized by their masters, to attend the preaching of a *white* minister. It was a state of things deplored by the Southern churches, for the law had been none of their doing. "There are over TWO MILLIONS of human beings in the condition of heathen,"

---

not recognized in law, were by no means unfamiliar (and under which the slave appears in practice to have had more initiative than the law theoretically gave him), see Richard B. Morris, "The Measure of Bondage in the Slave States," *Mississippi Valley Historical Review*, XLI (September, 1954), 219–40; see also Part IV, n. 115.

[65] Goodell, *American Slave Code*, p. 321.

[66] Ulrich B. Phillips (ed.), *A Documentary History of American Industrial Society* (Cleveland: Arthur H. Clark, 1910), I, 115.

[67] *Ibid.*, p. 127.

lamented the Presbyterian Synod of South Carolina and Georgia in 1833, "and some of them in worse condition."

In the present state of feeling in the South, a ministry of their own color could neither be obtained NOR TOLERATED. But do not the negroes have access to the gospel through the stated ministry of the whites? We answer, No. The negroes have no regular and efficient ministry: as a matter of course, no churches; neither is there sufficient room in the white churches for their accommodation.[68]

But the church could do nothing. Its rural congregations were full of humane and decent Christians, but as an institution of authority and power it had no real existence.

It is true that among the most attractive features of the plantation legend, dear to every Southerner with a sense of his past, were the paternal affection of the good master for his blacks and the warm sentiments entertained in Southern society at large for the faithful slave. The other side of the coin, then, might appear as something of a paradox: the most implacable race-consciousness yet observed in virtually any society. It was evolved in the Southern mind, one might say, as a simple syllogism, the precision of whose terms paralleled the precision of the system itself. All slaves are black; slaves are degraded and contemptible; therefore all blacks are degraded and contemptible and should be kept in a state of slavery. How had the simple syllogism come into being? That very strength and bulwark of American society, capitalism, unimpeded by prior arrangements and institutions, had stamped the status of slave upon the black with a clarity which elsewhere could never have been so profound, and had further defined the institution of slavery with such nicety that the slave *was,* in fact, degraded. That the black, as a species, was thus contemptible seemed to follow by observation. This assumption took on a life of its own in the attitudes of the people, and the very thought of such a creature existing outside the pale of their so aptly devised system filled the most reasonable of Southerners with fear and loathing. Quite apart from the demands of the system itself, this may account for many of the subsidiary social taboos—the increasing severity of the laws against manumission, the horror of miscegenation, the depressed condition of the free Negro and his peculiar place in

[68] Quoted in Goodell, *American Slave Code,* p. 334.

Southern society: all signs of how difficult it was to conceive a non-slave colored class. Nothing in their experience had prepared them for it; such a class was unnatural, logically awry, a blemish on the body politic, an anomaly for which there was no intellectual category.

There should be no such unresolved terms, no such unfactorable equations, in a society whose production economy had had such dynamic and unencumbered origins. Both reason and instinct had defined the Negro as a slave, and the slave as

that condition of a natural person, in which, by the operation of law, the application of his physical and mental powers depends, as far as possible, upon the will of another who is himself subject to the supreme power of the state, and in which he is incapable, in the view of the law, of acquiring or holding property, and of sustaining those relations out of which *relative* rights . . . proceed, except as the agent or instrument of another. In slavery, strictly so called, the supreme power of the state, in ignoring the personality of the slave, ignores his capacity for moral action, and commits the control of his conduct as a moral agent, to the master, together with the power of transferring his authority to another.[69]

The basic fact was, of course, that the slave himself was property. He and his fellow bondsmen had long since become

[69] Hurd, *Law of Freedom and Bondage,* I, 42–43. Such language would lead one to suppose that slavery was a condition which, by its very nature, at all times and in all places, should partake of the same legal and social necessities. But the usage of the ancient world, in which slavery was everywhere prevalent, was bound by no such necessities. Nor was slavery defined either with great clarity or great rigidity. There were so many degrees between "total" freedom and "total" slavery that the two tended to lose much of their meaning as opposites. Moreover, the stigma of slavery itself did not strike nearly so deep as in American slavery; in the latter, a man was either one thing or the other—slave or free. See William L. Westermann, "Between Slavery and Freedom," *American Historical Review,* L (January, 1945), 213–27. The difference that this made in the social attitudes of classical times toward slavery was considerable. "The lack in antiquity of any deep abhorrence of slavery as a social and economic evil may be explained in part," according to Professor Westermann, by the fact that "the change of legal status out of enslavement into liberty, by way of manumission, was as constant and as easy in Greco-Roman life as the reverse transition over the short passage from individual freedom of action into the constraints of nonfreedom, and the methods employed for making either transition were many." *Ibid.,* p. 215.

"chattels personal . . . to all intents, constructions and purposes whatsoever."[70]

In the slave system of the United States—so finely circumscribed and so cleanly self-contained—virtually all avenues of recourse for the slave, all lines of communication to society at large, originated and ended with the master. The system was unique, *sui generis*. The closest parallel to it at that time was to be found in the Latin-American colonies of Spain and Portugal. But the differences between the two systems are so much more striking than the similarities that we may with profit use them not as parallels but as contrasts. In the Spanish and Portuguese colonies, we are immediately impressed by the comparative lack of precision and logic governing the institution of slavery there; we find an exasperating dimness of line between the slave and free portions of society, a multiplicity of points of contact between the two, a confusing promiscuity of color, such as would never have been thinkable in our own country.[71] But before attempting to establish legal and customary classifications on the slave's condition in these places, in some manner corresponding to those we used for the United States, something should be said about the social and institutional setting in which slavery, in Spain and Portugal themselves, was both viewed and practiced.

Although the Spanish and Portuguese trade in Negro slaves would not become of primary importance until about the same period as did that of England, the civilization of the Iberian Peninsula was one in which slavery had long been familiar: laws, customs, and attitudes concerning it had been fixed for centuries. Indeed, the culture and traditions were rich in continuities with classical times—with the Romans themselves, who had known all about slavery. Slavery had been considered by Roman statesmen and publicists, and in succeeding centuries by the Latin

[70] Hurd, *Law of Freedom and Bondage,* I, 303.

[71] Four works upon which I have drawn heavily for my material on Latin-American slavery are Frank Tannenbaum's *Slave and Citizen* (New York: Knopf, 1947), Fr. Dieudonné Rinchon's *La traite et l'esclavage des Congolais par les Européens* (Wetteren, Belgium, 1929), Sir Harry Johnston's *The Negro in the New World* (London: Methuen, 1910), and Fernando Ortiz, *Los Negros esclavos* (Havana: Revista bimestra cubana, 1916).

church fathers. The church of Rome, in its Holy Scripture, preserved and perpetuated traditions in which the Jews of antiquity had not only held slaves but had also made endless rules for their treatment and governance. Many parts of the Justinian Code dealt with slavery. Moors, Jews, and even Spaniards had been held in slavery, a fact implicitly recognized in the codification of Spanish law undertaken in the thirteenth century by King Alfonso the Wise.[72] Thus the situation of the first Negro slaves, who probably came to the Iberian Peninsula about the middle of the fifteenth century, was at the very outset quite different from that of the first slaves to arrive in Virginia early in the seventeenth. For here they found already waiting a legal and social setting incredibly complex, thick with the experience of centuries, and peculiarly fitted to receive and absorb them.

The "logic" of this tradition, biblical and classical in its origins, would have been incomprehensible to publicists of nineteenth-century America, both North and South, even though each drew upon it for their arguments. In it, there was a clear recognition and implicit sanction of slavery; nowhere was it denied (and thus the Southerner was right); at the same time, held as it were in suspension, was the universal presumption that such servitude, violating the divine and natural equality of man, was "against both reason and nature"[73] (and here, of course, the Northerner was right). But the fact that these two contrary principles could be supported in such illogical equilibrium within the same body of law and custom, made it possible for the system of slavery to exist, both in Spain and in the New World colonies, in a form which differed immensely from that of the United States. That this was indeed possible requires further explanation, for even after a wide-scale plantation order, based on Negro slave labor, had been established in Latin America, the ancient

[72] This was a codification (*Las siete partidas del Rey Don Alfonso el Sabio*) which dealt extensively with slavery and "which in itself," according to Mr. Tannenbaum, "summarizes the Mediterranean legal *mores* of many centuries. . . ." *Slave and Citizen*, p. 45.

[73] "Slavery is a condition and institution made in antiquity, through which men, who were naturally free, enslave themselves and submit to the dominion of others against reason and nature." *Las siete Partidas*, quoted in *ibid.*, p. 45 n.

assumptions and legal sanctions governing slavery carried over into it with great tenacity and persistence.[74]

Of all the national states of western Europe, Spain, though dynastically united to a substantial degree late in the fifteenth century (and having even absorbed Portugal in the sixteenth),[75] remained, long into modern times, much the most "medieval." Its agriculture retained many of the subsistence features characteristic of manorial economy. Its social stability was guaranteed by that standing alliance of church and state upon which every feudal community rested; there, on a national scale, the Inquisition maintained at extravagant cost the dual secular-spiritual concept of society so characteristic of the Middle Ages and so repugnant to every modern idea. Moreover, having to deal with the Moslems on Spanish soil, the Spaniards had built crusades and the crusading temperament into their basic experience, where it actively remained long after the collapse of the other crusaders' states in Asia Minor. This fact had much to do with the failure to develop a banking and commercial class comparable to those existing elsewhere, for the chronic persecutions of the Moors and Jews deprived the kingdom of its most energetic and experienced businessmen. Banking services tended to be performed in very large part by foreigners, and Spanish wealth quickly found its way to places outside the realm. The monarchy's role in all such matters was conceived in a highly paternal and "illiberal" way, and laissez faire was just as unacceptable in economic life as was free-thinking in religion.

This royal paternalism was especially notable in colonial af-

[74] "In Spain, slavery existed before the Indies were discovered. More specifically, we find slavery in Iberia from the remotest times. . . . Spain was never without slaves. It is thus that the discovery of America and the naturally improvised political economy of the conquistadores and colonizers came face to face with the mold of slavery ready-made in the legal structure of the mother country.

"It happened otherwise in North America, where the colonies did not have *ab initio* a true slave law. This issued from the legislation of the colonies themselves. . . . Perhaps it is due to this circumstance that the slave legislation of the English colonies was more severe than the Spanish, and that the master's power to which the slave was subjected in the former was more absolute and uncontrollable." Ortiz, *Los Negros esclavos,* pp. 334–35.

[75] A union which lasted from 1580 to 1640.

fairs and shows a striking contrast to the permissive policies which allowed so wide a latitude of local autonomy in the English colonies. The royal houses of Spain and Portugal had been the first in the race for overseas colonies—the crown and grandees having been rather more oriented to "glory" than to "success"— but they in time found themselves outstripped by the English and Dutch and saw the fruits of their glory dribble away to London, Antwerp, and other successful centers of banking. This lack of economic efficiency was not unconnected with the very administrative efficiency that permitted the Spanish crown to maintain such rigid control over its American dependencies. The degree of supervision exercised over colonial life by the Council of the Indies at Madrid does not seem to have been sufficiently appreciated.[76] Add to this the power of the church, and the resulting setting may be seen as one hardly favorable to wide-scale enterprise. Even the establishment of great plantations in Cuba, Santo Domingo, Brazil, and elsewhere in the seventeenth and eighteenth centuries did not mean unmitigated capitalism, as would be the case under the free skies of Virginia, Maryland, and the Carolinas. The great difference lay in the fact that other institutional concerns were present besides those involved with production.[77]

No such dramatic transvaluation of social norms as occurred in seventeenth-century England to accommodate the new standards of the bourgeoisie would ever take place in Spain. And nowhere could the chivalric concept of the *hidalgo,* the man who

[76] Although the crown was not at all liberal in the actual financing of the early explorations, royal supervision in every other respect was simply a matter of policy; not only were all major officials crown-appointed but "routine activities were often regulated in detail by the voluminous legislation of a paternalistic monarchy," according to C. H. Haring. "No large project or change of official policy might be undertaken, no unaccustomed expenditure might be made from the royal treasury except in time of emergency, without first referring it to the Council of the Indies for approval." See C. H. Haring, *The Spanish Empire in America* (New York: Oxford University Press, 1947), pp. 120–23.

[77] The quasi-feudal nature of Spanish landholding, carried over to the colonies, is described in *ibid.,* pp. 258–59. "A minority of fortunate landowning creoles lived much like their Spanish ancestors, imbued with similar aristocratic prejudices, and with similar improvidence and lack of foresight." *Ibid.,* p. 258.

did no work with his hands and to whom business was contemptible, persist so tenaciously as in Spain and the Spanish colonies.[78] There, on the other hand, the concept of private property, peculiarly appropriate to the demands of an entrepreneurial class, would not develop with nearly the elaborateness that characterized it elsewhere. In at least one area—the master-slave relationship—this fact had very important consequences. For all the cruelty and bigotry of this quasi-medieval society, the balance between property rights and human rights stood in a vastly different ratio—much to the advantage of human rights —from that seen in the American South.

In the colonies of Latin America we are thus able to think of the church, the civil authority, and the property concerns of the planter-adventurer as constituting distinct and not always harmonious interests in society. The introduction of slaves into the colonies brought much discomfort to the royal conscience; when the trade in Negroes became of consequence, the monarchs gave it their growing concern, and it never occurred to them not to retain over it a heavy measure of royal control. Charles V, who had granted the first license to transport Negroes in quantity directly from Africa to America, turned against the principle late in his reign and ordered the freeing of all African slaves in Spanish America.[79] In 1570 King Sebastian of Portugal issued an order to the colonists of Brazil which forbade the taking of slaves except by "licit means," specifying that in any case they must be registered within two months or all authority over them be forfeited.[80] A century later it had become clear to the monarchs of Spain that both the demands of their colonists for labor and the revenue needs of the royal treasury required that the trade in African Negroes be accorded full legitimacy. But the king in 1679 still had to be assured "whether meetings of theologians and jurists have been held to determine whether it is licit to buy

[78] On *hidalguismo*, "the sense of nobility," see Américo Castro, *The Structure of Spanish History*, trans. Edmund L. King (Princeton: Princeton University Press, 1954), pp. 628–35.

[79] Haring, *Spanish Empire*, p. 219. It has to be added that one year after Charles's retirement to the monastery of Saint-Just in 1558, slavery and the slave trade was resumed.

[80] Rinchon, *La traite et l'esclavage*, pp. 140–41. This order applied to native Indians.

them as slaves and make asientos for them and whether there are any authors who have written on this particular question."[81] Again we find the king of Spain, in a *Real Cedula* of 1693, commanding the captain-general of Cuba to call upon all masters of slaves, and to "say to them in my name that they must not, for whatever motive, rigorously tighten the wage they receive from their slaves, for having been tried in other places, it has proved inconvenient harming the souls of these people. . . ." Since slavery was "a sufficient sorrow without at the same time suffering the distempered rigor of their master," any excesses were to be punished by applying "the necessary remedy."[82] The monarchy made terms when it met with the full force of this new enterprise—new at least with respect to its proportions. But the energy with which it imposed its own terms was drawn both from the ancient sanctions regarding servitude and from the traditional force of the crown's institutional prerogatives.

The other item in this equation was the presence of a powerful church with needs of its own. A considerable measure of its power as an institution naturally depended upon its position of leadership in matters touching the morals of society. The maintenance of that leadership required the church as a matter of course to insist on a dominant role in the formulation of all policy which might bear on the morality of the slave system and have consequences for the Faith. The terms it made with slavery paralleled those made by the crown and exhibited the same ambiguities. In effect, the church with one hand condemned slavery and with the other came to an understanding with it as a labor system. Its doctrine asserted in general that the practice of slavery and the slave trade was fraught with perils for those of the faithful who engaged in it and that they stood, at innumerable points, in danger of mortal sin. The immoralities connected with the trade compelled again and again the attention of church writers, and it was in this sense that the Franciscan Father Thomas Mercado had denounced it in 1587 as fostering

[81] "Résumé of the Origin of the Introduction of Slaves into Spanish America" (1685), quoted in Elizabeth Donnan, *Documents Illustrative of the History of the Slave Trade to America* (Washington: Carnegie Institution, 1930 ff.), I, 346.

[82] Quoted in Tannenbaum, *Slave and Citizen,* p. 89.

"two thousand falsehoods, a thousand robberies, and a thousand deceptions."[83] More temperately summarizing the most learned opinion of his age, Germain Fromageau, a doctor of the Sorbonne, declared in 1698 that "one can neither, in surety of conscience, buy nor sell Negroes, because in such commerce there is injustice."[84] In any case, as an eighteenth-century prelate, Cardinal Gerdil, categorically stated, "Slavery is not to be understood as conferring on one man the same power over another that men have over cattle. . . . For slavery does not abolish the natural equality of man. . . ."[85]

At the same time the church, in its character as an institution, functioning in the society of men, could not afford to proscribe slavery as unconditionally immoral, if for no other reason than that the majority of Christendom's overseas dominions would thus have been stained in depravity—a position which, for almost any procedural purposes, would have been absurdly untenable. Its casuists, therefore, readily found sanctions in tradition whereby slavery might exist under the church's official favor. Thus the Council of the Indies, after meetings with theologians, jurists, and prelates of the church, assured the king of Spain that

there cannot be any doubt as to the necessity of those slaves for the support of the kingdom of the Indies . . . ; and [that] with regard to the point of conscience, [the trade may continue] because of the reasons expressed, the authorities cited, and its longlived and general custom in the kingdoms of Castile, America, and Portugal, without any objection on the part of his Holiness or ecclesiastical state, but rather with the tolerance of all of them.[86]

The Jesuits would labor excessively in places such as Brazil to mitigate the evils of slavery; the papacy itself would denounce it in various ways in 1462, 1537, 1639, 1741, 1815, and 1839; at the

[83] *Ibid.*, p. 62.

[84] From *La dictionnaire des cas de conscience,* quoted in Rinchon, *La traite et l'esclavage,* p. 148.

[85] James J. Fox, "Ethical Aspect of Slavery," in Charles G. Hebermann and others (eds.), *The Catholic Encyclopedia* (New York: Encyclopedia Press, 1913), XIV, 40.

[86] "Minutes of the Council of the Indies" (1685), quoted in Donnan, *Documents,* I, 351.

same time the church "could no more have proclaimed the abolition of slavery," as Fr. Rinchon remarks, "than it could have imposed the eight-hour day or the rate of family incomes."[87]

Yet in the very act of certifying the practice of slavery, in admitting its economic necessity, and even in holding slaves of its own, the church had, as it were, bargained with the system so that its own institutional needs and its prerogatives in matters of morality might still be maintained at the visible maximum and protected against infringement. The effects of this determination are overwhelmingly evident in the actual workings of slavery in Latin America. They are evident, indeed, at nearly every point in the traffic itself, for the potent hand of the church fell upon the sequence of events long before it terminated in America. It had missionaries on the soil of Africa, proselytizing among the natives and operating great establishments there. It was highly sensitive to the possibility that the Faith, in the course of the trade, might be corrupted.[88] In 1685 the Inquisition, faced with an impending transaction which would turn over a portion of the trade to the Dutch, sternly urged the king that,

in case any contract is made with the Dutch, you will please to ordain that all necessary orders be provided and issued for the utmost care of the conservation and purity of our Holy Catholic Faith, because

[87] *La traite et l'esclavage,* p. 158.

[88] During the first quarter of the sixteenth century there was much royal soul-searching over the problem of what importation policy was most consistent with both the need for slaves and the need for maintaining the purity of the Indies in matters of faith. Nicolas Ovando, the new governor of Española, was forbidden in 1501 to bring in any but *ladinos* (Iberian Christian Negroes). Isabella suspended importations entirely in 1504; in 1505 Ferdinand, after Isabella's death, reintroduced importations of *ladinos.* In 1510, shipments of *bozales* (African Negroes not Christianized but as yet unsullied by Mohammedanism or Judaism) began being made from the Lisbon slave market—this class having been originally excluded. It was never permitted to come to a choice, however, between admitting or not admitting "infidel" slaves (Jewish or Mohammedan; they were always rigidly excluded); it was rather the question of whether they should be fully Christianized before or after importation to the Indies. When the first assiento was made in 1517 for shipments direct from Africa, the matter was automatically settled. José Antonio Saco, *Historia de la esclavitud de la raza africana en el Nuevo Mundo, y en especial en los paises américo-hispanos* (Barcelona: J. Jepus, 1879), pp. 61–69.

one can very justly fear that if the negroes come by way of the Dutch, they may be greatly imbued with doctrines and errors . . . and . . . this council should advise the inquisitors to exercise special vigilance.[89]

The contract was eventually made, but the Dutchman who received it was forced to take ten Capuchin monks to his African factories for the religious instruction of the Negroes, to support them, and to allow them to preach in public.[90] The Inquisition had a tribunal in the Indies which would punish any "heretic" (meaning Dutch or Flemish) who tried to introduce his creed there during the course of business.[91] Every slave bound for Brazil was to receive baptism and religious instruction before being put on board,[92] and upon reaching port every ship was boarded by a friar who examined the conscience, faith, and religion of the new arrivals. The friar was there "to investigate the individual's orthodoxy just as today the immigrant's health and race are investigated."[93]

It would be misleading to imply that slavery in the colonies drew its total character from the powerful influence of the church. But it may be asserted that the church, functioning in its capacity as guardian of morals, was responsible for whatever human rights were conserved for the slave within the grim system. What it came to was that three formidable interests—the crown, the planter, and the church—were deeply concerned with the system, that these concerns were in certain ways competing, and that the product of this balance of power left its profound impress on the actual legal and customary sanctions governing the status and treatment of slaves. These sanctions were by no means what they would have been had it been left to the planting class alone to develop them systematically with reference only to the requirements of a labor system. Let us examine them,

[89] "Report of the Council of the Inquisition to the King" (1685), quoted in Donnan, *Documents,* I, 339.

[90] "Minutes of the Council of the Indies" (1685), *ibid.,* pp. 348–49.

[91] *Ibid.,* p. 348. No one, according to the report, had hitherto been rash enough to attempt this.

[92] "[They] are catechised and receive baptism, a rite which has been found to console their minds under their unhappy circumstances." Carl Berns Wadström, *An Essay on Colonisation* . . . (London: Darton & Harvey, 1794), p. 125.

[93] Gilberto Freyre, *The Masters and the Slaves* (New York: Knopf, 1946), p. 41.

taking the same rough categories used with respect to the American South: term of servitude, marriage and the family, police and discipline, and property and other civil rights.

Neither in Brazil nor in Spanish America did slavery carry with it such precise and irrevocable categories of perpetual servitude, *"durante vita"* and "for all generations," as in the United States. The presumption in these countries, should the status of a colored person be in doubt, was that he was free rather than a slave.[94] There were in fact innumerable ways whereby a slave's servitude could be brought to an end. The chief of these was the very considerable fact that he might buy his own freedom. The Negro in Cuba or Mexico had the right to have his price declared and could, if he wished, purchase himself in instalments. Slaves escaping to Cuba to embrace Catholicism were protected by a special royal order of 1733 which was twice reissued. A slave unduly punished might be set at liberty by the magistrate. In Brazil the slave who was the parent of ten children might legally demand his or her freedom.[95] The medieval Spanish code had made a slave's service terminable under any number of contingencies—if he denounced cases of treason, murder, counterfeiting, or the rape of a virgin, or if he performed various other kinds of meritorious acts. Though all such practices did not find their way into the seventeenth- and eighteenth-century legal arrangements of Latin America, much of their spirit was perpetuated in the values, customs, and social expectations of that later period. It is important to appreciate the high social approval connected with the freeing of slaves. A great variety of happy family events—the birth of a son, the marriage of a daughter, anniversaries, national holidays—provided the occasion, and their ceremonial was frequently marked by the manumission of one or more virtuous servitors. It was considered a pious act to accept the responsibility of becoming godfather to a slave child, implying the moral obligation to arrange eventually for its freedom.

[94] "In the Cuban market freedom was the only commodity which could be bought untaxed; every negro against whom no one had proved a claim of servitude was deemed free. . . ." William Law Mathieson, *British Slavery and Its Abolition* (London: Longmans, Green, 1926), pp. 37–38.

[95] Johnston, *Negro in the New World,* p. 89.

Indeed, in Cuba and Brazil such freedom might be purchased for a nominal sum at the baptismal font.[96] All such manumissions had the strong approval of both church and state and were registered gratis by the government.[97]

In extending its moral authority over men of every condition, the church naturally insisted on bringing slave unions under the holy sacraments. Slaves were married in church and the banns published; marriage was a sacred rite and its sanctity protected in law. In the otherwise circumspect United States, the only category which the law could apply to conjugal relations between slaves—or to unions between master and slave—was concubinage. But concubinage, in Latin America, was condemned as licentious, adulterous, and immoral; safeguards against promiscuity were provided in the law,[98] and in Brazil the Jesuits labored mightily to regularize the libertinage of the master class by the sacrament of Christian marriage.[99] Moreover, slaves owned by different masters were not to be hindered from marrying, nor could they be kept separate after marriage. If the estates were distant, the wife was to go with her husband, and a fair price was to be fixed by impartial persons for her sale to the husband's master.[100] A slave might, without legal

[96] What I have said in this paragraph is virtually a paraphrase of the information which Mr. Tannenbaum has collected and so skilfully summarized on pp. 50, 53–54, 57–58 of *Slave and Citizen*.

[97] Johnston, *Negro in the New World*, p. 42.

[98] "The master of slaves must not allow the unlawful intercourse of the two sexes, but must encourage matrimony." Spanish slave code of 1789, quoted in *ibid.*, p. 44. Although slaves were allowed "to divert themselves innocently" on holy days, the males were to be kept apart from the females. *Ibid.*, p. 44.

[99] Freyre, *The Masters and the Slaves*, p. 85.

[100] Johnston, *Negro in the New World*, pp. 44–45. A diocesan synod of 1680 in Cuba issued weighty regulations on this subject which were supposed to supplement and have equal force with civil law. "Constitution 5 established that 'marriage should be free' and ordered that 'no master prohibit his slaves from marriage, nor impede those who cohabit therein, because we have found that many masters with little fear of God and in grave danger of their consciences, proscribe their slaves from marrying or impede their cohabitation with their married partners, with feigned pretexts'; and also prohibited 'that they go away to sell them outside the city, without that they take together husband and wife.'" Ortiz, *Los Negros esclavos*, p. 349. The church even made some concessions here to African

interference, marry a free person. The children of such a marriage, if the mother were free, were themselves free, inasmuch as children followed the condition of their mother.[101]

The master's disciplinary authority never had the completeness that it had in the United States, and nowhere did he enjoy powers of life and death over the slave's body. Under the Spanish code of 1789 slaves might be punished for failure to perform their duties, with prison, chains, or lashes, "which last must not exceed the number of twenty-five, and those must be given them in such manner as not to cause any contusion or effusion of blood: which punishments cannot be imposed on slaves but by their masters or the stewards."[102] For actual crimes a slave was to be tried in an ordinary court of justice like any free person,[103] and, conversely, the murder of a slave was to be prosecuted just as that of a free man would be.[104] Excessive punishments of slaves—causing "contusion, effusion of blood, or mutilation of members"—by plantation stewards were themselves punishable. Although gross violations of the law occurred, the law here was anything but the dead letter it proved to be in our own southern states. In the important administrative centers of both Brazil and the Spanish colonies there was an official protector of slaves, known variously as the syndic, procurador, or attorney-general, under whose jurisdiction came all matters relating to the treatment of slaves. His functions were nurtured by a well-articulated system of communications. The priests who made the regular rounds of the estates giving Christian instruction were required to obtain and render to him information from the slaves regarding their treatment, and investigation and the necessary steps would be taken accordingly. These priests were answerable to

tribal marriage arrangements, to the extent that a slave with multiple wives might—if the first-married wife's identity could not be ascertained—pick out the one he preferred and have his marriage with her solemnized under the sacraments. *Ibid.*, p. 349.

[101] Tannenbaum, *Slave and Citizen*, p. 56.

[102] Johnston, *Negro in the New World*, p. 45.

[103] The sentence, however, was apparently to be executed by the master. *Ibid.*, p. 45.

[104] *Ibid.*, pp. 45–46. The code does not make it clear whether the penalty would be the same against the slave's master as against another person. But in any case the murderer, master or other, was liable to prosecution.

no one else for their activities. In addition, the magistrates were to appoint "persons of good character" to visit the estates thrice yearly and conduct similar inquiries on similar matters. A further ingenious provision in the Spanish code caused all fines levied, for mistreatment and other excesses against slaves, to be divided up three ways: one-third went to the judge, one-third to the informer, and one-third to the "Fines Chest." Finally, the attorney-general and the justices themselves were made accountable to the crown for failure to carry out these ordinances. An implicit royal threat underlay all this; should the fines not have the desired effect and should the ordinances continue to be broken, "I," His Majesty promised, "will take my measures accordingly."[105]

As was implied in his right to purchase his own freedom, the slave in the Spanish and Portuguese colonies had the right to acquire and hold property. This meant something specific; in Brazil a master was obliged by law to give liberty to his slaves on all Sundays and holidays—which totaled eighty-five in the year—during which a slave might work for himself and accumulate money for his purchase price,[106] and the Spanish code of 1789 provided that slaves must be allowed two hours each day in which to be employed in "occupations for their own advantage."[107] In many places slaves were encouraged to hire themselves out regularly (there were skilled artisans among them as well as ordinary laborers), an arrangement which was to the advantage of both the master and the slave himself, since the latter was allowed to keep a percentage of the wage. Slaves even in rural areas might sell the produce of their gardens and retain

[105] *Ibid.*, pp. 45–46. The liberal code of 1789 was not uniformly enforced at first; Ortiz, indeed, insists—contradicting the earlier historian, Saco—that it was widely evaded until well into the nineteenth century. The colonists, however, eventually had to succumb to pressure from the Spanish government, and by the 1840's the code had been written into local police regulations in Cuba. Ortiz, *Los Negros esclavos,* pp. 363–64, 70. A full translation of the code in its municipal form is in *British and Foreign State Papers, 1842–1843,* XXXI (London, 1858), 393–99.

[106] It was not even uncommon for ex-slaves who had thus acquired their freedom to become actual slaveholders on their own account. Johnston, *Negro in the New World,* p. 90.

[107] *Ibid.*, p. 44.

the proceeds.[108] For all practical purposes slavery here had become, as Mr. Tannenbaum puts it, a contractual arrangement: it could be wiped out by a fixed purchase price and leave no taint. "There may have been no written contract between the two parties, but the state behaved, in effect, as if such a contract did exist, and used its powers to enforce it."[109] It was a contract in which the master owned a man's labor but not the man.

As for the privileges of religion, it was here not a question of the planting class "permitting" the slave, under rigidly specified conditions, to take part in divine worship. It was rather a matter of the church's insisting—under its own conditions—that masters bring their slaves to church and teach them religion. Such a man as the Mississippi planter who directed that the gospel preached to his slaves should be "in its original purity and simplicity" would have courted the full wrath of the Latin church. A Caribbean synod of 1622, whose *sanctiones* had the force of law, made lengthy provisions for the chastisement of masters who prevented their slaves from hearing Mass or receiving instruction on feast days.[110] Here the power of the Faith was such that master and slave stood equally humbled before it. "Every one who has slaves," according to the first item in the Spanish code, "is obliged to instruct them in the principles of the Roman Catholic religion and in the necessary truths in order that the slaves may be baptized within the (first) year of their residence in the Spanish dominions."[111] Certain assumptions were implied there-

[108] Tannenbaum, *Slave and Citizen*, pp. 58–61.

[109] *Ibid.*, p. 55. A practical application of this contractual aspect of slavery was the institution of *coartación* which developed in Cuba in the eighteenth century. This was an arrangement whereby the slave might buy his freedom in instalments. He would first have his price declared (if he and his master disagreed, the local courts would determine it), whereupon he made his first payment. After that point, the price could not be changed, and he could at the same time change masters at will, the new master simply paying the balance of his price. See Hubert H. S. Aimes, "Coartación: A Spanish Institution for the Advancement of Slaves into Freedmen," *Yale Review*, XVII (February, 1909), 412–31.

[110] Fr. Cipriano de Utrera, "El Concilio Dominicano de 1622, con una introducción histórica," *Boletín eclesiástico de la Arquidiócesis de Santo Domingo*, 1938–39, p. 40.

[111] Johnston, *Negro in the New World*, p. 43. Herbert Klein's excellent monograph, "Slavery in Cuba and Virginia: A Comparative History of

in which made it impossible that the slave in this culture should ever quite be considered as mere property, either in law or in society's customary habits of mind. These assumptions, perpetuated and fostered by the church, made all the difference in his treatment by society and its institutions, not only while a slave, but also if and when he should cease to be one. They were, in effect, that he was a man, that he had a soul as precious as any other man's, that he had a moral nature, that he was not only as susceptible to sin but also as eligible for grace as his master—that master and slave were brothers in Christ.

The Spaniards and Portuguese had the widespread reputation by the eighteenth century—whatever may have been the reasons—for being among all nations the best masters of slaves.[112] The standards for such a judgment cannot, of course, be made too simple. Were slaves "physically maltreated" in those countries? They could, conceivably, have been treated worse than in our own nineteenth-century South without altering the comparison,

---

the First Hundred Years" (M.A. thesis, University of Chicago, 1959), provides a wealth of detail and specific examples, all of which tend to confirm, in a case-study setting, the general assertions of the present work as well as those of Tannenbaum and Johnston. This is particularly true with regard to the ways in which royal and ecclesiastical power was exercised in the Spanish colonies.

[112] "The Spaniards, Portuguese and Danes are undoubtedly the best masters of slaves," wrote Carl Berns Wadström in 1794. The English and Dutch were in his opinion the worst. *Essay on Colonization*, p. 151 n. The Portuguese and Brazilians "rival the Spaniards for first place in the list of humane slave-holding nations," writes Sir Harry Johnston. "Slavery under the flag of Portugal (or Brazil) or of Spain was not a condition without hope, a life in hell, as it was for the most part in the British West Indies and, above all, Dutch Guiana and the Southern United States." *Negro in the New World,* p. 89. "The Spaniards themselves maltreated their slaves less than did the planters of the Antilles or of North America at a later period." P. Chemin-Dupontès, *Les Petites Antilles* (Paris: E. Guilmoto, 1909), quoted in *ibid.,* p. 42 n. Moreau de Saint-Méry, writing of the slaves of Spanish Santo Domingo, remarks, "To their masters they are more like companions than slaves." *Topographical and Political Description of the Spanish Part of Saint-Domingo* (Philadelphia, 1796), quoted in *ibid.,* p. 42 n. The French planters of Haiti and the Americans of Georgia both complained that the Spanish code of 1789 would (and did) induce their slaves to escape to the Spanish dominions. *Ibid.,* p. 46.

for even in cruelty the relationship was between man and man.[113]
Was there "race prejudice"? No one could be more arrogantly
proud of his racial purity than the Spaniard of Castile, and
theoretically there were rigid caste lines, but the finest Creole
families, the clergy, the army, the professions, were hopelessly
"defiled" by Negro blood;[114] the taboos were that vague in

[113] Most writers and students do seem to think that the system was
"milder" in the Spanish colonies and in Brazil, but nobody has ever
claimed that it was a life of ease and comfort. An interesting summary of
observers' opinions on this and other points is Margaret V. Nelson, "The
Negro in Brazil as Seen through the Chronicles of Travellers, 1800–1868,"
Journal of Negro History, XXX (April, 1945), 203–18. See also James F.
King, "Negro History in Continental Spanish America," *Journal of Negro
History*, XXIX (January, 1944), 7–23. "The fact is," as Donald Pierson
remarks, "that slavery in Brazil [and, one might add, in Spanish America
as well] was both mild *and* severe." The severe side of it, indeed, is discussed with very disagreeable particulars by Arthur Ramos in his *Negro
in Brazil* (Washington: Associated Publishers, 1939), pp. 20–22. It could
further be pointed out that comparisons, when made, were made most
frequently with the British colonies of the eighteenth century, especially
the British West Indies. In the United States, on the other hand, by (say)
1850, slavery in a "physical" sense was in general, probably, quite mild.
However, even if it had been milder here than anywhere else in the
Western Hemisphere, it would still be missing the point to make the
comparison in terms of physical comfort. In one case we would be dealing
with the cruelty of man to man, and, in the other, with the care, maintenance, and indulgence of men toward creatures who were legally and
morally *not* men—not in the sense that Christendom had traditionally
defined man's nature. It is for our purposes, in short, the *primary* relationship that matters. Masters and slaves in Brazil, according to João Ribeiro,
"were united into families, if not by law, at least by religion." Quoted in
Donald Pierson, *Negroes in Brazil* (Chicago: University of Chicago Press,
1942), p. 81.

[114] Even the legendary corruption of the Spanish upper classes was apparently biracial in the New World. Beye Cisneros of Mexico City, during
the course of the debates on the Spanish constitution of 1811, declared,
"I have known mulattoes who have become counts, marquises, *oidores,*
canons, colonels, and knights of the military orders through intrigue,
bribery, perjury, and falsification of public books and registers; and I have
observed that those who have reached these positions and distinctions by
reprehensible means, have been granted the corresponding honors without
repugnance, despite their mixed blood. . . ." James F. King, "The Colored
Castes and American Representation in the Cortes of Cádiz," *Hispanic
American Historical Review*, XXXIII (February, 1953), 56. The looseness
of practice which permitted such frequent "passings-over" was actually

practice. Was there squalor, filth, widespread depression of the masses? Much more so than with us—but there it was the class system and economic "underdevelopment," rather than the color barrier, that made the difference. In these countries the concept of "beyond the pale" applied primarily to beings outside the Christian fold rather than to those beyond the color line.[115]

We are not, then, dealing with a society steeped, like our own, in traditions of political and economic democracy. We are concerned only with a special and peculiar kind of fluidity—that of their slave systems—and in this alone lay a world of difference. It was a fluidity that permitted a transition from slavery to freedom that was smooth, organic, and continuing. Manumitting slaves, carrying as it did such high social approval, was done often, and the spectacle of large numbers of freedmen was familiar to the social scene. Such opportunities as were open to any member of the depressed classes who had talent and diligence were open as well to the ex-slave and his descendants. Thus color itself was no grave disability against taking one's place in free society; indeed, Anglo-Saxon travelers in nineteenth-century Brazil were amazed at the thoroughgoing mixture of races there. "I have passed black ladies in silks and jewelry," wrote Thomas Ewbank in the 1850's, "with male slaves in livery behind them. . . . Several have white husbands. The first doctor of the city is a colored man; so is the President of the Province."[116] Free Negroes had the same rights before the law as whites, and it was possible for the most energetic of their numbers to take immediate part in public and professional life. Among the Negroes and mulattoes of Brazil and the Spanish colonies—aside from the swarming numbers of skilled craftsmen

---

commended by the acting Captain-General of Venezuela in a dispatch to the Secretary of State for the Indies in 1815; "The State greatly gains," he wrote, "for the increase of the upper class, even though it be artificial, is to its interest." J. F. King, "A Royalist View of the Colored Castes in the Venezuelan War of Independence," *ibid.*, XXXIII (November, 1953), 528. See also Richard M. Morse, "The Negro in São Paulo, Brazil," *Journal of Negro History*, XXXVIII (July, 1953), 290–306.

[115] "The thing that barred an immigrant in those days was heterodoxy; the blot of heresy upon the soul and not any racial brand upon the body." Freyre, *The Masters and the Slaves*, pp. 40–41.

[116] *Life in Brazil, or the Land of the Cocoa and the Palm* (New York: Harper, 1856), p. 267.

—were soldiers, officers, musicians, poets, priests, and judges. "I am accustomed," said a delegate to the Cortes of Cádiz in 1811, "to seeing many engaged in all manner of careers."[117]

All such rights and opportunities existed *before* the abolition of slavery; and thus we may note it as no paradox that emancipation, when it finally did take place, was brought about in all these Latin-American countries "without violence, without bloodshed, and without civil war."[118]

The above set of contrasts, in addition to what it may tell us about slavery itself, could also be of use for a more general problem, that of the conservative role of institutions in any social structure. The principle has been observed in one setting where two or more powerful interests were present to limit each other; it has been tested negatively in a setting where a single interest was free to develop without such limits. The latter case was productive of consequences which could hardly be called, in the classical sense of the term, "conservative."

[117] King, "The Colored Castes and American Representation in the Cortes of Cádiz," p. 59. See also Irene Diggs, "Color in Colonial Spanish America," *Journal of Negro History*, XXXVIII (October, 1953), 403–26.

[118] Tannenbaum, *Slave and Citizen*, p. 106.

III

Slavery and Personality

PERSONALITY TYPES AND STEREOTYPES

An examination of American slavery, checked at certain critical points against a very different slave system, that of Latin America, reveals that a major key to many of the contrasts between them was an institutional key: The presence or absence of other powerful institutions in society made an immense difference in the character of slavery itself. In Latin America, the very tension and balance among three kinds of organizational concerns—church, crown, and plantation agriculture—prevented slavery from being carried by the planting class to its ultimate logic. For the slave, in terms of the space thus allowed for the development of men and women as moral beings, the result was an "open system": a system of contacts with free society through which ultimate absorption into that society could and did occur with great frequency. The rights of personality implicit in the ancient traditions of slavery and in the church's most venerable assumptions on the nature of the human soul were thus in a vital sense conserved, whereas to a staggering extent the very opposite was true in North American slavery. The latter system had developed virtually unchecked by institutions having anything like the power of their Latin counterparts; the legal structure which supported it, shaped only by the demands of a staple-raising capitalism, had defined with such nicety the slave's character as chattel that his character as a moral individual was left in the vaguest of legal obscurity. In this sense American slavery operated as a "closed" system—one in which, for the generality of slaves in their nature as men and women, *sub specie aeternitatis,* contacts with free society could occur only on the most narrowly circumscribed of terms. The next question is whether living within such a "closed system" might not have produced noticeable effects upon the slave's very personality.

The name "Sambo" has come to be synonymous with "race stereotype." Here is an automatic danger signal, warning that the analytical difficulties of asking questions about slave personality may not be nearly so great as the moral difficulties. The one inhibits the other; the morality of the matter has had a clogging effect on its theoretical development that may not be to the best interests of either. And yet theory on group personality is still in a stage rudimentary enough that this particular body of material—potentially illuminating—ought not to remain morally impounded any longer.

Is it possible to deal with "Sambo" as a type? The characteristics that have been claimed for the type come principally from Southern lore. Sambo, the typical plantation slave, was docile but irresponsible, loyal but lazy, humble but chronically given to lying and stealing; his behavior was full of infantile silliness and his talk inflated with childish exaggeration. His relationship with his master was one of utter dependence and childlike attachment: it was indeed this childlike quality that was the very key to his being. Although the merest hint of Sambo's "manhood" might fill the Southern breast with scorn, the child, "in his place," could be both exasperating and lovable.

Was he real or unreal? What order of existence, what rank of legitimacy, should be accorded him? Is there a "scientific" way to talk about this problem? For most Southerners in 1860 it went without saying not only that Sambo was real—that he was a dominant plantation type—but also that his characteristics were the clear product of racial inheritance. That was one way to deal with Sambo, a way that persisted a good many years after 1860. But in recent times, the discrediting, as unscientific, of racial explanations for any feature of plantation slavery has tended in the case of Sambo to discredit not simply the explanation itself but also the thing it was supposed to explain. Sambo is a mere stereotype—"stereotype" is itself a bad word, insinuating racial inferiority and invidious discrimination.[1] This modern

[1] The historian Samuel Eliot Morison was taken to task a few years ago by students of Queens College, Long Island, for his use of the name

[82]

approach to Sambo had a strong counterpart in the way Northern reformers thought about slavery in ante-bellum times: they thought that nothing could actually be said about the Negro's "true" nature because that nature was veiled by the institution of slavery. It could only be revealed by tearing away the veil.[2] In short, no order of reality could be given to assertions about slave character, because those assertions were illegitimately grounded on race, whereas their only basis was a corrupt and "unreal" institution. "To be sure," a recent writer concedes, "there were plenty of opportunists among the Negroes who played the role assigned to them, acted the clown, and curried the favor of their masters in order to win the maximum rewards within the system. . . ."[3] To impeach Sambo's legitimacy in this way is the next thing to talking him out of existence.

"Sambo" (in Volume I of his and H. S. Commager's text, *The Growth of the American Republic*) and for referring to the pre–Civil War Negroes as "a race with exasperating habits" and to the typical slave as "childlike, improvident, humorous, prevaricating, and superstitious." As a result, the use of the text at Queens was discontinued. See *Time,* February 26, 1951, pp. 48–49.

The following is from the "Concluding Summary" of one of the series of studies begun in the late 1930's under the inspiration of Gunnar Myrdal: "The description of the stereotypes held concerning the American Negro indicates the widespread tendency to look upon the Negro as inferior, and to ascribe to him qualities of intellect and personality which mark him off with some definiteness from the surrounding white American population . . . [;] not all these alleged characteristics of the Negro are uncomplimentary, but even those which may be regarded as favorable have the flavor of inferiority about them. When the Negro is praised, he is praised for his childlike qualities of happiness and good nature or for his artistic and musical gifts. . . . Negro writers do express much more frequently, as one would expect, the belief that whites and Negroes have essentially equal potentialities, and that it is only the accidents of training and economic opportunity which have produced temporary differences; even among Negro writers, however, some have accepted the prevailing stereotype." Otto Klineberg (ed.), *Characteristics of the American Negro* (New York: Harper, 1944). Instead of proposing an actual program of inquiry, the intentions of this line of thought appear to be primarily moral and its objectives to be of a normative sort: desistance from the use of stereotypes.

[2] See below, Part IV, pp. 190–91.

[3] Kenneth Stampp, "The Historian and Southern Negro Slavery," *American Historical Review,* LVII (April, 1952), 617.

There ought, however, to be still a third way of dealing with the Sambo picture, some formula for taking it seriously. The picture has far too many circumstantial details, its hues have been stroked in by too many different brushes, for it to be denounced as counterfeit. Too much folk-knowledge, too much plantation literature, too much of the Negro's own lore, have gone into its making to entitle one in good conscience to condemn it as "conspiracy." One searches in vain through the literature of the Latin-American slave systems for the "Sambo" of our tradition—the perpetual child incapable of maturity. How is this to be explained?[4] If Sambo is not a product of race (that "explanation" can be consigned to oblivion) and not simply a product of "slavery" in the abstract (other societies have had slavery),[5] then he must be related to our own peculiar variety

[4] There is such a word as "Zambo" in Latin America, but its meaning has no relation to our "Sambo." "A Zambo or Sambo (Spanish, *Zambo,* 'bandy-legged') is a cross between a *Negro* and an Amerindian (sometimes this name is given to the cross between a pure Negro and a mulatto, which the French called 'griffe')." Sir Harry Johnston, *The Negro in the New World* (London: Methuen, 1910), p. 3. I am not implying that racial stigma of some kind did not exist in South America (see above, pp. 77–78, n. 113); indeed, anthropological research has shown that the Latin-Americans were, and are, a good deal more conscious of "race" than such writers as Gilberto Freyre have been willing to admit. Even in Brazil, derogatory Negro stereotypes are common, and are apparently of long standing. On this point see Charles Wagley, *Race and Class in Rural Brazil* (Paris: UNESCO, 1952). On the other hand, it would be very difficult to find evidence in the literature of Brazil, or anywhere else in Latin America, of responsible men seriously maintaining that the Negro slave was constitutionally incapable of freedom. The views of a man like James H. Hammond, or for that matter the views of any average Southerner during the ante-bellum period, would have had little meaning in nineteenth-century Latin America. One is even inclined to think that these Latin-American stereotypes would compare more closely with the stereotypes of eastern and southern European immigrants that were held by certain classes in this country early in the twentieth century. See, e.g., Madison Grant's *Passing of the Great Race* (New York: Scribner, 1916). There are stereotypes and stereotypes: it would be quite safe to say that our "Sambo" far exceeds in tenacity and pervasiveness anything comparable in Latin America.

[5] It is, however, one thing to say that no longer are there any responsible men of science to be found advancing the racial argument, and quite another to assert that the argument is closed. In an odd sense we still find any number of statements indicating that the *other* side of the controversy

of it. And if Sambo is uniquely an American product, then his existence, and the reasons for his character, must be recognized in order to appreciate the very scope of our slave problem and its aftermath. The absoluteness with which such a personality ("real" or "unreal") had been stamped upon the plantation slave does much to make plausible the ante-bellum Southerner's difficulty in imagining that blacks anywhere could be anything but a degraded race—and it goes far to explain his failure to see any sense at all in abolitionism. It even casts light on the peculiar quality of abolitionism itself; it was so all-enveloping a problem in human personality that our abolitionists could literally not afford to recognize it. Virtually without exception, they met this dilemma either by sidetracking it altogether (they explicitly refused to advance plans for solving it, arguing that this would rob their message of its moral force) or by countering it with theories of infinite human perfectibility. The question of personality, therefore, becomes a crucial phase of the entire problem of slavery in the United States, having conceivably something to do with the difference—already alluded to—between an "open" and a "closed" system of slavery.

If it were taken for granted that a special type existed in significant numbers on American plantations, closer connections

---

is still being carried on, long after the bones of the enemy lie bleaching on the sands. For example, in the preface to a recent study on the American Negro by two distinguished psychologists, the authors define their "scientific position" by announcing that their book was "conceived and written on the premise that group characteristics are adaptive in nature and therefore not inborn, but acquired" and that "anyone who wishes to quote from [its] conclusions . . . to uphold any other thesis risks doing injustice to the material in the book, to the intentions of the authors, and to the Negro people." They then quote a kind of manifesto, signed by a group of prominent psychologists and social scientists, attesting that "as social scientists we know of no evidence that any ethnic group is inherently inferior." This is followed by a portion of the 1950 UNESCO "Statement on Race" which declares that "biological studies lend support to the ethic of universal brotherhood." From Abram Kardiner and Lionel Ovesey, *The Mark of Oppression: A Psychosocial Study of the American Negro* (New York: Norton, 1951), pp. v–vi. While these are sentiments which may (and must) be pronounced on any number of occasions among men of good will (the President regularly conceives it his duty to do this), their *scientific* content (which is the level at which they are here being offered) has long since ceased to be a matter of controversy.

might be made with a growing literature on personality and character types, the investigation of which has become a widespread, respectable, and productive enterprise among our psychologists and social scientists.[6] Realizing that, it might then seem not quite so dangerous to add that the type corresponded in its major outlines to "Sambo."

Let the above, then, be a preface to the argument of the present essay. It will be assumed that there were elements in the very structure of the plantation system—its "closed" character—that could sustain infantilism as a normal feature of behavior. These elements, having less to do with "cruelty" per se than simply with the sanctions of authority, were effective and pervasive enough to require that such infantilism be characterized as something much more basic than mere "accommodation." It will be assumed that the sanctions of the system were in themselves sufficient to produce a recognizable personality type.[7]

It should be understood that to identify a social type in this sense is still to generalize on a fairly crude level—and to insist for a limited purpose on the legitimacy of such generalizing is by no means to deny that, on more refined levels, a great profu-

[6] Among such studies are Robert K. Merton, "Bureaucratic Structure and Personality," *Social Forces,* XVIII (May, 1940), 560–68; Erich Fromm, *Man for Himself* (New York: Rinehart, 1947); David Riesman, *The Lonely Crowd* (New Haven: Yale University Press, 1950); and Theodore Adorno and Others, *The Authoritarian Personality* (New York: Harper, 1950)—a work which is itself subjected to examination in Richard Christie and Marie Jahoda (eds.), *Studies in the Scope and Method of "The Authoritarian Personality"* (Glencoe, Ill.: Free Press, 1954); and H. H. Gerth and C. Wright Mills, *Character and Social Structure: The Psychology of Social Institutions* (New York: Harcourt, Brace, 1953). For a consideration of this field in the broadest terms, see Alex Inkeles and Daniel J. Levinson, "National Character: The Study of Modal Personality and Sociocultural Systems," *Handbook of Social Psychology,* ed. Gardner Lindzey (Cambridge, Mass.: Addison-Wesley, 1954), II, 977–1020.

[7] The line between "accommodation" (as conscious hypocrisy) and behavior inextricable from basic personality, though the line certainly exists, is anything but a clear and simple matter of choice. There is reason to think that the one grades into the other, and vice versa, with considerable subtlety. In this connection, the most satisfactory theoretical mediating term between deliberate role-playing and "natural" role-playing might be found in role-psychology. See below, pp. 131–33.

sion of individual types might have been observed in slave society. Nor need it be claimed that the "Sambo" type, even in the relatively crude sense employed here, was a universal type. It was, however, a plantation type, and a plantation existence embraced well over half the slave population.[8] Two kinds of material will be used in the effort to picture the mechanisms whereby this adjustment to absolute power—an adjustment whose end product included infantile features of behavior—may have been effected. One is drawn from the theoretical knowledge presently available in social psychology, and the other, in the form of an analogy, is derived from some of the data that have come out of the German concentration camps. It is recognized in most theory that social behavior is regulated in some general way by adjustment to symbols of authority—however diversely "authority" may be defined either in theory or in culture itself—and that such adjustment is closely related to the very formation of personality. A corollary would be, of course, that the more diverse those symbols of authority may be, the greater is the permissible variety of adjustment to them—and the wider the margin of individuality, consequently, in the development of the self. The question here has to do with the wideness or narrowness of that margin on the ante-bellum plantation.

The other body of material, involving an experience undergone by several million men and women in the concentration camps of our own time, contains certain items of relevance to the problem here being considered. The experience was analogous to that of slavery and was one in which wide-scale instances of infantilization were observed. The material is sufficiently detailed, and sufficiently documented by men who not only took part in the experience itself but who were versed in the use of psychological theory for analyzing it, that the advantages of drawing upon such data for purposes of analogy seem to outweigh the possible risks.

[8] Although the majority of Southern slaveholders were not planters, the majority of slaves were owned by a planter minority. "Considerably more than half of them lived on plantation units of more than twenty slaves, and one-fourth lived on units of more than fifty. That the majority of slaves belonged to members of the planter class, and not to those who operated small farms with a single slave family, is a fact of crucial importance concerning the nature of bondage in the ante-bellum South." Stampp, *Peculiar Institution,* p. 31.

The introduction of this second body of material must to a certain extent govern the theoretical strategy itself. It has been recognized both implicitly and explicitly that the psychic impact and effects of the concentration-camp experience were not anticipated in existing theory and that consequently such theory would require some major supplementation.[9] It might be added, parenthetically, that almost any published discussion of this modern Inferno, no matter how learned, demonstrates how "theory," operating at such a level of shared human experience, tends to shed much of its technical trappings and to take on an almost literary quality. The experience showed, in any event, that infantile personality features could be induced in a relatively short time among large numbers of adult human beings coming from very diverse backgrounds. The particular strain which was thus placed upon prior theory consisted in the need to make room not only for the cultural and environmental sanctions that sustain personality (which in a sense Freudian theory already had) but also for a virtually unanticipated problem: actual change in the personality of masses of adults. It forced a reappraisal and new appreciation of how completely and effectively prior cultural sanctions for behavior and personality could be detached to make way for new and different sanctions, and of how adjustments could be made by individuals to a species of authority vastly different from any previously known. The revelation for theory was the process of detachment.

These cues, accordingly, will guide the argument on Negro slavery. Several million people were detached with a peculiar effectiveness from a great variety of cultural backgrounds in Africa—a detachment operating with infinitely more effectiveness upon those brought to North America than upon those who came to Latin America. It was achieved partly by the shock experience inherent in the very mode of procurement but more specifically by the type of authority-system to which they were introduced and to which they had to adjust for physical and psychic survival. The new adjustment, to absolute power in a closed system, involved infantilization, and the detachment was so complete that little trace of prior (and thus alternative) cultural sanctions for behavior and personality remained for the descendants of the

[9] See esp. below, p. 118 and n. 83.

first generation. For them, adjustment to clear and omnipresent authority could be more or less automatic—as much so, or as little, as it is for anyone whose adjustment to a social system begins at birth and to whom that system represents normality. We do not know how generally a full adjustment was made by the first generation of fresh slaves from Africa. But we do know —from a modern experience—that such an adjustment is possible, not only within the same generation but within two or three years. This proved possible for people in a full state of complex civilization, for men and women who were not black and not savages.

2

THE "AFRICAN CULTURE" ARGUMENT

While the widespread existence of "Sambo" on the ante-bellum plantation is being taken for granted, it is also taken for granted that no set of characteristics, Sambo-like or otherwise, may possibly be accounted for in terms of "race" or "inborn nature." But "race" is not the only explanation that has been offered for Negro character. Another, very much like it but based on assumptions about the "primitive" nature of African tribal culture, has also enjoyed considerable currency. In fact, with a warrant presumably more scientific, the "culture argument" managed to keep its respectability rather longer than did the one based on race, and to a great extent simply replaced it. But here, too, "inferiority" was in some sense taken as given and was in turn "explained" by generalizations about the low and savage state of the African tribal cultures from which the majority of slaves were originally taken.[10]

[10] Outstanding in this area are Joseph A. Tillinghast, *The Negro in Africa and America* (New York: American Economic Association, 1902); Jerome Dowd, *The Negro Races: A Sociological Study* (New York: Macmillan, 1907), and *The Negro in American Life* (New York: Century, 1926); and W. D. Weatherford, *The Negro from Africa to America* (New York: George H. Doran, 1924). Ulrich Phillips in his own thinking found it relatively easy to make the transition from "inferior race" to "inferior culture" as a basis for his convictions about the American Negro as a less than fully civilized being. This transition may be noted between Phillips' *American Negro Slavery* (1918) and his *Life and Labor in the Old South* (1929). See above, pp. 10 ff. and 17.

The "African culture" argument is a good deal more complex than the race argument and is thus not quite so easy to deal with or dispose of. Indeed, it has taken more than one form and has been put to benevolent as well as derogatory uses. But there is at least a basic assumption shared by all variations: the cultural forms of Africa, however they may be described, were carried over into New World slavery with enough persistence to make a substantial difference in the character and social habits of the American Negro. It is primarily this assumption that must be questioned.

One way to handle generalizations about African culture—and about the manner in which that culture may have influenced American plantation life and character types—would be simply to assert that the very cultural diversity among the African tribes involved in the slave trade makes it impossible to generalize at all. Indeed, taken in a practical sense—judging, that is, from the experience of the European slave traders—this in itself is a perfectly legitimate approach to the problem. The traders' descriptions of the captives they handled, and of the native peoples with whom they dealt, cannot give us much that is trustworthy in the way of anthropological data. But what is worthwhile about these accounts, the point that is really critical in them, is not their descriptive accuracy but their preoccupation with sheer variety.

Negroes were brought to the European traders from many different places, and the continent of Africa was vast. Not only were the trading stations scattered along an immense stretch of the west coast, but to each station it was usual for slave coffles to be brought from great distances inland, sometimes hundreds of miles.[11] The traders had to be endlessly sensitive to the great variety of religious customs, social and political arrangements,

[11] The area from which slaves were taken throughout the duration of the trade embraced roughly 2,300,000 square miles, or more than one-fifth of the entire continent of Africa. See the map in Franklin Frazier, *The Negro in the United States* (New York: Macmillan, 1949), p. 5. The coastline alone, along which the European trade was operated (a preponderance of which had by the 1770's been engrossed by the British), extended, according to Bryan Edwards, "upwards of 1,300 English leagues." The entire area was one "consisting of various countries, inhabited by a great number of savage nations, differing widely from each other, in govermnent, language, manners, and superstitions." Bryan Edwards, *The History, Civil and Commercial, of the British Colonies in the West Indies* (Philadelphia: James Humphreys, 1806), II, 252.

and languages of the people whom they had to meet.[12] Actually it was the very distances between tribes, the hopeless diversity of languages, and the Negroes' inability to communicate with one another, that was counted on to minimize the danger of insurrections on shipboard. William Smith advised that "the safest way is to trade with the different Nations, on either side of the River, and having some of every Sort on board, there will be no more likelihood of their succeeding in a Plot, than of finishing the tower of Babel."[13] Descriptions of individual types are endless, bordering often on the fanciful, but the main thing that emerges from them is the utter absence of any particular "African" type as such—least of all anything resembling "Sambo."[14]

[12] The Royal African Company insisted that its agents be constantly informed upon these matters and charged them with gathering information under an exhaustive variety of headings such as government, customs, language, laws, population, etc. See "Committee Report on the State of the Trade, 1721," in Donnan, *Documents,* II, 254–55. With regard to languages, for example, there were on the Gold Coast alone, no more than sixty miles in length, "seven or eight several languages," according to William Bosman, "so different that three or four of them are interchangeably unintelligible to any but the respective natives: The Negroes of Junmore, ten miles above Axim, cannot understand those of Egira, Abocroe, Ancober and Axim: There is indeed a vast difference in their Languages." *A New and Accurate Description of the Coast of Guinea* (London: J. Knapton, 1705), p. 130. From Whydah to Angola, wrote Bryan Edwards, "the dialects vary at almost every trading river." *History,* II, 255.

[13] William Smith, *A Voyage to Guinea* (2d ed.; London: J. Nourse, 1745), p. 28. This was also the advice of William Snelgrave to a shipmaster new to the trade: "And understanding from him, that he had never been on the coast of Guinea before, I took the liberty to observe to him, 'That as he had on board so many negroes of one town and language, it required the utmost care and management to keep them from mutinying. . . .'" William Snelgrave, *A New Account of Some Parts of Guinea, and the Slave Trade* (London: James, John and Paul Knapton, 1734), p. 187. "Cautions," wrote John Atkins, "where a Cargo is of one Language, is so much the more requisite." John Atkins, "Voyage of John Atkins to Guinea, 1721," in Donnan, *Documents,* II, 280. And as for distance, the native chiefs themselves found it desirable, according to Mungo Park, to take their victims from scattered localities, for, as he says, "the value of a slave in the eye of an African purchaser, increases in proportion to his distance from his native kingdom. . . ." Mungo Park, *Travels and Recent Discoveries, in the Interior Districts of Africa, in the Years, 1796 & 97* (New York: Alexander Brodie, 1801), p. 325.

[14] E.g., such descriptions may be found in "Voyage of John Atkins," Donnan, *Documents,* II, 267, 282–83; John Matthews, *A Voyage to the*

But it is hardly necessary to stop with the traders' accounts to establish the vast gulf between African culture and Negro life in North America. Indeed, there is a sufficient body of work available on the anthropology, history, and institutional life of West Africa to make it both possible, and profitable to take up the "culture argument" on its merits. We would discover that it is in fact possible to make certain kinds of generalizations about African culture, and that the more we find out, the greater is the sense of sheer contrast: the gulf between Africa and America is even wider than we imagined. We can suppose that the pseudo-anthropologists of the early 1900's must have begun, in their reasoning, not with Africa but with the depressed state of Negro existence in this country. They were thus prepared a priori, in their efforts to make connections, to find something comparable in the original tribal state. They were most sensitized, in short, not to sophistication or complexity, but rather to crudity, depravity, and primitivism.[15]

The anthropologist Melville Herskovits—though certain of his

River Sierra-Leone . . . (London: B. White and Son, 1788), pp. 92–93; Park, *Travels,* pp. 16–18 and *passim;* Edwards, *History,* II, 266–283; "John Barbot's Description of Guinea, 1682," Donnan, *Documents,* I, 286; Bosman, *New and Accurate Description,* pp. 65, 340–42; "The Slave Trade at Calabar, 1700–1705," Donnan, *Documents,* I, 286.

[15] Tillinghast was saying, in 1902: "The interval to be traversed . . . in passing from West African savagery to American civilization was so immense, that we must beware of losing true perspective in our view of the problem." *Negro in Africa and America,* p. 112. Again: "The question is: did American slavery develop in the negro his indolence, carelessness, brutality to animals, and aptness in deception, or did it merely fail to eradicate them as well as some better devised system might have done? Every characteristic just named we know to have been an integral part of the West African's nature long before any slaver ever touched our shore." *Ibid.,* p. 148. And Weatherford, twenty-two years later, in a book whose suggestive title is almost identical with Tillinghast's: "We believe that much of the present response of the Negro to social environment is influenced by the social heritage, not only from slavery but from the far African past. This is in no way an intimation that the Negro has not progressed far beyond that past. Indeed no one can read the story of his marvelous progress without great amazement. . . ." *Negro from Africa to America,* p. 20. The student of the American Negro, Weatherford innocently insists, "must be willing to judge him as to the distance he has traveled since he left his African home, rather than compared with the white man who had thousands of years the start." *Ibid.,* p. 42.

own conclusions have since been questioned—did much during the 1930's and 1940's to refocus the thinking on this whole general subject. He very properly saw that the work of such earlier writers as Dowd, Tillinghast, and Weatherford on the Negro in Africa, with its emphasis on superstition and savagery, had given much unwarranted support to racial stereotypes about the American Negro. Herskovits' *Myth of the Negro Past* was accordingly an effort both to destroy, as scientifically unusable, some of these dubious generalizations and to substitute for them sounder generalizations of his own based on a considerable amount of actual field work in Africa. The concrete findings of other investigators in the same area, taken together with the work of Herskovits, now constitute a body of knowledge that is well worth examining. Out of it, certain very significant patterns in West African tribal civilization may be distinguished, some of which should be noted here. Fifty years ago, if the American Negro was congratulated for anything, it was for his remarkable advancement from a state of primitive ignorance. Now, however, looking back upon the energy, vitality, and complex organization of West African tribal life, we are tempted to reverse the question altogether and to wonder how it was ever possible that all this native resourcefulness and vitality could have been brought to such a point of utter stultification in America.

Although slaves from many parts of Africa did ultimately find their way to Virginia and the Carolinas, it appears that the greatest numbers of them were drawn from the area that included the Niger delta, the Gold Coast, and Dahomey. Modern research has indicated, moreover, that the tribes of this region, despite considerable variation in languages and local customs, did share certain broad cultural characteristics.[16] For one thing, the

[16] This is discussed at length in Melville J. Herskovits, *The Myth of the Negro Past* (New York: Harper, 1941), esp. pp. 43–53, 81–85. The present writer is accepting without question the findings and generalizations put forth in the above work, insofar as they relate to the Negro in Africa. Quite another matter, however, is the effort made by Professor Herskovits to exhibit a wealth of African cultural survivals as having been retained in American Negro life. Here the author of *Myth of the Negro Past* seems in a peculiar sense to follow in the very footsteps of those writers whom he has attacked most freely. They, in their work, designated the American Negro's African heritage as a handicap; he, in his, makes great efforts to dignify that heritage and call attention to its worthiness. But the basic as-

basic mode of support throughout the entire region was agriculture. Unlike many of the Indian tribes of the New World, the West Africans had organized their agricultural economy to the point where a heavy concentration of population could be supported through cultivation of relatively limited areas. Agriculture here was thus more intensive and more purposeful than was the case with the preliterate peoples of North America. Nor was it purely woman's work; although the women did the cultivating, the heavy labor was performed by the men. Africa was no Garden of Eden; food could be produced only through hard work, and such traditions of toil and self-discipline as those of Dahomey are in sharp contrast not only to those of the migratory hunting cultures of America[17] but also to the legendary improvidence

---

sumption appears to be the same for both Herskovits and his predecessors: the Negro did in fact bring much of his African cultural background with him, and this background did substantially influence his subsequent life and behavior in this country. This assumption is not accepted in the present work. On the contrary, few ethnic groups seem to have been so thoroughly and effectively detached from their prior cultural connections as was the case in the Negro's transit from Africa to North America. This is the more striking when it is noted that "Africanisms" were much more effectively retained among similar groups going to South America. (See below, nn. 36–38.) It is the very thoroughness of such detachment, and the wide contrast between the way it operated in North America and Latin America, that seems to constitute a major problem for explanation.

[17] This may actually have some bearing on the reasons for the whites' uniform lack of success in enslaving the North American Indian. Indians would either escape or die in captivity; those sent to the West Indies simply pined away and expired in a matter of months. One explanation for this has a strong moral ring: it was a matter of pride; the Indian preferred death to servitude. But perhaps simple "primitivism"—a much profounder form of it than that of West African society—would be closer to the mark. Unlike the African Negro, the American Indian had absolutely no experience with intensive agriculture; the Indian economies of the eastern seaboard were based on hunting, fishing, and a very limited form of agriculture in which the land was cleared by fire and cultivated with sticks by the women. The men, meanwhile, occupied their time with hunting, trapping, visiting, and petty warfare. As a result the Indian was physically and psychologically incapable of adjusting to plantation life. That life was so utterly strange and foreign to him that there was literally nothing in it to sustain his will to live. See A. L. Kroeber, *Cultural and National Areas of Native North America* (Berkeley: University of California Press, 1939), pp. 93, 146–49; also Ruth Murray Underhill, *Red Man's America: A His-*

of the American plantation Negro. Indeed, the economies as a whole in this region were characterized by a high degree of specialization and division of labor. Ironworkers, weavers, carvers, and basketmakers were all clearly defined occupational groups, and their clothing, tools, and other products were made not simply for their own use but also for sale. These various features of West African economic life had a profound influence on the law, social organization, and religion of the entire area.[18]

Parallel with all this was a very intricate set of trading arrangements, the nature of which has not always been properly appreciated in discussions of American Negro slavery. Until very late in the eighteenth century, virtually no white men had ever seen anything of the African interior. This was due not to their own preference but to a widespread, highly organized, and successful determination on the part of the coastal tribes to keep them out. Except for the terminal points on the coast, the trade in slaves was for three centuries rigorously and exclusively controlled by the blacks. In Nigeria it was managed by the Oracle, a priestly institution not unlike the ancient Hellenic Oracle of Delphi. The prestige of the Oracle, and of the class of men that composed it, enabled this organization to assume control over the trade up and down the entire Niger region. It was necessary to evolve a highly complex network of understandings that would guarantee free passage through the territory of twenty or thirty different tribes. The Oracle, as a judicio-religious body, condemned hundreds of offenders of one kind or another to be sold into slavery, and their disappearance was accounted for locally by

---

tory of Indians in the United States (Chicago: University of Chicago Press, 1952), pp. 67, 87. With regard to the West African tribesman, on the other hand, this may be the one point—the agricultural tradition—at which his African background *did* make a major difference in his adjustment to life in America.

As for the "moral" implications of the Indian's "preferring death to servitude," these if reversed might turn out to be less simple than they seem. Cf. the point below about the "Moslems" in the concentration camps (n. 59); or the discussion of "give-up-itis" in the Korean prisoner-of-war camps in Eugene Kinkead, *In Every War but One* (New York: Norton, 1959), pp. 148–49.

[18] See particularly Melville J. Herskovits, *Dahomey: An Ancient West African Kingdom* (New York: J. J. Augustin, 1938), I, 29–77.

the explanation that they had been "eaten" by the Oracle. These victims, together with captives taken in local wars and raids, were regularly conducted to the coast, and for this trade in all its ramifications the Oracle acted as a kind of mediating agency between the coastal tribes and those of the interior. Such cooperative arrangements, effective over hundreds of square miles, made it possible to exclude the Europeans from the interior for centuries.[19]

Slavery, of course, existed in Africa. But there was a sharp distinction between the domestic slavery prevalent among the tribes themselves and the state into which the deported captives would ultimately be delivered by the Europeans. There was little in the one that could prepare a man for what he would experience in the other. The typical West African slave was a recognized member of a household and possessed numerous rights. "A slave," according to R. S. Rattray, writing of Ashanti society, "might marry; own property; himself own a slave; swear an 'oath'; be a competent witness; and ultimately might become heir to his master."[20]

A closely knit family structure stood at the base of all political, economic, and legal institutions, whose efficiency in turn depended on the discipline enforced within the family. Throughout West Africa the authority of the elders was accepted without question. Despite wide variation in political organization—ranging from small independent units to large empires—all assumed the rule of law rather than simple despotism. The king was never absolute; he ruled with the advice of a council of elders and in accordance with traditional law and custom. Just as authority was carefully graded from the family to the chief—and, in the larger units, to the king—so the law itself was administered by an intricate system of inferior and superior courts. African political institutions, moreover, were developed in sufficient complexity that they were able to provide stable governments for

[19] K. Onwuka Dike, *Trade and Politics in the Niger Delta, 1830–1885* (Oxford: Clarendon Press, 1956), pp. 37–46.

[20] R. S. Rattray, *Ashanti Law and Constitution* (Oxford: Clarendon Press, 1929), p. 38. See also *ibid.*, pp. 33–46; Herskovits, *Dahomey,* I, 99–100, and II, 97–98.

groups as large as two hundred thousand, some of them lasting for centuries.[21]

One of the most famous of these governments was the Ashanti, located in the heart of the slaving area. Ashanti emerged as a powerful feudal state about 1700, when one of the tribal rulers persuaded his fellow chiefs to recognize him as the *Asantehene,* king of all the Ashantis. A meaningful comparison between such a society and those of medieval Europe would be difficult, but the political federation of the Ashantis, their traditional constitution, their tax and revenue structure, and their military system—a system that enabled them to wage extended campaigns with armies as large as thirty or forty thousand—entitles one to argue that they must have had an institutional life at least as sophisticated as that of Anglo-Saxon England.[22]

But returning to the primary problem: no true picture, cursory or extended, of African culture seems to throw any light at all on the origins of what would emerge, in American plantation society, as the stereotyped "Sambo" personality. The typical West African tribesman was a distinctly warlike individual; he had a profound sense of family and family authority; he took hard work for granted; and he was accustomed to live by a highly

[21] See, e.g., C. K. Meek, *Law and Authority in a Nigerian Tribe: A Study in Indirect Rule* (London: Oxford University Press, 1937), pp. 88–164, 206–51; Rattray, *Ashanti Law and Constitution,* esp. pp. 75–98; and Herskovits, *Dahomey,* II, 3–48.

[22] In addition to the material in Rattray, see W. E. F. Ward, *A History of the Gold Coast* (London: George Allen & Unwin, 1948), pp. 107–19; and J. D. Fage, *An Introduction to the History of West Africa* (Cambridge: University Press, 1955), pp. 95–98. It was not primarily the rigors of disease and tropical climate that served to keep the Europeans out of the interior for so long, but rather the highly developed governmental and military systems of such West African nations as Ashanti, all of whom had at least one policy in common, an inflexible determination to prevent any non-African middlemen from cutting in on the internal slave trade. Nor was this area a "trackless wilderness"; it was much more thickly populated than was North America at the time of the first colonizing ventures and was crossed by a maze of heavily traveled trading routes. The power of Ashanti, for instance, continued until late in the nineteenth century when the Ashanti armies were finally defeated by the British after a long period, nearly a hundred years, of full-scale warfare. Ward's *History* deals at length with the relations of Ashanti and the British, and with the military campaigns that they waged against each other. See also Dike, *Trade and Politics,* pp. 7–10.

formalized set of rules which he himself often helped to administer. If he belonged to the upper classes of tribal society—as did many who later fell victim to the slave trade—he might have had considerable experience as a political or military leader. He was the product, in any case, of cultural traditions essentially heroic in nature.

Something very profound, therefore, would have had to intervene in order to obliterate all this and to produce, on the American plantation, a society of helpless dependents.

3

SHOCK AND DETACHMENT

We may suppose that every African who became a slave underwent an experience whose crude psychic impact must have been staggering and whose consequences superseded anything that had ever previously happened to him. Some effort should therefore be made to picture the series of shocks which must have accompanied the principal events of that enslavement.

The majority of slaves appear to have been taken in native wars,[23] which meant that no one—neither persons of high rank nor warriors of prowess—was guaranteed against capture and enslavement.[24] Great numbers were caught in surprise attacks

[23] There were other pretexts, such as crime or debt, but war was probably the most frequent mode of procurement. Snelgrave, New Account, p. 158; "John Barbot's Description," in Donnan, Documents, I, 284, 289, 294, 298; "Observations on the Slave Trade, 1789" [C. B. Wadström] in ibid., II, 599; Matthews, Voyage to Sierra-Leone, pp. 145-46, 163. See also below, n. 34.

[24] As to "character types," one might be tempted to suppose that as a rule it would be only the weaker and more submissive who allowed themselves to be taken into slavery. Yet it appears that a heavy proportion of the slaves were in fact drawn from among the most warlike. "In a country divided into a thousand petty states, mostly independent and jealous of each other; where every freeman is accustomed to arms, and fond of military achievements; where the youth who has practised the bow and spear from his infancy, longs for nothing so much as an opportunity to display his valour; it is natural to imagine that wars frequently originate from very frivolous provocation." Park, Travels, p. 328. "The most potent negroe," wrote William Bosman, "can't pretend to be insured from slavery; for if he ever ventures himself in the wars it may easily become his lot." New and Accurate Description, p. 183. It has often been pointed out that slavery already existed among the tribes themselves and that a considerable

upon their villages, and since the tribes acting as middlemen for the trade had come to depend on regular supplies of captives in order to maintain that function, the distinction between wars and raiding expeditions tended to be very dim.[25] The first shock, in an experience destined to endure many months and to leave its survivors irrevocably changed, was thus the shock of capture. It is an effort to remember that while enslavement occurred in Africa every day, to the individual it occurred just once.[26]

The second shock—the long march to the sea—drew out the nightmare for many weeks. Under the glaring sun, through the steaming jungle, they were driven along like beasts tied together by their necks; day after day, eight or more hours at a time, they would stagger barefoot over thorny underbrush, dried reeds, and stones. Hardship, thirst, brutalities, and near starvation penetrated the experience of each exhausted man and woman who reached the coast.[27] One traveler tells of seeing hundreds of bleaching skeletons strewn along one of the slave caravan routes.[28] But then the man who must interest us is the man who survived—he

---

proportion of Africans were used to it and had in fact been born into it. It may be doubted, however, if substantial numbers of *these* slaves came to America, for apparently the native chiefs tended to sell only their war captives to the Europeans and to keep their hereditary and customary slaves —together with their most docile captives—for themselves. Park, *Travels,* p. 332. It has even been asserted that in many places the tribal laws themselves forbade the selling of domestic slaves, except for crimes, though apparently it was simple enough to trump up an accusation if one wanted to get rid of a slave. Matthews, *Voyage to Sierra-Leone,* p. 153; Edwards, *History,* II, 312.

[25] "The Wars which the inhabitants of the interior parts of the country, beyond Senegal, Gambia, and Sierra Leona, carry on with each other, are chiefly of a predatory nature, and owe their origin to the yearly number of slaves, which the Mandingoes, or the inland traders suppose will be wanted by the vessels that will arrive on the coast." "Observations" [Wadström], in Donnan, *Documents,* II, 599.

[26] A number of excerpts describing these raids are cited in Thomas Fowell Buxton, *Letter on the Slave Trade to the Lord Viscount Melbourne* (London, 1838), pp. 34–38.

[27] Descriptions of the march may be found in Park, *Travels,* pp. 371 ff.; Buxton, *Letter,* pp. 41–44; Rinchon, *La traite et l'esclavage,* pp. 174–75; L. Degrandpré, *Voyage à la côte occidentale d'Afrique, fait dans les années 1786 et 1787* (Paris, 1801), II, 48–50.

[28] Buxton, *Letter,* p. 43.

who underwent the entire experience, of which this was only the beginning.

The next shock, aside from the fresh physical torments which accompanied it, was the sale to the European slavers. After being crowded into pens near the trading stations and kept there overnight, sometimes for days, the slaves were brought out for examination. Those rejected would be abandoned to starvation; the remaining ones—those who had been bought—were branded, given numbers inscribed on leaden tags, and herded on shipboard.[29]

The episode that followed—almost too protracted and stupefying to be called a mere "shock"—was the dread Middle Passage, brutalizing to any man, black or white, ever to be involved with it. The holds, packed with squirming and suffocating humanity, became stinking infernos of filth and pestilence. Stories of disease, death, and cruelty on the terrible two-month voyage abound in the testimony which did much toward ending the British slave trade forever.[30]

The final shock in the process of enslavement came with the Negro's introduction to the West Indies. Bryan Edwards, describ-

[29] "When these slaves come to fida, they are put in prison all together, and when we treat concerning buying them, they are all brought out together in a large plain; where, by our Chirurgeons, whose province it is, they are thoroughly examined, even to the smallest member, and that naked too both men and women, without the least distinction and modesty. Those which are approved as good are set on one side; and the lame or faulty are set by as *invalides,* which are here called *mackrons.* These are such as are above five and thirty years old, or are maimed in the arms, legs, hands or feet, have lost a tooth, are grey-haired, or have films over their eyes; as well as all those which are affected by any venereal distemper, or with several other diseases." Bosman, *New and Accurate Description,* p. 364. See also Degrandpré, *Voyage,* II, 53–56; Buxton, *Letter,* pp. 47–49; Rinchon, *La traite et l'esclavage,* pp. 188–89; "John Barbot's Description," in Donnan, *Documents,* I, 289, 295; Park, *Travels,* p. 360.

[30] Descriptions of the Middle Passage may be found in *An Abstract of the Evidence Delivered before a Select Committee of the House of Commons in the Years 1790, and 1791; on the Part of the Petitioners for the Abolition of the Slave Trade* (London, 1791); Alexander Falconbridge, *An Account of the Slave Trade on the Coast of Africa* (London: J. Phillips, 1788); Rinchon, *La traite et l'esclavage,* pp. 196–209; Edwards, *History,* II; Brantz Mayer, *Captain Canot* (New York: D. Appleton, 1854); Averil Mackenzie-Grieve, *The Last Years of the English Slave Trade, Liverpool 1750–1807* (London: Putnam, 1941).

ing the arrival of a slave ship, writes of how in times of labor scarcity crowds of people would come scrambling aboard, man-handling the slaves and throwing them into panic. The Jamaica legislature eventually "corrected the enormity" by enacting that the sales be held on shore. Edwards felt a certain mortification at seeing the Negroes exposed naked in public, similar to that felt by the trader Degrandpré at seeing them examined back at the African factories.[31] Yet here they did not seem to care. "They display . . . very few signs of lamentation for their past or of apprehension for their future condition; but . . . commonly express great eagerness to be sold."[32] The "seasoning" process which followed completed the series of steps whereby the African Negro became a slave.

The mortality had been very high. One-third of the numbers first taken, out of a total of perhaps fifteen million, had died on the march and at the trading stations; another third died during the Middle Passage and the seasoning.[33] Since a majority of the African-born slaves who came to the North American plantations did not come directly but were imported through the British West Indies, one may assume that the typical slave underwent an experience something like that just outlined. This was the man—one in three—who had come through it all and lived and was about to enter our "closed system." What would he be like if he survived and adjusted to that?

Actually, a great deal had happened to him already. Much of his past had been annihilated; nearly every prior connection had been severed. Not that he had really "forgotten" all these things— his family and kinship arrangements, his language, the tribal religion, the taboos, the name he had once borne, and so on—but none of it any longer carried much meaning. The old values, the sanctions, the standards, already unreal, could no longer furnish him guides for conduct, for adjusting to the expectations of a complete new life. Where then was he to look for new standards,

[31] Degrandpré, *Voyage*, II, 55–56.

[32] Edwards, *History*, II, 340. See also *Abstract of Evidence*, pp. 46–47, and Falconbridge, *Account*, pp. 33–36.

[33] Tannenbaum, *Slave and Citizen*, p. 28. As for the total exports of slaves from Africa throughout the entire period of the trade, estimates run as high as twenty million. "Even a conservative estimate," notes Mr. Tannenbaum, "would hardly cut this figure in half." *Ibid.*, p. 32.

new cues—who would furnish them now? He could now look to none but his master, the one man to whom the system had committed his entire being: the man upon whose will depended his food, his shelter, his sexual connections, whatever moral instruction he might be offered, whatever "success" was possible within the system, his very security—in short, everything.

The thoroughness with which African Negroes coming to America were detached from prior cultural sanctions should thus be partly explainable by the very shock sequence inherent in the technique of procurement. But it took something more than this to produce "Sambo," and it is possible to overrate—or at least to overgeneralize—this shock sequence in the effort to explain what followed.[34] A comparable experience was also undergone by slaves coming into Latin America, where very little that resembled our "Sambo" tradition would ever develop. We should also remember that, in either case, it was only the first generation that actually experienced these shocks. It could even be argued that the shock sequence is not an absolute necessity for explaining "Sambo" at all.

So whereas the Middle Passage and all that went with it must have been psychologically numbing, and should probably be regarded as a long thrust, at least, toward the end product, it has little meaning considered apart from what came later. It may be assumed that the process of detachment was completed—and, as it were, guaranteed—by the kind of "closed" authority-system into which the slave was introduced and to which he would have to adjust.[35] At any rate, a test of this detachment and its thoroughness is virtually ready-made. Everyone who has looked into the problem of African cultural features surviving among New World Negroes agrees that the contrast between North America

[34] Its rigors, at least prior to the sea passage, were clearly not experienced with uniform intensity by all. For example, Onwuka Dike claims that among the tribes east of the Niger, nearly as many, and perhaps even more, of the slaves sold to Europeans were procured by non-violent means, through the judgment of the Oracle, as were taken in wars. See Dike, *Trade and Politics,* pp. 40–41. It might also be added that the "long march" was probably not a universal experience either, since there was in West Africa a network of navigable rivers down which cargoes of slaves could be transported in canoes. On this point see *ibid.,* pp. 19–20.

[35] See above, pp. 37–63.

and Latin America is immense. In Brazil, survivals from African religion are not only to be encountered everywhere, but such carry-overs are so distinct that they may even be identified with particular tribal groups. "The Negro religions and cults," Arthur Ramos adds, "were not the only form of cultural expression which survived in Brazil. The number of folklore survivals is extremely large, the prolongation of social institutions, habits, practices and events from Africa."[36] Fernando Ortiz, writing of Cuba in 1905, saw the African witchcraft cults flourishing on the island as a formidable social problem.[37] One of our own anthropologists, on the other hand, despite much dedicated field work, has been put to great effort to prove that in North American Negro society any African cultural vestiges have survived at all.[38]

4

ADJUSTMENT TO ABSOLUTE POWER
IN THE CONCENTRATION CAMP

A certain amount of the mellowness in Ulrich Phillips' picture of ante-bellum plantation life has of necessity been discredited by recent efforts not only to refocus attention upon the brutalities of the slave system but also to dispose once and for all of Phillips' assumptions about the slave as a racially inferior being. And yet it is important—particularly in view of the analogy about to be

[36] Arthur Ramos, *The Negro in Brazil* (Washington: Associated Publishers, 1939), p. 94. Ramos devotes two full chapters to "The Cultural Heritage of the Brazilian Negro." Donald Pierson, in his *Negroes in Brazil* (Chicago: University of Chicago Press, 1942), likewise devotes two chapters to African influences in the customs of the Negroes of Bahia.

[37] Fernando Ortiz, *Los Negros Brujos* (Madrid: Libería de F. Fé, 1906). This entire book is devoted to occult African practices in Cuba, including a chapter called "The Future of Witchcraft."

[38] Herskovits, *Myth of the Negro Past*. The real aim of this study seems more often than not to be that of "promoting" African culture in the United States by insisting on its values instead of describing its actual survivals—which the author himself admits are decidedly on the scanty side compared with those to be found in Latin America. Such "Africanisms" do not seem to go much beyond esoteric vestiges of a suspiciously circumstantial nature, in speech rhythms, certain symbols in folk-tales, habits of "temporary mating," etc. Professor Herskovits reveals, perhaps unwittingly, that efforts to convince American Negro audiences that they do, in fact, have an African cultural heritage, have met with hostility and tension.

presented—to keep in mind that for all the system's cruelties there were still clear standards of patriarchal benevolence inherent in its human side, and that such standards were recognized as those of the best Southern families This aspect, despite the most drastic changes of emphasis, should continue to guarantee for Phillips' view more than just a modicum of legitimacy; the patriarchal quality, whatever measure of benevolence or lack of it one wants to impute to the regime, still holds a major key to its nature as a social system.

Introducing, therefore, certain elements of the German concentration-camp experience involves the risky business of trying to balance two necessities—emphasizing both the vast dissimilarities of the two regimes and the essentially limited purpose for which they are being brought together, and at the same time justifying the use of the analogy in the first place. The point is perhaps best made by insisting on an order of classification. The American plantation was not even in the metaphorical sense a "concentration camp"; nor was it even "like" a concentration camp, to the extent that any standards comparable to those governing the camps might be imputed to any sector of American society, at any time; but it should at least be permissible to turn the thing around—to speak of the concentration camp as a special and highly perverted instance of human slavery. Doing so, moreover, should actually be of some assistance in the strategy, now universally sanctioned, of demonstrating how little the products and consequences of slavery ever had to do with race. The only mass experience that Western people have had within recorded history comparable in any way with Negro slavery was undergone in the nether world of Nazism. The concentration camp was not only a perverted slave system; it was also—what is less obvious but even more to the point—a perverted patriarchy.

The system of the concentration camps was expressly devised in the 1930's by high officials of the German government to function as an instrument of terror. The first groups detained in the camps consisted of prominent enemies of the Nazi regime; later, when these had mostly been eliminated, it was still felt necessary that the system be institutionalized and made into a standing weapon of intimidation—which required a continuing flow of incoming prisoners. The categories of eligible persons were greatly widened to include all real, fancied, or "potential" opposition to the state. They were often selected on capricious and random grounds, and together they formed a cross-section of society which was virtually complete: criminals, workers, businessmen, professional people, middle-class Jews, even members of the aristocracy. The teeming camps thus held all kinds—not only the scum of the underworld but also countless men and women of culture and refinement. During the war a specialized objective was added, that of exterminating the Jewish populations of subject countries, which required special mass-production methods of which the gas chambers and crematories of Auschwitz-Birkenau were outstanding examples. Yet the basic technique was everywhere and at all times the same: the deliberate infliction of various forms of torture upon the incoming prisoners in such a way as to break their resistance and make way for their degradation as individuals. These brutalities were not merely "permitted" or "encouraged"; they were prescribed. Duty in the camps was a mandatory phase in the training of SS guards, and it was here that particular efforts were made to overcome their scruples and to develop in them a capacity for relishing spectacles of pain and anguish.

The concentration camps and everything that took place in them were veiled in the utmost isolation and secrecy. Of course complete secrecy was impossible, and a continuing stream of rumors circulated among the population. At the same time so repellent was the nature of these stories that in their enormity they transcended the experience of nearly everyone who heard them; in self-protection it was somehow necessary to persuade oneself that they could not really be true. The results, therefore, contained elements of the diabolical. The undenied existence of the camps cast a shadow of nameless dread over the entire population; on the other hand the *individual* who actually became a prisoner in one of them was in most cases devastated with fright and utterly demoralized to discover that what was happening to *him* was not less, but rather far more terrible than anything he had imagined. The shock sequence of "procurement," therefore, together with the initial phases of the prisoner's introduction to camp life, is not without significance in assessing some of the psychic effects upon those who survived as long-term inmates.

The arrest was typically made at night, preferably late; this was standing Gestapo policy, designed to heighten the element of shock, terror, and unreality surrounding the arrest. After a day or so in the police jail came the next major shock, that of being transported to the camp itself. "This transportation into the camp, and the 'initiation' into it," writes Bruno Bettelheim (an ex-inmate of Dachau and Buchenwald), "is often the first torture which the prisoner has ever experienced and is, as a rule, physically and psychologically the worst torture to which he will ever be exposed."[39] It involved a planned series of brutalities inflicted by guards making repeated rounds through the train over a twelve- to thirty-six-hour period during which the prisoner was prevented from resting. If transported in cattle cars instead of passenger cars, the prisoners were sealed in, under conditions not dissimilar to those of the Middle Passage.[40] Upon their arrival—if the camp was one in which mass exterminations were carried out —there might be sham ceremonies designed to reassure temporarily the exhausted prisoners, which meant that the fresh terrors in the offing would then strike them with redoubled impact. An SS officer might deliver an address, or a band might be playing popular tunes, and it would be in such a setting that the initial "selection" was made. The newcomers would file past an SS doctor who indicated, with a motion of the forefinger, whether they were to go to the left or to the right. To one side went those considered capable of heavy labor; to the other would go wide categories of "undesirables"; those in the latter group were being condemned to the gas chambers.[41] Those who remained would undergo the formalities of "registration," full of indignities, which culminated in the marking of each prisoner with a number.[42]

[39] Bruno Bettelheim, "Individual and Mass Behavior in Extreme Situations," *Journal of Abnormal Psychology*, XXXVIII (October, 1943), 424.

[40] A description of such a trip may be found in Olga Lengyel, *Five Chimneys: The Story of Auschwitz* (Chicago, 1947), pp. 7–10. See also Eugen Kogon, *The Theory and Practice of Hell* (New York: Farrar, Straus, 1946), p. 67.

[41] Elie Cohen, *Human Behavior in the Concentration Camp* (New York: Norton, 1953), pp. 118–22; Kogon, *Theory and Practice*, pp. 66–76; Lengyel, *Five Chimneys*, pp. 12–22.

[42] One aspect of this registration ceremony involved a sham "inspection" of the body, whose effect on the women prisoners in particular was apparently very profound. See Lengyel, *Five Chimneys*, p. 19; Ella Lingens-Reiner, *Prisoners of Fear* (London: Victor Gollancz, 1948), p. 26. This may be compared with Degrandpré's description of a similar "inspection"

There were certain physical and psychological strains of camp life, especially debilitating in the early stages, which should be classed with the introductory shock sequence. There was a state of chronic hunger whose pressures were unusually effective in detaching prior scruples of all kinds; even the sexual instincts no longer functioned in the face of the drive for food.[43] The man who at his pleasure could bestow or withhold food thus wielded, for that reason alone, abnormal power. Another strain at first was the demand for absolute obedience, the slightest deviation from which brought savage punishments.[44] The prisoner had to ask permission—by no means granted as a matter of course—even to defecate.[45] The power of the SS guard, as the prisoner was hourly reminded, was that of life and death over his body. A more exquisite form of pressure lay in the fact that the prisoner had never a moment of solitude: he no longer had a private existence; it was no longer possible, in any imaginable sense, for him to be an "individual."[46]

Another factor having deep disintegrative effects upon the prisoner was the prospect of a limitless future in the camp. In the immediate sense this meant that he could no longer make plans for the future. But there would eventually be a subtler meaning: it made the break with the outside world a *real* break; in time the

---

on the African slave coast in the 1780's; see his *Voyage,* II, 55–56. "Apart from the fact that for every newcomer his transformation into a 'prisoner' meant a degradation," writes an ex-prisoner of Auschwitz and Mauthausen, "there was also the *loss of his name.* That this was no trifling circumstance should be apparent from the great importance which, according to Freud, a man attaches to his name. This is, in Freud's view, sufficiently proven by 'the fact that savages regard a name as an essential part of a man's personality. . . .' Anyhow, whether one agrees with Freud or not, the loss of one's name is not without significance, for the name is a personal attribute. Because he no longer had a name, but had become a number, the prisoner belonged to the huge army of the nameless who peopled the concentration camp." Cohen, *Human Behavior,* pp. 145–46.

[43] *Ibid.,* pp. 134–35, 140–43.

[44] These punishments are discussed most vividly in Kogon, *Theory and Practice,* pp. 102–8, 207–11.

[45] Bettelheim, "Individual and Mass Behavior," p. 445.

[46] The effects of never being alone are noted in Cohen, *Human Behavior,* pp. 130–31, and David Rousset, *The Other Kingdom* (New York: Reynal & Hitchcock, 1947), p. 133.

"real" life would become the life of the camp, the outside world an abstraction. Had it been a limited detention, whose end could be calculated, one's outside relationships—one's roles, one's very "personality"—might temporarily have been laid aside, to be reclaimed more or less intact at the end of the term. Here, however, the prisoner was faced with the apparent impossibility of his old roles or even his old personality ever having any future at all; it became more and more difficult to imagine himself resuming them.[47] It was this that underlay the "egalitarianism" of the camps; old statuses had lost their meaning.[48] A final strain, which must have been particularly acute for the newcomer, was the omnipresent threat of death and the very unpredictable suddenness with which death might strike. Quite aside from the periodic gas-chamber selections, the guards in their sports and caprices were at liberty to kill any prisoner any time.[49]

In the face of all this, one might suppose that the very notion of an "adjustment" would be grotesque. The majority of those who entered the camps never came out again, but our concern here has to be with those who survived—an estimated 700,000 out of nearly eight million.[50] For them, the regime must be considered not as a system of death but as a way of life. These survivors did make an adjustment of some sort to the system; it is they themselves who report it. After the initial shocks, what was the nature of the "normality" that emerged?

[47] "When the author [Bettelheim] expressed to some of the old prisoners his astonishment that they seemed not interested in discussing their future life outside the camp, they frequently admitted that they could no longer visualize themselves living outside the camp, making free decisions, taking care of themselves and their families." Bettelheim, "Individual and Mass Behavior," p. 439.

[48] M. Rousset tells of how, on one of the death marches, a prisoner came to him bringing a French compatriot and begging his protection for the wretched man. "He told me that he was a lawyer from Toulouse, and it was only with the greatest difficulty that I kept from laughing aloud. For this social designation, *lawyer,* no longer fitted the poor wretch in the slightest. The incongruity of the thought was irresistibly comic. And it was the same with all of us." Rousset, *Other Kingdom,* p. 77.

[49] Kogon, *Theory and Practice,* p. 274; Cohen, *Human Behavior,* p. 155; Hilde O. Bluhm, "How Did They Survive?" *American Journal of Psychotherapy,* II (January, 1948), 5.

[50] Kogon, *Theory and Practice,* p. 277.

A dramatic species of psychic displacement seems to have occurred at the very outset. This experience, described as a kind of "splitting of personality," has been noted by most of the inmates who later wrote of their imprisonment. The very extremity of the initial tortures produced in the prisoner what actually amounted to a sense of detachment; these brutalities went so beyond his own experience that they became somehow incredible—they seemed to be happening no longer to him but almost to somone else. "[The author] has no doubt," writes Bruno Bettelheim, "that he was able to endure the transportation, and all that followed, because right from the beginning he became convinced that these horrible and degrading experiences somehow did not happen to 'him' as a subject, but only to 'him' as an object."[51] This subject-object "split" appears to have served a double function: not only was it an immediate psychic defense mechanism against shock,[52] but it also acted as the first thrust toward a new adjustment. This splitting-off of a special "self"—a self which endured the tortures but which was not the "real" self—also provided the first glimpse of a new personality which, being not "real," would not need to feel bound by the values which guided the individual in his former life. "The prisoners' feelings," according to Mr. Bettelheim, "could be summed up by the following sentence: 'What I am doing here, or what is happening to me, does not count at all; here everything is permissible as long and insofar as it contributes to helping me survive in the camp.' "[53]

One part of the prisoner's being was thus, under sharp stress, brought to the crude realization that he must thenceforth be governed by an entire new set of standards in order to live. Mrs. Lingens-Reiner puts it bluntly: "Will you survive, or shall I? As

[51] Bettelheim, "Individual and Mass Behavior," p. 431. See also Cohen, *Human Behavior,* pp. 116–17, 172.

[52] "Many kept their bearings only by a kind of split personality. They surrendered their bodies resistlessly to the terror, while their inner being withdrew and held aloof." Kogon, *Theory and Practice,* p. 71. "I arrived at that state of numbness where I was no longer sensitive to either club or whip. I lived through the rest of that scene almost as a spectator." Lengyel, *Five Chimneys,* p. 20.

[53] Bettelheim, "Individual and Mass Behavior," p. 432. "We camp prisoners," writes Mrs. Lingens-Reiner, "had only one yardstick: whatever helped our survival was good, and whatever threatened our survival was bad, and to be avoided." *Prisoners of Fear,* p. 142.

soon as one sensed that this was at stake everyone turned egotist."[54] ". . . I think it of primary importance," writes Dr. Cohen, "to take into account that the superego acquired new values in a concentration camp, so much at variance with those which the prisoner bore with him into camp that the latter faded."[55] But then this acquisition of "new values" did not all take place immediately; it was not until some time after the most acute period of stress was over that the new, "unreal" self would become at last the "real" one.

"If you survive the first three months you will survive the next three years." Such was the formula transmitted from the old prisoners to the new ones,[56] and its meaning lay in the fact that the first three months would generally determine a prisoner's capacity for survival and adaptation. "Be inconspicuous": this was the golden rule.[57] The prisoner who called attention to himself, even in such trivial matters as the wearing of glasses, risked doom. Any show of bravado, any heroics, any kind of resistance condemned a man instantly. There were no rewards for martyrdom: not only did the martyr himself suffer, but mass punishments were wreaked upon his fellow inmates. To "be inconspicuous" required a special kind of alertness—almost an animal instinct[58]— against the apathy which tended to follow the initial shocks.[59] To

[54] Lingens-Reiner, *Prisoners of Fear*, p. 23.

[55] *Human Behavior*, p. 136. The "superego," Freud's term for the "conscience," is discussed below, pp. 116–18.

[56] Bettelheim, "Individual and Mass Behavior," p. 438.

[57] Cohen, *Human Behavior*, p. 169.

[58] This should in no sense be considered as a calculating, "rational" alertness, but rather as something quite primitive. "Of myself," writes Dr. Cohen, "I know that I was not continuously occupied by the reflection: I am going to win through. The actions which contributed to my survival were performed instinctively rather than consciously. . . . Like animals warned by their instinct that danger is imminent, we would act instinctively at critical moments. These instinctive acts must, I think, be considered as manifestations of the life instinct. If the life instinct is not strong enough, the instinct will desert the individual, and instead of rising to the emergency, the individual will succumb, whereas a stronger life instinct would have seen him through." *Human Behavior*, p. 163.

[59] Those who had in fact succumbed to this apathy—who had given up the struggle, and for whom death would be a mere matter of time—were known as "Moslems." See above, n. 17.

give up the struggle for survival was to commit "passive suicide"; a careless mistake meant death. There were those, however, who did come through this phase and who managed an adjustment to the life of the camp. It was the striking contrasts between this group of two- and three-year veterans and the perpetual stream of newcomers which made it possible for men like Bettelheim and Cohen to speak of the "old prisoner" as a specific type.

The most immediate aspect of the old inmates' behavior which struck these observers was its *childlike* quality. "The prisoners developed types of behavior which are characteristic of infancy or early youth. Some of these behaviors developed slowly, others were immediately imposed on the prisoners and developed only in intensity as time went on."[60] Such infantile behavior took innumerable forms. The inmates' sexual impotence brought about a disappearance of sexuality in their talk;[61] instead, excretory functions occupied them endlessly. They lost many of the customary inhibitions as to soiling their beds and their persons.[62] Their humor was shot with silliness and they giggled like children when one of them would expel wind. Their relationships were highly unstable. "Prisoners would, like early adolescents, fight one another tooth and nail . . . only to become close friends within a few minutes."[63] Dishonesty became chronic. "Now they suddenly appeared to be pathological liars, to be unable to restrain themselves, to be unable to make objective evaluation, etc."[64] "In hundreds of ways," writes Colaço Belmonte, "the soldier, and to an even greater extent the prisoner of war, is given to understand that he is a child. . . . Then dishonesty, mendacity, egotistic actions in order to obtain more food or to get out of scrapes reach full de-

[60] Bettelheim, "Individual and Mass Behavior," p. 141.

[61] Says Dr. Cohen, "I am not asserting that sex was never discussed; it was, though not often. Frankl also states 'that in contrast to mass existence in other military communities . . . here (in the concentration camp) there is *no smut talk.*'" *Human Behavior,* p. 141.

[62] "With reference to this phenomenon Miss Bluhm has pointed out that it is not at all unusual that people in extraordinary circumstances, for example soldiers in wartime, 'are able to give up their habitual standards of cleanliness without deeper disturbance; yet only up to certain limits.' The rules of anal cleanliness, she adds, are not disregarded. 'Their neglect means return to instinctual behavior of childhood.'" *Ibid.,* p. 175.

[63] Bettelheim, "Individual and Mass Behavior," p. 445.

[64] *Ibid.,* p. 421.

velopment, and theft becomes a veritable affliction of camp life."[65] This was all true, according to Elie Cohen, in the concentration camp as well.[66] Benedikt Kautsky observed such things in his own behavior: "I myself can declare that often I saw myself as I used to be in my school days, when by sly dodges and clever pretexts we avoided being found out, or could 'organize' something."[67] Bruno Bettelheim remarks on the extravagance of the stories told by the prisoners to one another. "They were boastful, telling tales about what they had accomplished in their former lives, or how they succeeded in cheating foremen or guards, and how they sabotaged the work. Like children they felt not at all set back or ashamed when it became known that they had lied about their prowess."[68]

This development of childlike behavior in the old inmates was the counterpart of something even more striking that was happening to them: *"Only very few of the prisoners escaped a more or less intensive identification with the SS."*[69] As Mr. Bettelheim puts it: "A prisoner had reached the final stage of adjustment to the camp situation when he had changed his personality so as to accept as his own the values of the Gestapo."[70] The Bettelheim study furnishes a catalogue of examples. The old prisoners came to share the attitude of the SS toward the "unfit" prisoners; newcomers who behaved badly in the labor groups or who could not withstand the strain became a liability for the others, who were often instrumental in getting rid of them. Many old prisoners actually imitated the SS; they would sew and mend their uniforms in such a way as to make them look more like those of the SS— even though they risked punishment for it. "When asked why they did it, they admitted that they loved to look like . . . the guards." Some took great enjoyment in the fact that during roll call "they really had stood well at attention." There were cases of

[65] Quoted in Cohen, *Human Behavior*, p. 176.

[66] *Ibid.*   [67] *Ibid.*, p. 174.

[68] Bettelheim, "Individual and Mass Behavior," pp. 445-46. This same phenomenon is noted by Curt Bondy: "They tell great stories about what they have been before and what they have performed." "Problems of Internment Camps," *Journal of Abnormal and Social Psychology*, XXXVIII (October, 1943), 453-75.

[69] Cohen, *Human Behavior*, p. 177. Italics in original.

[70] Bettelheim, "Individual and Mass Behavior," p. 447.

nonsensical rules, made by the guards, which the older prisoners would continue to observe and try to force on the others long after the SS had forgotten them.[71] Even the most abstract ideals of the SS, such as their intense German nationalism and anti-Semitism, were often absorbed by the old inmates—a phenomenon observed among the politically well-educated and even among the Jews themselves.[72] The final quintessence of all this was seen in the "Kapo"—the prisoner who had been placed in a supervisory position over his fellow inmates. These creatures, many of them professional criminals, not only behaved with slavish servility to the SS, but the way in which they often outdid the SS in sheer brutality became one of the most durable features of the concentration-camp legend.

To all these men, reduced to complete and childish dependence upon their masters, the SS had actually become a father-symbol. "The SS man was all-powerful in the camp, he was the lord and master of the prisoner's life. As a cruel father he could, without fear of punishment, even kill the prisoner and as a gentle father he could scatter largesse and afford the prisoner his protection."[73] The result, admits Dr. Cohen, was that "for all of us the SS was a father image. . . ."[74] The closed system, in short, had become a kind of grotesque patriarchy.

[71] *Ibid.,* pp. 448–50. "Once, for instance, a guard on inspecting the prisoners' apparel found that the shoes of some of them were dirty on the inside. He ordered all prisoners to wash their shoes inside and out with water and soap. The heavy shoes treated this way became hard as stone. The order was never repeated, and many prisoners did not execute it when given. Nevertheless there were some old prisoners who not only continued to wash the inside of their shoes every day but cursed all others who did not do so as negligent and dirty. These prisoners firmly believed that the rules set down by the Gestapo were desirable standards of human behavior, at least in the camp situation." *Ibid.,* p. 450.

[72] *Ibid.* See also Cohen, *Human Behavior,* pp. 189–93, for a discussion of anti-Semitism among the Jews.

[73] Cohen, *Human Behavior,* pp. 176–77.

[74] *Ibid.,* p. 179. On this and other points I must also acknowledge my indebtedness to Mr. Ies Spetter, a former Dutch journalist now living in this country, who was imprisoned for a time at Auschwitz during World War II. Mr. Spetter permitted me to see an unpublished paper, "Some Thoughts on Victims and Criminals in the German Concentration Camps," which he wrote in 1954 at the New School for Social Research; and this, together with a number of conversations I had with him, added much to my understanding of concentration-camp psychology.

The literature provides us with three remarkable tests of the profundity of the experience which these prisoners had undergone and the thoroughness of the changes which had been brought about in them. One is the fact that few cases of real resistance were ever recorded, even among prisoners going to their death.

With a few altogether insignificant exceptions, the prisoners, no matter in what form they were led to execution, whether singly, in groups, or in masses, never fought back! . . . there were thousands who had by no means relapsed into fatal apathy. Nevertheless, in mass liquidations they went to their death with open eyes, without assaulting the enemy in a final paroxysm, without a sign of fight. Is this not in conflict with human nature, as we know it?[75]

Even upon liberation, when revenge against their tormentors at last became possible, mass uprisings very rarely occurred. "Even when the whole system was overthrown by the Allies," says David Rousset writing of Buchenwald, "nothing happened. . . . The American officer appointed to command of the camp was never called upon to cope with any inclination toward a popular movement. No such disposition existed."[76]

A second test of the system's effectiveness was the relative scarcity of suicides in the camps.[77] Though there were suicides, they tended to occur during the first days of internment, and only one mass suicide is known; it took place among a group of Jews at Mauthausen who leaped into a rock pit three days after their arrival.[78] For the majority of prisoners the simplicity of the urge to

[75] Kogon, *Theory and Practice,* p. 284.

[76] *The Other Kingdom,* p. 137.

[77] "In the preference camp Bergen Belsen, only four cases of attempted suicide were witnessed by Tas, three of which were saved with great effort, while in the Stammlager Auschwitz only one successful attempt came to my knowledge. This does not mean that there were not more, but their number was certainly small. Kaas, on the other hand, witnessed several attempted suicides in Buchenwald. He has remembered three that were successful (two by hanging, one by rushing into the electric fence). He also knows of prisoners who were known to be depressive cases, and who were shot down when during the night they had deliberately gone out of bounds. As compared with the large number of prisoners, the number of suicides, however, was very small." Cohen, *Human Behavior,* p. 158.

[78] Kogon, *Theory and Practice,* pp. 166–67. This occurred during fearful tortures at the quarry, where the Jews knew they were about to be killed anyway.

survive made suicide, a complex matter of personal initiative and decision, out of the question. Yet they could, when commanded by their masters, go to their death without resistance.

The third test lies in the very absence, among the prisoners, of hatred toward the SS. This is probably the hardest of all to understand. Yet the burning spirit of rebellion which many of their liberators expected to find would have had to be supported by fierce and smoldering emotions; such emotions were not there. "It is remarkable," one observer notes, "how little hatred of their wardens is revealed in their stories."[79]

5

THREE THEORIES OF PERSONALITY

The immense revelation for psychology in the concentration-camp literature has been the discovery of how elements of dramatic personality change could be brought about in masses of individuals. And yet it is not proper that the crude fact of "change" alone should dominate the conceptual image with which one emerges from this problem. "Change" per se, change that does not go beyond itself, is productive of nothing; it leaves only destruction, shock, and howling bedlam behind it unless some future basis of stability and order lies waiting to guarantee it and give it reality. So it is with the human psyche, which is apparently capable of making terms with a state other than liberty as we know it. The very dramatic features of the process just described may upset the nicety of this point. There is the related danger, moreover, of unduly stressing the individual psychology of the problem at the expense of its social psychology.

These hazards might be minimized by maintaining a conceptual distinction between two phases of the group experience. The process of detachment from prior standards of behavior and value is one of them, and is doubtless the more striking, but there must be another one. That such detachment can, by extension, involve the whole scope of an individual's culture is an implication for which the vocabulary of individual psychology was caught some-

[79] A. Hottinger, *Hungerkrankheit, Hungerödem, Hungertuberkulose,* p. 32, quoted in Cohen, *Human Behavior,* p. 197. "After the liberation many writers were struck by the callousness of the onetime prisoners, and particularly by their apathy when relating their experiences, even the most horrible." *Ibid.,* p. 144.

what unawares. Fluctuations in the state of the individual psyche could formerly be dealt with, or so it seemed, while taking for granted the more or less static nature of social organization, and with a minimum of reference to its features. That such organization might itself become an important variable was therefore a possibility not highly developed in theory, focused as theory was upon individual case histories to the invariable minimization of social and cultural setting. The other phase of the experience should be considered as the "stability" side of the problem, that phase which stabilized what the "shock" phase only opened the way for. This was essentially a process of adjustment to a standard of social normality, though in this case a drastic *re*adjustment and compressed within a very short time—a process which under typical conditions of individual and group existence is supposed to begin at birth and last a lifetime and be transmitted in many and diffuse ways from generation to generation. The adjustment is assumed to be slow and organic, and it normally is. Its numerous aspects extend much beyond psychology; those aspects have in the past been treated at great leisure within the rich provinces not only of psychology but of history, sociology, and literature as well. What rearrangement and compression of those provinces may be needed to accommodate a mass experience that not only involved profound individual shock but also required rapid assimilation to a drastically different form of social organization, can hardly be known. But perhaps the most conservative beginning may be made with existing psychological theory.

The theoretical system whose terminology was orthodox for most of the Europeans who have written about the camps was that of Freud. It was necessary for them to do a certain amount of improvising, since the scheme's existing framework provided only the narrowest leeway for dealing with such radical concepts as out-and-out change in personality. This was due to two kinds of limitations which the Freudian vocabulary places upon the notion of the "self." One is that the superego—that part of the self involved in social relationships, social values, expectations of others, and so on—is conceived as only a small and highly refined part of the "total" self. The other is the assumption that the content and character of the superego is laid down in childhood and undergoes relatively little basic alteration thereafter.[80] Yet a Freudian diagnosis of the concentration-camp inmate—whose social self, or superego, did appear to change and who seemed basically changed thereby—is, given these limitations, still possible. Elie Cohen, whose analysis is the most thorough of these, specifically states that "the superego acquired new values in a concentration camp."[81] The old values, according to Dr. Cohen, were first silenced by the shocks which produced "acute depersonalization" (the subject-object split: "It is not the real 'me' who is undergoing this"), and by the powerful drives of hunger and survival. Old values, thus set aside, could be replaced by new ones. It was a process made possible by "infantile regression"—regression to a previous condition of childlike dependency in which parental prohibitions once more became all-powerful and in which parental judgments might once more be internalized. In this way a new "father-image," personified in the SS guard, came into being. That the prisoner's identification with the SS could be so positive is explained by still another mechanism: the principle of "identi-

[80] "For just as the ego is a modified portion of the id as a result of contact with the outer world, the super-ego represents a modified portion of the ego, formed through experiences absorbed from the parents, especially from the father. The super-ego is the highest evolution attainable by man, and consists of a precipitate of all prohibitions and inhibitions, all the rules of conduct which are impressed on the child by his parents and by parental substitutes. The feeling of *conscience* depends altogether on the development of the super-ego." A. A. Brill, Introduction to *The Basic Writings of Sigmund Freud* (New York: Modern Library, 1938), pp. 12–13. "Its relation to the ego is not exhausted by the precept: 'You *ought to be* such and such (like your father); it also comprises the prohibition: 'You *must not be* such and such (like your father); that is, you may not do all that he does; many things are his prerogative.' " Sigmund Freud, *The Ego and the Id* (London: Hogarth Press, 1947), pp. 44–45. ". . . and here we have that higher nature, in this ego-ideal or super-ego, the representative of our relation to our parents. When we were little children we knew these higher natures, we admired them and feared them; and later we took them into ourselves." *Ibid.*, p. 47. "As a child grows up, the office of father is carried on by masters and by others in authority; the power of their injunctions and prohibitions remains vested in the ego-ideal and continues, in the form of conscience, to exercise the censorship of morals. The tension between the demands of conscience and the actual attainments of the ego is experienced as a sense of guilt. Social feelings rest on the foundation of identification with others, on the basis of an ego-ideal in common with them." *Ibid.*, p. 49.

[81] *Human Behavior,* p. 136.

fication with the aggressor." "A child," as Anna Freud writes, "interjects some characteristic of an anxiety-object and so assimilates an anxiety-experience which he has just undergone. . . . By impersonating the aggressor, assuming his attributes or imitating his aggression, the child transforms himself from the person threatened into the person who makes the threat."[82] In short, the child's only "defense" in the presence of a cruel, all-powerful father is the psychic defense of identification.

Now one could, still retaining the Freudian language, represent all this in somewhat less cumbersome terms by a slight modification of the metaphor. It could simply be said that under great stress the superego, like a bucket, is violently emptied of content and acquires, in a radically changed setting, new content. It would thus not be necessary to postulate a literal "regression" to childhood in order for this to occur. Something of the sort is suggested by Leo Alexander. "The psychiatrist stands in amazement," he writes, "before the thoroughness and completeness with which this perversion of essential superego values was accomplished in adults . . . [and] it may be that the decisive importance of childhood and youth in the formation of [these] values may have been overrated by psychiatrists in a society in which allegiance to these values in normal adult life was taken too much for granted because of the stability, religiousness, legality, and security of the 19th Century and early 20th Century society."[83]

---

[82] Anna Freud, *The Ego and the Mechanisms of Defence* (London: Hogarth Press, 1948), p. 121. "In some illustrative case reports, Clara Thompson stresses the vicious circle put in motion by this defense-mechanism. The stronger the need for identification, the more a person loses himself in his omnipotent enemy—the more helpless he becomes. The more helpless he feels, the stronger the identification, and—we may add—the more likely it is that he tries even to surpass the aggressiveness of his aggressor. This may explain the almost unbelievable phenomenon that prisoner-superiors sometimes acted more brutally than did members of the SS. . . . Identification with the aggressor represented the final stage of passive adaptation. It was a means of defense of a rather paradoxical nature: survival through surrender; protection again the fear of the enemy—by becoming part of him; overcoming helplessness—by regressing to childish dependence." Bluhm, "How Did They Survive?" pp. 24–25.

[83] Leo Alexander, "War Crimes: Their Social-Psychological Aspects," *American Journal of Psychiatry*, CV (September, 1948), 173. "The superego structure is . . . in peril whenever these established guiding forces weaken or are in the process of being undermined, shifted, or perverted,

A second theoretical scheme is better prepared for crisis and more closely geared to social environment than the Freudian adaptation indicated above, and it may consequently be more suitable for accommodating not only the concentration-camp experience but also the more general problem of plantation slave personality. This is the "interpersonal theory" developed by the late Harry Stack Sullivan. One may view this body of work as the response to a peculiarly American set of needs. The system of Freud, so aptly designed for a European society the stability of whose institutional and status relationships could always to a large extent be taken for granted, turns out to be less clearly adapted to the culture of the United States. The American psychiatrist has had to deal with individuals in a culture where the diffuse, shifting, and often uncertain quality of such relationships has always been more pronounced than in Europe. He has come to appreciate the extent to which these relationships actually support the individual's psychic balance—the full extent, that is, to which the self is "social" in its nature. Thus a psychology whose terms are flexible enough to permit altering social relationships to make actual differences in character structure would be a psychology especially promising for dealing with the present problem.[84]

Sullivan's great contribution was to offer a concept whereby the really critical determinants of personality might be isolated for purposes of observation. Out of the hopelessly immense totality of "influences" which in one way or another go to make up the personality, or "self," Sullivan designated one—the estimations and expectations of others—as the one promising to unlock the most

---

and becomes itself open to undermining, shifting, or perversion even in adult life—a fact which is probably more important than we have been aware of heretofore." *Ibid.*, p. 175.

[84] My use of Sullivan here does not imply a willingness to regard his work as a "refutation" to that of Freud, or even as an adequate substitute for it in all other situations. It lacks the imaginative scope which in Freud makes possible so great a range of cultural connections; in it we miss Freud's effort to deal as scientifically as possible with an infinite array of psychological and cultural phenomena; the fragmentary nature of Sullivan's work, its limited scope, its cloudy presentation, all present us with obstacles not to be surmounted overnight. This might well change as his ideas are elaborated and refined. But meanwhile it would be too much to ask that all connections be broken with the staggering amount of work already done on Freudian models.

secrets. He then made a second elimination: the *majority* of "others" in one's existence may for theoretical purposes be neglected; what counts is who the *significant* others are. Here, "significant others"[85] may be understood very crudely to mean those individuals who hold, or seem to hold, the keys to security in one's own personal situation, whatever its nature. Now as to the psychic processes whereby these "significant others" become an actual part of the personality, it may be said that the very sense of "self" first emerges in connection with anxiety about the attitudes of the most important persons in one's life (initially, the mother, father, and their surrogates—persons of more or less absolute authority), and automatic attempts are set in motion to adjust to these attitudes. In this way their approval, their disapproval, their estimates and appraisals, and indeed a whole range of their expectations become as it were internalized, and are reflected in one's very character. Of course as one "grows up," one acquires more and more significant others whose attitudes are diffuse and may indeed compete, and thus "significance," in Sullivan's sense, becomes subtler and less easy to define. The personality exfoliates; it takes on traits of distinction and, as we say, "individuality." The impact of particular significant others is less dramatic than in early life. But the pattern is a continuing one; new significant others do still appear, and theoretically it is conceivable that even in mature life the personality might be visibly affected by the arrival of such a one—supposing that this new significant other were vested with sufficient authority and power. In any event there are possibilities for fluidity and actual change inherent in this concept which earlier schemes have lacked.

The purest form of the process is to be observed in the development of children, not so much because of their "immaturity" as such (though their plasticity is great and the imprint of early

[85] Sullivan refined this concept from the earlier notion of the "generalized other" formulated by George Herbert Mead. "The organized community or social group [Mead wrote] which gives to the individual his unity of self may be called 'the generalized other.' The attitude of the generalized other is the attitude of the whole community. Thus, for example, in the case of such a social group as a ball team, the team is the generalized other in so far as it enters—as an organized process or social activity—into the experience of any one of the individual members of it." George H. Mead, *Mind, Self and Society: From the Standpoint of a Social Behaviorist* (Chicago: University of Chicago Press, 1934), p. 154.

experience goes deep), but rather because for them there are fewer significant others. For this reason—because the pattern is simpler and more easily controlled—much of Sullivan's attention was devoted to what happens in childhood. In any case let us say that unlike the adult, the child, being drastically limited in the selection of significant others, must operate in a "closed system."

Such are the elements which make for order and balance in the normal self: "significant others" plus "anxiety" in a special sense—conceived with not simply disruptive but also guiding, warning functions.[86] The structure of "interpersonal" theory thus has considerable room in it for conceptions of guided change— change for either beneficent or malevolent ends. One technique for managing such change would of course be the orthodox one of psychoanalysis; another, the actual changing of significant others.[87] Patrick Mullahy, a leading exponent of Sullivan, believes that in group therapy much is possible along these lines.[88] A

[86] The technical term, in Sullivan's terminology, for the mechanism represented by these two elements functioning in combination, is the individual's "self-dynamism." David Riesman has refined this concept; he has, with his "inner-directed, other-directed" polarity, considered the possibility of different kinds of "self-dynamisms." The self-dynamism which functions with reference to specific aims and which is formed and set early in life is characterized as the "gyroscope." On the other hand the self-dynamism which must function in a cultural situation of constantly shifting significant others and which must constantly adjust to them is pictured as the "radar." See *The Lonely Crowd, passim.* The principles summarized in this and the preceding paragraphs are to be found most clearly set forth in Harry Stack Sullivan, *Conceptions of Modern Psychiatry* (Washington: William Alanson White Psychiatric Foundation, 1945). Sullivan's relationship to the general development of theory is assessed in Patrick Mullahy, *Oedipus Myth and Complex: A Review of Psychoanalytic Theory* (New York: Hermitage House, 1948).

[87] Actually, one of the chief functions of psychoanalysis as it has been practiced from the beginning is simply given more explicit recognition here. The psychiatrist who helps the patient exhibit to himself attitudes and feelings systematically repressed—or "selectively ignored"—becomes in the process a new and trusted significant other.

[88] "Indeed . . . when the whole Sullivanian conception of the effect of significant others upon the origin and stability of self-conceptions is pushed farther, really revolutionary vistas of guided personality emerge. If the maintenance of certain characteristic patterns of interpersonal behavior depends upon their support by significant others, then to alter the composition of any person's community of significant others is the most direct and

demonic test of the whole hypothesis is available in the concentration camp.

Consider the camp prisoner—not the one who fell by the wayside but the one who was eventually to survive; consider the ways in which he was forced to adjust to the one significant other which he now had—the SS guard, who held absolute dominion over every aspect of his life. The very shock of his introduction was perfectly designed to dramatize this fact; he was brutally maltreated ("as by a cruel father"); the shadow of resistance would bring instant death. Daily life in the camp, with its fear and tensions, taught over and over the lesson of absolute power. It prepared the personality for a drastic shift in standards. It crushed whatever anxieties might have been drawn from prior standards; such standards had become meaningless. It focused the prisoner's attention constantly on the moods, attitudes, and standards of the only man who mattered. A truly childlike situation was thus created: utter and abject dependency on one, or on a rigidly limited few, significant others. All the conditions which in normal life would give the individual leeway—which allowed him to defend himself against a new and hostile significant other, no matter how powerful— were absent in the camp. No competition of significant others was possible; the prisoner's comrades for practical purposes were helpless to assist him.[89] He had no degree of independence, no lines to the outside, in any matter. Everything, every vital concern, focused on the SS: food, warmth, security, freedom from pain, all depended on the omnipotent significant other, all had to be worked out within the closed system. Nowhere was there a shred of privacy; everything one did was subject to SS supervision. The pressure was never absent. It is thus no wonder that the prisoners should become "as children." It is no wonder that their obedience became unquestioning, that they did not revolt, that they could not "hate" their masters. Their masters' attitudes

---

drastic way of altering his 'personality.' This can be done. Indeed, it is being done, with impressive results, by the many types of therapeutic groups, or quasi-families of significant new others, which have come up in the past few years." Patrick Mullahy (ed.), *The Contributions of Harry Stack Sullivan* (New York: Hermitage House, 1952), p. 193.

[89] It should be noted that there were certain important exceptions. See below, pp. 134–35.

had become *internalized* as a part of their very selves; those attitudes and standards now dominated all others that they had. They had, indeed, been "changed."

There still exists a third conceptual framework within which these phenomena may be considered. It is to be found in the growing field of "role psychology." This psychology is not at all incompatible with interpersonal theory; the two might easily be fitted into the same system.[90] But it might be strategically desirable, for several reasons, to segregate them for purposes of discussion. One such reason is the extraordinary degree to which role psychology shifts the focus of attention upon the individual's cultural and institutional environment rather than upon his "self." At the same time it gives us a manageable concept—that of "role"—for mediating between the two. As a mechanism, the role enables us to isolate the unique contribution of culture and institutions toward maintaining the psychic balance of the individual. In it, we see formalized for the individual a range of choices in models of behavior and expression, each with its particular style, quality, and attributes. The relationship between the "role" and the "self," though not yet clear, is intimate; it is at least possible at certain levels of inquiry to look upon the individual as the variable and upon the roles extended him as the stable factor.[91] We thus have a potentially durable link between individual psychology and the study of culture. It might even be said, inasmuch as its key term is directly borrowed from the theater, that role psychology offers in workable form the long-awaited connection—apparently missed by Ernest Jones in his *Hamlet* study—between the insights of the classical dramatists

[90] An outstanding instance of authorities who are exponents of both is of that of H. H. Gerth and C. Wright Mills, whose study *Character and Social Structure* ranges very widely in both interpersonal theory and role psychology and uses them interchangeably.

[91] Conceptually, the purest illustration of this notion might be seen in such an analogy as the following. Sarah Bernhardt, playing in *Phèdre,* enacted a role which had not altered since it was set down by Racine two centuries before her time, and she was neither the first woman who spoke those lines, nor was she the last. Nor, indeed, was *Phèdre* her only triumph. Such was Bernhardt's genius, such was her infinite plasticity, that she moved from immutable role to immutable role in the classic drama, making of each, as critic and theatergoer alike agreed, a masterpiece. Now Bernhardt herself is gone, yet the lines remain, waiting to be transfigured by some new genius.

and those of the contemporary social theorist.[92] But be that as it may, for our present problem, the concentration camp, it suggests the most flexible account of how the ex-prisoners may have succeeded in resuming their places in normal life.

Let us note certain of the leading terms.[93] A "social role" is definable in its simplest sense as the behavior expected of persons specifically located in specific social groups.[94] A distinction is kept between "expectations" and "behavior"; the expectations of a role (embodied in the "script") theoretically exist in advance and are defined by the organization, the institution, or by society at large. Behavior (the "performance") refers to the manner in which the role is played. Another distinction involves roles which are "pervasive" and those which are "limited." A pervasive role

[92] In the resources of dramatic literature a variety of insights may await the "social scientist" equipped with both the imagination and the conceptual tools for exploiting them, and the emergence of role-psychology may represent the most promising step yet taken in this direction. A previous area of contact has been in the realm of Freudian psychology, but this has never been a very natural or comfortable meeting ground for either the analyst or the literary critic. For example, in Shakespeare's *Hamlet* there is the problem, both psychological and dramatic, of Hamlet's inability to kill his uncle. Dr. Ernest Jones (in *Hamlet and Oedipus*) reduces all the play's tensions to a single Freudian complex. It should be at once more "scientific" and more "literary," however, to consider the problem in terms of role-conflict (Hamlet as prince, son, nephew, lover, etc., has multiple roles which keep getting in the way of one another). Francis Fergusson, though he uses other terminology, in effect does this in his *Idea of a Theater*.

[93] In this paragraph I duplicate and paraphrase material from Eugene and Ruth Hartley, *Fundamentals of Social Psychology* (New York: Knopf, 1952), chap. xvi. See also David C. McClelland, *Personality* (New York: Sloane, 1951), pp. 289–332. Both these books are, strictly speaking, "texts," but this point could be misleading, inasmuch as the whole subject is one not normally studied at an "elementary" level anywhere. At the same time a highly successful effort has been made in each of these works to formulate the role concept with clarity and simplicity, and this makes their formulations peculiarly relevant to the empirical facts of the present problem. It may be that the very simplicity of the roles in both the plantation and concentration-camp settings accounts for this coincidence. Another reason why I am inclined to put a special premium on simplicity here is my conviction that the role concept has a range of "literary" overtones, potentially exploitable in realms other than psychology. For a recent general statement, see Theodore R. Sarbin, "Role Theory," *Handbook of Social Psychology*, I, 223–58.

[94] Hartley, *Fundamentals of Social Psychology*, p. 485.

is extensive in scope ("female citizen") and not only influences but also sets bounds upon the other sorts of roles available to the individual ("mother," "nurse," but not "husband," "soldier"); a limited role ("purchaser," "patient") is transitory and intermittent. A further concept is that of "role clarity." Some roles are more specifically defined than others; their impact upon performance (and, indeed, upon the personality of the performer) depends on the clarity of their definition. Finally, it is asserted that those roles which carry with them the clearest and most automatic rewards and punishments are those which will be (as it were) most "artistically" played.

What sorts of things might this explain? It might illuminate the process whereby the child develops his personality in terms not only of the roles which his parents offer him but of those which he "picks up" elsewhere and tries on. It could show how society, in its coercive character, lays down patterns of behavior with which it expects the individual to comply. It suggests the way in which society, now turning its benevolent face to the individual, tenders him alternatives and defines for him the style appropriate to their fulfilment. It provides us with a further term for the definition of personality itself: there appears an extent to which we can say that personality is actually made up of the roles which the individual plays.[95] And here, once more assuming "change" to be possible, we have in certain ways the least cumbersome terms for plotting its course.

The application of the model to the concentration camp should be simple and obvious. What was expected of the man entering the role of camp prisoner was laid down for him upon arrival:

"Here you are not in a penitentiary or prison but in a place of instruction. Order and discipline are here the highest law. If you ever want to see freedom again, you must submit to a severe training.

[95] "Personality development is not exclusively a matter of socialization. Rather, it represents the organism's more or less integrated way of adapting to *all* the influences that come its way—both inner and outer influences, both social and nonsocial ones. Social influences, however, are essential to human personality, and socialization accounts for a very great deal of personality development.

"From this point of view it would not be surprising to find that many personality disturbances represent some sort of breakdown or reversal of the socialization process." Theodore M. Newcomb, *Social Psychology* (New York: Dryden Press, 1950), p. 475.

. . . But woe to those who do not obey our iron discipline. Our methods are thorough! Here there is no compromise and no mercy. The slightest resistance will be ruthlessly suppressed. Here we sweep with an iron broom!"[96]

Expectation and performance must coincide exactly; the lines were to be read literally; the missing of a single cue meant extinction. The role was pervasive; it vetoed any other role and smashed all prior ones. "Role clarity"—the clarity here was blinding; its definition was burned into the prisoner by every detail of his existence:

In normal life the adult enjoys a certain measure of independence; within the limits set by society he has a considerable measure of liberty. Nobody orders him when and what to eat, where to take up his residence or what to wear, neither to take his rest on Sunday nor when to have his bath, nor when to go to bed. He is not beaten during his work, he need not ask permission to go to the W.C., he is not continually kept on the run, he does not feel that the work he is doing is silly or childish, he is not confined behind barbed wire, he is not counted twice a day or more, he is not left unprotected against the actions of his fellow citizens, he looks after his family and the education of his children.

How altogether different was the life of the concentration-camp prisoner! What to do during each part of the day was arranged for him, and decisions were made about him from which there was no appeal. He was impotent and suffered from bedwetting, and because of his chronic diarrhea he soiled his underwear. . . . The dependence of the prisoner on the SS . . . may be compared to the dependence of children on their parents. . . .[97]

The impact of this role, coinciding as it does in a hundred ways with that of the child, has already been observed. Its rewards were brutally simple—life rather than death; its punishments were automatic. By the survivors it was—it had to be—a role *well played*.

Nor was it simple, upon liberation, to shed the role. Many of the inmates, to be sure, did have prior roles which they could resume, former significant others to whom they might reorient themselves, a repressed superego which might once more be

[96] Quoted in Leon Szalet, *Experiment "E"* (New York: Didier, 1945), p. 138.

[97] Cohen, *Human Behavior*, pp. 173–74.

resurrected. To this extent they were not "lost souls." But to the extent that their entire personalities, their total selves, had been involved in this experience, to the extent that old arrangements had been disrupted, that society itself had been overturned while they had been away, a "return" was fraught with innumerable obstacles.[98]

[98] Theodore Newcomb is the only non-Freudian coming to my attention who has considered the concentration camp in the terms of social psychology. He draws analogies between the ex-inmates' problems of readjustment and those of returning prisoners of war. "With the return of large numbers of British prisoners of war . . . from German and Japanese camps, toward the end of World War II, it soon became apparent that thousands of them were having serious difficulties of readjustment. It was first assumed that they were victims of war neuroses. But this assumption had to be abandoned when it was discovered that their symptoms were in most cases not those of the commonly recognized neuroses. Most of the men having difficulty, moreover, did not have the kinds of personalities which would have predisposed them to neurotic disorders. Psychiatrists then began to wonder whether their disturbances represented only a temporary phase of the men's return to civilian life. But the difficulties were neither temporary nor 'self-correcting.' 'Even when men had been back for 18 months or even longer, serious and persistent difficulties were reported in something like one-third of the men.' . . . All in all . . . the authors were led to the conclusion that the returning war prisoner's troubles did not lie entirely within himself. They represented the strains and stresses of becoming *re*socialized in a culture which was not only different from what it had been but was radically different from that to which the men had become accustomed during their years of capture." "When a deliberate attempt is made to change the personality, as in psychotherapy, success brings with it changes in role patterns. When the role prescriptions are changed—as for . . . concentration-camp inmates—personality changes also occur. When forcible changes in role prescriptions are removed, the degree to which the previous personality is 'resumed' depends upon the degree to which the individual finds it possible to resume his earlier role patterns." Newcomb, *Social Psychology,* pp. 476–77, 482.

Social workers faced with the task of rehabilitating former concentration-camp prisoners rapidly discovered that sympathy and understanding were not enough. The normal superego values of many of the prisoners had been so thoroughly smashed that adult standards of behavior for them were quite out of the question. Their behavior, indeed, was often most childlike. They made extreme demands, based not on actual physical needs but rather on the fear that they might be left out, or that others might receive more than they. Those who regained their equilibrium most quickly were the ones who were able to begin new lives in social environments that provided clear limits, precise standards, steady goals, and specific roles to play. Adjustment was not easy, however, even for the most fortunate. On

It is hoped that the very hideousness of a special example of slavery has not disqualified it as a test for certain features of a far milder and more benevolent form of slavery. But it should still be possible to say, with regard to the individuals who lived as slaves within the respective systems, that just as on one level there is every difference between a wretched childhood and a carefree one, there are, for other purposes, limited features which the one may be said to have shared with the other.

Both were closed systems from which all standards based on prior connections had been effectively detached. A working adjustment to either system required a childlike conformity, a limited choice of "significant others." Cruelty per se cannot be considered the primary key to this; of far greater importance was the simple "closedness" of the system, in which all lines of authority descended from the master and in which alternative social bases that might have supported alternative standards were systematically suppressed.[99] The individual, consequently, for his very psychic security, had to picture his master in some way as

---

the collective farms of Israel, for example, it was understood that former concentration-camp inmates would be "unable to control their greed for food" for a number of months. During that time, concern for their neighbors' sensibilities was more than one could expect. Paul Friedman, "The Road Back for the DP's" *Commentary*, VI (December, 1948), 502–10; Eva Rosenfeld, "Institutional Change in Israeli Collectives" (Ph.D. diss., Columbia University, 1952), p. 278.

[99] The experience of American prisoners taken by the Chinese during the Korean War seems to indicate that profound changes in behavior and values, if not in basic personality itself, can be effected without the use of physical torture or extreme deprivation. The Chinese were able to get large numbers of Americans to act as informers and to co-operate in numerous ways in the effort to indoctrinate all the prisoners with Communist propaganda. The technique contained two key elements. One was that all formal and informal authority structures within the group were systematically destroyed; this was done by isolating officers, non-commissioned officers, and any enlisted men who gave indications of leadership capacities. The other element involved the continual emphasizing of the captors' power and influence by judicious manipulation of petty rewards and punishments and by subtle hints of the greater rewards and more severe punishments (repatriation or non-repatriation) that rested with the pleasure of those in authority. See Edgar H. Schein, "Some Observations on Chinese Methods of Handling Prisoners of War," *Public Opinion Quarterly*, XX (Spring, 1956), 321–27.

the "good father,"[100] even when, as in the concentration camp, it made no sense at all.[101] But why should it not have made sense for many a simple plantation Negro whose master did exhibit,

[100] In a system as tightly closed as the plantation or the concentration camp, the slave's or prisoner's position of absolute dependency virtually compels him to see the authority-figure as somehow really "good." Indeed, all the evil in his life may flow from this man—but then so also must everything of any value. Here is the seat of the only "good" he knows, and to maintain his psychic balance he must persuade himself that the good is in some way dominant. A threat to this illusion is thus in a real sense a threat to his very existence. It is a common experience among social workers dealing with neglected and maltreated children to have a child desperately insist on his love for a cruel and brutal parent and beg that he be allowed to remain with that parent. The most dramatic feature of this situation is the cruelty which it involves, but the mechanism which inspires the devotion is not the cruelty of the parent but rather the abnormal dependency of the child. A classic example of this mechanism in operation may be seen in the case of Varvara Petrovna, mother of Ivan Turgenev. Mme Turgenev "ruled over her serfs with a rod of iron." She demanded utter obedience and total submission. The slightest infraction of her rules brought the most severe punishment: "A maid who did not offer her a cup of tea in the proper manner was sent off to some remote village and perhaps separated from her family forever; gardeners who failed to prevent the plucking of a tulip in one of the flower beds before the house were ordered to be flogged; a sevant whom she suspected of a mutinous disposition was sent off to Siberia." Her family and her most devoted servants were treated in much the same manner. "Indeed," wrote Varvara Zhitova, the adopted daughter of Mme Turgenev, "those who loved her and were most devoted to her suffered most of all." Yet in spite of her brutality she was adored by the very people she tyrannized. David Magarshack describes how once when thrashing her eldest son she nearly fainted with sadistic excitement, whereupon "little Nicholas, forgetting his punishment, bawled at the top of his voice: 'Water! Water for mummy!'" Mme Zhitova, who knew Mme Turgenev's cruelty intimately and was herself the constant victim of her tyranny, wrote: "In spite of this, I loved her passionately, and when I was, though rarely, separated from her, I felt lonely and unhappy." Even Mme Turgenev's maid Agatha, whose children were sent to another village, when still infants so that Agatha might devote all her time to her mistress, could say years later, "Yes, she caused me much grief. I suffered much from her, but all the same I loved her! She was a real lady!" V. Zhitova, *The Turgenev Family*, trans. A. S. Mills (London: Havill Press, 1954), p. 25; David Magarshack, *Turgenev: A Life* (New York: Grove, 1954), pp. 14, 16, 22.

[101] Bruno Bettelheim tells us of the fantastic efforts of the old prisoners to believe in the benevolence of the officers of the SS. "They insisted that these officers [hid] behind their rough surface a feeling of justice and pro-

in all the ways that could be expected, the features of the good father who was really "good"? If the concentration camp could produce in two or three years the results that it did, one wonders how much more pervasive must have been those attitudes, expectations, and values which had, certainly, their benevolent side and which were accepted and transmitted over generations.

For the Negro child, in particular, the plantation offered no really satisfactory father-image other than the master. The "real" father was virtually without authority over his child, since discipline, parental responsibility, and control of rewards and punishments all rested in other hands; the slave father could not even protect the mother of his children except by appealing directly to the master. Indeed, the mother's own role loomed far larger for the slave child than did that of the father. She controlled those few activities—household care, preparation of food, and rearing of children—that were left to the slave family. For that matter, the very etiquette of plantation life removed even the honorific attributes of fatherhood from the Negro male, who was addressed as "boy"—until, when the vigorous years of his prime were past, he was allowed to assume the title of "uncle."

From the master's viewpoint, slaves had been defined in law as property, and the master's power over his property must be absolute. But then this property was still human property. These slaves might never be quite as human as *he* was, but still there were certain standards that could be laid down for their behavior: obedience, fidelity, humility, docility, cheerfulness, and so on. Industry and diligence would of course be demanded, but a final element in the master's situation would undoubtedly qualify that expectation. Absolute power for him meant absolute dependency for the slave—the dependency not of the developing child but of the perpetual child. For the master, the role most aptly fitting

---

priety; he, or they, were supposed to be genuinely interested in the prisoners and even trying, in a small way, to help them. Since nothing of these supposed feelings and efforts ever became apparent, it was explained that he hid them so effectively because otherwise he would not be able to help the prisoners. The eagerness of these prisoners to find reasons for their claims was pitiful. A whole legend was woven around the fact that of two officers inspecting a barrack one had cleaned his shoes from mud before entering. He probably did it automatically, but it was interpreted as a rebuff of the other officer and a clear demonstration of how he felt about the concentration camp." Bettelheim, "Individual and Mass Behavior," p. 451.

such a relationship would naturally be that of the father. As a father he could be either harsh or kind, as he chose, but as a *wise* father he would have, we may suspect, a sense of the limits of his situation. He must be ready to cope with *all* the qualities of the child, exasperating as well as ingratiating. He might conceivably have to expect in this child—besides his loyalty, docility, humility, cheerfulness, and (under supervision) his diligence—such additional qualities as irresponsibility, playfulness, silliness, laziness, and (quite possibly) tendencies to lying and stealing. Should the entire prediction prove accurate, the result would be something resembling "Sambo."

The social and psychological sanctions of role-playing may in the last analysis prove to be the most satisfactory of the several approaches to Sambo, for, without doubt, of all the roles in American life that of Sambo was by far the most pervasive. The outlines of the role might be sketched in by crude necessity, but what of the finer shades? The sanctions against overstepping it were bleak enough,[102] but the rewards—the sweet applause, as it were, for performing it with sincerity and feeling—were something to be appreciated on quite another level. The law, untuned to the deeper harmonies, could command the player to be present for the occasion, and the whip might even warn against his missing the grosser cues, but could those things really insure the performance that melted all hearts? Yet there was many and many a performance, and the audiences (whose standards were high) appear to have been for the most part well pleased. They were actually viewing their own masterpiece. Much labor had been lavished upon this chef d'oeuvre, the most genial resources of Southern society had been available for the work; touch after touch had been applied throughout the years, and the result— embodied not in the unfeeling law but in the richest layers of Southern lore—had been the product of an exquisitely rounded collective creativity. And indeed, in a sense that somehow transcended the merely ironic, it was a labor of love. "I love the simple and unadulterated slave, with his geniality, his mirth, his swagger, and his nonsense," wrote Edward Pollard. "I love to look upon his countenance shining with content and grease; I

---

[102] Professor Stampp, in a chapter called "To Make Them Stand in Fear," describes the planter's resources for dealing with a recalcitrant slave. *Peculiar Institution,* pp. 141–91.

love to study his affectionate heart; I love to mark that peculiarity in him, which beneath all his buffoonery exhibits him as a creature of the tenderest sensibilities, mingling his joys and his sorrows with those of his master's home.[103] Love, even on those terms, was surely no inconsequential reward.

But what were the terms? The Negro was to be a child forever. "The Negro . . . in his true nature, is always a boy, let him be ever so old. . . ."[104] "He is . . . a dependent upon the white race; dependent for guidance and direction even to the procurement of his most indispensable necessaries. Apart from this protection he has the helplessness of a child—without foresight, without faculty of contrivance, without thrift of any kind."[105] Not only was he a child; he was a happy child. Few Southern writers failed to describe with obvious fondness the bubbling gaiety of a plantation holiday or the perpetual good humor that seemed to mark the Negro character, the good humor of an everlasting childhood.

The role, of course, must have been rather harder for the earliest generations of slaves to learn. "Accommodation," according to John Dollard, "involves the renunciation of protest or aggression against undesirable conditions of life and the organization of the character so that protest does not appear, but acceptance does. It may come to pass in the end that the unwelcome force is idealized, that one identifies with it and takes it into the personality; it sometimes even happens that what is at first resented and feared is finally loved."[106]

[103] Edward A. Pollard, *Black Diamonds Gathered in the Darkey Homes of the South* (New York: Pudney & Russel, 1859), p. 58.

[104] *Ibid.*, p. viii.

[105] John Pendleton Kennedy, *Swallow Barn* (Philadelphia: Carey & Lea, 1832).

[106] John Dollard, *Caste and Class in a Southern Town* (2d ed.; New York: Harper, 1949), p. 255. The lore of "accommodation," taken just in itself, is very rich and is, needless to say, morally very complex. It suggests a delicate psychological balance. On the one hand, as the Dollard citation above implies, accommodation is fraught with dangers for the personalities of those who engage in it. On the other hand, as Bruno Bettelheim has reminded me, this involves a principle that goes well beyond American Negro society and is to be found deeply imbedded in European traditions: the principle of how the powerless can manipulate the powerful through aggressive stupidity, literal-mindedness, servile fawning, and irresponsibility. In this sense the immovably stupid "Good Soldier Schweik" and the

Might the process, on the other hand, be reversed? It is hard to imagine its being reversed overnight. The same role might still be played in the years after slavery—we are told that it was[107] —and yet it was played to more vulgar audiences with cruder standards, who paid much less for what they saw. The lines might be repeated more and more mechanically, with less and less conviction; the incentives to perfection could become hazy and blurred, and the excellent old piece could degenerate over time into low farce. There could come a point, conceivably, with the old zest gone, that it was no longer worth the candle. The day might come at last when it dawned on a man's full waking consciousness that he had really grown up, that he was, after all, only playing a part.

6

MECHANISMS OF RESISTANCE TO ABSOLUTE POWER

One might say a great deal more than has been said here about mass behavior and mass manifestations of personality, and the picture would still amount to little more than a grotesque cartoon of humanity were not some recognition given to the ineffable difference made in any social system by men and women pos-

---

fawning Negro in Richard Wright's *Black Boy* who allowed the white man to kick him for a quarter partake of the same tradition. Each has a technique whereby he can in a real sense exploit his powerful superiors, feel contempt for them, and suffer in the process no great damage to his own pride. Jewish lore, as is well known, teems with this sort of thing. There was much of it also in the traditional relationships between peasants and nobles in central Europe.

Still, all this required the existence of some sort of alternative forces for moral and psychological orientation. The problem of the Negro in slavery times involved the virtual absence of such forces. It was with the end of slavery, presumably, that they would first begin to present themselves in generally usable form—a man's neighbors, the Loyal Leagues, white politicians, and so on. It would be in these circumstances that the essentially intermediate technique of accommodation could be used as a protective device beneath which a more independent personality might develop.

[107] Even Negro officeholders during Reconstruction, according to Francis B. Simkins, "were known to observe carefully the etiquette of the Southern caste system." "New Viewpoints of Southern Reconstruction," *Journal of Southern History,* V (February, 1939), 52.

sessing what is recognized, anywhere and at any time, simply as character. With that, one arrives at something too qualitatively fine to come very much within the crude categories of the present discussion; but although it is impossible to generalize with any proper justice about the incidence of "character" in its moral, irreducible, individual sense, it may still be possible to conclude with a note or two on the social conditions, the breadth or narrowness of their compass, within which character can find expression.

Why should it be, turning once more to Latin America, that there one finds no Sambo, no social tradition, that is, in which slaves were defined by virtually complete consensus as children incapable of being trusted with the full privileges of freedom and adulthood?[108] There, the system surely had its brutalities. The slaves arriving there from Africa had also undergone the capture, the sale, the Middle Passage. They too had been uprooted from a prior culture, from a life very different from the one in which they now found themselves. There, however, the system was not closed.

Here again the concentration camp, paradoxically enough, can be instructive. There were in the camps a very small minority of the survivors who had undergone an experience different in crucial ways from that of the others, an experience which protected them from the full impact of the closed system. These people, mainly by virtue of wretched little jobs in the camp administration which offered them a minute measure of privilege, were able to carry on "underground" activities. In a practical sense the actual operations of such "undergrounds" as were possible may seem to us unheroic and limited: stealing blankets; "organizing" a few bandages, a little medicine, from the camp hospital; black market arrangements with a guard for a bit of extra food and protection for oneself and one's comrades; the circulation of news; and other such apparently trifling activities. But for the psychological balance of those involved, such activities were vital; they made possible a fundamentally different adjustment to the camp. To a prisoner so engaged, there were others who mattered, who gave real point to his existence—the SS was no longer the *only* one. Conversely, the role of the child was

[108] See above, n. 4.

not the only one he played. He could take initiative; he could give as well as receive protection; he did things which had meaning in adult terms. He had, in short, alternative roles; this was a fact which made such a prisoner's transition from his old life to that of the camp less agonizing and destructive; those very prisoners, moreover, appear to have been the ones who could, upon liberation, resume normal lives most easily. It is, in fact, these people—not those of the ranks—who have described the camps to us.[109]

It was just such a difference—indeed, a much greater one—that separated the typical slave in Latin America from the typical slave in the United States. Though he too had experienced the Middle Passage, he was entering a society where alternatives were significantly more diverse than those awaiting his kinsman in North America. Concerned in some sense with his status were distinct and at certain points competing institutions. This involved multiple and often competing "significant others." His master was, of course, clearly the chief one—but not the only one. There could, in fact, be a considerable number: the friar who boarded his ship to examine his conscience, the confessor; the priest who made the rounds and who might report irregularities in treatment to the *procurador;* the zealous Jesuit quick to

[109] Virtually all the ex-prisoners whose writing I have made use of were men and women who had certain privileges (as clerks, physicians, and the like) in the camps. Many of the same persons were also active in the "underground" and could offer some measure of leadership and support for others. That is to say, both the objectivity necessary for making useful observations and the latitude enabling one to exercise some leadership were made possible by a certain degree of protection not available to the rank and file.

I should add, however, that a notable exception was the case of Bruno Bettelheim, who throughout the period of his detention had no privileged position of any kind which could afford him what I am calling an "alternative role" to play. And yet I do not think that it would be stretching the point too far to insist that he did in fact have such a role, one which was literally self-created: that of the scientific observer. In him, the scientist's objectivity, his feeling for clinical detail and sense of personal detachment, amounted virtually to a passion. It would not be fair, however, to expect such a degree of personal autonomy as this in other cases, except for a very few. I am told, for instance, that the behavior of many members of this "underground" toward their fellow prisoners was itself by no means above moral reproach. The depths to which the system could corrupt a man, it must be remembered, were profound.

resent a master's intrusion upon such sacred matters as marriage and worship (a resentment of no small consequence to the master); the local magistrate, with his eye on the king's official protector of slaves, who would find himself in trouble were the laws too widely evaded; the king's informer who received one-third of the fines. For the slave the result was a certain latitude; the lines did not all converge on one man; the slave's personality, accordingly, did not have to focus on a single role. He was, true enough, primarily a slave. Yet he might in fact perform multiple roles. He could be a husband and a father (for the American slave these roles had virtually no meaning); open to him also were such activities as artisan, peddler, petty merchant, truck gardener (the law reserved to him the necessary time and a share of the proceeds, but such arrangements were against the law for Sambo); he could be a communicant in the church, a member of a religious fraternity[110] (roles guaranteed by the most powerful institution in Latin America—comparable privileges in the American South depended on a master's pleasure). These roles were all legitimized and protected *outside* the plantation; they offered a diversity of channels for the development of personality. Not only did the individual have multiple roles open to him as a slave, but the very nature of these roles made possible a certain range of aspirations should he some day become free. He could have a fantasy-life not limited to catfish and watermelons; it was within his conception to become a priest, an independent farmer, a successful merchant, a military officer.[111] The slave could actually—to an extent quite unthinkable in the United States—conceive of himself *as a rebel*. Bloody slave revolts, actual wars, took place in Latin America; nothing on this order occurred in the United States.[112] But even without a rebellion, society

[110] See Tannenbaum, *Slave and Citizen,* pp. 64–65.

[111] *Ibid.,* pp. 4 ff., 56–57, 90–93; see also Johnston, *Negro in the New World,* p. 90.

[112] Compared with the countless uprisings of the Brazilian Negroes, the slave revolts in our own country appear rather desperate and futile. Only three emerge as worthy of any note, and their seriousness—even when described by a sympathetic historian like Herbert Aptheker—depends largely on the supposed plans of the rebels rather than on the things they actually did. The best organized of such "revolts," those of Vesey and Gabriel, were easily suppressed, while the most dramatic of them—the Nat Turner Rebellion—was characterized by little more than aimless butchery. The Brazilian

here had a network of customary arrangements, rooted in antiquity, which made possible at many points a smooth transition of status from slave to free and which provided much social space for the exfoliation of individual character.

To the typical slave on the ante-bellum plantation in the United States, society of course offered no such alternatives. But that is hardly to say that something of an "underground"—something rather more, indeed, than an underground—could not exist in Southern slave society. And there were those in it who hardly fitted the picture of "Sambo."

The American slave system, compared with that of Latin America, was closed and circumscribed, but, like all social systems, its arrangements were less perfect in practice than they appeared to be in theory. It was possible for significant numbers of slaves, in varying degrees, to escape the full impact of the system and its coercions upon personality. The house servant, the urban mechanic, the slave who arranged his own employment and paid his master a stipulated sum each week, were all figuratively members of the "underground."[113] Even among those

---

revolts, on the other hand, were marked by imagination and a sense of direction, and they often involved large-scale military operations. One is impressed both by their scope and their variety. They range from the legendary Palmares Republic of the seventeenth century (a Negro state organized by escaped slaves and successfully defended for over fifty years), to the bloody revolts of the Moslem Negroes of Bahia which, between 1807 and 1835, five times paralyzed a substantial portion of Brazil. Many such wars were launched from the *quilombos* (fortified villages built deep in the jungles by escaped slaves to defend themselves from recapture); there were also the popular rebellions in which the Negroes of an entire area would take part. One is immediately struck by the heroic stature of the Negro leaders: no allowances of any sort need be made for them; they are impressive from any point of view. Arthur Ramos has described a number of them, including Zambi, a fabulous figure of the Palmares Republic; Luiza Mahin, mother of the Negro poet Luiz Gama and "one of the most outstanding leaders of the 1835 insurrection"; and Manoel Francisco dos Anjos Fereira, whose followers in the *Balaiada* (a movement which drew its name from "Baliao," his own nickname) held the *entire province* of Maranhão for three years. Their brilliance, gallantry, and warlike accomplishments give to their histories an almost legendary quality. On the other hand, one could not begin to think of Nat Turner in such a connection. See Ramos, *The Negro in Brazil,* pp. 24–53; Herbert Aptheker, *American Negro Slave Revolts* (New York: Columbia University, 1943), *passim*.

[113] See below, Part IV, n. 115.

working on large plantations, the skilled craftsman or the responsible slave foreman had a measure of independence not shared by his simpler brethren. Even the single slave family owned by a small farmer had a status much closer to that of house servants than to that of a plantation labor gang. For all such people there was a margin of space denied to the majority; the system's authority-structure claimed their bodies but not quite their souls.

Out of such groups an individual as complex and as highly developed as William Johnson, the Natchez barber, might emerge. Johnson's diary reveals a personality that one recognizes instantly as a type—but a type whose values came from a sector of society very different from that which formed Sambo. Johnson is the young man on the make, the ambitious free-enterpriser of American legend. He began life as a slave, was manumitted at the age of eleven, and rose from a poor apprentice barber to become one of the wealthiest and most influential Negroes in ante-bellum Mississippi. He was respected by white and black alike, and counted among his friends some of the leading public men of the state.[114]

It is of great interest to note that although the danger of slave revolts (like Communist conspiracies in our own day) was much overrated by touchy Southerners; the revolts that actually did occur were in no instance planned by plantation laborers but rather by Negroes whose qualities of leadership were developed well outside the full coercions of the plantation authority-system. Gabriel, who led the revolt of 1800, was a blacksmith who lived a few miles outside Richmond; Denmark Vesey, leading spirit of the 1822 plot at Charleston, was a freed Negro artisan who had been born in Africa and served several years aboard a slave-trading vessel; and Nat Turner, the Virginia slave who fomented the massacre of 1831, was a literate preacher of recognized intelligence. Of the plots that have been convincingly substantiated (whether they came to anything or not), the majority originated in urban centers.[115]

[114] See William R. Hogan and Edwin A. Davis (eds.), *William Johnson's Natchez: The Ante-Bellum Diary of a Free Negro* (Baton Rouge: Louisiana State University Press, 1951), esp. pp. 1–64.

[115] Aptheker, *American Negro Slave Revolts,* pp. 220, 268–69, 295–96, and *passim.*

For a time during Reconstruction, a Negro elite of sorts did emerge in the South. Many of its members were Northern Negroes, but the Southern ex-slaves who also comprised it seem in general to have emerged from the categories just indicated. Vernon Wharton, writing of Mississippi, says:

A large portion of the minor Negro leaders were preachers, lawyers, or teachers from the free states or from Canada. Their education and their independent attitude gained for them immediate favor and leadership. Of the natives who became their rivals, the majority had been urban slaves, blacksmiths, carpenters, clerks, or waiters in hotels and boarding houses; a few of them had been favored body-servants of affluent whites.[116]

The William Johnsons and Denmark Veseys have been accorded, though belatedly, their due honor. They are, indeed, all too easily identified, thanks to the system that enabled them as individuals to be so conspicuous and so exceptional and, as members of a group, so few.

[116] Vernon L. Wharton, *The Negro in Mississippi, 1865–1890* (Chapel Hill: University of North Carolina Press, 1942), p. 164.

IV

Slavery and the Intellectual

I

INSTITUTIONS AND INSIGHTS

When a society is confronted by a problem so profound as that of slavery—a problem of such magnitude and of such ancient origins—one supposes that all the wisdom available should in the very course of things strain toward its solution. But then where was wisdom, in the solution found for this problem? Need that "solution" have been so dire and tragic? Its seeming bloody inevitability has tormented our historians for generations. "For Americans in 1861," one of them asserts, ". . . war was easier than wisdom and courage."[1] It should thus be appropriate to take up at this point the question of wisdom itself. What makes "wisdom" possible? What are the daily conditions which enable the men of thought and feeling in a society to function responsibly? If a society's intellectual resources are to remain grounded in reality, if they are to be at hand in a form appropriate to the problems of the day, what are the prerequisites? These questions may be considered with regard to the society of the United States in the years following 1830 by resuming, in a somewhat different connection, the discussion begun in Part II.[2]

In that period the dominant social problem became the problem of slavery. If for no other reason, it was the concrete fact of strong sentiment everywhere else in the Western world which made it so. It may be taken as given, in the face of increasing antislavery pressures from Europe, that some sort of resolution was sooner or later bound to occur, and that the problem was

[1] Allan Nevins, *The Emergence of Lincoln* (New York: Scribner, 1950), II, 471.

[2] See above, pp. 27–34.

one which to an increasing extent would engage the energies of an entire society. To what extent, then, in this society, was it possible for *intellectual* energies to be engaged?

As for the South, it may be wondered whether the intellectual resources of that region were really available, or whether, to the Southerner, slavery *could* in the strictest sense of the word be a "problem." By 1830 the commitment of the South to capitalist agriculture—to the production of a staple crop for a world market—was the dominant fact of Southern life. In the cotton kingdom it was no longer possible to consider slavery as a social issue in which there were real alternatives; it was not possible in the sense that it had been in Jefferson's Virginia, where slavery in an economic sense had become considerably less than an unmixed blessing. To men of the nineteenth-century cotton kingdom, slavery was apparently a success. Other things being equal, it is in the nature of societies in good working order, as Richard Hofstadter has said, that "they do not foster ideas . . . hostile to their fundamental working arrangements." Very little criticism of slavery was to be heard in Alabama or Mississippi; slavery there had become much too profitable. Whatever pressures did or could exist there to force a critical analysis of slavery were canceled, moreover, by slavery's sectional character. That slavery was present in one region and not in another was quite enough, for one purpose at least, to create two distinct cultures. With antislavery sentiment dwindling in the South and heightening in the North, the Southerner faced a situation in which all the hostile criticism was coming from the outside. A whole series of loyalties was thus automatically called into question. For these reasons there was no longer generally to be found the man best equipped to deal with slavery intellectually—a man such as Thomas Jefferson whose mind operated under the balanced tensions created not only by a repugnance to the system but also by a commitment to it.

By the 1830's the closest thing to an intellectual community in the United States consisted of men with no concrete commitment to the system at all. They were men who had no close commitment to any of society's institutions. They were truly men without responsibility.

The intellectual center of gravity had by this time somehow shifted. Its present location was not the Virginia Tidewater, not

Philadelphia, not really New York, not even, in fact, quite Boston. The nearest approach to such a center had withdrawn, rather symbolically, to a place *just outside* Boston, to the town of Concord. Living in Concord, or spending much time there, were persons all of whose names are now familiar: Ralph Waldo Emerson, Henry Thoreau, Bronson Alcott, George Ripley, Margaret Fuller, Theodore Parker, William Henry Channing, and others. These persons lived in a radically different age, and did their thinking in a radically changed setting, from that of such earlier intellectuals as Jefferson, Hamilton, Madison, and Adams.

The age had several characteristics which set it apart from that of forty years before and which left a decided mark upon its spiritual life. It has already been noted that this was an age featured by the breakdown of a number of key social institutions. During his own lifetime, the mature American of 1830 had seen stripped of their power all the establishments which a generation or so earlier had seemed to represent order—the church, the bar, the Federalist party, and the eastern merchant aristocracy.[3] It was an age in which the individual had become an almost mystical symbol of promise. "In all my lectures," Emerson declared, "I have taught one doctrine, namely the infinitude of the private man."[4] It was also one in which nearly every form of public expression had taken on a prodigious quality of abstraction. Finally, it was an age which throbbed with the impulse to reform.

Some of this requires a certain amount of elaboration. Institutions, for example: what difference might the presence or absence of institutions, their thinness or thickness, make in the texture of a man's thought? It was this very question that Henry James asked with regard to Hawthorne and what Hawthorne lacked. His famous answer was outrageously concrete:

The negative side of the spectacle on which Hawthorne looked out, in his contemplative saunterings and reveries, might, indeed, with a little ingenuity, be made almost ludicrous; one might enumerate the items of high civilization, as it exists in other countries, which are absent from the texture of American life, until it should become a won-

[3] See above, pp. 27-34.

[4] *Journals of Ralph Waldo Emerson,* ed. Edward Waldo Emerson and Waldo Emerson Forbes (Boston: Houghton Mifflin, 1909-14), V, 380.

der to know what was left. No State, in the European sense of the word, and indeed barely a specific national name. No sovereign, no court, no personal loyalty, no aristocracy, no church, no clergy, no army, no diplomatic service, no country gentlemen, no palaces, no castles, nor manors, nor old country houses, nor parsonages, nor thatched cottages, nor ivied ruins; no cathedrals, nor abbeys, nor little Norman churches; no great universities nor public schools—no Oxford, nor Eton, nor Harrow; no literature, no novels, no museums, no pictures, no political society, no sporting class—no Epsom nor Ascot! . . . The natural remark, in the almost lurid light of such an indictment, would be that if these things are left out, everything is left out.[5]

Sociologically, there seems to be much reason for taking James's statement seriously, however idiosyncratic its expression. What he might be saying is that artistic and intellectual activity at large must be nourished by a rich and complex profusion of "things," things which ought to have a certain sanction in antiquity—by no means a trivial point in itself. But there is an even larger principle involved, one to which "things" and "antiquity" are certainly related, but in rather a secondary way (Hawthorne's Salem was, after all, very old); the heart of the matter could be that these "facts" and "things" which James so valued were the signs, agents, and products of social institutions, of continuing institutions upon which one could count for mooring posts, for points of view, for centers of focus. It could be said that institutions define a society's culture, that they provide the stable channels, for better or worse, within which the intellectual must have his business—if, that is, his work is to have real consequences for society and if he himself is to have a positive function there. Institutions with power produce the "things" not only upon which one leans but also against which one pushes; they provide the standards whereby, for men of sensibility, one part of society may be judged and tested against another. The lack of them, moreover, removes the thinker not only from the places where power resides but also from the very *idea* of power and how it is used. "Power" is transformed into an abstraction. Such a condition in Emerson's time "ratified the general heresy," as R. P. Blackmur has put it, "that the arts and learning can be divorced from the power and resources of society

[5] Henry James, *Hawthorne* (New York: Harper, 1879), pp. 42–43.

without danger to both." "The danger," Mr. Blackmur asserts, "is social impotence."[6]

Society, institutions, power—all became abstractions, both in letters and in popular oratory. Where now was the setting in which the thinker might locate man, the object of his contemplation? The transcendent "individual" must be placed not in the society over which he had symbolically triumphed but in a transcendental universe—man himself became an abstraction. Success, energy, and power had for Americans made abstractions of everything; no one really needed to know or remember what had made them possible.

The very conception of their history itself which Americans could hold at this time was non-institutional, and this may shed some light on the abstract nature of both their thought and their morality. There were, for instance, at least two points of view (besides those of Lord North and George III) from which Americans might have analyzed their Revolution. One was indicated by the language of the Declaration:

We hold these truths to be self-evident, that all men are created equal, that they are endowed by their Creator with certain inalienable Rights. . . . That whenever any Form of Government becomes destructive of these ends, it is the Right of the People to alter and abolish it, and to institute new Government. . . .

It was to some extent necessary that the revolutionary generation should conceive its great enterprise in such terms: mounting oppression and the right to smash all connections and begin anew. But there was another viewpoint, that of Edmund Burke. Burke's line of vision was fully English, and he had little use for the above sentiments; yet he was not unfriendly to the Revolution. He was always aware how relatively little was being smashed. He knew that the revolt of the Americans had sprung from a rude disruption of orderly expectations, that they were in fact struggling to conserve the institutions they already had, and that the very strength of those institutions pretty much guaranteed, in one form or another, that the Americans would

[6] R. P. Blackmur, "The American Literary Expatriate," in David F. Bowers (ed.), *Foreign Influences in American Life* (New York: Peter Smith, 1952), p. 133.

succeed.[7] Yet it was very difficult for any American to picture his Revolution on such grounds—grounds of "stability" rather than "change"—and for good reasons which Burke himself would have been the first to understand. The clearest social thought comes when basic institutional arrangements are threatened, and when revolutionists are truly forced to change these institutions, they become highly sensitive to them. But the American Revolution never really made this demand on its intellectuals. Its political and military leaders operated within institutional patterns long familiar to them, and, intellectually, all the Revolution required were the abstract ideals necessary to keep it going. Practically, it was an organizational genius for self-government ac-

[7] As for the causes of the conflict, Burke's analysis focused upon a disruption in the serene order of things, rather than a course of oppression which had at last become intolerable. "After the repeal of the Stamp Act, 'the colonies fell . . . into their ancient state of *unsuspecting confidence in the mother country.'* This unsuspecting confidence is the true centre of gravity amongst mankind, about which all the parts are at rest. It is this *unsuspecting confidence* that removes all difficulties, and reconciles all the contradictions which occur in the complexity of all ancient puzzled political establishments. . . . If [our] undefined power has become odious since that time, and full of horror to the colonies, it is because the *unsuspicious confidence* is lost, and the parental affection, in the bosom of whose boundless authority they reposed their privileges, is become estranged and hostile." The institutions which the colonies were now fighting to conserve had become too settled, too well-established, and too powerful to be subdued any longer on a question of "principle." "You have the ground you encamp on, and you have no more." Such institutions, moreover, were worth far more in Burke's eyes than the price that would be required to crush them: "I would expect ten times more benefit to this kingdom from the affection of America, though under a separate establishment, than from her perfect submission to the crown and Parliament, accompanied by her terror, disgust, and abhorrence. Bodies tied together by so unnatural a bond of union as mutual hatred are only connected to their ruin." He would thus (though being above all things a good Englishman) place his approval on the Revolution rather than try to preserve a connection that would in the very process have become worthless to the mother country: "You impair the object by your very endeavours to preserve it." "Letter to the Sheriffs of Bristol, 1777," in *Works of the Right Honorable Edmund Burke* (Boston: Little, Brown, 1865), II, 205, 234-36, and *passim;* see also "Speech on Conciliation with the Colonies," *ibid.,* p. 119 and *passim.* The judgment was thus based on circumstances rather than "principles"—which (no matter what kind of principles) in themselves never impressed Burke in the least. Such habits of mind are explicitly discussed in the opening passages of his "Reflections on the Revolution in France," *ibid.,* III, 240.

quired over generations that brought it to a successful conclusion. There were "changes," to be sure, but the major changes, which the Revolution did little more than legitimize, had already been accomplished over half a century before. It is an axiom in the theory of revolutions that an "orthodox" revolution, in the European sense, undergoes at least two phases. The first is that phase of militancy where ideals and slogans must be produced and proclaimed for the inspiration of the revolutionary movement. Necessary though they are, however, these ideals, being abstract and primarily moral in their nature, represent only one side of the movement's objectives; beyond a certain point there is danger that the abstractions may be taken too literally and may thus threaten the future stability of the revolutionary state. At this point—"Thermidor"—it may become necessary to eliminate the dedicated sloganeers, the Robespierres and Trotskys associated with the militant phase, and to formulate the objectives of the new state in more rational and pacific form. In our own Revolution this never occurred. Instead, the slogans themselves became enshrined in the minds and hearts of Americans, and to the generations that followed there seemed little reason why they should not be adequate to explain all the basic facts of the national experience.[8]

There had been one moment, indeed, when institutional arrangements had hung in the balance, and it was during this time that our best social thinking occurred. In the Philadelphia convention of 1787 and during the period of ratification that followed, men with specific stakes in society, men attached to institutions and with a vested interest in one another's presence,

[8] It might be added that the Declaration had been regarded all along not so much as a revolutionary manifesto, in the classic sense, but rather as a legal brief wherein the plaintiff epitomizes the reasons for a contemplated separation. Those elements in the revolutionary movement who might have been led to take the more sweeping assertions of universal equality too literally—the Tom Paines and Sam Adamses—had less, rather than more, influence as the movement developed into a drawn-out war. The Declaration's *obiter dicta* would thus never really be challenged one way or the other, and the Revolution never required a "Thermidor." As a result, the American people could accept the Declaration more or less *in toto* as a statement of the political theory on which the Republic rested, and if any test of its soundness were required, it was met by the success of the Revolution.

men aware of being engaged with concrete problems of power, wrote and debated a constitution and produced a treatise in political science—*The Federalist*—which remain as yet unmatched. They had, in short, all the prerequisites for intellectual efficiency. With much to push against and with both the opportunity and the necessity for testing their conceptions against those of one another, the common character of their work avoided much duplication of effort and eliminated the need for returning continually to first principles. But once again the very brilliant success of these men's efforts made it unnecessary to preserve the party they created, and made it possible for posterity to canonize their concrete achievement—the Constitution—into a shining moral abstraction. In short, a "withering-away of the state," at least in men's minds, never occurred more decisively than it did here; and we are brought back once more to the problem of "wisdom" and what, if anything, men in those days presumed to be wisdom's support. That support, as Emerson announced, was simply "character":

To educate the wise man, the State exists; and with the appearance of the wise man, the State expires. The appearance of character makes the State unnecessary. The wise man is the State. He needs no army, fort, or navy,—he loves men too well; no bribe, or feast, or palace, to draw friends to him: no vantage ground, no favorable circumstance. He needs no library, for he has not done thinking; no church, for he is a prophet; no statute book, for he is the lawgiver; no money, for he is value; no road, for he is at home where he is; no experience, for the life of the creator . . . looks from his eyes.[9]

2

INTELLECTUALS WITHOUT RESPONSIBILITY

The thinkers of Concord, who in the later thirties and forties would create an intellectual attitude at least coherent enough to be given a name—"Transcendentalism"—were men without connections. Almost without exception, they had no ties with the sources of wealth; there were no lawyers or jurists among them; none of them ever sat in a government post; none was a member of Congress; they took next to no part in politics at all; indeed,

[9] "Politics," in *Emerson's Complete Works* (Cambridge: Riverside Press, 1883), III, *Essays, Second Series,* 206–7.

as Emerson remarked, "They do not even like to vote."[10] Not one of them wielded even the limited influence of a professor; they were scarcely on good terms with nearby Harvard itself, though all were well educated and several of them had studied there. They were all deeply concerned with religion and a number were ministers. Yet even here the bias was strongly anti-institutional, antiformal, and individualistic.

Emerson had quit his Unitarian pastorate in 1832 in the conviction that he could administer the Lord's Supper only if the bread and wine were omitted from it; attacking the organized church as dead and worthless in his 1838 Divinity School address, he became *persona non grata* at Harvard and remained so for thirty years. George Ripley, declaring that "the truth of religion does not depend on tradition, nor historical facts, but has an unerring witness in the soul,"[11] resigned from his pulpit in 1841 amid the protests of his admiring parishioners. Orestes Brownson had first joined the Presbyterian church but had remained in it for only two years, becoming a Universalist in 1824 and later a Universalist minister, though after a series of broils with other Universalists he drifted about as a freelance and eventually back to the church as a Unitarian. After four years of this he organized his own church, the "society for Christian Union and Progress"; then, having attacked both Protestantism and Catholicism in *New Views of Christianity, Society, and the Church* (1836), Brownson shocked New England liberals in 1844 by joining the Catholic church and violently attacking all its enemies. Theodore Parker was also a Unitarian minister but was never able to get along with other Unitarians. The Unitarians themselves had done what they could to get away from forms, traditions, and miracles, but Parker harassed them mercilessly for too much dependence on authority and for developing their own orthodoxies. Their organizational stability in Boston, loose and uncertain at best, was constantly being threatened by such episodes as Parker's attacks on the Divinity School, his denunciation of

[10] "The Transcendentalist," in *Works*, I, *Nature, Addresses and Lectures*, 326.

[11] "Letter to the Church in Purchase Street," in O. B. Frothingham, *George Ripley* (Boston: Houghton Mifflin, 1882), pp. 84–85.

the Hollis Street Council,[12] and his demand, in an ordination sermon in 1841, that "we worship as Jesus did, with no mediator, with nothing between us and the Father of all."[13] Parker never actually abandoned the pulpit, but a new church was founded for him which he ran on his own terms after having resigned his pastorate in West Roxbury. William Henry Channing, nephew of the founder of Unitarianism, William Ellery Channing, was constantly in and out of the church. He tried unsuccessfully in 1837 to organize a free church; he resigned a Unitarian pastorate after less than two years because he suspected Christianity of not being a divine institution and the Gospels of being unreliable; for two years Channing led an independent religious society in New York which fell apart when he went to Brook Farm in 1845, though he stayed there only a few months. After heading the "Religious Union of Associationists," whose object was the reign of love among mankind and which lasted about three years, Channing in middle life lapsed back into Unitarianism. The pathetic Jones Very, a poet of sorts as well as a man of religion, impressed the other Transcendentalists for a time with his intoxicated mysticism, but after his youthful inspiration had worn off he was unable to preach well because of shyness; aside from two temporary pastorates, Very lived the last forty years of his life in virtual retirement, a self-confessed "failure." At one time he had even been suspected of madness and had actually spent five weeks in an asylum, where he had successfully preached to the inmates his doctrine of "will-less existence." The only ministers connected with the Transcendentalist circle who retained at all times a stable relationship with the church were James Freeman Clarke and Frederic Henry Hedge, both of whom remained within the Unitarian fold and in later years took active roles in public life.

Certain features already mentioned as having become especially

[12] The Reverend John Pierpont in 1842 had denounced brewers and wine-bibbers from his pulpit and had actually called them by name. A council of clergymen rebuked Pierpont for using intemperate language, whereupon Parker denounced the council's decision as a "Jesuitical document in the interest of the liquor trade." See "The Hollis Street Council," *The Dial,* III (October, 1842), 201–21.

[13] Theodore Parker, *The Transient and Permanent in Christianity* (Boston: American Unitarian Association, 1908), p. 30.

characteristic of the period at large—its abandonment of older institutional patterns, its exaltation of the individual and his limitless potentialities, the high-flown abstraction which national success permitted in public expression, the receptivity (charged with tension and guilt) toward the reform schemes which flourished in the middle thirties and early forties—all these features found their close counterparts in the attitudes and thought of the Transcendentalists. Their "revolt against the age" could be conceived and acted out only along lines which the age itself had laid down for them.

The anti-institutional impulse so strikingly evident even in the ministers' relationship with their own churches was also to be seen in the Transcendentalists' attitude toward institutions in general. "The difficulty," wrote Emerson, "is that we do not make a world of our own, but fall into institutions already made, and have to accommodate ourselves to them to be useful at all, and this accommodation is, I say, a loss of so much integrity and, of course, of so much power."[14] This echoed the earlier thoughts of William Ellery Channing, who had declared, "Most of our civil institutions grow out of our corruptions."[15] The church as an institution was corrupt, and most of the Transcendentalists attacked it as such. "I hear a preacher announce for his text and topic the expediency of one of the institutions of his church. Do I not know beforehand that not possibly can he say a new and spontaneous word?"[16] Look not to the church for the meaning of Christianity, urged Theodore Parker, but to Jesus Himself: "He founds no institution as a monument of his words."[17] They turned their hostility not only upon the church but upon other establishments. Trade was denounced as an institutionalized web of corruption. Theodore Parker was not against businessmen as individuals ("Not all the merchants were bad," remarks his biographer)[18] but was very hard on them as

[14] *Journals*, II, 448–49.

[15] Quoted in John Reinhardt, "The Evolution of William Ellery Channing's Sociopolitical Ideas," *American Literature*, XXVI (May, 1954), 157.

[16] "Self-Reliance," in *Works*, II, *Essays, First Series*, 55–56.

[17] Parker, *The Transient and Permanent*, p. 2.

[18] Henry S. Commager, *Theodore Parker* (Boston: Beacon Press, 1936), p. 183.

a class. "All is the reflection of this most powerful class. The truths that are told are for them, and the lies."[19] Emerson said similar things about "the system," though he too made allowances for decent *individuals*.[20] The Transcendentalists attacked all institutions and stood aloof from them—church, trade, even government itself. Especially noteworthy, as Perry Miller observes, was Henry Thoreau's "comprehensive resignation from all institutions he had never joined."[21] Everywhere a man goes, Thoreau complained, "men will pursue and paw him with their dirty institutions, and, if they can, constrain him to belong to their desperate odd-fellow society."[22]

Here we get a sense of how dramatic was the contrast between these men and those of two generations earlier, and of how differently they looked at things. Thoreau's refusal to pay a poll tax, while sojourning at Walden, resulted in his being lodged overnight in the Concord jail, and the episode inspired him to declare, "I was never molested by any person but those who represented the State."[23] It was that very "State," of course, which had made it possible for Henry Thoreau to remain unmolested by any but itself—and that but once. The flourishing

[19] "A Sermon of Merchants," in Perry Miller (ed.), *The Transcendentalists: An Anthology* (Cambridge: Harvard University Press, 1950), p. 454.

[20] "I content myself with the fact that the general system of our trade (apart from the blacker traits, which, I hope, are exceptions denounced and unshared by all reputable men), is a system of selfishness; is not dictated by the high sentiments of human nature; is not measured by the exact law of reciprocity, much less by the sentiments of love and heroism, but is a system of distrust, of concealment, of superior keenness, not of giving but of taking advantage." "Man the Reformer," in *Works*, I, 222.

[21] *The Transcendentalists*, p. 258. Society's very instruments of communication were depraved: railroads ("We do not ride on the railroad; it rides upon us"), the post office ("There are very few important communications made through it"), or newspapers ("I never read any memorable news in a newspaper"). *Writings of Henry David Thoreau*, ed. B. Torrey and F. B. Sanborn (Boston: Houghton Mifflin, 1893–1900), II, *Walden, or Life in the Woods*, 102–3.

[22] *Ibid.* "This, our respectable daily life, on which . . . our institutions are founded, is in fact the veriest illusion, and will vanish like the baseless fabric of a vision. . . ." *Writings*, VI, *Familiar Letters*, 162.

[23] *Writings*, II, *Walden*, 190.

success of such a "State," there in the heart of New England, now enabled its philosophers to contemplate the institutions it could do without and to hold up, as a serious philosophical alternative, the question of whether or not it needed any at all. Could he have foreseen it, this might well have confounded Theodore Parker's grandfather, who had commanded the militia on Lexington Green. And whereas few prose lyrics in praise of nature have so endeared themselves to us as Thoreau's *Walden* has, we might still ask whether *Walden,* as a paradigm of the good society, would have made much sense to James Madison.

It followed that the prime seat of virtue lay in the individual himself: "Transcendentalism says, the Man is all."[24] "What faculties slumber within," exclaimed William Ellery Channing, "weighed down by the chains of custom!"[25] To Frederic Henry Hedge, who inspired the first meetings of the "Transcendental Club," it was upon the individual that men must place the supreme hope of progress. "Let us ground it on universal Man, on the sight of the human will, and on the might of the human will, and on the boundless resources of the human mind."[26] A theory of infinite perfectibility flowed quite naturally from this, and the fellow seekers eagerly discussed its various possibilities. "I believe in Eternal Progression," wrote Margaret Fuller to James Freeman Clarke; "I believe in a God, a Beauty and Perfection to which I am to strive all my life for assimilation."[27] George Ripley insisted that "man has the power of conceiving a perfection higher than he has ever reached. Not only so. He can make this perfection a distinct object of pursuit."[28] The same thought was

[24] *Journals,* VII, 268.

[25] Quoted in Van Wyck Brooks, *The Life of Emerson* (New York: Dutton, 1932), p. 37.

[26] "Progress of Society," in Miller, *Transcendentalists,* p. 74. "Character," according to the "Orphic Sayings" of Bronson Alcott, "is the only legitimate institution; the only regal influence." *The Dial,* I (July, 1840), 91. Emerson, in "Self-Reliance," exhorted the young man to throw aside the curtains of dead institutions and free his soul: ". . . under all these screens I have difficulty to detect the precise man you are. . . ." *Works,* II, 55.

[27] *Memoirs of Margaret Fuller Ossoli,* ed. R. W. Emerson, W. H. Channing, and J. F. Clarke (London: R. Bentley, 1852), I, 177.

[28] George Ripley, *Discourse on the Philosophy of Religion* (Boston: J. Munroe, 1836), p. 39.

announced by Bronson Alcott in even loftier terms: "Every soul feels at times the possibility of becoming a God; she cannot rest in the human, she aspires after the God-like. This instinctive tendency is an authentic augury of its own fulfillment. Men shall become Gods."[29] It was on the theme of individual perfectibility that the Transcendentalists' leading ideas on education were based.[30]

Did he [the Transcendentalist] take up the cause of education, it was as a believer in the latent capacity of every child, boy or girl; as an earnest wisher that such capacity might be stimulated by the best methods, and directed to the best ends. . . . Mr. Alcott's school . . . would have achieved such remarkable results had more faithful trial of its methods been possible.[31]

Even the agricultural communities (Brook Farm and Fruitlands) in which some of the Transcendentalists took part were conceived not as collective institutions but rather as "united individuals" gathered together to make self-perfection easier and to provide, as Elizabeth Peabody put it, "LEISURE TO LIVE IN ALL THE FACULTIES OF THE SOUL."[32] William Henry Channing put the aspirations of

[29] *Dial,* I (July, 1840), 87.

[30] "It was the design of Providence," reasoned Sampson Reed, "that the infant mind should possess the germ of every science. If it were not so, they could hardly be learned." Elizabeth Peabody declared, "There is not a single thing that cannot be studied with comparative ease, by a child, who can be taught what faculties he must use, and how they are to be brought to bear on the subject, and what influence on those faculties the subject will have, after it is mastered." Sampson Reed, *Observations on the Growth of the Mind* (Boston: Crosby, Nichols, 1859), p. 45; Elizabeth Peabody, *Record of a School: Exemplifying the General Principles of Spiritual Culture* (Boston: Russel, Shattuck, 1836), p. xxi.

[31] Octavius Brooks Frothingham, *Transcendentalism in New England* (New York: Putnam, 1876), p. 156. Frothingham had personal recollections of many of the Transcendentalists.

[32] Elizabeth Peabody, "Plan of the West Roxbury Community," *The Dial,* II (January, 1842), 364. William Ellery Channing thought that the depressed condition of laborers after the 1837 panic was due to "the want of a strict economy"—they should have been realizing their true selves in cultural improvement. "Sure I am," he wrote, "that, were they to study plainness of dress and simplicity of living, for the purpose of their own true elevation, they would surpass in intellect, in taste, in honorable qualities, and in present enjoyment, that great proportion of the prosperous who are softened into indulgence or enslaved to empty show. By such

the whole group into a formula: "Trust, dare, and be; infinite good is ready for your asking; seek and find."[33]

That the age permitted its philosophers to abstract "man" so completely from his culture, with no sense of how much was thereby being taken for granted, should go far to explain the overwhelming abstractness of the Transcendentalists' thinking about everything—not only about "man" but about existence itself. Transcendentalists, George Ripley declared, are so called "because they believe in an order of truths which transcends the sphere of the external sense. Their leading idea is the supremacy of mind over matter."[34] Frederic Henry Hedge managed to write whole passages on "society" in which there was not a single concrete word.[35] The lovable Bronson Alcott almost lived on abstractions. Emerson, with a certain mellow tolerance, noted of Alcott in his journal, "Particulars—particular thoughts, sentences, facts even—cannot interest him, except as for a moment they take their place as a ray from his orb. The Whole,—Nature proceeding from himself, is what he studies." Emerson would be astonished, "having left him in the morning with one set of opinions, to find him in the evening totally escaped from all recollection of them. . . ."[36] Although life at the Alcotts' had its genial side, the abstractions of the philosopher brought actual suffering to others. "At the very time," writes Harold Goddard, "when Alcott was entering in his Journal, 'All day discussing the endless infinite themes,'

self-denial, how might the burden of labor be lightened, and time and strength redeemed for improvement!" *The Works of William E. Channing, D.D.* (Boston, 1855), V, 211.

[33] *Memoirs of Margaret Fuller Ossoli,* II, 13.

[34] "Letter to the Church in Purchase Street," in Frothingham, *Ripley,* p. 84.

[35] "For, what is society, It is not a single people or generation, it is not a collection of individuals as such; but it is an intimate union of individuals, voluntarily coöperating for the common good, actuated by social feelings, governed by social principles, and urged onward by social improvements. Society, in this sense, has always been advancing, not uniformly, indeed, far from it,—sometimes the motion has not been perceptible, sometimes, it may be, there has been no motion at all,—but it has never lost ground;—whenever it has moved at all, it has moved forward." "Progress of Society," in Miller, *Transcendentalists,* p. 73.

[36] *Journals,* IV, 72; VI, 175. "Alcott drank water," commented Frederika Bremer, "and we drank fog."

Mrs. Alcott was doing the endless finite chores."[37] At Fruitlands, Alcott and Charles Lane, in their heroic project of liberating the soul from its fetters of tradition and form, succeeded in shackling the household in an iron discipline which drove Mrs. Alcott close to distraction. "I am almost suffocated," she wrote furtively in her own journal, "in this atmosphere of restriction and form." The spartan diet was hard on her teeth, which were "very bad," and part of the routine involved everyone's keeping his hands "from each other's bodies."

All these causes have combined to make me somewhat irritable. . . . They all seem most stupidly obtuse on the causes of this occasional prostration of my judgment and faculties. I hope the solution of the problem will not be revealed to them too late for my recovery or their atonement for this invasion of my rights as a woman and a mother. Give me one day of practical philosophy. It is worth a century of speculation and discussion.[38]

But it was the restless Margaret Fuller, a woman of extraordinary intellectual capacities and strong sensibilities, who was the tragic figure of the Transcendentalists. The kindly reserve of Emerson, the dubious inspirations of the younger Channing, the vaporings of Alcott, the pale imitations in plaster at the Boston Athenaeum—to poor ardent Margaret there was nothing very *resistant* about all this. Almost too late, like a Henry James heroine, she found what she needed in the thick life of Europe and in a love affair amid the passions of the Italian revolution of 1848. "Had I only come ten years earlier! Now my life must be a failure, so much strength has been wasted on abstractions, which only came because I grew not in the right soil."[39] The idyl was pathetically short, for very soon she had it all taken from her— husband, baby, her own life—in a storm at sea.[40]

[37] Harold Clarke Goddard, *Studies in New England Transcendentalism* (New York: Columbia University Press, 1908), p. 158. Alcott's daughter Louisa May, when once asked to define a "philosopher," replied, "My definition is of a man up in a balloon, with his family and friends holding the ropes which confine him to earth and trying to haul him down." *Ibid.*, p. 158.

[38] Odell Shepard, *Pedlar's Progress: The Life of Bronson Alcott* (Boston: Little, Brown, 1938), pp. 348, 351–53.

[39] *Memoirs,* II, 225.

[40] All three were drowned in a shipwreck off Fire Island, New York, in 1850.

The final element of interest to us in the thinking of the Transcendentalists—its overtone of guilt—was symptomatic of the reform impulses of the period. "I pray for the opportunity and will," wrote the anguished William Henry Channing to his mother in January, 1837, "to put forth all my powers rightly for the increase of good. . . . Self-satisfaction, or rather an easy conscience, I never yet enjoyed, and never deserved to, though perhaps I have by nature a self-tormenting disposition."[41] George Ripley's resignation from the pulpit was inspired by the conviction that his views did not have the reforming influence there that they should have had. "Blame me for it if you will," he wrote to his congregation in 1840, "but I cannot behold the degradation, the ignorance, the poverty, the vice, and the ruin of the soul, which is everywhere displayed in the very bosom of Christian society in our own city, while men look idly on, without a shudder."[42] Theodore Parker also worried over his relationship to the evils of the day. "It is a good thing, no doubt," he reflected, "that I should read the Greek Anthology and cultivate myself in my leisure, as a musk-melon ripens in the sun, but why should I be the only one of a thousand who has this chance?"[43] Even the serene Emerson was moved to exclaim, "Am I not too protected a person? Is there not a wide disparity between the lot of me and the lot of thee, my poor brother, my poor sister?"[44] Overwhelmed, for instance, by the evils of business life, Emerson was led to construct a web of guilt from which no one could be exempt.

We are all implicated of course in this charge; it is only necessary to ask a few questions as to the progress of the articles of commerce from the fields where they grew, to our houses, to become aware that we eat and drink and wear perjury and fraud in a hundrd commodities. . . .

But by coming out of trade you have not cleared yourself. The trail of the serpent reaches into all the lucrative professions and practices of man. Each has its own wrongs. Each finds a tender and very intelligent conscience a disqualification for success. . . . Inextricable seem to be the twinings and tendrils of this evil, and we all involve our-

[41] Octavius B. Frothingham, *Memoir of William Henry Channing* (Boston: Houghton Mifflin, 1886), pp. 125–26.

[42] Frothingham, *Ripley*, p. 74.

[43] Quoted in Commager, *Theodore Parker*, p. 163.

[44] "New England Reformers," in *Works*, III, *Essays, Second Series*, 244.

selves in it the deeper by forming connections, by wives and children, by benefits and debts.[45]

"What is a man born for," he insisted, "but to be a Reformer, a Re-maker of what man has made; a renouncer of lies; a restorer of truth and good, imitating that great Nature which embosoms us all . . . ?"[46]

Such expressions were indicative of a phenomenon which was becoming noticeably widespread. It was apparent by the mid-1830's—with the appearance of Transcendentalism, of abolitionism, of the reform-conscious Jacksonian "workingmen's parties"—that America was entering an extraordinary period of reform. The drive, momentarily halted with the panic and depression of the late thirties, burst forth once more in the forties in a veritable fury of reform projects of every imaginable sort—temperance, millenarianism, perfectionism, spiritualistic Shakerism, utopianism, pacifism. It could probably be said that much of the aggression which such activities surely generated found its satisfaction in the splurge of Manifest Destiny and war with Mexico in the middle and late forties, for by the 1850's a great number of the reform schemes so absorbing a few years earlier had lost their vitality. By then the field was vacated, so far as most people were concerned, to a single reform preoccupation—antislavery. That movement, present in some form since the early thirties and inflamed rather than alleviated by the exertions of the Mexican War, grew to formidable proportions in the 1850's.

3

SIN, GUILTY INNOCENCE, AND REFORM

The point being examined here is the relationship of intellect to the question of slavery in the United States from the 1830's on. It has been asserted, with regard to the functioning of intellect in culture at large, that a state of vital tension among the institutions of that culture makes a very great difference in the focus or lack of focus which its intellectual activity is to have. Some sort of daily orientation to institutions seems to be needed for the thinker to develop a sensitivity to the terms upon which they are main-

[45] "Man the Reformer," in *Works*, I, 221, 223–24.
[46] *Ibid.*, p. 236.

tained (and, conversely, subverted); only thus are questions of power and social policy likely to take on for him a quality of concreteness. It has been further asserted, by way of example, that the most notable intellectual expression of the 1830's and 1840's in the United States—Transcendentalism—was quite unable in this respect to "transcend" its culture and its age at all: that, far from "revolting" against the age, Transcendentalism embodied in aggravated form certain of its most remarkable features—its anti-institutionalism, its individual perfectionism, its abstraction, and its guilt and reforming zeal.[47] Moreover, the intellectual features of the reform movement most relevant to this inquiry—abolitionism—very strikingly duplicated those very features just enumerated, particularly guilt and its counterpart, moral aggression.

But before spelling this out, it will be necessary to make a final digression in order to give some special attention to the last-named of these qualities—social guilt and its various adjuncts. Reform movements in the United States appear to have been given a unique character by reason of the special part played in them by guilt; we should therefore examine some of the conditions which have typically made reform movements possible in this country.

It should in the first place be recognized that in the history of American reform no direct correlation can be found between the extent of any given social evil and the intensity of the reform activity directed against it. It is frequently to be observed that some of the most notorious of abuses have been allowed to go unchallenged while others comparatively superficial may be attacked with inordinate energy, or that continuing ills may have been ignored at one time and ferociously denounced at another. Something more than the mere existence of such ills is therefore needed to explain the action which they may evoke.

[47] John W. Ward, in "Two Versions of Individualism" (a paper read at the 1957 meeting of the American Historical Association), pointed out the very close resemblance between the popular thought of the Jacksonian era and the leading ideas of the Transcendentalists. "The body of assumptions made explicit in Emerson's thought," he said, "are implicit in contemporary political theory, religious thought, and the celebration of the Old Hero, Andrew Jackson himself." Thoreau's *Walden*, Professor Ward added, "can stand for us as a kind of cultural metaphor, expressing an emotion that had a deep hold on the imagination of the time."

The first element that a typical American reform situation appears to require is some sort of disruption of expectations, not necessarily connected with the actual objects of reform. This may be brought about in more than one way. One such way could be a depression bringing unemployment and sharp cutbacks in a variety of projects. But such a disruption might equally well be accomplished by a sharp upturn in prosperity, with its sweeping rearrangements of status and the dramatic appearance of a multitude of unsuspected possibilities. However, either way—and such a qualification might actually be called the second element needed for a reform situation—there must be *some* maneuvering space, an absence of *total* crisis conditions. A total involvement of energies in a crisis would leave none for a reform movement.[48]

A further element typifying reform activity in America has been the absence of clear institutional arrangements for channeling radical energy. We have never had a traditional orientation for such activity; no institutionalized radicalism has ever existed here. For those who, like Bismarck, have known how to read them, such arrangements in European society—for instance, the social-democratic and quasi-revolutionary parties—have tended to

[48] This is a principle well known to labor leaders of the present day; it is one of their rules of thumb that the ideal setting for organizing activity is not in the trough of a depression, when poverty and hard times have become a reality (nor for that matter in a time of steady prosperity), but rather when things are either on the way up or on the way down. The classic statement of this idea was made by the French sociologist Émile Durkheim. Durkheim's problem was exactly parallel: tension produced by disrupted expectations. To measure this, he used the most extreme index he could find: the suicide rate in a given society. That rate increases, he discovered, not only with a sharp drop but also with a sharp upturn in prosperity. "If . . . industrial or financial crises increase suicides, this is not because they cause poverty, since crises of prosperity have the same result; it is because they are crises, that is, disturbances of the collective order. Every disturbance of equilibrium, even though it achieves greater comfort *and a heightening of general vitality,* is an impulse to voluntary death. Whenever serious readjustments take place in the social order, whether or not due to a sudden growth or to an unexpected catastrophe, men are more inclined to self-destruction." Émile Durkheim, *Suicide,* trans. John A. Spaulding and George Simpson (Glencoe, Ill.: Free Press, 1951), p. 246 (italics added). Thus the seemingly paradoxical connection between reform movements and suicide (each involving a form of aggression) lies in a condition from which either one or the other may be likely to result.

act as more or less dependable barometers of society's ills and discontents. The absence of anything of the sort in the America of the thirties and forties may in some measure account for the wild and unfocused quality of the various reform impulses of that period. This lack of channels seems to produce in the reformers a constant reconsideration of first principles, an urge to develop a great variety of new organizations,[49] and an overwhelming illusion of the individual's power to change society. While European radical movements have tended very often to *over*emphasize the institutional structure of their activity,[50] the case in the United States has never been anything but the opposite. The initial burst of energy is typically dissipated for lack of a structure, and instead of leaving some residue of an organization, it leaves, more often than not, nothing at all.

Still another element of interest is the role of the intellectual in a reform situation. In Europe, the intellectual institutionally connected—with church, labor movement, or the like—is seen to act, in a crisis, along specified lines. He produces explanations for the followers of the institution, and his formulations, as a matter of course, give the institution a central place in the solution of the crisis. Certain things are thus expected of the intellectual; his role has specifications. The intellectual without connections, chronically the case in America, finds himself in a fundamentally different position. Society normally asks little or nothing of him; a reform situation, on the other hand, seems to present him with a role. Yet even here the only pressures exerted on him involve the maintenance of a steady stream of new and exciting ideas; his

[49] Alexis de Tocqueville, traveling in the United States during a great reform epoch—the 1830's—was greatly struck by this. "The political associations that exist in the United States," he wrote, "are only a single feature in the midst of the immense assemblage of associations in that country. Americans of all ages, all conditions, and all dispositions constantly form associations. . . . If it is proposed to inculcate some truth or to foster some feeling by the encouragement of a great example, they form a society. Wherever at the head of some new undertaking you see the government in France, or a man of rank in England, in the United States you will be sure to find an association." *Democracy in America* (New York: Knopf, 1945), II, 106.

[50] Robert Michels, *Political Parties,* trans. Eden and Cedar Paul (Glencoe, Ill.: Free Press, 1949), describes and analyzes the inevitable bureaucratization of European Social Democratic movements.

only measurement of effect must be that of audience appeal; his principal question must continue to be, How many are listening? The pressures he does not feel are the concrete demands of an institution as such; he feels no direct responsibility for a clientele; he has, in short, no vested interest. The result for the intellectual is a situation of no limits. His reform thinking will tend to be erratic, emotional, compulsive, and abstract.

It is in such a setting that guilt—always a necessary element in any reform movement anywhere—comes to assume a unique and disporportionate role in American reform activity. A gnawing sense of responsibility for the ills of society at large appears to be experienced most readily in this country by groups relatively sheltered, by groups without connections and without clear and legitimate functions (a prime example being furnished by the Transcendentalists), and by people who have seen older and honored standards transformed, modified, or thrown aside.

Reforming energy, or a sense of social responsibility, could be designated in terms other than "guilt." But the conditions of American society have made such energy peculiarly a personal, an individual, phenomenon. It is the absence of clear channels for the harnessing of these drives that has made it so. Contrasted with the civilizations of Europe, our Protestant culture with its strong secular inclinations has been conspicuous for its lack of institutions, religious or secular, among whose functions has been the absorption and transformation of guilt. Guilt must be borne as an individual burden to a degree not to be observed elsewhere. Guilt in a structured situation has formalized outlets, limits within which it may be expressed constructively and with effect. Otherwise, it has no such channels. It will thus accumulate, like static electricity; it becomes aggressive, unstable, hard to control, often destructive. Guilt may at this point be transformed into implacable moral aggression: hatred of both the sinner and the sin.

The morally implacable American has always been seen by the European as somehow unpredictable and dangerous. On the other hand, the European, to that same American, has immemorially evoked suspicions of cynicism, expediency, and corruption. This is because, between ourselves and the Europeans, the most basic conceptions of morality—of sin, of "the good" and "the bad"—have traditionally lain poles apart. All such conceptions have inevitably been formulated, in our culture, from the viewpoint of the individual looking outward; the individual in America has historically insisted upon his right to define sin for himself. The complex life of Europe, lived out century after century in the same place, has never been able to afford this. There, it has traditionally been regarded as much too dangerous to intrust the definition of iniquity to inspired itinerant preachers and young men on the make. Too much has been at stake: it is through the eyes of society that such matters have been seen; it is society's voice that has articulated them; it is within society's institutions that such formulations have been set down, conserved, and woven into the ancient fabric of custom. Between America and Europe a staggering range of cultural differences rests upon this single point: the meaning of "sin."

Let us picture, if possible, a stark "sin situation": the quasi-feudal community of pre-nineteenth-century Europe. Here we find a setting in which the perversion of power, always possible, could and did have immediate consequences—a setting in which the strong might at any time exploit the weak. Here the social arrangements, tightly knit, could afford little *physical* latitude; it was rarely possible for the oppressed to uproot themselves and move away. The setting, thus, was one in which "sin" meant something concrete—one in which terms had to be made with sin then and there. Sin was defined; arrangements in law and custom were worked out in the course of things for construing the responsibilities of the strong and providing for the protection of the weak—the sacraments, *noblesse oblige,* "the right ordering of things." People who have thus lived with sin for centuries have become intimately acquainted with it; shock does not come to them so easily; their methods of dealing with sin do not appear as callous to themselves as to the innocent.

If, on the other hand, there were such a thing as a pure "innocence situation," it might look very much like nineteenth-century America. There, space and mobility prevented the development of a tight social structure in which one had to accept exploitation, aggression, lust, and avarice as a daily problem. There, in a symbolic if not quite a literal sense, the very space and mobility might offer something of a bargaining situation, functioning not only as a "safety valve" for the exploited but also as a warning to the exploiter. Such a setting is not the same as that in which the oppressed, having no such latitude as a possible alternative, must protect themselves by an intricate set of customs and standards which take into account the existence of sin—of man's tendency to exploit man. The result would be a different kind of conscience with dramatically different standards. The "innocence situation" in certain respects can make, and always has made, higher moral demands; for here the evidence seems to show, as it did to the Transcendentalists, that man's "nature" is indeed normally good. "Sin" thus becomes an abstraction, vague and sinister. One might still talk of greed and lust, but not concretely; social sins are indeed committed, but are somehow plotted in the dark by unseen forces. Such sins seem actually worse than if intimacy with them were more direct. Moreover, as social sin diminishes in concreteness and acquires an overwhelming emphasis on individual rather than social morality, sin is internalized and made "personal"; sins are invented which concern only oneself and the social consequences of which are relatively limited.[51]

It now remains only to ask what might happen when people to whom daily aggression is not a perennial problem, people who have no knowledge of the traditional mechanisms whereby such aggression is habitually controlled, are then brought face to face with concrete instances of violence, cruelty, lust, and injustice. The individual whose culture does not contain formalized arrangements for the handling of such matters feels himself personally involved. He pictures direct retribution; this being impossible, he is oppressed by the accumulation of guilt without means of outlet. Having no experience with limited ways of com-

[51] I am here referring to the sins of consumption—the consumption, for example, of those narcotics (alcohol, nicotine, and so on) which may be socially tolerated but which appear at the same time to symbolize personal corruption. The same is true of certain amusements (dancing, cards, the theater) which, through society's eyes, function to divert the lusts of the flesh into harmless channels but which, from a "personal" viewpoint, seem to represent—if not actually to embody—those very lusts. Even fornication has traditionally been regarded among us more as a matter of personal defilement than as an act having possible social consequences. Actually all this should be said in the past tense. It was a wholesome morality, so long as relatively few strains were put on it, but its breakdown, having taken place over the first half of the present century, is now all but complete, except in areas of comparative isolation. Unavoidably, but unfortunately, the breakdown was accompanied by a kind of cynicism heavily laced with naïveté, and it left many wounds.

ing to terms with exploitation, being pressed by cumulative and undischarged guilt, he makes an emotional demand for a total solution. Destroy the evil, he cries; root it up, wipe it out.

Such, then, are some of the considerations which make guilt a primary thing to watch in American reform movements. The easing of guilt is always a most important hidden function of such movements, and with this as a disproportionate element in their maintenance, we have a test for movements that seem to disintegrate without accomplishing anything; guilt may have been absorbed and discharged in ways which make unnecessary a literal attainment of the objective.[52] Let us now return to the reform movement which did not end that way—the one in which guilt was not pacifically discharged, in which nothing happened to alleviate its fever, its mounting aggression, its ultimate demand for a literal, a root-and-branch, solution.

4

THE TRANSCENDENTALIST AS ABOLITIONIST

It is not the primary aim here to exhibit the Transcendentalists as sole spiritual predecessors to the abolitionists. But there are at least two major reasons for according the Transcendentalists the attention which they have thus far received. The first is the historical fact that theirs was the closest thing to a concerted intellectual effort to be found in pre–Civil War America. Any other movement concerned with social policy, looking for intellectual cues, would have found no more distinguished a colloquium in which to seek them than the Transcendental circle of Concord. It was there, if anywhere, that "wisdom" was to be revealed; the best anywhere would be no better than that available at Concord. The most formidable of antislavery movements might thus have

[52] Such an example may be found in the Progressive Era of the early twentieth century, during which Theodore Roosevelt served so admirable a function as the symbolic focus for reform. Among the most notable impulses of that period was the antitrust movement, prosecuted with such strenuosity by the President and with such minimal objective consequences. His successor, President Taft, who had none of Roosevelt's flair, was very unpopular among reformers, though his administration prosecuted twice as many antitrust suits and in half the time. For a discussion of the "guilt" theme, see Richard Hofstadter's *Age of Reform* (New York: Knopf, 1955), pp. 173–212.

gathered its strength from the strength of the Transcendentalists, while its weaknesses would very likely have been their weaknesses. In any case, whatever the actual intentions, the abolitionists could not have duplicated the intellectual pattern of the Transcendentalists more precisely if they had tried.

The other reason for making key figures of the Transcendentalists lies in the fact, already noted, that the very time at which they flourished coincides with the launching of the great reform impulses. The tensions and dislocations of the age were nowhere more fully felt than in New England, the region in which they lived. It was an age in which they, and many others on the eastern seaboard less sensitive than they, were witnessing rapid economic and political changes not easy to understand. There were extraordinary developments in transportation during the 1830–40 decade; the great new markets created by the new roads, canals, and railroads built during those years were forcing radically changed relationships upon local merchants, craftsmen, and farmers, who were having to compete more and more on regional than on local terms. In this same decade occurred the greatest expansion in small factories of any comparable period prior to the Civil War—a development which tended to disrupt old stabilized craft arrangements in which mechanic and customer had been used to dealing directly with each other. It was also in the 1830's that the full impact of the frontier was felt; nothing like the population increase in the Old Northwest during that decade had hitherto been seen; the population of that region, negligible in 1800, now exceeded that of New England. These movements of population, plus their sheer physical increase, made themselves felt in drastic changes in political relationships; political experience was forced upon groups that had previously never needed to acquire it. The democratized relationships which emerged with the appearance of new political arrangements—universal suffrage, the mass party, and the political machine—were not the same ones familiar to Federalist New England a generation earlier; they required a fundamentally different adjustment to government. The economic madness of the thirties—the internal improvements mania and the land boom—dazzled thousands with a whole new range of opportunities and aspirations. It was a sharply upturning prosperity situation with a thousand new alternatives for action; it was at the same time one in which limits were being broken ev-

erywhere, in which traditional expectations were disrupted profoundly—a classic instance of that tension-producing state which
Émile Durkheim named *"anomie."*[53] It was against such a background that Transcendentalism and other reform movements
first appeared, and abolitionism began to flourish.[54] Expectations

[53] This was the term, roughly meaning "broken limits" which Durkheim borrowed from the Greek to designate the kind of setting crucial
to his theory of suicide. See above, n. 48.

[54] This might account for a heightened receptivity to reform ideas
among people in general, but it does not necessarily explain why the
leaders of reform might be more likely to come from some groups than
from others. This problem was first considered by Frank Tracy Carlton
in a remarkably perceptive essay, written over fifty years ago, which is
very applicable to the Transcendentalists. Carlton called attention to the
psychological stresses that are likely to occur within old ruling groups
in an era of economic change. "The diversion of business into new
channels and the rise of new political and social ideals," he wrote, "left
a portion of the old leaders and their families stranded and outside the
active business and social current of events. An old ruling class was
'dying out in a blaze of intellectual fireworks.' . . . A class which is
losing its hold upon social and economic supremacy invariably produces
humanitarian leaders." Frank T. Carlton, "Humanitarianism, Past and
Present," *International Journal of Ethics,* XVII (October, 1906), 52.
Avery Craven, in his *Coming of the Civil War* (New York: Scribner,
1942; rev. ed., Chicago: University of Chicago Press, 1957), implicitly
accepted Carlton's reasoning on the motivations of humanitarianism.
(See chap. vi, "The Northern Attack on Slavery.") Such general assertions could of course lead to misleading conclusions regarding the origins
of the anxieties and tensions exhibited by the Transcendentalists. It might
be assumed, in their case, that careers of dignity, prestige, and power—
those of jurist, statesman, merchant, or minister—were no longer open
to them, that positions of leadership in the community, formerly taken
by fathers or grandfathers who had followed such careers, were now
closed to the sons. But here we have a difficulty. Most of the Transcendentalist group (quite aside from prior family connections) were men of
high ability and learning; there was no inherent reason why they should
have been "prevented" from occupying such careers—the careers per se
were actually more numerous than ever. There were more factories, more
businesses, heightened demands for politicians and lawyers with the
democratization of politics and the bar, and new churches were springing
up every day. Indeed, most of the Transcendentalists were—or had been—
ministers themselves. And yet the argument, if properly qualified, has a
validity which is well worth unraveling. Such careers *were* indeed more
"available" than ever, but the very dynamics of this fact resulted in a
relative devaluation of the roles associated with them. The respect which

were actually disrupted two ways, not only by turning sharply upward but also, with the sudden panic of 1837 and the subsequent depression, by dropping acutely. After the crisis years of 1838 and 1839, in which there was relatively little reform activity, the humanitarian projects burst forth once more in the early forties in greater profusion and with greater intensity than ever.

By the 1840's many of the Transcendentalists were themselves in effect becoming abolitionists. To a certain extent they had been introduced to antislavery by their elder mentor, William Ellery Channing. They had shared at first Channing's repugnance to the more aggressive Garrisonian type of abolitionism, but as time went on they moved irresistibly toward more and more extreme positions. And as they did so, it is remarkable to note how their approach to slavery followed the same pattern as their approach to everything else.

We see once more their unwillingness to think in institutional terms. Theodore Parker, for instance, who had as wide an audience as any of the group, would not really think of slavery as an institution. Parker had read more widely in that subject than any man of his time; he knew all about slavery in Latin America and about the great variations which it had assumed in the ancient world; there is little that we now know on the law of slavery in this country and elsewhere that Theodore Parker could not have written a century ago. But although Parker used this information again and again in his attacks on slavery, as may be seen in his numerous papers and lectures on that subject,[55] he never stopped to analyze the way these variations may have pivoted upon radically differing institutional arrangements. Nor did he ever give serious thought to specific improvements in the slave's condition

---

such roles once carried in the community had been downgraded. Thus the young man of talent, learning, and sensibility with ties to an earlier era—either of family or simply of local tradition—was just not attracted to those careers in the way he might once have been (in the career of Henry Adams, at a later period in our history, we have the most poignant symbol of this). In *this* sense such a group as the Transcendentalists could quite properly be called a "displaced elite." The latest, best, and most precise version of the argument is David Donald's "Toward a Reconsideration of Abolitionists," in *Lincoln Reconsidered: Essays on the Civil War Era* (New York: Knopf, 1956), pp. 19–36.

[55] *Works of Theodore Parker* (Boston: American Unitarian Association, 1907–13), [V], *The Slave Power.*

by concentrating on specific features of the institution of American slavery. He was fully aware, for example, that marriage was sacred and inviolate in most other slave cultures, and although he attacked the American system on this basis, among others, he never thought of such a feature as a specific object of reform and of focusing his energies upon that. He used it instead as a justification for full emancipation; he used his learning in the role of moral agitator, not of intellectual.[56]

Not only did these men fail to analyze slavery itself as an institution, but they failed equally to consider and exploit institutional means for subverting it. The primary choice as it appeared to most of them was simply, "Shall I oppose it, or shall I ignore it?" If the former, their action consisted principally in speaking out in public against it. Their relationship with abolition societies was never anything but equivocal. Neither Emerson nor Thoreau ever joined any of them; William Henry Channing and Frederic Hedge in the thirties joined a short-lived organization which had been formed to counter not only slavery but also Garrisonian abolition; James Freeman Clarke often attended meetings of the Anti-Slavery Society and made speeches there, but he was little concerned with the matter of nominal membership. Theodore Parker was of course his own one-man society. They gave little thought to the use of existing institutions—of the potentialities, say, of the national church organizations—which was certainly no accident, for they had little regard for their own Unitarian church ("corpse-cold") as an institution dedicated to moral regeneration: "this icehouse of Unitarianism," Emerson had called it, "all external."[57] Their pulpits were in effect platforms for personal agitation. Organization was distrusted more or less for its own sake.

[56] This unusual obtuseness to the possibility of piecemeal reform could readily be understood in a single-minded fanatic like Garrison, but Parker was a man of extraordinary talents and a wide breadth of knowledge and interests; it is such cases as his that impel one to examine the social and institutional conditions amid which moral and intellectual energy is expended. Parker had had fifteen years of experience in New England reform movements before he turned his attention to slavery, and he had good reason to know that major changes in social institutions are not brought about in a day. And yet in the case of slavery the only solution he ever recognized was full and immediate emancipation. See Commager, *Parker*, p. 201, on the delay in Parker's concern over slavery.

[57] *Journals*, VI, 218.

Every "cause," Emerson thought—abolition, Unitarianism, or what not—"becomes speedily a little shop, where the article, let it have been at first never so subtle and ethereal, is now made up into portable and convenient cakes, and retailed in small quantities to suit purchasers."[58] Henry Thoreau disdained the use of any institutions at all for combating slavery—even the resources of government itself:

I do not hesitate to say, that those who call themselves Abolitionists should at once effectively withdraw their support, both in person and property, from the government of Massachusetts. . . . I think that it is enough if they have God on their side, without waiting for that other one.[59]

It was thus very difficult for the Transcendentalists to think of slavery reform as anything but an individual concern—a question between a man and his own conscience.

I know this well [wrote Thoreau], that if one thousand, if one hundred, if ten men whom I could name,—if ten *honest* men only, —ay, if *one* HONEST man, in this State of Massachusetts, *ceasing to hold slaves,* were actually to withdraw from this copartnership, and be locked up in the county jail therefor, it would be the abolition of slavery in America.[60]

A strongly individualistic approach to the subject was generally matched by a conception of the object—the slave—which was itself individualistic. The Transcendentalists were preoccupied with the natural essence of the slave, when they considered him at all. The question was not so much what the institution had made of him but what it prevented him from being—his naked, inviolate self. Thus, referring to "faculties," "moral genius," and "intellect," they asked whether the Negro were naturally "inferior" and decided that, as James Freeman Clarke insisted, it was "a mistake to speak of the African as an inferior race to the Caucasian."[61] This, for Emerson (convinced by the exploits of Toussaint L'Ouverture that the Negro was indeed a man) settled the principal issue: "Here is man: and if you have man, black or white is an insignif-

<hr/>

[58] "The Transcendentalist," in *Works,* I, 327.

[59] "Civil Disobedience," in *Writings,* X, *Miscellanies,* 147.

[60] *Ibid.,* p. 148.

[61] *Slavery in the United States: A Sermon Delivered on Thanksgiving Day, 1842* (Boston: B. H. Greene, 1843), p. 23.

icance. The intellect,—that is miraculous! Who has it, has the talisman: his skin and bones, though they were of the color of night, are transparent, and everlasting stars shine through, with attractive beams."[62] The Negro was a man, and it was thus only the corrupt institution of slavery which stood between him and the infinite potentialities residing in every man, potentialities which might be unfolded by the benefits of education. "The black child," Clarke predicted, "will learn to read and write as fast or faster than the white child, having equal advantages."[63] But by focusing upon "race" rather than culture, they could ignore a range of possibilities: that a man's humanity, such as he has, lies not in his naked essence but in his culture—and that when a corrupt culture has corrupted his "nature," it is less than half a solution simply to strip away his culture and leave him *truly* naked.

The tendency was in every sense away from concreteness. It was not really a question of subverting the institution of slavery, which would have amounted to compromise; little thought was given to the concrete terms on which the child's "infinite potentialities" might be developed—no plans were really formulated for that—but rather what it came to was simply the question of whether slavery was right or wrong. Subordinating everything to its rightness or wrongness was the theme of all the Transcendentalists' sermons; slavery became not really a social problem but a moral abstraction. And once they came to the decision that it was wrong, which they all did, the burden of guilt for its continued existence became theirs and that of their hearers.

[62] "Address Delivered in Concord on the Anniversary of the Emancipation of the Negroes in the British West Indies, August 1, 1844," *Works,* XI, 172. Emerson, carrying the doctrine of self-reliance even into this question, came rather close to saying that the Negro should really emancipate himself, now that the principal fact—that of his innate humanity—had been established. "All the songs and newspapers and money-subscriptions and vituperation of such as do not think with us, will avail nothing against a fact. I say to you, you must save yourself, black or white, man or woman; other help is none. I esteem the occasion of this jubilee to be the proud discovery that the black race can contend with the white; that, in the great anthem which we call history, a piece of many parts and vast compass, after playing a long time a very low and subdued accompaniment, they perceive the time arrived when they can strike in with effect and take a master's part in the music." *Ibid.,* pp. 172–73.

[63] Clarke, *Slavery,* p. 24.

Was this primarily a matter of temperament? Were their minds innately predisposed to abstraction? To guilty torment? It is not vital that we know this. We are more interested in the mechanics of their social situation. In a reform setting guilt may and naturally does operate as one salutary stimulus to action. But there is an essential difference between a case of that sort and the one in which guilt is the only dynamic element sustaining action. The difference lies in what is to be done with objective alternatives in thought and procedure. When such alternatives can be launched through institutional channels as specific policy proposals, they have some chance of issuing in action and of being tested and modified in the process, of being translated by a series of formal and informal stages into policy itself. The point is reached where such policy will take its cue not so much from the conscience as from the facts. But what becomes of objective alternatives and "the facts" without such channels? They are short-circuited: every new bit of information, instead of clarifying choices for action, is simply transformed into another increment of static guilt. It was just so with these men. They could proceed only in a vicious circle; new knowledge meant added knowledge of evil, which could only mean fresh torment for the seekers.

How this process worked is nowhere better seen than in the thinking of William Ellery Channing, the gentle preceptor of the Transcendentalists. Channing in the mid-1830's had written a remarkably perceptive analysis of slavery in which he clearly saw what the institution had made of the Negro as a man—that it had stripped him of self-respect, that amid its arrangements he had been "trained to cowardice and low vices," and that where adult morality was not demanded of him he was prey to every kind of licentiousness, intemperance, dishonesty, and theft. He saw that all this was in the problem's foreground—that while slavery was "radically, essentially evil," the fixing of guilt was by no means its most pressing urgency. "Because a great injury is done to another, it does not follow that he who does it is a depraved man," he wrote. "Our ancestors at the North were concerned in the slave trade. . . . Were they, therefore, the offscouring of the earth? Were not some of them among the best of their times?" Channing, in urging that slavery be undermined by specific improvements, took what was virtually a functional approach to the institution: "It cannot, like other institutions, be perpetuated by

[171]

being improved. To improve it is to prepare the way for its subversion."[64]

But that was in 1835, and the argument was doomed to a short life, even in Channing's own mind. Six years later Channing was scarcely the same man. In 1835 he had written, with calm reasonableness, "Let it not be said, that when new light is offered him [the slaveholder], he is criminal in rejecting it. Are we all willing to receive new light?" Yet he now charged, in 1841, that "a people, upholding or in any way giving countenance to slavery, contract guilt in proportion to the light which is thrown on the injustice and evils of this institution . . . [and] the weight of guilt on this nation is great and increasing." The "light" to which he referred was as follows:

The wars, the sacked and burning villages, the kidnapping and murders of Africa, which begin this horrible history; the crowded hold, the chains, stench, suffocation, burning thirst, and agonies of the slave ship; the loathsome diseases and enormous waste of life in the middle passage; the wrongs and sufferings, of the plantation, with its reign of terror and force, its unbridled lust, its violations of domestic rights and charities—these all are revealed.

"To shut our eyes against all this," he warned, "to shut our ears and hearts . . . this, surely, is a guilt which the justice of God cannot wink at, and on which insulted humanity, religion, and freedom call down fearful retribution."[65]

What had happened? Channing's treatise of 1835, which went through several editions, had been enthusiastically commended in antislavery circles. But it was only in the argument's simplest and most abstract form—its assertion that slavery was an evil—that it was actually accepted, even by Channing's closest followers, to say nothing of his wider audience, and it was on this basis that it was both praised and attacked. The fact was that there was no way for Channing's argument in all its ramifications to fall into the hands of institutions which could process it into concrete proposals of policy; the history of an idea from thought to action is, to repeat, clearly more than one step. In a society dominated by institutions it would be conceivable that the social guilt generated

[64] William Ellery Channing, *Slavery* (4th ed.; Boston: J. Munroe, 1836), pp. 51–53, 56–58, 68–69, 118.

[65] William Ellery Channing, *Emancipation* (New York: American Anti-Slavery Society, 1841), pp. 38–39.

by such polemics might find release at specific points and in measured increments; ideas might be adjusted in accordance with the institution's actual experience in dealing with them. But a society as devoid of structure as Channing's had little to offer him in the way of such a testing ground; the best he could do with his ideas was to throw them out on the general public, where they could only be received and dealt with at the level of simple moral abstraction. Ideas in such a form can feed only on themselves and on the psychic tensions which they produce, and to maintain the level of excitement they must be made less and less qualified. Thus we may suppose that Channing, in order to maintain his audience (and perhaps his own self-respect), would have had to respond to increasing pressures for making the moral side of his position more and more extravagant. With no tests other than audience response—with no *visible* progress being made in changing the institution of slavery—the only thing that more knowledge and awareness of it could produce would be an added burden of guilt both in his followers and in himself. And for that matter, Channing's own basic commitment to a philosophy inherently individualistic must have made whatever hold he had on his original insight a very tenuous one at best.

With the other Transcendentalists it was the same. Channing's nephew, William Henry Channing, had counseled himself, sometime between 1831 and 1833: "Not excitement. Calm, deep, solemn question. Sympathy with slave-owner. What can he do? Sympathy with the slave." He would subsequently pencil "shame" and "alas" alongside his early writings on that subject. Upon reading *Uncle Tom's Cabin* he would exclaim in anguish,

O Heaven! How patient are God and nature with human diabolism! It seems to me that I have never begun to do anything for antislavery yet. And now, with one's whole heart bleeding, what can we do? . . . How this book must cut a true-hearted Southerner to the quick!—cut us all, for we verily are all guilty together.[66]

Certain groups had at one point advanced an objective scheme of compensated emancipation which threw Channing into great alarm because he was afraid it might really succeed. Such was the matter-of-factness of the plan, and so intense was Channing's absorption with penitence and atonement rather than policy, that he

[66] Frothingham, *Memoir*, p. 259.

was actually moved in 1853 to write a long and agitated letter to Salmon P. Chase urging some means of preventing it—some nobler plan of "common sacrifice" for slavery's removal, shared equally ("We are all guilty"), "in which sacrifice of course the slaveholders must bear their full proportion"[67] James Freeman Clarke, in praising the elder Channing's early essay on slavery, had written serenely in 1836, "Though the system of slavery is a wrong one, I deny that to hold slaves is always to commit sin."[68] But though greatly opposed at this time to guilt-mongering Garrisonians, Clarke in the forties changed his mind after "seeing something of their grand and noble work";[69] by 1859, declaring that "either Slavery is right or it is wrong"—that there could be "no intermediate answer"—he announced: "There is an 'irrepressible conflict' between Freedom and Slavery. The opposition is radical and entire; there can be no peace nor permanent truce between them, till one has conquered the other."[70] Meanwhile, Theodore Parker savagely lashed guilty Bostonians, Northerners, Southerners, every citizen of the United States and his ancestors and for all generations, and himself; such was *his* intellectual contribution to the problem of slavery:

Think of the nation's deed, done continually and afresh. God shall hear the voice of your brother's blood, long crying from the ground;

[67] *Ibid.*, pp. 261–62. Channing even at this late date was still afraid of colonization schemes (as well as compensated emancipation) and thought that they too should be forestalled.

[68] James Freeman Clarke, *Autobiography, Diary, and Correspondence,* ed. Edward Everett Hale (Boston: Houghton Mifflin, 1891), p. 220.

[69] *Ibid.*, p. 221.

[70] "Causes and Consequences of the Affair at Harpers Ferry" (sermon, printed as pamphlet, Boston, 1859), p. 4. Even Emerson and Thoreau, neither of whom would join any antislavery societies (Thoreau would not join anything), had themselves, by the 1850's, become more or less chronic prey to guilt over slavery and to thoughts of atonement. Emerson burned with "painful auguring" at the news of the Fugitive Slave Law and thought that the wealth of Boston should be used "to be clean of it." "I would pay a little of my estate with joy," he wrote in his journal, "for this calamity darkens my days." *Journals,* VIII, 202. John Brown's martyrdom threw Henry Thoreau into agonies. " 'But he won't gain anything by it,' " he mocked. "Well, no, I don't suppose he could get four-and-sixpence a day for being hung, take the year round; but then he stands a chance to save a considerable part of his soul. . . ." "A Plea for Captain John Brown," in *Writings,* X, *Miscellanies,* 208.

His justice asks you even now, "America, where is thy brother?" This is the answer which America must give: "Lo, he is there in the rice-swamps of the South, in her fields teeming with cotton and the luxuriant cane. He was weak and I seized him; naked and I bound him; ignorant, poor and savage, and I over-mastered him. I laid on his feebler shoulders my grievous yoke. I have chained him with my fetters; beat him with my whip. Other tyrants had dominion over him, but my finger was on his human flesh. I am fed with his toil; fat, voluptuous on his sweat, and tears, and blood. I stole the father, stole also the sons, and set them to toil; his wife and daughters are a pleasant spoil to me. Behold the children also of thy servant and his handmaidens—sons swarthier than their sire. Askest thou for the African? I have made him a beast. Lo, there Thou hast what is thine."[71]

5

THE ABOLITIONIST AS TRANSCENDENTALIST

If intellectual cues for the solution of social problems were to come from anywhere, one supposes that it would be from within such a circle as this. Whether their cues were actually followed or not makes little difference; what does matter is that the thinking of those men whom we specifically remember as abolitionists—whose claim on history rests on their association with the abolitionist movement as such—should follow the very same pattern.

The anti-institutionalism so characteristic of the Transcendentalists reached heights of extravagance in the speeches and writings of the radical abolitionists. "The difficulty of the present day and with us is," declared Wendell Phillips, "we are bullied by institutions."[72] They attacked the church both North and South as the "refuge and hiding-place" of slavery;[73] the sects—particularly

[71] *The Slave Power*, pp. 116–17.

[72] "Public Opinion," in *Speeches, Lectures, and Letters* (Boston: Lee & Shepard, 1892), p. 46.

[73] *Anti-Slavery Bugle,* June 20, 1845; quoted in Arthur Young Lloyd, *The Slavery Controversy* (Chapel Hill: University of North Carolina Press, 1939), p. 94. The *Bugle* asserted that to attack the church would thus be to strike at the "monster" itself—slavery. This was one of the central features of abolitionist doctrine. "The abolitionists of the United States . . . have been fully convinced that the American churches were mainly answerable for the continuance of American slavery. . . ." *Slavery and the Internal Slave Trade in the United States of America; Being Replies to Questions Transmitted by the Committee of the British*

the Methodist[74]—were denounced singly and severally, and Stephen Symonds Foster condemned the entire clergy as a "brotherhood of thieves."[75] Foster also reviled both Whig and Democratic parties for countenancing slavery;[76] Edmund Quincy, Wendell Phillips, and William Lloyd Garrison repudiated the Constitution itself; resolution after resolution was passed in various societies

and Foreign Anti-Slavery Society (London, 1841), p. 196. This is by no means to say that abolitionists did not use the pulpit in their attacks; on the contrary, the churches functioned as indispensable sounding boards for the moral energy of these reformers. But it was perfectly possible, and not at all inconsistent, to attack the *institutional* character of religious establishments without implicating the specific *local* congregation before whom one stood or the specific pulpit from which one preached. Christians were not in this period being asked to dissolve their own fellowship or to raze their buildings, but they *were* exhorted to throw out as much of their institutional baggage as possible, so that they might approach closer to God; they were urged to consider themselves as forming not so much an institution as an assembly of individual souls seeking purification. It was characteristic of the age, with the democratization of religion, that broad organizations should be breaking down into narrower ones, that ecclesiastical traditions, forms, and "confining usages" should be denounced not only as shackling to the individual spirit but also as so much dead weight upon society at large—encumbrances whose very inertia resisted the clearing-away of society's corruptions, among which was the institution of slavery. It was in such a sense that the extent of the church's institutionalization appeared the very extent of slavery's irremovability.

[74] Garrison called it "a cage of unclean birds," S. S. Foster said that it was "more corrupt than any house of ill-fame in the city of New York," and the *Anti-Slavery Bugle* pronounced it "the most diabolical of all the associations, of our nation." Gilbert Hobbs Barnes, *The Anti-Slavery Impulse, 1830–1844* (New York: Appleton-Century, 1933), p. 93; Lloyd, *Slavery Controversy,* p. 96.

[75] Stephen S. Foster, *The Brotherhood of Thieves* (Concord, N.H.: Parker Pillsbury, 1886).

[76] "The man who votes with either of the great political parties does necessarily legalize slavery, both of these parties being pledged not only to execute all the provision of the Constitution in favor of slavery, but to go even farther, and perpetuate the system, with all it abominations, in the District of Columbia. . . .

"No intelligent person, man or woman, who is in concert with the Whig or Democratic party, or who votes for any other than an uncompromising abolitionist for civil office, or silently countenances such voting, can say, in truth, he is innocent of these crimes." *Ibid.,* pp. 25, 27.

condemning the Union ("No Union with Slaveholders"); and Garrison actually "nominated Jesus Christ to the Presidency of the United States and the World."[77]

No matter [wrote Garrison], though . . . every party should be torn by dissensions, every sect dashed into fragments, the national compact dissolved, the land filled with the horrors of a civil and a servile war—still, slavery must be buried in the grave of infamy, beyond the possibility of a resurrection. If the State cannot survive the anti-slavery agitation, then let the State perish. If the Church must be cast down by the strugglings of Humanity to be free, then let the Church fall, and its fragments be scattered to the four winds of heaven, never more to curse the earth. If the American Union cannot be maintained, except by immolating human freedom on the altar of tyranny, then let the American Union be consumed by a living thunderbolt, and no tear be shed over its ashes. If the Republic must be blotted out from the roll of nations, by proclaiming liberty to the captives, then let the Republic sink beneath the waves of oblivion, and a shout of joy, louder than the voice of many waters, fill the universe at its extinction.[78]

An anti-institutional attitude so pronounced as this could hardly be confined merely to doctrine. It was bound to have disintegrating effects on the organizational development of the very societies which promoted it. Whereas such societies did indeed flourish and expand in the early and middle 1830's, the truth is that the life of *institutional* antislavery was doomed to brevity: the story of abolitionism's spread is not, after all, that of the strengthening of the societies as such. On the contrary, the national organization, after a luminous but short career, was all but extinguished during the depression years of the late thirties and never really recovered. The story of the movement is to be found elsewhere.

We have elsewhere noted that the democratization of all the major institutions once familiar to American life had to a profound degree worked to undermine those same institutions, and that in a larger sense such institutional breakdown was the very condition, or price, of national success.[79] But, in at least one area, the price of democracy was very high. For a fatal process was at

[77] Barnes, *Anti-Slavery Impulse,* p. 93.

[78] "No Compromise with Slavery," *Selections from the Writings and Speeches of William Lloyd Garrison* (Boston: R. F. Wallcut, 1852), p. 139.

[79] See above, pp. 142–46.

work, and that process was nothing less than the very democratization, North and South, of the controversy over slavery. The tragic flaw of an otherwise singularly favored society was the absence of mechanisms for checking such a development—the absence of mechanisms which might permit a range of alternatives in sentiment and idea to be crystallized and maintained and which might prevent the development of a lowest common denominator of feeling in each section, widely enough shared as to provide a democratic ground for war.[80]

An appreciation of this depends to some extent upon chronology. Viewing in sequence a little of the movement's early career, we are given a sense of how it was that action became less and less institutional precisely as it became more and more democratized. As of, say, 1835 the spectrum of antislavery sentiment could still, for conceptual purposes, be divided into four rough categories. The first of these, colonization, involved an enterprise which had been founded under the most distinguished sponsorship. The American Colonization Society, established in 1817 under the presidency of Judge Bushrod Washington, had numbered among its prominent adherents such men as John Marshall, James Madison, James Monroe, and Henry Clay, and its program—the deportation of the Negro race to Liberia—had at first commanded wide support both North and South. By proposing to get rid of the free Negroes (an unwanted element in the slaveholding community) the plan was offered to the South as a safeguard for slavery, and at the same time, since it promised to make manumissions more feasible, more acceptable, and therefore more numerous, it was promoted in the North as an antislavery program. A second variety of antislavery might be called *philosophical abolitionism*—the position held by such writers as Francis Wayland and William Ellery Channing. Wayland and Channing both acknowledged that insofar as slavery partook of evil it ought to be abandoned; yet each was impressed by the great likelihood that

[80] There was, actually, one such mechanism: the political party system, which stood unique and unprotected. If a separate essay on politics were to be included in this work, it would emphasize the way in which the conservative function of this one institution was eventually broken down —though only under the most merciless pressure and after the most prodigious resistance—by the combined forces of proslavery and antislavery.

this would not happen immediately, and accordingly each gave attention to the improvement of the institution and of relations between master and slave.[81]

A third position was *gradual immediatism,* or "immediate emancipation gradually accomplished." This was the doctrine formulated by the New York Committee for a National Anti-Slavery Society, which had been organized in 1831 under the auspices of the philanthropic brothers Arthur and Lewis Tappan and which included such ardent abolitionists as Simeon Jocelyn, William Goodell, Joshua Leavitt, Theodore Dwight Weld, and, later, the reformed slaveholder James G. Birney. This group was the nucleus from which in 1833 was formed the American Anti-Slavery Society. Inspired by the success of British abolitionists in their efforts to bring about immediate emancipation in the West Indies,[82] yet sensible of the social turmoil sure to attend such a program if effected in the Southern states, the committee brought forth a modification of the British formula for their own purposes. They conceived that edicts of emancipation, promulgated immediately, might then be followed, not by immediate and unconditional civil and political rights, but rather by a series of grad-

[81] Channing's early views have already been touched upon (above, pp. 171–72). Wayland was president of Brown University and professor of moral philosophy there. His *Elements of Moral Science* was for some time a standard text in colleges both North and South. In it he asserted that in principle slavery was evil, but he also recognized that the moral problems which slavery raised were not to be disposed of merely by saying that they would not exist if slavery were done away with; until the time when slavery might be abolished, a master-slave morality had to be provided for, recognized, and adhered to. "Thus, we see, that the Christian religion not only forbids slavery, but that it also provides the only method in which, after it has once been established, it may be abolished, and that with entire safety and benefit to both parties. By instilling the right moral dispositions into the bosom of the master and of the slave, it teaches the one the duty of reciprocity, and the other the duty of submission; and thus, without tumult, without disorder, without revenge, but by the real moral improvement of both parties, restores both to the relation towards each other intended by their Creator." *Elements of Moral Science* (New York: Cooke & Co., 1835), p. 229.

[82] As a matter of fact, British emancipation was anything but "immediate," when the movement is regarded as a whole. It was the culmination of unremitting effort carried on over a period of many years. Only in the final stages was it possible to call for immediate emancipation. See below, pp. 202–4.

uated stages, such as peonage or apprenticeship, whereby the slave might ultimately be prepared for full civic status. A final form of antislavery, the simplest and most direct, was *immediate and unqualified emancipation*. This was the doctrine of William Lloyd Garrison and his followers, and it had been laid down in the first number of Garrison's *Liberator* in 1831.

The chronology of the societies during the 1830's is the story of how all these positions would blur together in men's minds: of how the distinctions between them would for practical purposes break down almost completely, of how, in the ranks of organized antislavery, abolitionism per se would usurp the field from colonization, and of how "gradual immediatism" would merge with "immediate immediatism." The year 1831 saw the appearance of the *Liberator* and a tiny New England Anti-Slavery Society dominated by Garrison; it also saw the formation of the New York Committee. These groups differed sharply in their principles and were mutually hostile, but both organizations attacked the Colonization Society with great energy. Colonization, its impracticality becoming daily more obvious, and its moral footing—equivocal to say the least—having made it less and less satisfying to the Northerner who had any interest in slavery, was by the end of that decade thoroughly discredited as a tenable antislavery position.[83] In 1833 a national abolition organization was established

[83] For the aims and program of the colonizationists, see Early Lee Fox, *The American Colonization Society, 1817–1840* (Baltimore: Johns Hopkins Press, 1919), pp. 142–45. Fox and other writers have claimed that the leaders of this movement were practical men who recognized the need for a gradualist program. While there is much to be said for this viewpoint—perhaps more than has in fact been said—the society's ultimate vulnerability lay in the fact that its program was designed for men who felt guilty about slavery but did not want to do anything drastic about altering the institution itself. With the intensification of antislavery feeling in the 1830's, the colonizationists found themselves without resources for protecting their movement against the moral pressures of radical abolitionism. As their own moral purposes were more and more called into question, the moderates tended to lose their energy; at the same time, the society's best antislavery organizers, such as James G. Birney, were irresistibly co-opted into more radical groups. The work no longer provided the personal satisfactions required by a really dedicated man. The conversion process in Birney's case is described in Betty Fladeland, *James Gillespie Birney: Slaveholder to Abolitionist* (Ithaca: Cornell University Press, 1955), pp. 75–89. See esp. Birney's letter to the Colonization Society giving the reasons for his resignation, *ibid.*, p. 85. For the ease with

—the American Anti-Slavery Society—in which the Tappans and their New York allies were the moving spirits but at whose first convention Garrison usurped the limelight. Garrison had just returned from England, where the British abolitionists, in the glow of their own success, had conferred upon him their apostolic blessing, Garrison having convinced them that it was in fact he who was the major figure of American abolitionism. His alliance with the new society was, however, an uneasy one, for Garrison continued to preach unqualified immediatism while the New York formula of gradual immediatism remained for the time being the society's official doctrine. But the subtleties of that formula soon proved embarrassing.

The following year, 1834, saw Theodore Dwight Weld, the society's most persuasive agent, quietly at work among the students of Lane Seminary, a theological school in Cincinnati which had been heavily endowed by the Tappans. In May of that year a great debate was conducted by the student body to consider the merits of abolition. The meeting, actually more a revival than a "debate," lasted eighteen nights, and after much prayerful inquiry the majority, some of whom were Southerners, experienced conversion and "a profound sense of personal guilt for the system of slavery."[84] They resolved to labor as a group in the cause of "im-

---

which Garrison (whose "practical" successes in other respects were not impressive) crushed the colonization movement in New England, see Roman J. Zorn, "The New England Anti-Slavery Society: Pioneer Abolition Organization," *Journal of Negro History*, XLIII (July, 1957), 157–76.

[84] The words in quotation marks are those of Gilbert Barnes. Mr. Barnes's book, *The Antislavery Impulse*, is far and away the most perceptive on this subject. The above paragraphs draw heavily on his material and on his conception of antislavery in its organized phase. Recent works which are also very useful (in addition to the Fladeland biography of Birney cited above, n. 83) are Benjamin P. Thomas, *Theodore Weld, Crusader for Freedom* (New Brunswick: Rutgers University Press, 1950); and Russel B. Nye, *William Lloyd Garrison and the Humanitarian Reformers* (Boston: Little, Brown, 1955). The best argument in defense of pure extremist agitation is Richard Hofstadter's essay on Wendell Phillips in *The American Political Tradition* (New York: Knopf, 1949), pp. 135–61. Hofstadter's point, made with considerable astuteness, is that the patrician Phillips understood the unique role of the agitator in a democratic society, was willing to accept its limitations, and played it with perception and finesse.

mediate emancipation gradually carried out."[85] When President Lyman Beecher and the trustees disapproved of their plans (to the consternation of the Tappans), fifty-three of the students withdrew, leaving the seminary virtually empty, and in 1835 moved into newly founded Oberlin College. The Lane rebels eventually covered a tremendous territory in the Middle West, holding revivals and making thousands of converts. They were easily the most effective of any single group working in the cause. Yet the very intensity of their devotion and the technique of their activity required that in matters of doctrine they should be as simple and direct as possible. They could attack colonization, which they did to great effect (they had already seduced a leading colonizationist, James G. Birney, into their ranks); but the very nature of the conversion which they were working to achieve in their hearers was such that intellectual arguments and positive plans of their own actually menaced their objectives (Weld had been specifically instructed to stay away from plans);[86] they disavowed Garrisonism, which was too radical, but they found that the New York doctrine to which they were committed was much too subtle and smacked of sophistry.[87] The magic word "immediate" was the key to their dilemma (how could emancipation be immediate and yet not immediate?), and they very quickly discovered the solution: *immediate repentance of sin*—all else would follow. It was on this basis that they achieved their successes. But

[85] A variation of this formula, carrying the same meaning, was "gradual emancipation, immediately begun."

[86] "Do not allow yourself to be drawn away from the main object, to exhibit a detailed PLAN of abolition; for men's consciences will be greatly relieved from the feeling of present duty, by any objections or difficulties which they can find or fancy in your plan." "Particular Instructions to T. D. Weld upon his commission as Agent for the year 1834," in Gilbert Barnes and Dwight Dumond (eds.), *Letters of Theodore Dwight Weld, Angelina Grimké Weld, and Sarah Grimké, 1822–1844* (New York: Appleton-Century, 1934), I, 126.

[87] "Abolitionists," wrote William Jay, "are constantly called on for a plan of emancipation. They have little encouragement to respond to the call. If they propose the simple plan of proclaiming by act of the State Legislatures the immediate and unqualified abolition of slavery, they are denounced as reckless incendiaries. If they intimate that abolition does not necessarily inhibit all compulsory labor . . . they are reproached with wishing to substitute one kind of slavery for another." Quoted in Barnes, *Anti-Slavery Impulse*, p. 102.

from this formula to Garrison's it was, of course, the merest step. The New York office ultimately recognized this, and at length the word went out that qualified emancipation was to be abandoned in favor of unconditional immediatism.

It might well be said that the theme which dominated the declining phase of *nationally organized* abolition activity was, after all, that of Garrisonian individualism triumphant. Garrison and his methods were peculiarly suited not only to stamping the movement in his image and giving it his tone but also to splitting the movement's institutional structure. "Garrisonism" was in the last analysis deeply subversive of antislavery's efforts to develop and consolidate organized power. The man himself, with his egocentric singleness of mind, antagonized most of those who tried to combine with him in any action requiring concerted effort. As a result virtually all such enterprises with which his name was connected acquired, as Theodore Weld wrote, a "vague and indefinite odium." Garrison's own New England Anti-Slavery Society, which had never in any case been much concerned with field operations,[88] split wide apart over the venom of his attacks on the clergy, and the movement all over New England fell into disrepute. By the late thirties the vitality of the American Anti-Slavery Society itself had been sufficiently sapped by Garrison's reputation that it was quite unable to weather out the depression years which followed the 1837 panic. By a touch of irony the meeting of 1840, at which the society's final dissolution was to have taken place, was captured by Garrison with a boatload of hastily commissioned "delegates" brought down from Lynn on an outing. Nearly all the state auxiliaries promptly withdrew, but

[88] The society was mainly a forum for speechmaking. "Observers from elsewhere invariably remarked the absence from its proceedings of the usual business of central societies: reports from local societies, details of the year's efforts in the field, and plans for future operations." *Ibid.*, p. 88. Ironically, however, Garrison himself found it necessary at one point to suppress one of his own followers, Nathaniel Peabody Rogers, when Rogers began spelling out Garrison's anti-institutionalism in so many words. As editor of the *Herald of Freedom,* Rogers advocated not only no-government (which Garrison approved), but no-committee and no-organization as well; whereupon Garrison moved in with the help of Stephen S. Foster and wrested control of the paper from Rogers and gave it to Parker Pillsbury. See Louis Filler, "Parker Pillsbury: An Anti-Slavery Apostle," *New England Quarterly,* XIX (September, 1946), 315–37.

this did not disturb Garrison; he was at last in full control. Yet the society which he had thus "rescued" was by then nothing more than a name.

Garrison's personal legend had been built up at the expense of organized antislavery. It is thus that one may deny his having "represented" in any functioning sense the majority of abolitionists and at the same time exhibit him as the living symbol of abolitionism, so far as the country at large was concerned. He had alienated hundreds by personal contact; his name was deeply distasteful to most middling citizens of the North and anathema to the entire South. But this very fact had made him famous; to think of abolitionism was to think of Garrison. Besides, he had spoken out early; he did have a vocal personal following, and for thousands of local abolitionists who had never seen him and who cared nothing for societies, his name was magic. It was a personal notoriety; he was profoundly the individual, anything but the organizer. As Gilbert Barnes writes, "He was equipped by taste and temperament for free-lance journalism and for nothing else. As a journalist he was brilliant and provocative; as a leader for the antislavery host he was a name, an embodied motto, a figurehead of fanaticism."[89]

"Garrisonism" might thus carry a number of meanings—radical doctrines, intransigence, intolerance, fanaticism—but what is chiefly of interest here is the way it symbolizes the direction in which antislavery, Garrison or no Garrison, was bound to move, even as it spread. That direction was from complexity of doctrine to simplicity, from organization to fragmentation, from consolidated effort to effort dispersed, diffuse, and pervasive. Whatever institutional character antislavery might have had, either as colonization or abolition, had broken down by the 1840's. Nor was this the only institutional breakdown of the period, for it was also in the 1840's that whatever last opportunity there may have been, in the interest of the slave, to exploit the power of the national church organizations disappeared forever. By that time the Methodists and Baptists had quarreled over slavery and split into sectional wings, Northern and Southern.[90]

[89] Barnes, *Anti-Slavery Impulse,* p. 58.

[90] The Methodists split in 1844 and the Baptists in 1845. The Presbyterians did not divide along completely sectional lines until 1861, but the schism of

But while antislavery sentiment and action were thus becoming less and less institutional, they were becoming at the same time— almost in inverse ratio—more widely shared. It had been made increasingly clear that the societies conceived their fundamental purpose to be that of spreading the antislavery gospel rather than of striking for the most vulnerable spots in slavery itself. There were now forces at work which made for a diffusion of the issue in such a way that it no longer needed to be carried by the societies; the ground upon which one might conceivably hold antislavery views was being tremendously broadened. The mechanism whereby this was brought about has been denoted in our own time, quite accurately, as the "fellow-traveler" principle.

The process operated somewhat as follows: Relatively few were actually prepared to take unequivocal abolitionist positions, but moral pressures, coming from everywhere in the civilized world and reflected intensely from our own abolitionists, were more and more insistent that Northerners recognize in some form the evils of slavery. Functional substitutes for abolitionism, that is, were coming increasingly into demand. And this growing need for some satisfactory mode of self-expression was in fact being provided for by the appearance of other issues and other forms of action—in some cases broader, and in all cases more acceptable— to which abolitionism could be linked but in which more and more persons could participate.

One such issue, shaped by a series of incidents occurring in the thirties, might be summarized sweepingly under the headings of freedom of speech, freedom of assembly, freedom of the press, and individual justice. The affair of Prudence Crandall's school had

---

1837 was due, at least in part, to growing tension over the slavery issue. This is not to say, of course, that the Northern and Southern church organizations thereby became impotent; it was rather that they no longer retained the kind of institutional commitments that transcended sectional interests and that might mediate in any way between the respective Northern and Southern moral positions on slavery. William Warren Sweet, *Methodism in American History* (New York: Methodist Book Concern, 1933), pp. 229–75; Charles Baumer Swaney, *Episcopal Methodism and Slavery* (Boston: Richard C. Badger, 1926), pp. 117–85; Mary Burnham Putnam, *The Baptists and Slavery, 1840–1845* (Ann Arbor: George Wahr, 1913); Edmund Arthur Moore, *Robert J. Breckenridge and the Slavery Aspect of the Presbyterian Schism of 1837* (Chicago: University of Chicago Libraries, 1934).

involved the attempt in 1833 by a Quaker teacher of Canterbury, Connecticut, to admit Negro girls to her school and had ended by the enactment of a state law forbidding the teaching of nonresident colored pupils and by the brief imprisonment of Miss Crandall for having disobeyed it. Whereas popular feeling was overwhelmingly hostile to her activity, her case, which had to go to a superior court before being decided against her, was something of a *cause célèbre* and attracted wide attention among humanitarians. More effective was the episode of the Boston mob and its handling of Garrison in 1835. At that time it was still possible for abolition meetings to arouse popular violence, and on the day that the English abolitionist George Thompson was scheduled to speak, a mob vainly searching for Thompson found Garrison instead and laid rough hands on him. After being dragged through the streets at a rope's end, Garrison was rescued and lodged in the city jail for his own safety. The result was a determination by the city of Boston thereafter to afford proper protection for abolition meetings. A similar riot in Utica on the same day brought the wealthy landowner Gerrit Smith (who took the besieged abolitionists under his own roof) into the ranks of antislavery. A further persecution was the attempt of the Connecticut General Association of Congregational Ministers, embodied in a resolution of 1836, to bar from their pulpits any itinerant lecturers not bearing the proper ecclesiastical credentials. Many strolling antislavery orators went about testing the right of free speech against this "Connecticut gag law," as it was called, and won much attention and publicity for themselves.

The culmination of all such incidents was the murder of the abolitionist editor Elijah Lovejoy by a mob at Alton, Illinois, in 1837. This was deeply shocking to a major portion of the American public and marked something of a turning point in sentiment. Indignant mass meetings were held everywhere, and the most famous of them, the great rally at Faneuil Hall in Boston, overflowed with the city's most respectable citizens. The principal speaker was the beloved Doctor Channing, and the occasion marked the conversion to abolition of the patrician Wendell Phillips. The mounting public concern which followed all these incidents, insofar as they constituted a unified sequence, did not manifestly involve the rightness or wrongness of abolitionism. Indeed, no less than the Bill of Rights itself was at stake, and, just as at other times in our history, the least excitable of conservatives were quick to rise in defense of those fundamental rights.[91]

A second issue, involving antislavery but claiming public attention under a wider principle, was that of the right of petition. This episode, enacted in the United States Congress over the years 1836–44, had as its hero none other than the venerable John Quincy Adams. Antislavery petitions, touching all sides of the question, had begun pouring into the House of Representatives in such numbers, threatening the disruption of all normal business, that a House resolution of 1836 ordered that all such petitions be laid on the table without debate. Adams, a member of the House since the end of his presidency, fought this so-called gag rule with such caustic ferocity, making impromptu speeches on every possible occasion, that he was the despair of all members who wished, for whatever reason, to keep antislavery itself from becoming a disruptive issue on the floor of the House. An attempt to censure him in 1842 miscarried and resulted in a triumph for the old man, who conducted his own defense. His chief ally, Joshua Giddings of Ohio, was, in fact, successfully censured during the same session, but when Giddings resigned and was promptly re-elected by his constituency (a district already thoroughly canvassed by the Lane rebels), the antipetition forces retired in chagrin. The gag rule was eventually repealed in 1844. The significant fact, however, was that throughout this period showers of antislavery petitions were flying through communities all over the North. They were circulated by thousands of volunteer workers, including substantial numbers of women who had for the first time found a satisfying mode of civic activity in which they could engage with reasonable propriety. To all these newly recruited citizens, inspired by the spectacle of an ex-president defending a question of manifest right, theirs seemed an enterprise sanctioned by the soundest of constitutional principles.[92]

[91] An excellent study of this phase (the process whereby antislavery sentiment grew by associating itself with other libertarian values) is Russel B. Nye, *Fettered Freedom: Civil Liberties and the Slavery Controversy* (East Lansing: Michigan State College Press, 1949).

[92] The fact that a minor debate is still waged over whether Adams was a "secret abolitionist" (Avery Craven, for instance, takes for granted that he was; Adams' latest biographer, Samuel Bemis, thinks that he was not) is rather ironic, and would doubtless have delighted the old Puritan. One cannot imagine anyone else as the subject of such a debate. On the one

Still another form of activity which absorbed the energies of numerous individuals was the "underground railroad," a well-articulated network of routes and stations, especially thick in the Middle West, for speeding fugitive slaves on their way to the Canadian border. The "U.G.R.R." had been in operation since the early 1820's, but its activity was greatly stepped up beginning about 1840. Here, in all senses, was a "fellow-traveler" movement par excellence.[93]

hand, Adams, like many another New Englander, was convinced of the sin in slavery, and the need to act out that conviction was very strong; on the other hand, he was temperamentally a conservative in all matters involving institutions, law, and the uses of power. Quite conceivably he may have disdained ever saying to himself, "I am an abolitionist" (if he had, he would probably have said it to others also). But in practice, he was of course the very prince of fellow travelers. John Minor Botts of Virginia asserted that the battle "made more abolitionists in one year, by identifying the right of petition with the question of slavery, than the abolitionists would have made for themselves in twenty-five years." See Samuel Flagg Bemis, *John Quincy Adams and the Union* (New York: Knopf, 1956), pp. 326–83, 416–48; and Nye, *Fettered Freedom,* pp. 32–53. For Adams' diabolical parliamentary tricks in the House, and his superior intelligence in using them, Harold Lieberman's unpublished M.A. thesis, "John Quincy Adams, Slavery, and the Right of Petition" (University of Chicago, 1949), is especially good.

[93] Wilbur H. Siebert, *The Underground Railroad from Slavery to Freedom* (New York: Macmillan, 1899), p. 39. The value of this work and the same author's *Mysteries of Ohio's Underground Railroads* (Columbus: Long's College Book Co., 1951) lies in Mr. Siebert's many interviews in the 1890's with persons who had once been active in the Ohio U.G.R.R. See also R. C. Smedley, *History of the Underground Railroad in Chester and the Neighboring Counties of Pennsylvania* (Lancaster, Pa.: Lancaster Journal, 1883), which likewise benefits from contemporary sources. The most recent study is William Breyfogle, *Make Free: The Story of the Underground Railroad* (Philadelphia: J. B. Lippincott, 1958). One may suspect that the real importance of the U.G.R.R. lay not in what it did for the slaves—the total number who were transported into Canada was hardly overwhelming—but rather in what it did for the people involved in the transporting. On the one hand, it gave an opportunity for substantial numbers of people to move beyond the stage of talk and agitation in opposing slavery, and, on the other, it drew in, willy-nilly, a great many who were not by temperament agitators and talkers. The transport of a single slave across New England or the Midwest might involve hundreds of people, if only in the knowledge that a neighbor was breaking the law; and to offer one's assistance in the slightest way could make the difference between doing nothing and a decisive emotional commitment to the entire antislavery

That all such issues and activities were participated in amid a certain amount of public disapproval—indeed, at first considerable —should not deceive us. Such enterprises have traditionally depended, for part of their motive power, on being undertaken in a spirit of "dissent," even though the element of actual dissent (as more and more join) may turn out to involve "heresies" shared by a sizable part of the community. Such activity must in any event have some opposition or it will not be satisfying. At the same time it should be obvious that when substantial numbers are participating, the commitment itself has become a limited one; it may be risky, but not too risky, and the extent of the risks can be measured and graded.[94]

Finally, the broadest of all such issues, emerging after the Mexican War, was that of "free soil"—an antislavery position so widely shared that by 1860 it could command political majorities in every Northern state but one. It was with this issue that the democratization of antislavery had become complete.

The remainder of our paradigm of antislavery thought with its four explanatory categories—anti-institutionalism, individualism, abstraction, and guilt—is speedily traversed. Various implications of the first of these, anti-institutionalism, have already been noted, and in the process certain things have been said of its counterpart, individualism. As more and more individuals entered the antislavery movement at one level or another, the movement became

---

cause. This principle was well understood in the resistance movements in Europe during World War II. To the extent that men could be persuaded to accept even the most minor roles in the underground, the tendency of the population to compromise or collaborate with the Germans was decisively reduced.

[94] The American Communists of course did much to exploit this principle of limited or "graded" involvement. Getting a man into a series of reform activities was often to commit him emotionally to a movement which he might never actually join. In the case of the abolitionists, one wonders whether their movement ever contained more than a small core of men who might actually be called "revolutionaries." There were the Garrisons and Phillipses of course, but then Weld, Birney, the Grimkés, and many others were of a very familiar and recognizable type; they were by temperament and instinct reformers. That the reform movement itself became "revolutionary" may be argued, though it would probably be more accurate to say that it was *democratized* and that a movement to resist it was likewise democratized.

less and less institutional in character; moreover, between institutional solidarity on the one hand and individual satisfaction and self-expression on the other, the balance would invariably swing to the latter.

Now this very individualism also penetrated, in spite of itself, to the debate over the slave. That debate, focusing as it did upon the Negro's "nature" and "innate capacities," in effect bypassed the nature of the institution within which he acted out his daily life. "The negro is a child in his nature," an anonymous Southerner had written in 1836, "and the white man is to him as a father."[95] He was cheerful and gay, a trait which John Pendleton Kennedy called "constitutional and perennial";[96] he was imitative and adaptable ("The African adapts himself with greater readiness to circumstances than the white man"),[97] docile and lacking in pride and courage: "The slave, besotted, servile, accustomed to degradation, and habituated to regard his master with deference and awe, does not presume to dream of contending with him."[98] He was lazy and dishonest: "All history proves that idleness and vice is the only liberty the African aspires to, either in his own country or as a slave in Christian lands."[99] He was irresponsible ("the most improvident race in the world, and must have a superior mind to guide them"),[100] and yet in the last analysis affectionate and loyal. "They look up to their liberal and generous masters, and their mistresses, with a feeling absolutely fond and filial."[101] Slavery, in short, was really the only state in which such a creature could exist. "He is happier . . . as a slave," wrote the Southerner of *The South Vindicated,* "than he could be as a freeman. This is the result of the peculiarities of his character."[102]

[95] *The South Vindicated from the Treason and Fanaticism of the Northern Abolitionists* (Philadelphia: H. Manly, 1836), p. 304.

[96] *Swallow Barn* (New York: Putnam, 1929 printing), p. 379.

[97] Lucien B. Chase, *English Serfdom and American Slavery* (New York: H. Long & Bro., 1854), p. 202.

[98] *South Vindicated,* p. 299.

[99] Mrs. Henry R. Schoolcraft, *The Black Gauntlet: A Tale of Plantation Life in South Carolina* (Philadelphia: Lippincott, 1860), pp. 49–50.

[100] Mrs. Caroline Rush, *The North and South, or, Slavery and Its Consequences* (Philadelphia: Crissey & Markley, 1852), p. 226.

[101] *South Vindicated,* p. 79.

[102] *Ibid.,* p. 81.

The Northern reformer accepted the argument on the Southerner's terms by reversing it, and attempted to refute it with that logic of individual perfectibility upon which the humanitarianism of the day drew so deeply. Lydia Maria Child admitted the existence of ignorance among the Negroes, but insisted that their desire to be otherwise would increase "just in proportion as they are free. The fault is in their *unnatural* situation, not in themselves."[103] Mrs. Child, pointing to the existence of numerous merchants, priests, and doctors in Brazil who had once been slaves, drew the inference not that this was due to institutional differences between American and Brazilian slavery but rather that it was simply freedom which had made the difference. She thought that freedom, followed by universal education, was the remedy and that it was only prejudice that prevented "the improvement of a large portion of the human race."[104] Emancipation, according to William Jay, would have instant salutary effects upon the Negroes; it would "stimulate their morals, quicken their intelligence, and convert a dangerous, idle, and vicious population into wholesome citizens." The transition from slave to free labor might, he thought, be "effected instantaneously, and with scarcely any perceptible interruption of the ordinary pursuits of life."[105] S. B. Treadwell wrote:

If all the slaves in the United States should have their shackles knocked off, and endowed with the privileges of freemen to-morrow, and barely paid a fair compensation for their labour, (which would also be far better for their masters) they would at once be as capable, from the honest avails of their labour of supporting themselves and their families, in their accustomed mode of living, as any class of people in the world. Of this there can be no question.[106]

[103] *An Appeal in Favor of the Class of Americans Called Africans* (Boston: Allen & Ticknor, 1833), p. 181.

[104] *Ibid.,* pp. 92, 139, 143.

[105] *Miscellaneous Writings on Slavery* (Boston: J. P. Jewett, 1853), p. 195. Jay thought that the opportunity to make wage contracts would actually improve relations between Negro and white: "The very consciousness . . . that justice is done to both parties, will remove their mutual suspicions and animosities, and substitute in their place feelings of kindness and confidence." *Ibid.,* p. 198.

[106] *American Liberties and American Slavery* (New York: John S. Taylor, 1838), pp. 184–85.

It was, and is, perfectly possible to accept both the descriptive accuracy of what the Southerner saw and the attainability, in theory, of what the Northerner hoped for. But not at the level of "the individual and his innate capacities"; to argue it out at that level (innate racial inferiority versus innate human perfectibility) was not only to freeze all hope of mutual understanding but actually to rule out of the argument a formidable social institution. Here was the ante-bellum form of a now-venerable debate—the debate over "Sambo." Finally, the controversy, never very concrete, was raised to empyrean heights of abstraction as both sides resorted to Bible criticism. Each searched the sacred texts, one to show slavery as "consistent with the precepts of patriarchs, apostles, and prophets,"[107] the other to prove "The Book and Slavery Irreconcilable,"[108] and of course each found the appropriate passages.

What it came down to, after all, was a problem of morality whose intellectual content had become more and more attenuated. It was really the abolitionist, with guilt as both powerful stimulus and powerful weapon, who understood most surely—if only by instinct—the means which would carry the issue furthest. Alternately he writhed and thundered. "My brother," wrote Weld with quiet intensity to James G. Birney,

God's terrors have begun to blaze upon the guilty nation. If repentance, speedy, deep and *national* do[es] not forestall Jehovah's judgments, they will break upon us from the thickening air and the heaving earth and the voice of a brothers blood crying from the ground will peal against the wrathful heavens and shake down ruin as a fig tree casteth her untimely fruit. May God purify us, gird us for the conflict, give us faith and then we shall stand unscathed by the flames which blaze around us.[109]

[107] Resolution of the Charleston Union Presbytery, quoted in Lloyd, *Slavery Controversy*, pp. 170–71.

[108] Title of a book by the Rev. George Bourne. The "Bible argument" bulks large on both sides, as may be seen in any pro- and antislavery bibliography.

[109] Weld to Birney, December 22, 1835, in Dwight L. Dumond (ed.), *Letters of James Gillespie Birney, 1831–1857* (New York: Appleton-Century, 1938), I, 289. For a discussion of this "guilt" mechanism in its extreme form, see Hazel Catherine Wolf, *On Freedom's Altar: The Martyr Complex in the Abolition Movement* (Madison: University of Wisconsin Press, 1952).

"How ought I to feel and speak?" Garrison demanded meanwhile, in apocalyptic accents.

My soul should be, as it is, on fire. I should thunder—I should lighten. I should blow the trumpet of alarm, long and loud. I should use just such language as is most descriptive of the crime. I should imitate the example of Christ, who, when he had to do with people of like manners, called them sharply by their proper names—such as, an adulterous and perverse generation, a brood of vipers, hypocrites, children of the devil, who could not escape the damnation of hell.[110]

The Southerner of course, whose own moral tradition was not so very different from Weld's and Garrison's, also writhed. "If you would reform the Southern man," protested Joseph Stiles, "say, if you please, that his explanations do not entirely satisfy you; but say something of them; give them some regard, some weight. For he knows, and so do you, that his views and feelings are such as an intelligent and honest man may well entertain."[111] But the Southerner's guilt could do little other than turn defensive. Nehemiah Adams, a Northern minister who returned from a Southern visit with greatly modified views on Southern morals, had conversed with a slaveholder "of liberal education and great influence at the south, and withal an extreme defender of the system of slavery." Adams was much impressed by this man's words: "If the north had directed its strength against the evils of slavery instead of assailing it as a sin *per se,* it could not have survived to the present day."[112] While doubtless not worth much as *post hoc* prediction, the statement is an admirable little map of what had happened to Southern squeamishness on the subject of slavery.

6

CHOICES

It is of the nature of tragedy that while the choices it offers are most sharply and painfully limited, such choices must still exist. Were this not so, situations which we call "tragic" would have

[110] "Vindication of the Liberator," *Selections,* p. 180.

[111] *Modern Reform Examined; or, The Union of North and South on the Subject of Slavery* (Philadelphia: Lippincott, 1858).

[112] *A South-Side View of Slavery; or, Three Months at the South, in 1854* (3d ed.; Boston: T. R. Marvin; Sanborn, Carter & Bazin, 1855), p. 157.

little analytic merit and no dramatic essence. It can hardly be doubted that the estrangement of North and South over slavery, and the consequences of it, offer us what is potentially the most distinguished subject available in our history. That it might have ended otherwise is a shadowy possibility that will trouble our minds forever. That there may have been alternatives—that choices were at least conceivable—makes it a subject not quite foreordained and fatal, but tragic.

What openings might there have been for intellectuals and agitators to play meaningful roles in the controversy? What specific alternatives might they have pressed for? "Moderation" was not really an alternative; the difficulty was not harshness of tone; "moderate abolition" would mean nothing at all. The true difficulty lay in the absence of any sense of the *limits* within which the problem would have to be handled, limits functioning to exhibit not only the impossible but also the possible. Yet in the 1830's those limits, for anyone really looking for them, would not have been very hard to find.

The major limit was the fact of slavery's expansion in the Southwest and the commitment of this area, more than any other, to slave labor. There was no way of side-stepping such a fact as this; it would be the basic thing that reformers would be working with. Here was the area in which the reformer would have to expect abuse for virtually everything he said; it was here that he would make the least difference. The second fact, however, was that in other areas of the South—in the older planting states—an earlier commitment to slavery had been to some extent undermined during the first quarter of the century. Distinctions, that is, would have to be made; the slaveholding South could not realistically be considered as a unit. It was here (in Virginia, North Carolina, Kentucky) that the system's weaknesses would be most exposed to whatever reform activity was feasible. The final test of the problem's limits was to be found in the deep hostility still existing at that time, not merely in the South but in the North itself, toward out-and-out abolitionism. The potential explosiveness of that issue, taken as a whole, was a thing recognized somehow by almost everyone. Potential support for a concrete policy would have to be calculated with this in mind.

What it all pointed to, if the system were eventually to be removed without bloodshed, was a catalogue of preliminaries—a series of separate short-term reforms rather than root-and-branch abolition. It is not difficult to conceive a few of the specific measures which might have been advanced. One such project, and here the national church organizations could afford to be implacable, would be that of bringing the slave into the Christian fold and under the eye of the church, of insisting that he be offered a spiritual life marked by dignity and be given instruction in Christian morality. For the slave, such arrangements would have functioned not merely as personal consolation but also as institutional leverage, as a claim on society. This tradition in the Latin states impresses us by its subversive effects upon slavery, and we are struck, on the other hand, by the buffoonery, the lack of dignity and moral power, which characterizes much of the legend of plantation religion in our own South.[113] The sanctity of the family could have been insisted upon as a basic principle of Christian practice, not simply to decrease personal anguish, but to establish another level of human dignity that society would, in some sense or other, be called upon to recognize. Conversely, were it a matter of official doctrine (as it was in Latin America) that the slave, for all his servile degradation, had been endowed with a moral

[113] "The tradition in the main . . . utilizes the spectacular and the comic rather than the genuine. A favorite device is the use of queer exegesis; in Annie Hobson's *In Old Alabama* a darkey places the story of Daniel and the lions in a sweet potato patch; . . . in Dunbar's *Trial Sermons on Bull Skin* a minister explains that the prepared table for the psalmist was really a 'possum dinner: in Russell's well known poem, the negro gives a biblical origin for the banjo. . . . One of the most widely established conventions concerning the darkey's religion is its total severance from moral conduct, the easy dissociation, let us say, of faith and works. The fundamental dogma seems to be a continuing in sin that grace may abound. From the divine in *Miss Ravenel's Conversion,* who offended easily the seventh commandment in a test of the permanence of heavenly pardon, to the ecclesiastic of *The Leopard's Spots* who devoutly stole chickens in order that the everlasting mercy might have large opportunity to exercise itself, the record of negro religion is chiefly a burlesque." Francis P. Gaines, *The Southern Plantation* (New York: Columbia University Press, 1924), pp. 195–96. No matter how heavily one discounts the accuracy of such a tradition's details (unless, of course, one simply asserts that there is no truth in it), the range of spiritual aspirations which it offered the Negro cannot for a moment be compared with its counterpart in white culture. Such a tradition, treated sympathetically, reveals its own plane of dignity and much depth of feeling, yet its loftiest manifestation still remains at about the level of *Green Pastures.*

personality as sacred as his master's, such precepts as those touching Christian marriage could hardly have been taken so lightly. There might have been a movement to write into law the best Southern practice as to the treatment of the slave's person—not only to mitigate personal cruelty but to establish still a further claim, institutionally formalized before all society, for the slave's humanity. The South's own jurists admitted the desirability of such a step,[114] which meant that here was another area containing some latitude. Arrangements might further have been proposed for a program of incentives—such as the slave's use of free time to accumulate his purchase price, or freedom for meritorious service—which might, from the master's own point of view, improve the system.[115] Such a policy might not noticeably improve the slave's own "standard of living," but it would set up formal channels of communication between himself and free society which were not previously there.

The presence of all these things in Latin America gives a clear indication of what might have been the consequences for the Negro community had they existed in this country. They would not have been mere incidentals. By humanizing the Negro, by making property-holding legal, by regularizing procedures of

[114] The "perfectly unprotected and helpless position of the slave," according to T. R. R. Cobb of Georgia, ". . . is one of the most vulnerable points in the system of negro slavery, and should be farther guarded by legislation." *An Inquiry into the Law of Negro Slavery in the United States of America* (Philadelphia: T. & J. W. Johnson, 1858), I, 97–98.

[115] This would not have been a complete innovation in the South; indeed, a basis for it was already in existence there. In many places, particularly where plantation agriculture had become unprofitable, it was not uncommon that an industrious slave be permitted to hire himself out. Although such an arrangement was against the law, the slave would agree to pay his master a fixed sum each year, and in return he would be allowed to make the best bargain he could for his labor. This gave the slave the opportunity to choose his employer and to control his earnings. Here was a long step in the direction of practical freedom. Every state in the South had legislation against self-hiring, but in certain areas the economic advantages were clear enough to the parties concerned that it continued unabated up to the Civil War. Could this practice have been formalized and widely encouraged, it is not difficult to imagine its eventual impact on the institution of slavery. See Richard B. Morris, "The Measure of Bondage in the Slave States," *Mississippi Valley Historical Review*, XLI (September, 1954), 219–40.

manumission, social space would be provided; there would be a basis for the emergence of a Negro elite of leadership.[116] A series of contacts with free society would thus have been established, and in such a setting many of the difficulties of a general emancipation, should such an event some day occur, would have been absorbed in advance. Even *debating* such a program, item by item, would be a different thing entirely from debating the relative merits or evils of slavery as a whole; it would be far more easy to defend the entire system of slavery than to defend the denial of religious instruction or the removal of children from their mothers.

Actually, there was not a single one of these schemes that was not proposed in some form or other during the pre–Civil War generation and that has not been repeatedly considered by historians ever since. Indeed, the British example was there for anyone concerned with procedure; theirs was a program very similar to the one just outlined; their approach in softening up the system for final emancipation followed a pattern much resembling that just suggested.

And yet the setting made all the difference. It is one thing to point out that such proposals were there and quite another to find a setting in the America of the 1830's capable of receiving them, of testing them, of debating them, of transforming them into something more than mere proposals. It is something of a shock to realize that one cannot imagine a setting within which, for example, the proposals of Channing could be approached as a reasoned body of doctrine rather than as moral formulas, or in which it would have seemed natural to contrast Virginia and Mississippi, rather than North and South, with regard to slavery and its liabilities. The institutionally formed habits of mind needed to appraise the tactics of the British abolitionists were available neither to Garrison nor to other Americans interested in antislavery. None of them could really comprehend the meaning of Buxton's and Wilberforce's operations—operations whose key qualities included a sense of what the Negro ought to be like after emancipation and a sense of what was needed to bring it about without disruption. In contrast to the British antislavery program, whose every item was hammered

[116] See above, pp. 137–38.

out by daily experience over a period of years, any concrete proposal made by an American could only be thrown into the void.

For it to have been otherwise, a myriad of intermediate relationships would have been required. The reformers might have taken as their standards the standards of the best Southern families. What might this have had to offer the slaveowner of the older planting states who still felt guilt over his position as a holder of slaves? It could offer him a clear role as model slaveholder, a role which would have had at least one manifest function and two hidden ones. Not only would it carry prestige and general recognition, but it might also provide constructive channels for his sense of guilt and at the same time set the pattern for the system's ultimate dissolution. It was precisely here—not in the cotton kingdom but in the border states and older seaboard slave areas—that an enormously sensitive spot existed. On the one hand it made little sense to put economic pressure on the planters of these states, and on the other it was folly to accuse them of sin and make them guiltier. Incentives for taking action could never result from any such pressures. But moral incentives for improvement (rather than naked abolition) could operate quite differently, since here the system was a good deal less secure than in Alabama and Mississippi. It was in such an area that reform might most effectively be generated. It was here, for instance, that colonization had made the greatest headway; it was in this area, even, that actual antislavery activity, before the rise of Northern abolitionism, had been most prominent.

The resources of intellect and experience available to each shade of emancipationist feeling, from Massachusetts to Virginia, might have been considerable had there been some cultural matrix capable of containing them all. To operate with purpose and meaning in such a situation, the intellectual and reforming publicist would certainly have needed not only to know of but to understand the experience being undergone at that same period by the British. The intellectual's role would also have involved knowing what was happening to the slave system in Latin America, and having some rough idea of the reasons. It would further have involved a relationship to the humane slaveholder which need not inevitably have been one of "friendly sympathy" but would certainly have had to be one of responsibility, of sensitivity to his requirements. One thinks, in this connection, of the hard-bitten Englishman Wilberforce, who, for all his merciless campaigning for emancipation, could still be appalled at a premature proposal in the House of Commons to do away with the whip as the badge of authority in the West Indies. If any experiments were to be made on the system—such as a program of education for slaves, an attempt to demonstrate the advantages of property-holding for slaves, a range of moral incentives (on the Dabney plantation they insisted on weddings)—it would have to be within such a relationship that such experiments would be planned and publicized.

Had the national churches remained united and sensitive to the uses of power, it might have made considerable difference as to the choices made by religious groups in the matter of slavery. The Lane Seminary debate of the mid-1830's, for example —what was the nature of the choice made there? The students had begun the famous meeting by reasoning together, by questioning, with prayerful inquiry, into the nature of their moral duty. Might they not have arrived at a different decision? Suppose they had still resolved to go out in the service of Christ, as they conceived it, and to labor for the slave's welfare, but not as abolitionists? The Southern brethren might then have gone into the South, there announcing that on no account were they to be confused with abolitionists, that their unshakable purpose was simply to bring Christ to the slave and to minister to the needs of his soul. They might thus have taken a leaf from the Jesuits; they might really have dedicated themselves, that being their wish, to an arduous but noble work. But of course there was no setting in which they could do this, in which they might say, evil is with us and we must work with it. They could not actually think of the slave in his present condition; they could only be overwhelmed by the sense of sin and guilt of slaveholding. Thus was stifled any sense they may have had of the needs of souls other than their own. More than Garrison it was they who, with the revival that followed, would find the formula—sin and guilt— that would drive the entire South in the same direction.

One may note, finally, the question of what might be called "degrees of commitment." We have already referred to tendencies everywhere at work which acted to break down the barriers protecting one type of sentiment on slavery from another, which acted to merge differing points of view instead of permitting them to instruct each other, which dissolved them in a common moral atmosphere and made them indistinguishable. Yet even so, this was not true to quite the extent in the North that it was in the South. In the North it was at least in some measure possible to express in action varying degrees of hostility to slavery, depending on preferences, temperament, and depth of feeling. In the South there was no real counterpart to this; there were no corresponding degrees of either pro- *or* antislavery sentiment which could hold up long enough to be identifiable, which could be crystallized, maintained, and acted out. In the North, one's activity could focus on such things as the defense of free speech, free press, and freedom of assembly; there was the circulation of petitions; there was the underground railroad. Even the underground railroad involved a limited personalized experience, that of helping a wretched creature on his way; it was not a total commitment; it was one which was fraught with certain risks but which had its rewards. Its hypothetical counterpart would have been the case of the planter (pro- or antislavery) who might resolve to educate his slaves, law or no law; who might determine to let them work for themselves, law or no law; who might insist that the local parish provide for their spiritual needs, ridicule or no ridicule. Again, all of this certainly did occur in the South. But something would have been required to make a satisfying experience of it—something that was not there. It would have needed at least a scattered community of guilty slaveholders, in the sense that the scattered stations of the underground railroad formed a "community," who were willing to incur some displeasure in their neighborhoods but whose activity would in a wider sense be recognized as virtuous, not only among themselves but by antislavery people everywhere.

What it all came to, finally, was that every such alternative became unreal, if not impossible. What made it so?

In every "tragic" situation a set of choices exists which might conceivably bring the conflict to a solution. Suppose Hamlet had destroyed his uncle in the first act? Suppose Othello had made his own investigations? But now let us admit that such questions, though by no means idle, have running through them a touch of the academic. To ask them is to confirm the rules of tragedy but also to contravene them, because in tragedy two elements are in mortal but uneven conflict: one involves the choices that exist; the other involves the circumstances which predispose the principals to choose one set of alternatives rather than another. It is with the latter that we must finally make our terms.

A recurrent theme in our histories continues to affront us: their intimation that the failure of American society to solve the problem of slavery without bloodshed was somehow the failure of men to curb their passions—that it was in some sense a breaking-loose of Northern radicalism and Southern fire-eating, a matter of too much "slogan-making" and "propaganda" (as the late Professor Randall put it) and not enough "moderation and understanding."[117] But a healthy culture can afford this. Indeed, such a culture must have its fanaticism and moral passion in order that its moderation and sagacity may be given point and meaning. We should say that the difficulty lay elsewhere—that the great falling-short in American society was precisely its lack of proper channels for the launching either of its passion or its moderation, either of its propaganda, its slogan-making, or its deepest counsels of understanding.

There was no church with a national scope, which in its concern with the nation's morals would be forced to operate on intersectional terms. There were no national universities to focus intellectual activity, no intellectual matrix within which the most pressing problems of the day would have had to be debated on national grounds and on their merits. There was no national focus of social and financial power (the only possible American equivalent to a ruling class): no national vested business interest such as a national bank (the nearest approach to such a thing had been smashed during the Jackson administration); no established mercantile axis powerful enough to resist a sectional movement; no seaboard social axis reaching from Boston to Charleston, whose vested loyalties might have gone deeper than local ones. There was no national bar which would, with its vested interest in standards, be forced to meet the legal complications of slavery in a national way. Indeed, there were not even sectional (to say nothing of national) abolition societies—no organization which carried anything resembling power, or which lasted long enough

[117] J. G. Randall, *The Civil War and Reconstruction* (Boston: D. C. Heath, 1937), p. vii.

to accomplish anything against slavery. Those that existed were contemptible in their impotence.

Very different was the case in England. There, no matter what men did, they did it in a setting in which they could hardly avoid thinking and acting institutionally. They behaved this way whether oppressing their poor or reforming their factories, manipulating their rotten boroughs or organizing their Reform Bills, massacring the Peterloo "rabble" or celebrating Christmas Eve at Oxford and Westminster. For whatever purpose it might be, the channels, the patterns of habit, the established points of orientation, awaited them on every side. There was the Church of England, which reached deep into the daily life of every community and which also managed the ceremonial of the greatest occasions of state. Alongside it stood the nonconforming sects, which themselves maintained strong national establishments. There were the national universities (behind which stood the great public schools) through which was funneled a substantial portion of the future leaders in all areas of the national life. There was the ruling class, fluid enough in its recruitment to maintain its vitality, whose appurtenances of power, exhibited in a hundred ways, were yet clear enough to command the recognition of all society. It was the class through which all major matters of policy had to be channeled, and it had great independence in shaping the form in which such policy would emerge. There was a tradition of bench and bar, emanating from the King's Bench, with a set of customs, standards, training, and a body of law, all reaching far back into British experience—a tradition which made it not only possible, but natural, that men should conceive the actual terms upon which law would be put into practice at the very time such law was being enacted. The elites of these and other institutions crossed one another's paths a dozen times a year. All this, in terms of social structure, was of course what James had in mind in his "lurid indictment" of the United States: "No sovereign, no court . . . no aristocracy, no church . . . no great universities nor public schools—no Oxford, nor Eton, nor Harrow; . . . no political society, no sporting class—no Epsom nor Ascot!"

The antislavery movement in England had an array of resources, and habits of mind appropriate to them, which were in no way available to Americans. The differences between the two movements were no mere differences of formula (the formulas themselves were superficially similar); the crucial differences were those which existed between two cultures.

The British abolitionists made use of every institution, every center of power, that they had at hand. The movement had a continuity of leadership which dated from the initial agitation against the slave trade in the 1780's and remained intact until the final abolition of slavery itself in the 1830's. Its key names were those of William Wilberforce and Thomas Fowell Buxton, who between them carried on the campaign in all its stages against slavery for over fifty years. Both were men of substance and weighty connections. Wilberforce, a wealthy squire of Wimbledon and scion of a prominent mercantile family of Hull, had entrée to the most brilliant society of his day. His closest friend and co-worker as a young man was no less a personage than the younger Pitt (they had been at Cambridge together), and for his first assaults on the trade he had the active support of such men as Burke, Fox, Castlereagh, Canning, and the Duke of Wellington. He himself was the Member for Yorkshire in the House of Commons throughout most of his public career. Buxton, who labored with Wilberforce for many years and inherited the older man's leadership in the final stages of the struggle, was the eldest son of a Norfolk squire and was himself a successful brewer. He served in Parliament as the Member for Weymouth.

The "immediate emancipation" formula which Garrison adopted from the British reformers in the early 1830's was simply the product of the movement's closing phase; slavery in the West Indies, when finally abolished, had been softened by the cumulative effort of a half-century, an effort consistently directed from the same sources. It had begun with the outlawing of the trade (not accomplished until 1806), followed by tireless work to achieve international enforcement (during which Wilberforce himself corresponded and negotiated with numerous heads of state including the pope, Prince Talleyrand, and the tsar of Russia); from here the reformers had proceeded, in the 1820's, to a program for the melioration of the plantation system itself and for the emancipation of newborn children, a part of which (but by no means all) was achieved after interminable debate in the

House of Commons. In the 1830's they undertook to press for full emancipation by means of monetary compensation and an intermediate five-year plan of apprenticeship, a program which was passed in Commons after an item-by-item struggle in the summer of 1833. After two years the government, annoyed by the obstructions of the colonial assemblies in carrying out the program, could finally at a stroke end slavery once and for all.

Confronted throughout by formidable opposition from Tory, military, West Indian, and High Church elements, Wilberforce and Buxton had quite naturally moved against it with other sources of power, similarly organized. Against proslavery peers they could rally their own antislavery peers; against West Indian power they could oppose the interests of the East India Company; they could combat High Church intransigence, especially after Wilberforce's conversion, with the phalanx of Low Church power then at their disposal. Available to them were some of the finest legal minds of the day. Numerous reform organizations supported the cause, most redoubtable of which was the London Anti-Slavery Society with its royal and noble patrons, and the movement's intellectual reinforcements (Buxton and Wilberforce were themselves men of learning and acumen) featured such names as those of Thomas Clarkson, Jeremy Bentham, Henry Brougham (later Lord Brougham), James Stephen, and later his sons Sir James and Sir George, and the Macaulays, Zachary and his son Thomas, later Lord Macaulay.[118] Thus bulwarked, the leaders had ample protection from pressures of sentiment on either side of them. Much of that sentiment, needless to say, was more moderate than their own, and some of it, indeed, was much more radical.

In contrast to these planners, these intellectuals, these men of affairs, who was poor Garrison? What matter was it that he had received the benign blessing of the dying Wilberforce? What plans had he, what were *his* resources—other than the impotent

[118] Much excellent material on the movement is to be found in R. Coupland, *Wilberforce, A Narrative* (Oxford: Clarendon Press, 1923); *Memoirs of Sir Thomas Fowell Buxton, Bart.*, ed. Charles Buxton (London: J. Murray, 1855); R. H. Mottram, *Buxton the Liberator* (London: Hutchinson, 1946); and Frank J. Klingberg, *The Anti-Slavery Movement in England: A Study in English Humanitarianism* (New Haven: Yale University Press, 1926).

fury of his own poisoned pen? Where were the men of power who might have supported him a generation before (even assuming a vocabulary they could have shared, which was dubious): the Washingtons, Jeffersons, Randolphs, Henrys, Madisons, and Monroes, whose hatred of slavery had been a product not of moral abstractions but of intimate acquaintance? All were gone by the 1840's; yet it hardly mattered, for the roles which their successors might have played—the model slaveholder, the man whose views other men respected, the man of learning whose wisdom had been shaped by affairs—were roles which society no longer recognized.

Our antislavery movement was for practical purposes devoid of intellectual nourishment. There was no real way for intellectual productions to avoid being democratized, no way of testing their merit other than by casting them upon the market place; the market place was where they had to pay their way. There were no limited areas within which ideas could be judged as ideas, policy as policy, and not as something else, no structure within which ideas and policies might have had their identity protected from mass pressures long enough to compete with one another rather than with moral formulas. In its ultimate stages antislavery, to reach a point where it could measurably influence public policy, had to find a lowest common denominator: the formula of "free soil." It had to be in such a form that by 1860 substantial majorities in the Northern states might be found thinking alike—sufficiently alike, at least, to bring a new party into power. By that time what little intellectual leadership antislavery had ever possessed had long since lost control. This was the extent to which the wisdom of an Emerson was needed by the America of that generation, for all the difference it made. In such circumstances an intellectual elite—a real elite, with a clear sense of its own function and equipped to play the needed roles—could hardly have been either recruited or maintained.

The reasons for such an elite's never appearing were anything but accidental. There was no way for intellectuals to be located institutionally and thus be sensitized to power and the meaning of power. They could not conceive of competing institutions in a state of tension; tensions in that sense were not really there. No bargaining relationship could thus exist between them and the institution of slavery. Intellect itself had been "sectionalized";

[205]

the closest thing to a community of intellectuals was to be found at Concord, but such men were not national intellectuals; they had no community with Southern counterparts. Those counterparts would have been located in Virginia and elsewhere in the upper South, where slavery had already come under pressures other than those created by moral aggression from the outside.

These men, cut off from the source of power, with virtually no vested connections, far removed from that institution with which they became increasingly concerned, thus had few tests other than their own consciences and those of their average fellow citizens, to prevent their thought from moving to the simplest of moral abstractions. The very nature of that thought—anti-institutional, individualistic, abstract, and charged with guilt—blocked off all concrete approaches to the problems of society.

7

POSTSCRIPT: SLAVERY, CONSENSUS, AND THE SOUTHERN INTELLECT

The intellectual history of the American pre–Civil War generation does seem to have been made, to a very great extent, in New England. But for the specific question of slavery, does this not leave a substantial part of the story out? Were there not men in the South who concerned themselves, as "intellectuals" in some sense, with this, the primary problem of Southern life? The problem was, after all, fully debated by members of the Virginia legislature at the very time the first organized antislavery activity was being launched from New York and New England. And is it not possible to identify, as thinkers, such men as Calhoun, Dew, Simms, Fitzhugh, and Tucker, and to grant that they made the most profound effort to think not only about slavery but about society itself? The men did exist; they did apparently make the effort; the work, tucked away in old books, remains. In assessing the legitimacy of such work, as thought, some attention should be given to the conditions under which it was done.

From the 1830's on, the thinking that went into the Southern proslavery position operated under disabilities at least as grave as those which governed antislavery thought in the North. It is historically true that the need to defend an institution, a social order, or a way of life has at times produced some of the best conservative thinking in the Western world; an optimum setting for self-discernment seems to have been created by the very tensions and pressures of crisis.[119] But that did not happen in the American South. The minute re-examination of Southern slavery which ought in principle to have occurred—no matter how it should turn out, *pro* or *anti*—did not occur at all. The most outstanding of the proslavery statements, even with their flashes of logical genius on such matters as the nature of industrial capitalism, were precisely those which, on slavery itself, were the least equivocal and the most rigid, single-minded, and doctrinaire. The fact that the dialectic was not really an internal one, that the only assaults on slavery to which men in the South paid any attention were coming from the outside—*this* was the problem, not slavery itself, that both engaged and somehow sapped these men's energies. They were thus unable, in the fullest sense, to think about slavery. At most, they thought in the vicinity of slavery.

It does not necessarily follow, however, as some have claimed, that the true fathers of the proslavery argument were the antislavery zealots of New England, or that it required the fanaticism of a William Lloyd Garrison to mobilize the South in defense of an otherwise dying institution. One doctrinaire attitude can tell us a great deal about its opposite, and so in this case, but the proslavery position, as a matter of chronology, goes back well before Garrison's *Liberator*. That position, though Northern polemics did much to bring it into focus, had been in the making for the better part of a generation.

It is quite true that, despite a general commitment to slavery, the state of the Southern mind up to about 1830 was complicated by various undercurrents of an antislavery nature. But it was hardly a question of battle lines; the South's intellectual life was never truly featured by the existence of recognized pro- and antislavery "factions." The closest the South would come to such a condition of things was a kind of schism in the Southern soul,

---

[119] See above, pp. 145–47. Possibly the best example of a thorough conservative re-examination of a social order, made in time of stress, is that of Edmund Burke. Burke wrote during a period when the French Revolution augured the most profound threat not only to his own society but to those of all Europe.

a schism which at one time made for complexity—as opposed to the relative simplicity of later times—but hardly for decision. The man of reason and good will in the Jeffersonian and immediate post-Jeffersonian South tried again and again to balance within himself two conflicting sets of feelings about slavery. On the one hand was the sentiment, widely shared at the end of the eighteenth century, that the institution was uneconomic, morally dubious, and a burden on both the slaveholder and the community. That the Negro, on the other hand, lacked the capacity to care for himself as a free American was a conviction that slavery's strongest opponents, not excluding Thomas Jefferson, could seldom escape.[120]

This conflict was never actually resolved. Despite the example which Washington, Randolph, and others had tried to give in the way of emancipation experiments, such efforts were seldom more than sporadic, and most men came to take for granted that it was beyond their power to do anything much about altering the institution of slavery. The one major way in which humane Southern slaveholders could try squaring this accommodation process with their own consciences was to support the American Colonization Society. The dilemma of the emancipated Negro's lack of fitness for adulthood and freedom in the local community could be settled through the society's plan for shipping him out of the country. That program might thus enable a man to be an emancipationist and at the same time not force him to challenge his own basic social arrangements. The society's program, as an idea, retained its hold until the early 1830's, but its concrete accomplishments were extremely meager throughout.

[120] "I advance it . . . as a suspicion only," Jefferson wrote reluctantly in 1781, "that the blacks, whether originally a distinct race, or made distinct by time and circumstances, are inferior to the whites in the endowments both of body and mind." *Notes on the State of Virginia,* ed. William Peden (Chapel Hill: University of North Carolina Press, 1955), p. 143; see also *ibid.,* pp. 286–88. Jefferson apparently continued to hope that he was wrong on this point. "Nobody wishes more than I do," he wrote to a Negro mathematician and surveyor in 1791, "to see such proofs as you exhibit, that nature has given to our black brethren, talents equal to those of the other colors of men, and that the appearance of a want of them is owing merely to the degraded condition of their existence, both in Africa and America." Jefferson to Benjamin Banneker, August 30, 1791, *Writings of Thomas Jefferson,* ed. Albert E. Bergh (Washington: Thomas Jefferson Memorial Association, 1905), VIII, 241.

Meanwhile, the economics of slavery had altered with the rapid expansion of cotton into the lower South in the period following the War of 1812. For the first time in many decades, slave labor could now represent something unequivocally profitable and become a factor of high value for large numbers of people,[121] especially in the new Gulf states. Many an old Virginia family might still be unwilling to sell its Negroes down the river, but sending a younger son South with enough surplus slaves to open a new plantation could be on quite another moral plane. Both, actually, occurred with increasing frequency. The hostility to slavery that had been common in Jeffersonian times became more and more abstract and, after a final flareup in the early 1830's, all but disappeared.

Several sets of conditions in Virginia combined, first, to bring the question of emancipation out for final review, and then to settle it, to all intents and purposes, forever. One of these was an economic recession during which the prices of tobacco, cotton, and slaves had remained low for several years.[122] In addition, the Census of 1830 had appeared to give some basis for the fear that an inordinate surplus of Negro slaves, not being sold outside the state, was accumulating within it, and that their rate of increase had become greater than that of the white population. This had an especially irritating effect on the yeoman-farmer districts of western Virginia. There, as in other upland areas of the South, the antislavery feeling that existed was a product not of humanitarianism but simply of race hostility, hostility to the Tidewater, and a strong reluctance to receive substantial numbers of new Negroes into their midst.[123] Then the news, in August, 1831, of Nat Turner's rebellion in Southampton County, Virginia, gave rise to the wildest emotions everywhere.

The meeting of the Virginia legislature in December, 1831,

[121] On this general question of slavery's "profitability," see Appendix.

[122] Lewis Cecil Gray, *History of Agriculture in the Southern States to 1860* (Washington, D.C.: Carnegie Institution of Washington, 1933), II, 767; U. B. Phillips, *American Negro Slavery* (New York: Appleton, 1918), p. 370.

[123] Joseph Clarke Robert, *The Road from Monticello: A Study of the Virginia Slavery Debate of 1832* ("Historical Papers of the Trinity College Historical Society," XXIV [Durham: Duke University Press, 1941]), pp. 8–11. The underrepresented western districts also favored reduction of the Negro population in the Tidewater counties.

thus occurred amid circumstances in which men found their thoughts and feelings in a highly unsettled state and in which their talk might conceivably erupt in any of several directions. Such were the circumstances—a general sense that "something ought to be done"—in which the famous debates took place. The legislature that year happened to be full of high-spirited young men, including the son of John Marshall and the grandson of Thomas Jefferson. These scions of antislavery planter families, anxious to launch their political careers on a strong antislavery note, managed to strike up enough of an alliance with upland delegates of the western counties to cause a considerable amount of difficulty before they were finally brought to a halt. They condemned slavery and urged, with great vivacity, a publicly financed program of emancipation and colonization. The debate lasted about two weeks, during which the antislavery forces appeared to have gained substantial support, but at length it was voted that the question be delayed until the next session. The community's "conservative good sense" needed no more of a breather than that, in order to reassert itself, and nothing more came of the scheme thereafter.[124]

Any sentiment of an antislavery sort had, as a matter of fact, been more or less hollowed out well before this time. The strongest voices in the Virginia legislature—men of high principle whose families had been active in the Colonization Society, as well as the dirt-farming folk of the west—were all united in one thing: Negroes constituted an unwelcome element in Southern life. At no point was it proposed simply to give the slaves their liberty and let it go at that; the last thing anyone wanted was a free Negro population in Virginia. Consequently, all that these men could really offer in the face of such an evil, and the only solution they had for the badness of slavery, was to get rid of

[124] The debates, and the conservative reaction that followed them, are discussed at length in *ibid.*, pp. 15–50. Very symptomatic of this reaction, coinciding as it did with a marked economic upturn in 1832, were heavy victories for the conservatives in the spring elections and the wide effect of Thomas R. Dew's pamphlet, *Review of the Debates in the Virginia Legislature of 1831 and 1832*. Dew, a professor of political economy and other subjects at William and Mary College, temperately but most effectively chided the young delegates for their (as he thought) reckless and unseemly zeal in urging that slavery, a beneficent (as he tried to prove) institution, be banished from Virginia.

their Negroes altogether.[125] It was not simply the adverse vote, moreover, but subsequent events that settled remaining doubts and placed their schemes of colonization finally beyond the realm of practicality. Matters were set to rights very shortly thereafter when in 1832 prices—and the profitable export of slaves from Virginia to the lower South—took a sharp upturn.[126]

The decade of the 1830's saw the completion of a consensus throughout Southern society on the subject of slavery that became ever broader and deeper. What the abolitionist blasts of Garrison and the others could then do, and did with peculiar effectiveness,

[125] There were varying degrees of antislavery sentiment expressed—some of considerable sharpness—and various kinds of emancipationist proposals offered, but in the end they all came down to the same solution, deportation. See Robert, *Road from Monticello*, pp. 15–36, 57–112.

[126] This economic recovery, especially as it affected slavery, was most dramatic, and should be accorded very great weight in explaining how Southern antislavery feeling, turning a definite corner at this time, began its swift and final decline into insignificance. It was in this very period that prices in the key items—tobacco, cotton, and slaves—began to soar. The warehouse price of tobacco in Virginia had by 1837 more than doubled what it was in 1830, and in cotton, the New York price went from 9½ cents a pound in 1832 to 17½ cents in 1835. For slaves, the low point in Virginia had been reached in the period 1825–29, when a prime field hand sold for $400. By 1835, however, the price had risen to $650, and by 1837, to $1100. See Gray, *History of Agriculture,* II, 765–68; Phillips, *American Negro Slavery,* table opposite p. 370.

And yet this situation, so far as it affected the status of slavery in Virginia, becomes even more striking when it is connected with what was happening to slave prices in the Gulf area. For example, the New Orleans price by 1832 had already reached $1,025 (substantially higher than in Virginia), which in Virginia had the effect not only of raising prices but of giving an unprecedented stimulus to the export of slaves from Virginia to the lower South—an agreeable functional substitute, to say the least, for state-financed schemes of colonization. At no time was this trade heavier than it became between 1832 and 1836; during the entire 1830–40 decade some 120,000 Negroes were exported from Virginia; and by 1840 the Negro majority in that state had been reduced from 81,000 to 68,000, despite an actual drop in the white population. *Ibid.,* p. 370; Winfield H. Collins, *The Domestic Slave Trade of the Southern States* (New York: Broadway Publishing Co., 1904), pp. 49–50; Frederic Bancroft, *Slave-Trading in the Old South* (Baltimore: J. H. Furst Co., 1931), pp. 385–86. Consequently one may well understand how the only really convincing antislavery argument in Virginia—the threat of a surplus Negro population—was pulled away with what amounted to breath-taking suddenness, never to be reinstated.

was to bring that consensus to an acute pitch of self-awareness. The "argument," such as it had been, was all but closed. And now, the fact that the abolitionists were virtually all Northerners —and that their attacks were so violent and uncompromising— could hardly have been better suited for a general mobilization of sectional patriotism. Indeed, there was nothing in the abolitionist program of immediate emancipation that even made connections with whatever antislavery sentiment still persisted in such areas as western Virginia, Tennessee, and North Carolina. All that Garrison and Phillips could do with the people of these places was to repel and alienate them. And so it would be with the most humane and sensitive planter, wherever he might be found; such a man was just as much Garrison's target as was the most brutal slave-beater in Mississippi. Be he ever so ridden with doubts about the morality and justice of slavery, the fanatics of New England seemed to leave him with little choice. What was he to do with *his* guilt? He could do as the abolitionists demanded and get rid of his slaves; he might then, as Birney did, go North and proselytize. He would not have had much company. Or, he might simply discharge his sense of guilt by turning upon his tormentors. With that, he entered a growing phalanx of Southerners, high, low, and middling.[127]

The existence of thoroughgoing consensus in a democratic community appears to create two sorts of conditions for the functioning of intellect. One is sternly coercive, the other, wildly permissive. On the one hand, consensus narrows the alternatives with which thought may deal; on the other, it removes all manner of limits—limits of discrimination, circumspection, and

[127] This mechanism was well described by a sympathetic Northern visitor, Nehemiah Adams. "To the question of why various things are not done to improve the condition of the blacks," he wrote, "the perpetual answer from men and women who seek no apology for indolence and cupidity is, 'We are afraid of your abolitionists. Whoever moves for redress in any of these things is warned that he is playing into the hands of northern fanatics.' " An example was the fate of a bill in one of the state legislatures for placing a limit on the age under which a slave child could not be sold. The killing argument had nothing to do with humanity, but was simply, "It is a concession to the abolitionists." The man who drafted the bill told Adams that his measure "was voted down under the influence of appeals and warnings . . . against northern exultation." *South-Side View of Slavery,* pp. 108, 113.

discipline—on the alternatives that remain. The former function is probably better understood than the latter; both, however, were fully at work in the intellectual life of the ante-bellum South.

When Tocqueville wrote out his ideas on the "tyranny of the majority" over matters of thought, he was specifically using America as his model. The "most absolute monarchs in Europe," he declared, "cannot prevent certain opinions hostile to their authority from circulating in secret through their dominions, and even in their courts." But, he continued,

It is not so in America; as long as the majority is still undecided, discussion is carried on; but as soon as its decision is irrevocably pronounced, every one is silent, and the friends as well as the opponents of the measure unite in assenting to its propriety. . . .

The authority of a king is physical, and controls the actions of men without subduing their will. But the majority possesses a power which is physical and moral at the same time, which acts upon the will as much as upon the actions, and represses not only all contest, but all controversy.

It is a process in which "the body is left free, and the soul is enslaved."[128]

Such was the process whereby the young bloods of Virginia in 1831, and any who shared their views, to say nothing of men who may have entertained truly radical ones, were finally silenced. We cannot know for certain that they stopped thinking; most certainly they stopped speaking.

Before considering the other, the permissive, function of democratic consensus, it should be granted that the very effort which

[128] Tocqueville, *Democracy in America,* I, 263–64. Cf. the following passage from John Stuart Mill: "Like other tyrannies, the tyranny of the majority was at first . . . held in dread, chiefly as operating through the acts of the public authorities. But reflecting persons perceived that when society is itself the tyrant—society collectively, over the separate individuals who compose it—its means of tyrannizing are not restricted to the acts which it may do by the hands of its public functionaries. Society can and does execute its own mandates: and if it issues wrong mandates instead of right, or any mandates at all in things with which it ought not to meddle, it practices a social tyranny more formidable than many kinds of political oppression, since, though not usually upheld by such extreme penalties, it leaves fewer means of escape, penetrating much more deeply into the details of life, and enslaving the soul itself." *On Liberty and Other Essays,* introd. Emery Neff (New York: Macmillan, 1926), p. 7.

went into the proslavery argument did force ante-bellum Southern thinkers to view society in certain ways that were not congenial to the generality of Americans at the time, ways that would doubtless not have been hit upon otherwise. More than one recent writer has discerned the odd affinity between some of these men's social commentaries and those of Karl Marx himself. Insofar as a burgeoning industrial order was conceived as the enemy, the South did in its way confront that order with its busiest critics. John C. Calhoun, to mention the most eminent of them, worried the subject to death, but "he also set forth," as Richard Hofstadter has said, "a system of social analysis that is worthy of considerable respect." Calhoun was perfectly willing to recognize the exploitative potentialities of industrial capitalism; class revolution was to him quite conceivable—as it was to Marx and other European thinkers—in consequence of what he assumed as capital's tendency to concentrate itself while wearing out its ever expendable supply of "free" labor. The point, for him, was that the irresponsibility of wage employment for the employee was absent under chattel slavery.

A number of other Southerners followed, or paralleled, Calhoun in this line of thinking, and in the course of it produced observations of at least a proto-sociological sort. Especially noteworthy in this respect were such men as George Fitzhugh, Thomas R. Dew, George Frederick Holmes, and Henry Hughes. In all times and in all societies, they argued, were forces that made for authority on one side and subordination on the other. Under feudalism, the principle worked through a kind of "natural" ordering of class and function, of responsibilities and duties; under capitalism, the ordering process is accomplished only through the untrammeled motive of gain, with the exploitation and ultimate starvation of labor as its result. This was the condition toward which the Northern laboring classes were headed— if they were not hopelessly mired in it already—and the Southern arrangement of outright lifetime bondage could thus be seen as the truly humane, rational, and beneficent solution for the subordinated orders. So long as capital *owned* labor, the owner had not only a responsibility for, but a vested interest in, the laborer's well-being. The argument, in such writings as those of Simms, Hammond, and Tucker, envisioned an aristocratic idyl of productive leisure and protected labor; under the "sociologists" and political economists it also brought forth a labor, as opposed to a property, theory of value.[129]

To the extent that the thinker, in order to acquire insights into a society, must stand a little off, or at least see his society in a kind of double vision, to such an extent may it be said that these Southerners were able to see things about American society that to Northerners were more or less invisible. As we have already noted, the Northerner's sense of structure, of authority, of labor and property and institutions, had atrophied to the point of childishness in an expanding universe of individual enterprise, when it came to assessing these things intellectually. The South-

[129] Clear evidence of Calhoun's conviction that labor and capital in a free society are by nature antagonistic may be found in his "Speech on the Reception of Abolition Petitions" delivered in the Senate on February 6, 1837, as well as in his "Disquisition on Gevernment." *Works of John C. Calhoun,* ed. Richard K. Crallé (New York: Appleton, 1854–61), I, 46; II, 632. Richard N. Current traces this and other "Marxist" elements in Calhoun's letters, reports, conversations, and speeches in "John C. Calhoun, Philosopher of Reaction," *Antioch Review,* III (Summer, 1943), 223–34; see also Richard Hofstadter's essay, "John C. Calhoun: The Marx of the Master Class," in *The American Political Tradition,* pp. 67–91.

Other works that together form the quintessence of the South's intellectual effort in defense of slavery are: George Fitzhugh, *A Sociology for the South; or, The Failure of Free Society* (Richmond: A. Morris, 1854), and *Cannibals All! or, Slaves without Masters* (Richmond: A. Morris, 1857); Henry Hughes, *A Treatise on Sociology, Theoretical and Practical* (Philadelphia: Lippincott, Grambo, 1854); *The Pro-Slavery Argument; as Maintained by . . . Chancellor Harper, Governor Hammond, Dr. Simms, and Professor Dew* (Charleston: Walker, Richards, 1852); and *Cotton Is King, and Pro-Slavery Arguments: Comprising the Writings of Hammond, Harper, Christy, Stringfellow, Hodge, Bledsoe, and Cartwright . . .* (Augusta: Pritchard, Abbott & Loomis, 1860).

Especially useful, as analyses of some or all of this work, are Joseph Dorfman, *The Economic Mind in American Civilization, 1606–1865* (New York: Viking Press, 1946), II, 881–956; Clement Eaton, *Freedom of Thought in the Old South* (Durham: Duke University Press, 1940); Louis Hartz, *The Liberal Tradition in America: An Interpretation of American Political Thought since the Revolution* (New York: Harcourt, Brace, 1955), pp. 145–200; William Sumner Jenkins, *Pro-Slavery Thought in the Old South* (Chapel Hill: University of North Carolina Press, 1935); and Harvey Wish, *George Fitzhugh, Propagandist of the Old South* (Baton Rouge: Louisiana State University Press, 1943). C. Vann Woodward's subtle essay, "George Fitzhugh, Sui Generis" (the introduction to a new edition of Fitzhugh's *Cannibals All!* scheduled for publication in 1960 by Harvard University Press), considers the margin within which Fitzhugh was *not* coerced by the proslavery argument.

erner, being just enough out of phase with the drift of society at large, was anything but ready to take it all uncritically for granted. And yet, as Louis Hartz remarks of Fitzhugh, all around this intellectual heave-to in behalf of slavery lingers the echo of the mad genius. All these perceptions about the nature and conditions of free labor under property-grounded laissez-faire capitalism were well and good. But they were gained not so much through a critical contrast with slavery as through a general agreement to stop thinking about slavery altogether; the failure of any free workers to present themselves for enslavement can serve as one test of how much the analysis may have added to Americans' understanding of themselves. "Everything that the Southerners had said," observes Mr. Hartz, "was superlatively a matter of degree. . . ."[130]

Whether this were true "conservative" thought—or, indeed, "thought" of any kind as it is commonly carried on—may be judged from a glance at a British conservative thinker who was full of sympathy for the slaveholding South and who was the closest British counterpart to the American proslavery writers. Thomas Carlyle, in his own writings, had opposed emancipation in the West Indies and had vigorously attacked the "misguided philanthropists" who held forth at London's Exeter Hall. Carlyle was much praised and widely quoted in the American South, and he himself appeared not unwilling to lend his pen to the Southerners in defense of their institutions. But he had his conditions. *Some* account must be taken of slavery as it now existed, and something had to be done; intellect, without its Exeter Hall, was to him unthinkable. "Give me leave, in my dim light, but in my real sympathy with your affairs," he wrote to his friend Beverley Tucker,

to hint . . . [a] thought I have. It is, that this clamour from your "Exeter Hall" and ours, which few persons can regard with less reverence than I, was nevertheless a thing *ncessary*. My notion is, that the relation of the white man to the black is *not* at present a just one, according to the Law of the Eternal; and though "abolition" is by no means the way to remedy it . . . yet, beyond all question, remedied it must be; and peace upon it is not possible till a remedy be found, and begin to be visibly applied. "A servant hired *for life,* instead of by the day or month": I have often wondered that wise and just men in your

130 Hartz, *Liberal Tradition,* p. 186.

region (of whom I believe there are many) had not come upon a great many methods, or at least some methods better than those yet in use, of justly enunciating this relation. . . .[131]

This could strike Tucker only as a rather unpleasant digression. He passed Carlyle's letter on to Hammond, remarking, "He has still prejudices growing out of perverted statements which in England pass for truth, but his thoughts and feelings are strongly drawn to the subject."[132] Complexity of such a sort, at this stage, was hardly what Tucker, Hammond, or any Southerner wanted from Carlyle, who was asking them to use intellect in the service of their own problems. And so it was, that in the end all that these men actually took from their British friend was his "real sympathy" with their affairs.

In reality, the contour of this body of thought was governed by the fact that the South was talking no longer to the world, or even to the North, but to itself. It is this fact—the fact of internal consensus and the peculiar lack of true challenge-points at any level of Southern society—that gives the proslavery polemic its special distinction. Consensus, while withdrawing one kind of liberty, conferred in its place another kind which had not previously been there. The mind could now conceive the enemy in any size or shape it chose; specters were utterly free to range, thrive, and proliferate.

Only in such a setting of nightmare does it seem plausible, for example, that one of the most non-intellectual of paradoxes should have developed in men's writing and talk regarding the Negro slave and his present and hypothetical behavior. On the one hand, the ideal picture of Southern life was one of contentment, of plantations teeming with faithful and happy black children young and old—helpless, purposeless children incapable of sustained and unsupervised initiative. On the other hand was the picture of doom; the hint of freedom, whispered by designing

[131] Carlyle to N. Beverley Tucker, October 31, 1850, quoted in Jenkins, *Pro-Slavery Thought,* p. 307. Cf. Carlyle, "Occasional Discourse on the Nigger Question," in *Critical and Miscellaneous Essays* (London: Chapman & Hall, 1888), III, 463–92. This fiercely conservative essay, whose white-supremacy doctrines were so heartening to American proslavery publicists, first appeared as a magazine article in 1849.

[132] Tucker to J. H. Hammond, January 2, 1851, Hammond MSS, Library of Congress.

abolitionists, would galvanize the sleeping monster in every slave, arouse bloody revolts, and bring hordes of black primitives bent on murder and destruction. For the first picture, though it tended to blur alongside the other, there was at least a substantial amount of evidence; for the second, which grew in luridness the longer men stared at it, there was next to none.

A heavy and cramping tension thus exists in most of the formal writings. The spokesmen did not want it supposed for an instant that the South was unable to control its slave population or that the inferior creatures were anything but pleased with their happy condition. But on the other hand, in order that the abolitionist menace might be given reality and concreteness in their own community, the Southerners could only murmur of insurrection as the price of non-vigilance. Any talk of liberation, on whatever terms, would open doors to the unspeakable. "A merrier being does not exist on the face of the globe, than the negro slave of the U. States," wrote Professor Dew, one of the earliest and least troubled of the proslavery essayists. And yet he warned: "Let the wily philanthropist but come and whisper into the ears of such a slave that his situation is degrading and his lot a miserable one ... and that moment, like the serpent that entered the garden of Eden, he destroys his happiness and his usefulness." Rebuking the emancipationists in the Virginia legislature, Dew wrote of their schemes: "They are admirably calculated to excite plots, murders and insurrections; whether gradual or rapid in their operation, this is the inevitable tendency."[133] William Gilmore Simms insisted in 1837:

Perhaps there is nothing in the world that the people of the South less apprehend, than ... the insurrection of their negroes. The attempts of this people at this object have been singularly infrequent, and perhaps never would be dreamed of, were their bad passions not appealed to by the abolitionists or their emissaries. They are not a warlike people; are, indeed, rather a timid race. . . .[134]

[133] "Professor Dew on Slavery," reprint of Dew's *Review of the Debates in the Virginia Legislature of 1831 and 1832*, in *Pro-Slavery Argument*, pp. 444, 459–60.

[134] "The Morals of Slavery," in *ibid.*, pp. 242–43. Simms, novelist and littérateur of Charleston, edited the *Southern Quarterly Review*. This essay originally appeared in the *Southern Literary Messenger* in 1837 as a review of, and attack on, the writings of Harriet Martineau and others.

The irritability mounts. Chancellor William Harper of South Carolina took note, in 1837, of insinuations that his countrymen were "nightly reposing over a mine [of potential revolt], which may at any moment explode," whereupon he himself exploded. He declared that "if any thing is certain in human affairs, it is certain and from the most obvious considerations, that we are more secure in this respect than any civilized and fully peopled society upon the face of the earth." Later in his essay, however, Harper observed gloomily that it was doubtless through "the exertions of the *amis des noirs* in France" that "the horrors of St. Domingo were perpetrated."[135] One of the most lyrical passages in praise of slavery was penned by Governor Hammond of South Carolina:

And our patriarchal scheme of domestic servitude is indeed well calculated to awaken the higher and finer feelings of our nature. It is not wanting in its enthusiasm and its poetry. The relations of the most beloved and honored chief . . . are frigid and unfelt compared with those existing between the master and his slaves—who served his father, and rocked his cradle, or have been born into his household, and look forward to serve his children—who have been through life the props of his fortune, and the objects of his care—who have partaken of his griefs, and looked to him for comfort in their own—whose sickness he has so frequently watched over and relieved—whose holidays he has so often made joyous by his bounties and his presence; for whose welfare, when absent, his anxious solicitude never ceases, and whose hearty and affectionate greetings never fail to welcome him home. In this cold, calculating, ambitious world of ours, there are few ties more heartfelt, or of more benignant influence, than those which mutually bind the master and the slave, under our ancient system, handed down from the father of Israel.

And yet in the same essay Hammond, rhetorically addressing the abolitionists, demands: "Allow our slaves to read your writings, stimulating them to cut our throats! Can you believe us to be such unspeakable fools?"[136]

[135] "Harper on Slavery," *ibid.*, pp. 74–75, 97; reprinted as "Slavery in the Light of Social Ethics," in *Cotton Is King, and Pro-Slavery Arguments*, pp. 607–8, 625. "Santo Domingo," in this and other writings, refers to the terrible uprising of free Negroes and slaves in Haiti during the French Revolution, culminating in the massacre of hundreds of whites and, ultimately, in the island's winning its independence.

[136] This painful ambiguity is evident throughout Hammond's essay: "I do not mean by all this to say that we are in a state of actual alarm and

By the 1850's the argument had become mechanical. In Albert Taylor Bledsoe's "Liberty and Slavery," it was only a single step from a peaceful countryside (upon which the author contented himself by simply quoting Hammond) to the hideous specter of Santo Domingo. Emancipation, Bledsoe announced, "would furnish the elements of the most horrible civil war the world has ever witnessed."

> As Robespierre caused it to be proclaimed to the free blacks of St. Domingo that they were naturally entitled to all the rights and privileges of citizens; as Mr. Seward proclaimed the same doctrine to the free blacks of New York; so there would be kind benefactors enough to propagate the same sentiments among our colored population. . . . If the object of such agitators were . . . to stir up scenes of strife and blood, it might be easily attained. . . .[137]

Such imaginings took even more fantastic form in the popular mind. Despite the fact that after 1831 no more slave insurrections were seen in the South, it was precisely then that the South became most victimized by its own fears, being "racked at intervals," as Clement Eaton writes, "by dark rumors and imagined plots." These periodic upheavals over suspected revolts—characterized by furious vigilante hunts and wild confusion, all based on mirage—constitute one of the more bizarre chapters in Southern history. Indeed, the very absence of slave uprisings all during this period, and thus their very imaginary character, may have been the real key to their frightfulness. "Negro insurrection," wrote a skeptical resident of Falmouth, Virginia,

> is the name for every horror, simply because it is one of which the Southerners know nothing. . . . The present generation has seen noth-

---

fear of our slaves; but under existing circumstances we should be ineffably stupid not to increase our vigilance and strengthen our hands." Then later he declares that the system is not "in decay," that it "flourishes in full and growing vigor"—yet should the bond be broken "but for a day," then the full cycle of revolution would begin, to be ended only by a blood bath like that of Santo Domingo. "Hammond's Letters on Slavery," *Pro-Slavery Argument*, pp. 124, 127, 147–50, 161; reprinted as "Slavery in the Light of Political Science," in *Cotton Is King, and Pro-Slavery Arguments*, pp. 649, 651, 667–69, 678. This essay consisted originally of two letters addressed to the British abolitionist Thomas Clarkson, written early in 1845.

[137] *Cotton Is King*, p. 412. Bledsoe was professor of mathematics at the University of Virginia. "Liberty and Slavery" was written in 1856.

ing of the kind. That is the very reason why there is such a horror and a panic about it: it is a vague, mysterious, and unknown evil.[138]

It was a matter, moreover, not of division but of consensus, consensus in its ultimate stage of democratization; the "black terror" now meant virtually the same thing to everyone.

In trying to explain the mounting passions of the period, more than one writer has declared, with a kind of desperate irritability, that the South's fears were simply "unreal." Though this in itself may not explain much, there is good reason to conclude that the South's horror of insurrection was a product not of real insurrection but, oddly enough, of a united mind. *This*—its own unanimity—was what the South had girded itself and rigged all its alarms to defend. It was now, in short, not so much physical peril that Southerners most feared, but something else; they feared subversion.[139] The fear itself, if not its object, was real enough; Southern newspapers, month after month, teemed with evidence of it. Those old papers thus leave ironic traps for us, even today. We have a monograph on slave revolts, written in scholarly modern times, that can offer nothing but this kind of "evidence"—fear of subversion—for a multitude of "revolts" that never materialized. At the bottom of nearly every imaginary "plot" was an imaginary abolitionist—a "foreign agent" or a domestic fellow traveler.[140]

[138] Moncure D. Conway, quoted in Wish, *George Fitzhugh,* p. 63. It is also interesting to note Frederick Law Olmsted's observation that the places where the whites posted the weakest guard were actually the areas where the Negro population was densest. See *A Journey in the Back Country* (New York: Mason Bros., 1860), p. 377.

[139] This was, in effect, what Olmsted reported. "The real object of the systematic mail robbery which is maintained throughout the South, and the censorship of the press which is otherwise attempted, was once betrayed by a somewhat distinguished Southern editor, Duff Green, in the *United States Telegraph,* in the following words:

" 'The real danger of this [slave insurrection] is remote. We believe we have most to fear from the organized action upon the consciences and fears of the slaveholders themselves; from the insinuation of . . . dangerous heresies into our schools, our pulpits, and our domestic circles. It is only by alarming the consciences of the weak and feeble, and diffusing among our people a morbid sensibility on the question of slavery, that the Abolitionists can accomplish their object.' " Olmsted, *The Cotton Kingdom,* ed. and introd. A. M. Schlesinger (New York: Knopf, 1953), p. 579 n.

[140] Herbert Aptheker, *American Negro Slave Revolts* (New York: Columbia University Press, 1943), esp. pp. 325–58. This book, much of

An elusive attribute of internal danger is that at the moment when a society is most fully committed to resist it, the "danger" itself has for that very reason become least dangerous. Conversely, then, it is hardly a paradox that the farther away the enemy is, the more menacing he seems and the more devilish are the shapes he assumes; and this is because all, not just a few, are hunting him everywhere in their midst. If he is imagined to be lurking under every bed, it is because no one meets him face to face any more in the market place. If he were indeed real and present, some men—the community's intellectuals at least—might try to reason with him. But a democratic people no longer "reasons" with itself when it is all of the same mind. Men will then only warn and exhort each other, that their solidarity may be yet more perfect. The South's intellectuals, after the 1830's, did really little more than this. And when the enemy's reality disappears, when his concreteness recedes, then intellect itself, with nothing more to resist it and give it resonance, merges with the mass and stultifies, and shadows become monsters.

---

whose evidence consists of unsubstantiated rumors in ante-bellum rural newspapers, is thus rather unreliable for judging how seriously any of these "revolts" should be taken. The book does, however, bring out one striking fact about the period: whereas the "real" rebellions of the pre-1835 period (those of Gabriel, Vesey, and Turner) were instigated by Negroes, the "unreal" ones in the following period almost invariably involved white men—white abolitionists, that is, created by the Southern imagination. The same point is made in Edwin A. Miles, "The Mississippi Slave Insurrection Scare of 1835," *Journal of Negro History*, XLII (January, 1957), 48–60. See also Eaton, *Freedom of Thought*, pp. 89–117. One of the heavy coercions upon the Southern mind in this period was the fact that men were expected to believe in these dangers, their patriotism actually coming under suspicion if they failed to. There was no premium—as would tend to be the case in the midst of real peril—on cool-headedness. In 1835 one Virgil A. Stewart, in a pamphlet full of lies, spread stories across the state of Mississippi about an impending slave revolt in which white Northerners were supposedly implicated. "He was looked upon by many as a great public benefactor," wrote Henry S. Foote many years later, "and those who dared even to question the actual existence of the dangers which he depictured were suspected of a criminal insensibility to the supposed perils of the hour, or were denounced as traitors to the slaveholding interests of the South." *Casket of Reminiscences* (Washington: Chronicle Publishing Co., 1874), p. 251.

V

Slavery and Ideology
(1971)

I

When I first became interested in the subject of slavery more than fifteen years ago, I was greatly struck by what seemed to me the "closed" character of the argument as it had been carried on by publicists and scholars over several prior generations. "To the present day," I said in the opening pages of my book, "the rhythm of 'right' and 'wrong' which characterized antebellum discourse on the subject of slavery has retained much of its original simplicity and vigor." It seemed then that some effort needed to be made to break the grip of the old argument, and to interrupt this persistent "rhythm of 'right' and 'wrong.'" That is, I did not believe that further insights were to be gained by continuing the discourse as though the brutality and inhumanity of American Negro slavery were still a matter of question. On those terms, I felt, the debate had been settled. I urged that the terms now be changed, and that the debate be continued on newer and less familiar ground. Specifically, I believed that by examining the implications of cross-cultural comparisons, and by raising the issue of institutions and their impact upon individuals, one might thereby loosen the coercions of the old debate and open up new lines of exploration. Since that time, such explorations have in fact occurred, and a new debate has replaced the old. The present occasion, to which I have been invited to contribute, bears impressive testimonial of this.[1]

And yet this same occasion, dealing as it does with my own

[1] The occasion referred to was the preparation of Ann J. Lane, ed., *The Debate over Slavery: Stanley Elkins and His Critics* (Urbana: University of Illinois Press, 1971).

work, confronts me with certain ironic embarrassments. I began that work in an effort to break out of a closed cycle, but hardly foresaw that the time might come when I would be locked in another, this time partly of my own making. The terms of today's debate are very different from what they were then. But the debate itself, and the rhythm of it, have now taken on qualities uncomfortably similar to those I found so coercive when I first began. That I myself should be largely responsible for a state of things comparable to the one I originally resisted hardly makes the embarrassment less acute. Consequently, I have come to think that it would be not at all a bad thing if the terms were once again changed.

How all this came about, and how the outlines of the present debate emerged, may be seen from the critical writings to which my work has given rise. This criticism falls into three broad categories. How significant, it asks, were the differences between North American and Latin American slavery? How adequate is such an analogy as the Nazi concentration camp, with its implications for human personality, when applied to the complex reality of American Negro slavery? What real bearing does the idea of anti-institutionalism in American life have on the problem of American abolitionism? These three questions, of course, encompass a good many others, as a close reading of the critical essays will reveal. The criticism has been formidable, salutary, and enormously instructive. At the same time it does form a certain pattern, and has created a new rhythm of its own.

I am thus faced with certain choices regarding what the present occasion requires of me. One choice would be simply to take up the principal commentaries, point by point, and "answer" them seriatim. From the standpoint of their quality, justice would certainly seem to call for some such effort. But here I would be confronted with endless difficulties. For one thing, certain of the criticisms, being correct, are by the same token unanswerable. But as for the rest, were I to approach them on their merits, I would be forced to undertake a range of supplementary investigation and scholarship that would be well beyond my competence. Faced with that, I should be powerfully tempted to beg off, concede the field, and go about other business. And yet I do retain certain convictions about my own work, and the number of concessions I am willing to make does have its limits.

Another choice would be to proceed as though all the criticism were helpful, at least in its effect, and to try to project what my book might have been like if I had had the benefit of it beforehand —or if, instead of having written it then, I were writing it now. But it took little reflection to make the artificiality of such a course apparent. In subsequent editions of their work, few authors have been known to change a single word of what they originally wrote, and I think I can now understand why. The very criticism they have received, the subsequent knowledge they have acquired, the afterthoughts they have entertained, all make it literally impossible to imagine what it would be like to start over. At the same time, why should it be assumed that the conceptual framework which I found meaningful ten years ago, and within which the question is still being debated, is necessarily the most serviceable one for future debates? Conceivably it is not; others are surely possible.

All of which leads to a third alternative, one that to me seems much more constructive than either of the others. What my critics have written is important, and must be taken account of. But I wish to do this with other purposes in mind than simply "vindicating" *Slavery*. I should like to make certain predictions about the future course of the argument. I am assuming that the present one has taken on a certain repetitiveness and acquired certain locked-in features, that this could in time become dangerously stultifying, and that the cycle once more can and should be broken. A new object of interest—the phenomenon of ideology—has arisen in other areas of historical study within the past five years. Ideology is a subject that has to be thought about and written about with standards we are only beginning to get used to. It is this phenomenon and this interest, I should guess, that may create new or altered perspectives in the study of slavery.

2

In the years since I made my proposal, following the lead of Frank Tannenbaum's *Slave and Citizen,* that many important insights were to be derived from comparisons of North American and Latin American slavery, there has been considerable dispute over what such comparisons, if systematically carried out, might be expected to yield. Underlying this debate, if I may simplify it momentarily, is a philosophical question having to do with method. It is a question not simply of models of explanation, but of why one constructs such "models" in the first place, and of what it is one wants to explain with them. In this instance, concerning the slave systems in Anglo-American and Latin American cultures, there are a number of writers—most prominently David Brion Davis, and to a qualified degree Eugene Genovese—who believe that the broad similarities between these systems are more significant than the differences. I, on the other hand, was for more impressed by the contrasts, and laid out my discussion accordingly.

I was struck by the way in which the arrangements of law, custom, and institutions—including those of religion—in the American South evolved along lines so precisely parallel with, and supportive of, the full development of slavery and plantation capitalism. It was apparent that no official contrary standards could emerge in Southern society which might interfere with such a system or complicate its workings. The logic of all this was embodied in a racism the massive consistency of which kept that society united behind slavery while it existed, and continued to operate as a barrier to full freedom long after slavery was dead. In the way in which law, custom, and institutions impinged on slavery in Latin American society, on the other hand, I could perceive no such parallelism, no such logic, no such consistency. The complexities of the slave system there, and the subtle gradations in racial attitudes which accompanied it, are baffling to any American who tries to penetrate them, conditioned as he is to the comparative simplicities of his own society's experience with slavery. To the outside observer, then as now, the Latin American slave population somehow did not seem as totally "enslaved" as it logically ought to have been, since men and women kept leaving it by a variety of exits; nor did color, as a barrier to advancement in free society, operate with anything like the inexorability that his own historical experience would lead him to expect. But why? Why this difference? The question was deeply interesting to me, as it was to Tannenbaum.

In order to deal with it, I lumped the entire Hispanic American and Luso-Brazilian experience together, as Tannenbaum had done, for the purpose of the comparison with the American South. I reasoned that there must have been countervailing institutional forces in both these Latin cultures, generating standards not always consonant with those of chattel slavery, that served both to blunt the full force of slavery itself and to blur the line between slavery and freedom. In attempting to locate such forces I found, or thought I had found, what I was looking for in the form of a royal officialdom which saw to the enforcement of a body of law governing the treatment of slaves and protecting their rights, as well as of a Church whose interest it was to see that all men—slaves included—should be gathered together in the Faith. This rather abstract framework—overly abstract, perhaps—does seem to have been borne out fairly well by studies since made by others of parts of the Spanish Empire.[2] But the same framework, as critics have pointed out to me, cannot be applied to Brazil in anything like the same way. The Portuguese Crown never had the effectiveness in Brazil that the Spanish Crown at the height of its power could claim over its own New World colonies. Repeated royal edicts from Lisbon against the mistreatment of slaves, for example, had minimal results, and expectations of legal redress for abuses were chronically precarious. In the boom plantation areas—the coffee regions of Brazil and even the sugar estates of nineteenth-century Cuba—slavery was full of horrors. Nor did the Church in Brazil, in its official, institutional capacity, have quite the direct impact upon slave life that my schematic treatment seemed to suggest, at least not on the plantations. Nearly all planters maintained private chapels, but despite the heavy Catholic symbolism that characterized daily life and personal relations among masters and slaves, priests were found only on the larger estates, while on most others clerical visits were very irregular. And although the Church's official position was one of racial equality, it was much breached in practice, and the Church's zeal for mitigating the rigors of Negro slavery was hardly on a level with its opposition to Amerindian slavery.[3]

[2] E.g., Herbert S. Klein, *Slavery in the Americas: A Comparative Study of Cuba and Virginia* (Chicago: University of Chicago Press, 1967); Norman Meiklejohn, "The Observance of Negro Slave Legislation in Colonial Nueva Granada" (Ph.D. diss., Columbia University, 1968).

[3] These points are stressed in Eugene D. Genovese, "Rebelliousness and Docility in the Negro Slave: A Critique of the Elkins Thesis," *Civil War History*, XIII (December, 1967), 293–314; David Brion Davis, *The Problem of Slavery in Western Culture* (Ithaca: Cornell University Press, 1966), pp. 223–90; Marvin Harris, *Patterns of Race in the Americas* (New York:

A purely institutional scheme, therefore, if it were to embrace satisfactorily the conditions and impact of slavery in both Brazil and the Spanish colonies, would need to be arranged in a form both more enlarged and more refined than the one proposed in my own brief discussion. I remain—not perversely, I think—more convinced than ever that this is entirely possible. But since for my particular purposes the social end-products of both systems were functionally interchangeable, I was not moved as much as I should have been to pursue such refinements at the time. Had I done so, I would not have required the law and official authority in Brazil to bear quite so many of the burdens, and would have supplemented this with a far heavier emphasis than I gave to the authority of tradition and custom, about which there is a variety of evidence. As for the Brazilian Church, picturing it as a single institution speaking with a single voice is misleading, certainly with regard to the many points at which it touched slavery. A proper picture of the Church's true authority in this realm would require proportionally greater emphasis on the subsidiary institutions which it fostered and protected—most prominently the Negro lay brotherhoods—as well as on the variety of ways in which personal relations were affected by Catholic practice. For forcing me to think such modifications through (I shall say more about them shortly), I have particularly to thank Genovese and Davis, whatever the discomfiture they may have caused me.

The very surge, however, that has gone into their line of criticism, salutary as it is, has generated certain side effects that discomfit me for quite other reasons, and that are not so salutary. What they should have taxed me for was making insufficient discriminations within Latin American society—and in a very limited sense, they have. But more fundamentally their effort is to break down my entire scheme of contrasts with North America through the technique of citing exceptions, the cumulative effect of which is to blur *all* discriminations—discriminations so strikingly gross as to have been perfectly obvious to every outsider who observed and wrote about slavery in nineteenth-century Brazil.

Walker and Co., 1964); Stanley J. Stein, *Vassouras: A Brazilian Coffee County, 1850–1900* (Cambridge: Harvard University Press, 1957), pp. 132–95; and C. R. Boxer, *Race Relations in the Portuguese Colonial Empire, 1415–1825* (Oxford: Clarendon Press, 1963).

Let me revert for a moment to the philosophical question I mentioned earlier regarding assumptions about method: the question of what it is that one expects to accomplish with the comparative approach to historical problems. My conviction on this is that the usefulness of comparison as an analytical device, great as it is, cannot be made to extend beyond fairly restricted purposes. For instance, a case can certainly be made for analogies, if one uses them metaphorically and does not claim too much for them. Or, a comparative survey whose aim is to exhibit a series of sharp contrasts, say between two or more sets of cultural phenomena, seems equally defensible. The critical test they have to meet is simply that of effectiveness: what such devices do for heightening perception. On the other hand, a comparative effort whose primary attention is upon the broad parallels and similarities between cultures will always end, it seems to me, not by heightening perception at all, but by dulling it. To the extent that Davis and Genovese have emphasized the features that slave systems everywhere have had in common—placing the United States, whose system was the most socially damaging of modern times, side by side with Brazil, where the social consequences of slavery were dramatically different—to that extent do they reduce and homogenize the slave experience of the entire Western Hemisphere. I cannot see the gain in this, and I would urge with all due respect that such a drift be resisted. It would be regrettable if, after all our discourse, we should find ourselves back where we started.[4]

One must, at any rate, protect the clarity of one's gross perceptions. Among the very grossest of these, when it is a question of comparing the slave society of Brazil with that of North America, is that concerning the rate and frequency of manumissions. Of the total Negro population of the American slave states in 1860, more than 90 per cent were still in slavery; in Brazil at the same time, more than half were already free, and the proportion of free to slave, which had been steadily rising since the eighteenth

[4] In justice to Genovese I should note that when in his opinion "homogenization" has gone too far, he too feels impelled to move against it. I refer to his sharp critique of Carl Degler's paper, "Slavery in the United States and Brazil: An Essay in Comparative History," read at the annual meeting of the Organization of American Historians at Philadelphia, April 19, 1969, and published in *American Historical Review,* LXXV (April, 1970), 1004–28.

century, would continue to do so over the ensuing 28 years.[5] This is the key fact one has to work with; everything of consequence regarding the entire problem is directly related to it. The very high rate of manumission in Brazil throughout the period of slavery, and, conversely, the large and ever increasing numbers of former slaves functioning in free society there, affected the position not only of freedmen but of persons still in slavery. It affected, in short, the whole character of the slave system; it was a social fact, moreover, that simply did not exist in the United States. And fundamentally it was upon this basis, rather than on grounds of physical treatment, that observers invariably referred to the Brazilian slave system as the "mildest" in the Western Hemisphere.

How are we to account for this, and what are we to make of it? As for the law and its enforcement in Brazil, no modern study has as yet been made, and until one is, generalizations can hardly be made with much precision. We do know from the recent studies of colonial Bahia by A. J. R. Russell-Wood that aggrieved slaves found direct access to the sovereign remarkably simple. But though Spix and Martius, Walsh, Koster, and Mansfeldt insisted that masters were liable to punishment for abusing their slaves,[6] in-

---

[5] In comparison to the steady rise in the numbers of free colored in relation to slaves in Brazil throughout this period, the free-slave ratio among the total colored in the United States (for the entire country) remained strikingly stable. Indeed, by 1860 it had actually declined to 11.0 per cent from the 11.9 per cent of 1850 and 13.4 per cent of 1840. On the other hand, an examination of early manuscript census materials in Brazil has led Herbert Klein to estimate that in the closing years of the eighteenth century the proportion of free men within the total colored population already ran as high as 50 per cent in the peripheral regions and between 20 percent and 30 per cent in the major slave-plantation areas. *Negro Population in the United States, 1790–1915* (New York: Arno Press, 1968), pp. 53–57; Herbert S. Klein, "The Colored Freedmen in Brazilian Slave Society," *Journal of Social History*, III (Fall, 1969), 30–52.

[6] A. J. R. Russell-Wood, *Fidalgos and Philanthropists: The Santa Casa da Misericórdia of Bahia, 1550–1755* (Berkeley: University of California Press, 1968), pp. 139, 257; and "Class, Creed and Colour in Colonial Bahia: A Study in Prejudice," *Race*, IX (October, 1967), 133–57. "One curious aspect of the relationship between slave and sovereign was the facility with which any slave and coloured person could appeal directly to the king." *Ibid.*, 151. J. B. von Spix and C. F. P. von Martius. *Travels in Brazil in the Years 1817–1820* (London: Longmans, 1824), I, 179; R. Walsh, *Notices of Brazil in 1828 and 1829* (Boston: Richardson, 1831), II, 189; Henry Koster,

stances of cruelty, some bordering on the bizarre, were frequent. Or, in view of the frequency of self-purchase, even most Brazilians seem to have been under the impression that a master was legally obliged to free a slave who could present his purchase price. Apparently no such law existed.[7] But here it was custom and public opinion, applauding *all* forms of manumission, that had the virtual force of law. (Newspaper notices of manumissions were carried under the heading of "Acts Worthy of Praise.")[8] One must, moreover, take account not only of what the law did, but of what it did not do. In the American South there were actual prohibitions in law, as well as sanctions of public opinion, against manumission, against the holding of property, and against the educating of slaves. Such prohibitions were unknown in Brazil.

The very conditions of city life, with enormous numbers of both slave and free colored concentrated in urban centers, represented another fragmenting influence upon Brazilian slavery. The employment—and self-employment—of slaves as stevedores, boatmen, peddlers, artisans, skilled craftsmen, and small tradesmen had a variety of consequences both inside and outside the system. With the right to retain a portion of their earnings,

Travels in Brazil (London: Longmans, 1817), II, 237; Julius Mansfeldt, *Meine Reise nach Brasilien im Jahre 1821* (Magdeburg: E. Bansch, 1828), p. 92.

The only study ever done on Brazilian slave law, originally published in 1866 and recently reprinted, is Agostinho Marques Perdigão, *A escravidão no Brasil: ensaio historico-juridico-social* (São Paulo: Edições Cultura, 1944), 2v. It is a study of the jurisprudence of the subject and a commentary on the codes, and is therefore of value for what it reveals of the society's systems of belief (see below), but it contains no systematic information on enforcement. It is comparable to John Codman Hurd's *Law of Freedom and Bondage* and Thomas R. R. Cobb's *Inquiry into the Law of Negro Slavery* for the United States.

[7] Mary W. Williams, "The Treatment of Negro Slaves in the Brazilian Empire: A Comparison with the United States of America," *Journal of Negro History*, XV (July, 1930), 332–33; W. D. Christie, *Notes on Brazilian Questions* (London: Macmillan, 1865), p. 178.

[8] Sir Richard F. Burton, *Explorations of the Highlands of the Brazil* (London: Tinsley, 1869), I, 271–72; Walter Colton, *Deck and Port; or, Incidents of a Cruise in the United States Frigate Congress* . . . (New York: D. W. Evans, 1860), p. 112; Pierre Verger, *Flux et reflux de la traite des nègres entre le Golfe de Bénin et Bahia de Todos os Santos du dix-septième au dix-neuvième siècle* (Paris: Mouton, 1968), pp. 516–18.

these individuals regularly bought their way out of slavery, which meant a systematic leakage of ambitious, economically productive non-whites into free society. Moreover, the diversity of roles which these persons could play while still in slavery meant an ongoing rehearsal, as it were, for freedom, and this in turn meant that the shock of transition, either on the individual or on the environing society, was bound to be minimal. The apprenticing of slave craftsmen side by side with free colored apprentices, their subsequent practice of their trade in company with freedmen, and their eventual entry as free men themselves into a world in which all the skilled crafts were dominated by men of color, constitutes the representative example of how the process worked.[9] And the cities themselves were the very places where sentiments least friendly to slavery were fostered. For example, the officer class, largely recruited from the cities, came more and more to resent the use of the army to capture runaway slaves, and the military schools were centers of abolitionism for many years before emancipation. Nor should this be surprising, with a large part of the army's rank and file, and even a proportion of the officers, being made up of Negroes and mulattoes. In the cities of the American South, on the other hand, the conditions of life for slaves were by mid-century being consciously made more and more restricted.[10]

And yet it was the Catholic Church, however diffusely its

[9] "I have now seen slaves working as carpenters, masons, pavers, printers, sign and ornamental painters, carriage and cabinet makers, fabricators of military ornaments, lamp-makers, silversmiths, jewelers, and lithographers. It is also a fact that sculptures in stone and saintly images in wood are often done admirably by slaves and free blacks. . . . *All* kinds of trades are carried on by black journeymen and boys." Thomas Ewbank, *Life in Brazil: or, A Journal of a Visit to the Land of the Cocoa and the Palm* (New York: Harper, 1856), p. 195. See also Koster, *Travels,* II, 219–20, 260–61; Spix and Martius, *Travels,* I, 197–98; John Luccock, *Notes on Rio de Janeiro and the Southern Parts of Brazil . . . from 1808 to 1818* (London: S. Leigh, 1820), p. 201.

[10] Richard Graham, "Causes for the Abolition of Negro Slavery in Brazil: An Interpretive Essay," *Hispanic American Historical Review,* XLVI (May 1966), 127, 134; Koster, *Travels,* I, 59–60; Klein, "Colored Freedmen," pp. 31–33; C. S. Stewart, *Brazil and La Plata: The Personal Record of a Cruise* (New York: Putnam, 1856), p. 296; Richard C. Wade, *Slavery in the Cities: The South, 1820–1860* (New York: Oxford, 1964), pp. 243–46.

power may have been exerted, that accounted for the major contrasts in character between the slave system of Brazil and that of the United States. The coercive power of the Church in the Spanish dominions was certainly more direct than in Brazil, and the numbers and quality of the priesthood were higher. But it may be doubted whether the influence of Catholic values and Catholic practice was for that reason any the less pervasive. One of the laws that seems not to have been evaded in Brazil was that requiring Catholic instruction and baptism within a year of the newly imported slave's arrival. Family prayers on the estates, morning and night (priest or no priest), the frequent feast days, and the custom of asking and receiving blessings all seem to have created a special set of personal relationships between masters and slaves, unfailingly commented upon by observer after observer. The many religious holidays, during which it was universally understood that slaves, urban or rural, were free to work for themselves, represented a custom that was not lightly breached. The all-embracing quality of the Faith was noted with wonder by the Protestant John Turnbull, visiting Bahia in 1800: "We found . . . that there was one country in the world in which religion was fashionable, the churches being crowded with all ranks of people, from the meanest slave to his excellency the governor himself."[11]

It was, moreover, unquestionably the Church that created the moral climate for frequent manumissions. The testimony is overwhelming: manumission was a pious deed, a Catholic duty, an "Act Worthy of Praise." It was done on a variety of occasions: a marriage, a birthday, a church festival, the making of a will. The freeing of a slave infant at baptism—whether through the custom

[11] Klein, "Colored Freedmen," p. 40; Williams, "Treatment of Negro Slaves," pp. 330–31; John Turnbull, *A Voyage Round the World in the Years 1800, 1801, 1802, 1803, and 1804* . . . (London: Phillips, 1805), I, 23; Koster, *Travels*, II, 239; Thomas Lindley, *Narrative of a Voyage to Brazil* . . . (London: J. Johnson, 1805), p. 176; J. B. Debret, *Voyage pittoresque et historique au Brésil* . . . *depuis 1816 jusqu'en 1831* . . . (Paris: Firmin Didot, 1834–39), II, 100, 104; III, 129; Maria Graham, *Journal of a Voyage to Brazil, and Residence There, during* . . . *1821, 1822, 1823* (London: Longman, 1824), p. 196. "The people of Brazil, brought more in contact with their slaves, from the mildness of their disposition, and from the effects of their religion which unites them together, mix more with them than in other countries. . . ." Alexander Caldcleugh, *Travels in South America during the Years 1819–20–21* (London: John Murray, 1825), I, 89.

of godparenthood or the practice of free fathers liberating their offspring by slave mothers—was very common. It is no mere coincidence that the great majority of such occasions took place under the direct auspices and encouragement of the Church.[12]

Whereas in locating the sources of the Church's institutional power in Spanish America one looks first to the official hierarchy, in Brazil the counterpart is not so obvious. And yet the power was there, and it may well have been organized in such a way that for day-to-day purposes its impact on the slave system itself was even more effective. A major bulwark, social and financial, to Catholicism and the Catholic establishment in Brazil was the large number of lay brotherhoods that flourished under the aegis and protection of the Church. These brotherhoods served the widest variety of social, benevolent, and charitable functions, extending to the actual building and furnishing of churches, and each played a prominent part in municipal religious life, which included the great public festivals and processions. A number of the brotherhoods were open to slaves, free Negroes, and mulattoes, and these probably did more to mold a self-conscious community of the slaves than did any other social mechanism. "The urban counterpart of the *quilombo*," one writer asserts, "was the brotherhood." The Negro brotherhoods gave their members a set of close fraternal ties with a wide company of fellow Catholics, saw to it that masses and a decent burial were provided for those who died, and maintained a regular fund for purchasing the freedom of those who were in slavery. They spoke in a variety of ways for the interests of their membership, and their influence was frequently exerted with the authorities in cases of injustice. The most powerful Negro brotherhood in Bahia, Our Lady of the Rosary, became, according to Russell-Wood, "the mouthpiece for Negro rights."[13]

[12] Herbert S. Klein, "The Integration of the Negro into Latin American Society," paper read at Wayne State University, May 5, 1969, MS.; Koster, *Travels*, II, 234–36; Barbara Rose Trosko, "The Liberto in Bahia before Abolition" (M.A. thesis, Columbia University, 1967), pp. 42–43.

[13] Roger Bastide, *Les religions africaines au Brésil: vers une sociologie des interpénétrations de civilisations* (Paris: Presses Universitaires, 1960), pp. 73, 158–74; Gilberto Freyre, "Some Aspects of the Social Development of Portuguese America," in Charles C. Griffin, ed., *Concerning Latin American Culture* (New York: Columbia University Press, 1940), pp. 92–93; Manoel S. Cardozo, "The Lay Brotherhoods of Colonial Bahia," *Catholic Historical*

The power of the Portuguese Crown to impose its own terms upon the slave system of colonial Brazil could not rival that of the Spanish Crown in Spanish America. Nor could the Brazilian Empire, after 1822, achieve much in the way of centralized authority without the support of the planter class. Yet the fact remains that the interests of the Imperial government with regard to slavery were not those of the *fazendeiros*. For one thing, Brazil's very claims to national sovereignty remained perennially insecure throughout the middle decades of the nineteenth century in the face of constant pressure from the British over the slave trade, the enforcement of slave-trade treaties, and the issue of slavery itself. To such pressures, exerted as they were not only through diplomacy but with the actual use of the Royal Navy, the Brazilian Crown, planters or no planters, found it both expedient and necessary to adjust. Moreover, Dom Pedro II himself, throughout much of his enlightened reign of nearly fifty years, was an ardent abolitionist and made little secret of it. Frequent cues from the Throne did much to establish the emancipationist climate of that reign: the Emperor's freeing of his inherited slaves upon his accession, his personal visit of congratulation to the Benedictines of Rio when they emancipated theirs, his insistence upon freedom for those who served in the Paraguayan War, and his pressure upon the ministry, from the 1860's on, to prepare plans for full emancipation. The 1867 Speech from the Throne was a clear indication to the nation at large that slavery was on its way out. In the end, Pedro II's leadership in this realm may have done much to bring down the monarchy itself, but it also had a great deal to do with bringing down slavery.[14]

Review, XXXIII (April, 1947), 12–30; Verger, *Flux et reflux*, pp. 518–21, 527–28. "For ostensibly religious purposes the Church supported these Negro brotherhoods. Behind this support, however, was its decision to allow the Negroes to protect and defend themselves by forming guilds for their collective efforts towards personal liberty." Trosko, "Liberto in Bahia," pp. 43–44. The quotations are from Russell-Wood, *Fidalgos and Philanthropists*, pp. 142, and "Class, Creed and Colour," p. 153. The *quilombos* were fortified villages of escaped slaves, the term being used here in the sense of a sanctuary.

[14] Richard Graham, "Causes for Abolition," pp. 129–32; Mary W. Williams, *Dom Pedro the Magnanimous: Second Emperor of Brazil* (Chapel Hill: University of North Carolina Press, 1937), pp. 264–87.

In any event, one might have toured the Southern United States from end to end, any time after the mid-1830's, searching in vain for a state governor—or any other prominent public official—willing to take a single step, or to say a single public word, hostile to slavery.

A further test of the Brazilian slave system is surely to be found in the state of race relations in Brazilian society both during and after slavery. The amazement of visitors, especially Americans, at finding "no distinction between white and black, or any of the intermediate colors, which can act as a bar to social intercourse or political advancement," is a repeated and well-known feature of all the travel accounts. There was no segregation in omnibuses, trains, restaurants, or places of entertainment. In the coffee room at the opera house in Rio, wrote Ruschenberger in the 1830's, "Blacks and Whites were gay and noisy, eating and drinking together, apparently on the most intimate terms of equality." Agassiz reported that the students at the elite Colégio Dom Pedro II "were of all colors, from black through intermediate shades to white, and even one of the teachers . . . of a higher class in Latin was a negro." The fastest growing element in nineteenth-century Brazilian society was the free colored—not through natural increase but through miscegenation and manumission—and before the end of slavery the colored were well represented in every major oocupation and profession. The process had already been in motion more than two centuries before, when Henrique Dias and several of his Negro captains were awarded titles of nobility and admitted into Iberian military orders for their exploits in the wars against the Dutch. "African blood," wrote John Codman after a visit in 1866, "runs freely through marble halls, as well as in the lowest gutters." To a Brazilian slave looking toward freedom, there existed a variety of models of aspiration everywhere around him. To the American slave, viewing the degraded free Negro in his own society, such models were dismally few. And so they would remain for many years after Emancipation—certainly in contrast to the freely mixed society of post-Imperial Brazil.[15]

[15] John Codman, *Ten Months in Brazil: With Incidents of Voyages and Travels* . . . (Boston: Lee and Shepard, 1867), p. 153; [William S. W. Rusehenberger], *Three Years in the Pacific: Including Notices of Brazil, Chile, Bolivia, and Peru* (Philadelphia: Carey, Lea and Blanchard, 1834), p. 43; Louis and Elizabeth Agassiz, *A Journey in Brazil* (Boston: Fields,

I am well aware that the innumerable accounts of humane race relations in Brazil, from slavery times down to the present day—from the writings of Henry Koster and Thomas Ewbank in the nineteenth century to those of Gilberto Freyre, Donald Pierson, Frank Tannenbaum, and Charles Wagley in our own time—have at length induced in a number of scholars a certain fretfulness. Race, they point out, *has* been a factor, and still is; prejudice and discrimination *have* played their part in the ordering of Brazilian social arrangements.[16] It is very true that they have. But in what

---

Osgood, 1869), p. 124; Klein, "Colored Freedmen," p. 31. "Thus, if a man have freedom, money, and merit, no matter how black may be his skin, no place in society is refused him." D. P. Kidder and J. C. Fletcher, *Brazil and the Brazilians, Portrayed in Historical and Descriptive Sketches* (Philadelphia: Childs and Peterson, 1857), p. 133. "A Southern lady (the wife of the very popular United States Consul at Rio during the administration of President Pierce) used to say that 'the very paradise of the negroes was Brazil; for there they possess a warm climate, and, if they choose, may make their way up in the world, in a manner which can never be the case in the United States." *Ibid.,* p. 133n. According to Stewart, "color does not fix the social position here, as with us at home. . . . A slave is a menial, not because he is black, but because he is a slave." *Brazil and La Plata,* p. 296. W. D. Christie, whose position as British minister required him to be officially jaundiced against Brazilian slavery, conceded that "colour is no obstacle to advancement." *Notes,* p. 78.

[16] In this connection special mention should be made of the "São Paulo school" of sociology in contemporary Brazil. The "Paulistas" came into being as a self-conscious group largely as a result of a series of studies in race relations in various regions of Brazil financed by UNESCO in the 1950's. In some of these studies the findings reveal a pattern of mild and humane relations generally consistent with that described earlier by Donald Pierson. This category includes the work of Thales de Azevedo (Bahia), Luiz de Aguiar Costa Pinto (Rio de Janeiro), and Charles Wagley (northeast interior). The study done in the south by Roger Bastide and Florestan Fernandes of the University of São Paulo, however, placed much more stress on discrimination, both in historical experience and in contemporary life. Their students, Octavio Ianni and Fernando Henrique Cardoso, have subsequently published work similar in spirit. Summary statements in English which embody the Paulista viewpoint are: O. Ianni, "Race and Class in Brazil," *Présence Africaine,* XXV, no. 53 (1st qu., 1965), 105–19; F. H. Cardoso, "Colour Prejudice in Brazil," *ibid.,* pp. 120–28; and F. Fernandes, "The Weight of the Past," *Daedalus,* XCVI (Spring, 1967), 560–79. Fernandes' book *A integreção do negro na sociedade de classes,* originally published in 1965, has recently been condensed and translated into English as *The Negro in Brazilian Society* (New York: Columbia University Press, 1969).

context, and compared to what? Not in any context of comparison that includes the United States. To stress "prejudice" in Brazil, and to equate this with prejudice everywhere, including the American South, seems downright perverse. I am quite certain that insights as to the workings of these two cultures—insofar as they are to be reached by any comparative techniques—will not come through this kind of emphasis. Whatever we do, in short, we ought not to homogenize: not in the realm of slavery and race relations, where they concern Brazil on the one side and the United States on the other, not if we want to learn anything really important about either.

But having said all this, I am brought back to a conviction I expressed at the beginning: it is time the argument were moved to another plane entirely. I would guess, from indications already in the air, that when this occurs it will take the form of broad-scale and intensive researches in the realm of ideology. Ideology is of course related to, and has greatly encroached upon, much of what we have done up to now. But we have barely scratched the surface.

Ideology in its most inclusive sense is a massive end-product— a configuration, a total *gestalt*—of a society's historical experience, its norms, its values, its fears and prejudices, its material interests, and its habits of mind. The world-views of societies, or of groups within societies, are inferrable not only from their formal writings but from their bodies of law, political arrangements, social customs, ceremonial behavior, imaginative literature, and responses to real or imagined crisis. We do know something—though we could stand to know a great deal more—about the ideological dynamics that have moved our own society from time to time. But how much do we know, in this respect, of Latin American society? What do we have in systematic and comprehensive form that seeks to place in ideological context the emotional, moral, and intellectual responses of these societies, say, to problems of slavery and race? There is at present little that I know of.[17] A projection or

17 The work of Gilberto Freyre on Brazil might be regarded as an exception, though it could be objected (I think properly) that its principal value lies not so much in systematic analysis but rather in whatever inferences are to be drawn (in this case, with regard to social ideology) from the author's suggestive and wide-ranging impressionism.

two, however, might be ventured as to the categories and components that will make up such inquiries when they do appear, as they surely will.

A major one would be class, with all the vestigial precapitalist attitudes that went with it. Taking into account, as one must, that color has been an item of strong prejudice in all Western societies including those of Latin America, one might well ask how such an element as race tended to be contained, modified, and even transformed over time by assumptions about rank, hierarchy, and class. What were those assumptions, what was their historic background in the experience of Spain and Portugal, and how were they expressed?[18] In the case, say, of Brazil, what sort of psychological protection did a complex class system provide for the society at large against the spectacle of a steady infusion of free blacks and mulattoes into its social and economic life? They must have been considerable, in view of that society's very limited inclination to hold the line at any given point on such matters as freedom of movement, holding of property, commercial activity, education, miscegenation, and manumission.

Another ideological category most certainly would concern the Church and Catholic culture. The "climate of moral opinion," "the ability of the Catholic Church to help shape the ethos of slave society" (to use Genovese's words), is a great subject for study in itself. The Church made its terms with slavery. But what was the tone and style with which it did so? What was the quality of the Iberian experience that accounts for the Church's extraordinary impulse to *absorb*? Many things would come under some such heading: the acculturation of Moors, Jews, and Negroes; the extension of the sacraments to all men; the syncretization of African cults under the Church's aegis; the encouragement of slave and free colored religious brotherhoods. What sort of attitudes grew out of all this, and how were they expressed? What was the form taken by those convictions about paternity that moved so many free fathers to liberate their slave children at baptism, or that pro-

[18] Some suggestions in this realm are contained in Richard M. Morse, "Toward a Theory of Spanish American Government," *Journal of the History of Ideas,* XV (January, 1954), 71–93. Another such effort is Alexandre Lobato, "Permanence and Change in Overseas Portuguese Thought," in Raymond S. Sayers, ed., *Portugal and Brazil in Transition* (Minneapolis: University of Minnesota Press, 1968), 93–107.

tected a slave's free time, or that placed such approval on manumission? What was it that made the Church and the relationships associated with it the "primary factors," as one student finds, "in the assimilated liberto's life"?[19] And finally, we need to know more than we do about the ways in which Catholic norms left their impress upon the slave codes themselves. The degree to which the codes were enforced in different times and places, under the stress of varying local conditions, constitutes one kind of historical problem. But another concerns the things such codes can tell us, whatever those conditions, about what a society *believed*.[20]

Then there is the fascinating question— particularly in the case of Brazil—of a society's racial picture of itself, and of what effect this may have on its attitudes about "race" in general. Earlier notions about racial purity in Brazil, as we know, tended to break down over time. There has been much speculation as to the causes. The heritage of experience with the Moors, widespread habits of miscegenation owing to the scarcity of white women in the early days, the tolerance of enveloping Catholic values, and so on—there is no certain formula as to how to strike the balance.[21] But we do know something about the results, and in a general way how the society feels about them now.

[19] "Undeniably, the outstanding aspect of the last wills and testaments [of freed slaves] was the religious proclamation of their Catholic faith. For example, the African Felizberta Maria de Jesus declared she was a member of the Irmandades of São Benedicto, Santa Efiginia, of Jesus, Maria e José, of the Carmo, of the Rosário de João Pereira and the Rosário e Baixa de Sapateiros!" Trosko, "Liberto in Bahia," p. 65.

[20] See again Morse, "Theory," pp. 72–73. Professor Morse, a strong opponent of "homogenization," questions the tendency of some American historians to assimilate the experience of slavery in Brazil and that in the United States to anything resembling a common or comparable cultural context. In a critique of the paper by Carl Degler mentioned above (see footnote 3), he says: "[W]e must recognize that generalizations about slavery, race relations, forms of prejudice and discrimination, rebellions and protest movements will be random and incoherent unless they can be related to [the] central premises of belief systems which prevailed in the respective societies."

[21] Attempts to strike such a balance include H. Hoetink, *The Two Variants in Caribbean Race Relations: A Contribution to the Sociology of Segmented Societies* (London: Institute of Race Relations, 1967); and Pierre L. van den Berghe, *Race and Racism: A Comparative Perspective* (New York: Wiley, 1967).

Even while slavery still existed in Brazil, according to Thomas Skidmore, virtually no one believed in the actual biological inferiority of the colored peoples. Race, accordingly, had little to do with that, but it did have something to do with social inferiority. It was therefore desirable to "whiten" the dark-skinned people—an ideal, indeed, which for generations had had its practical application. It was done either through talent and money, which simply redefined a man as "white" when he was really dark, or it was done through miscegenation. Miscegenation was thus a good thing because it "whitened" (whereas in the United States it was a bad thing because it darkened). It was such a way of looking at their own society, for example, that permitted Brazilian intellectuals, despite their feelings of cultural inferiority, to resist the coercions of European racist thought in the years prior to World War I. Patriotism and national pride had no choice but to defend the mixed Brazilian type, who by then was clearly beyond all hope of racial "purity."[22]

With this entire ideological *gestalt*—historical and contemporary—reconstructed, one may be in a position to understand both why ordinary Brazilians find discussions of the "race problem" in the United States incomprehensible, and why a modern Brazilian intellectual should find it so natural to conclude one of his books by serenely referring to his country as "more and more a racial democracy."[23] And going back to slavery times, one can better assess the chances, say, of the *fazendeiro* class's imposing a contrary set of standards on the rest of Brazilian society, beyond a pale and apologetic version of the "necessary evil" argument. Thus with ideology as the governing concept, it becomes easier to see that whereas fragmenting such a *gestalt* by concentration upon counter examples may be useful for some purposes, for others it is gravely misleading. For it *is* a kind of totality, the whole being

[22] Thomas E. Skidmore, "Brazilian Intellectuals and the Problem of Race, 1870–1930," Graduate Center for Latin American Studies, Vanderbilt University, Occasional Paper no. 6, 1969.

[23] Donald Pierson, *Negroes in Brazil: A Study of Race Contact at Bahia,* 2nd ed. (Carbondale: Southern Illinois University Press, 1967), pp. xxix–xxx; Gilberto Freyre, *The Mansions and the Shanties: The Making of Modern Brazil* (New York: Knopf, 1963), p. 431. "Brazilians," according to Charles Wagley, "can still call their society a racial democracy." *Race and Class in Rural Brazil,* 2nd ed. (New York: UNESCO, 1963), p. 2.

more significant than the parts, and serves to exhibit in relief those very distinctions between cultures that are most worth grasping.

Moreover, one may, if one wishes, view ideologies comparatively. One may examine with fresh appreciation the slave ideology of the antebellum American South, supported as it was not only by the South's leading "theorists"—Calhoun, Fitzhugh, Simms, Hammond, and all the rest—as well as by every argument on racial inferiority then known, but also by every social, political, legal, and religious institution which that society contained.

3

No section of my book has been the subject of so much discussion and criticism as the one entiled "Slavery and Personality." In it, I proposed an analogy between North American slavery in the nineteenth century and the Nazi concentration camps of the twentieth, using the analogy both to draw implications for human personality in an extreme relationship of power and dependency, and to explore the psychological setting in which a childish "Sambo" type might have been fostered among large numbers of American slaves. There have been numerous objections to this. Some have resisted the implication that the slave system could have been as psychologically coercive as the concentration camp image, with all its emotional impact, suggests. There have been many difficulties over Sambo. How prevalent was Sambo as a type—or, for that matter, was he even real? To what extent were Sambo-like characteristics truly internalized, and to what extent were such characteristics, when they appeared, simply a deliberate response to the expectations of white men?

Discussion on all this was originally very heated, and enough of it occurred while the book was still in manuscript that I was able to comment on the main outlines of it in an appendix to the first edition. Since that time, however—though the basic objections continue to be those made from the beginning—the discussion has become much more subtle and sophisticated. It has been conceded that the use of analogy in itself, as an analytical device, is legitimate. The critical question has shifted to that of whether the particular analogy I used is necessarily the most effective one for the purpose. Certain refinements on my theoretical apparatus have been proposed using institutions less extreme than the concentration camp, the better to account for the variety of behavior and personality patterns to be observed within the institution of slavery. Here I have found the essays by George Fredrickson and Christopher Lasch, and by Roy Bryce-Laporte, very illuminating.

But before proceeding to their work, I shall have to say something about that of Genovese.[24] Genovese's critique of this section falls somewhat outside the pattern just referred to, inasmuch as it forms an integral part of his discussion of the previous section and is consistent with his argument that slavery in all times and places has produced similar effects. Unlike many of the critics, Genovese is willing to concede the reality of Sambo—he calls it the "slavish personality"—but insists that such a type was not unique to American slavery. Citing evidence from various cultures, including Brazilian and even Arabic, he asserts that Sambo existed wherever slavery existed.

Genovese further argues that my notion of absolute power, in relation to the complex realm of alternatives and probabilities that constituted the historical reality of slavery, was not sufficiently discriminating to deal either with the many spaces in the system or with a range of deviant behavior, including rebelliousness, among the slaves themselves. My "greatest weakness," he says, is my "inability to accept the principle of contradiction, to realize that all historical phenomena must be regarded as constituting a process of becoming, and that, therefore, the other-sidedness of the most totalitarian conditions may in fact represent the unfolding of their negation." The contradictions within Sambo, for instance, might very well reach the point of transforming him, under certain conditions, into a Nat Turner.

I gather that Genovese would actually concede me a very large part of my argument, were he not somehow convinced that I have established a "deterministic model" which consistency will not allow me to modify. He would even concede me "more American than Latin American Sambos" if the contrast "could be reduced to a matter of degree," though my own model would then "fall."

[24] "Rebelliousness and Docility," cited above. The other two are George M. Fredrickson and Christopher Lasch, "Resistance to Slavery," *Civil War History*, XIII (December, 1967), 315–29, and Roy S. Bryce-Laporte, "The Conceptualization of the American Slave Plantation as a Total Institution" (Ph.D. diss., UCLA, 1968).

But it was never my intention to establish a deterministic model, and I would be more than happy to settle for "degrees." (For instance, something less than absolute power produces something less than absolute dependency.) I have said as much throughout my book, and I do not think my argument would "fall" if I said so again.[25]

I assumed all along that any sustained relationship of power and dependency in human affairs can have consequences which are psychologically infantilizing (the degree of the one depending, as I said, on the degree of the other), and I am not surprised at the evidence Genovese has produced from other slave societies that show this. Nor need such evidence be restricted always to slavery. But it is one thing to cite instances, and quite another to conclude from them that a cultural tradition as extended and deep-rooted as that of Sambo in the American South can be postulated for any society in which slavery existed. *That* case is as yet not proven, and if it were to be, more flexible techniques would be needed for doing it than those he has used. A study of the Negro in Brazilian literature, for example, reveals no such tradition. There, the slave appears in a variety of types: he is filthy and bestial; he is a fighting ruffian; he is resourceful, intelligent, heroic. But there are no lovable, irresponsible Sambos. The literature of the American plantation, on the other hand, as I have elsewhere suggested, tells a very different story.[26]

[25] E.g., "The American slave system, compared with that of Latin America, was closed and circumscribed, but, like all social systems, its arrangements were less perfect in practice than they appeared to be in theory. It was possible for significant numbers of slaves, in varying degrees, to escape the full impact of the system and its coercions upon personality" (p. 137).

[26] Nowhere in antebellum American fiction have I seen the typical "faithful slave" portrayed, as he is in Brazilian, as one who will *fight* for his master or mistress and perform heroic acts. The *bad* Brazilian slave, on the other hand, is a treacherous beast of prey. (The bad female slave is unfaithful to all her lovers.) See Raymond S. Sayers, *The Negro in Brazilian Literature* (New York: Hispanic Institute, 1956), pp. 81, 148–51, 174–75, and *passim*. "In Brazilian literature there is no Uncle Remus and there is no tradition of happy days on the old plantation." *Ibid.*, p. 224. To the Portuguese, African Negroes were, to be sure, inferior beings, but not Sambo types. "Deformed, horrible, cruel, bestial, ferocious, these are the characteristics attributed to the Negroes by Barros, Castanheda, Góis, and Osório."

I would agree that the day-to-day reality of American slavery contained many more contradictions than my discussion seemed to allow for. But to formalize this idea and to erect "contradiction" itself into a principle of explanation, historical or any other kind, is something (here Genovese is quite right) that I am hardly prepared to accept. The metaphysical side of Marxist theory, unlike many another side, is one I could never take very seriously or regard as very scientific. Genovese takes my argument to task "because it proves too much and encompasses more forms of behavior than can usefully be managed under a single rubric." And yet he does much the same thing, going even further and with theoretical underpinning far more questionable, when he argues that Sambo—having internalized *all* the contradictory elements of the system—could, if "the psychological balance was jarred," rise up and become the negation of himself (Nat Turner), the total dependent becoming the total rebel.

With this, I fear, Genovese has shouldered a very cumbersome dialectical apparatus and at the same time pushed the argument down a road that leads nowhere. Rebellions have never been a major issue in the history of American slavery, and he himself has said as much elsewhere.[27] There were none of any consequence after 1831, and the historical Nat Turner, from all indications, was himself anything but a Sambo. He was psychologically able to do what he did precisely because he was so situated in the system that he could resist the full impact of its Samboizing coercions. Moreover, Turner was an exception. There were few like him, and *this* is the thing that has to be explained. Genovese has not yet, to my satisfaction, located the true mechanism of rebellion, such as it was, on the North American continent; nor does he seem willing to consider the full extent to which the South was able to organize itself—militarily, psychologically, ideologically— to discourage *all* forms of resistance, well short of open rebellion.

Jose Honório Rodrigues, *Brazil and Africa* (Berkeley: University of California Press, 1965), p. 6.

[27] "The Nat Turner Case," *New York Review of Books,* (September 12, 1968), pp. 34–37. An excellent study of the very special social conditions required to produce a rebel in the American context—in this case, Gabriel Prosser—is Gerald W. Mullin, "Patterns of Slave Behavior in Eighteenth Century Virginia" (Ph.D. diss., Berkeley, Calif., 1968), Ch. 6.

There was a strain toward consistency in the South's own self-mobilization here that I, for one, have not been able to perceive to a like degree in any other slave society.

An argument to which I find it somewhat easier to adjust my own thinking is that based on Erving Goffman's theory of "total institutions."[28] George Fredrickson and Christopher Lasch in their essay, and Roy Bryce-Laporte in his, have proposed this theory as a more refined substitute for my concentration camp analogy. They do so on the ground that it allows for a wider range of slave behavior, embracing various forms of independence and non-co-operation with the slave-holding regime. The line of thought they propose is one I find most suggestive.

According to Fredrickson and Lasch, such "total institutions" as asylums and prisons, being more flexible, are for that reason better than the concentration camp for purposes of analogy with the slave plantation. They are especially useful in analyzing resistance to the system. They allow not only for a large measure of psychological coercion and for a scarcity of open revolts, but also for a considerable variety of adjustments short of full internalization of the system's values. Fredrickson and Lasch cite Goffman's four categories of the inmate's adjustment: (1) situational withdrawal (apathy); (2) colonization (a kind of practical adjustment to the world of the total institution); (3) conversion (internalization of the institution's definition of him); and (4) intransigence (a sometimes violent but essentially personal and therefore largely non-political rejection of the institution). The inmate can alternate in these roles, occasionally even playing all of them at once—unlike the case of the concentration camp, where the choice is simply that of situational withdrawal (and death) or of conversion. Such a formulation allows for a wide range in between, as well as for the real problems of discipline—such problems, that is, as a limited sense of obligation to obey, the need for rewards and punishments, and the expediency of various compromises within the system. In such a setting the long-time inmates become the "master opportunists," the "virtuosos of the system" whose personal style is "playing it cool," those who, "neither docile nor rebellious . . . , spend their lives in skillful and somewhat cynical attempts to beat

[28] See Erving Goffman, *Asylums: Essays on the Social Situation of Mental Patients and Other Inmates* (Chicago: Aldine Publishing Co., 1961).

[246]

the system at its own game." The point of all this, of course, is that theoretically it should apply to slavery as well.

Bryce-Laporte's work, indeed, is an effort, more detailed and extended than that of Fredrickson and Lasch, to adapt the theory of total institutions to North American slavery. Bryce-Laporte is especially interested in the possibility of some kind of independent subculture in the slave community, and in the conditions under which such a culture might function. Following Goffman, he postulates two major categories of adjustment made by the inmates of a total institution, adjustments which by analogy applied, he believes, to slave society as well. One consists of "primary adjustments," or those which correspond directly to the roles officially demanded by the institution. The other concerns the "secondary adjustments"—the behavior patterns that either deviate from or run counter to the official role-expectations. Bryce-Laporte is particularly concerned with the "secondary adjustments." He further subdivides these into "contained" and "disruptive," the former being adjustments not prescribed by the institution but representing no direct threat to it, and the latter, those either actually or potentially dangerous to the institution. This complex of both "contained" and "disruptive" secondary adjustments that any total institution creates goes to make up its "underlife."

Bryce-Laporte has no extravagant illusions as to the "political" character of this underlife. Such a character would require stable and sustained group loyalties, which would in turn create a strong degree of independent social control. But he does believe that the plantation system permitted, overlooked, or tolerated a series of activities—religious services, spirituals, folk tales, holidays—which allowed the slave a measure of protection for his individual autonomy and which blunted the full impact of the system upon his personality. The slave family, moreover, truncated as it was, represented a truly subversive element, a crucial factor in the underlife of the plantation. All in all, Bryce-Laporte believes, the underlife could sustain the widest and subtlest variety of activity, including the activity of protest: "slowing down work, misuse of implements, resistance to acculturation, apologetic and fantasy folklore, religion and exorcism, malingering, running away, suicide, infanticide, stealing, poisoning, murder, and arson."

Bryce-Laporte's specific criticism of me is similar to that of Fredrickson and Lasch. He denies, as do they, that the psychological impact of the slave system, heavy as it may have been, "reached the dimensions of creating a prevailing and crystallized *personality*." He thinks that if slaves had fully succumbed to the conditions of the system "they would have been all zombiefied or psychologically dead," that the typical adjustment lay somewhere between this and intransigence, and that Sambo was a product of role-playing rather than a true internalization of the master class's picture of him.[29]

The great virtue of this work is that in it the problem of *resistance* is at last fully contained, and contained within a theoretical framework far more subtle and scientific than any previously devised. It makes many useful conceptual distinctions. It does not require "revolutionary" or even "political" activity; nonetheless it leaves room for a wide range of overt, covert, and even unconscious forms of resistance. Nor do I think my own work, generally speaking, need be regarded as incompatible with it. To be sure, there are certain points on which Fredrickson and Lasch and Bryce-Laporte obviously would not agree, and I shall have to comment on those points. Yet I made a number of efforts in the course of my book to provide spaces into which just such a theory might fit, however crudely in comparison to their work I may have roughed them in.[30]

I am particularly intrigued by the conceptual possibilities Bryce-Laporte has outlined—to which should be added the findings of Sterling Stuckey on slave folklore—for an "underlife," a subculture

[29] I ought, in passing, to correct at least one misreading of my text. Bryce-Laporte, following Ralph Ellison, believes I extended the Sambo personality to present-day Negro Americans. This is simply not true; indeed, such an extension would have contradicted my entire argument. If one is accounting for dependent personalities in terms of a peculiarly coercive slave system, then it ought to follow that those same personalities would be profoundly affected in the reverse direction by the collapse of that system. The historical evidence, moreover, tends to bear this out; for confirmation one need only examine the experience of emancipation and Reconstruction. I have elaborated this point in Nathan Huggins, Martin Kilson, and Daniel Fox, eds., *Key Issues in the Afro-American Experience* (New York: Harcourt Brace Jovanovich, 1971), I, 138–40 *et seq.*

[30] *Slavery*, pp. 133–39. Another writer who has experimented with Goffman's theories in connection with slavery is Raymond T. Smith, "Social Stratification, Cultural Pluralism, and Integration in West Indian Societies," S. Lewis and T. G. Mathews, eds., *Caribbean Integration: Papers on Social, Political, and Economic Integration* (Rio Piedras, P.R.: Institute of Caribbean Science, 1967), pp. 226–58.

of great richness and variety. The suggestions of Bryce-Laporte and others on music, conjuring, prayer meetings, and escape lore, the descriptions of Negro night life in the cities by Richard Wade, Stuckey's studies of double meanings in work songs, spirituals, and the Brer Rabbit cycle—all these represent a vast treasury of materials, much of it still waiting to be mined.[31] Nor, incidentally, do I see why such a concept as "underlife" cannot itself be extended to comparative examinations—say, with Latin America. The terminology would be particularly congenial to such a setting; Catholic cultures have traditionally taken "underlife" for granted and have in fact encouraged it. Bryce-Laporte argues, for example, that although an underlife does not ordinarily change an institution by revolution, it can, over time, force a series of long-term evolutionary adjustments. We do not as yet know how much of this occurred in America, but it certainly occurred in Brazil. The wild *candomblés,* the cults of black madonnas and black saints, the African folk festivals that could dominate the routine of a Brazilian city for days, the activities of the black brotherhoods— together, all such aspects of slave underlife in time altered not only Brazilian Catholicism but also Brazilian slavery.

But the great problem, returning once more to the main argument, is that of "infantilization" and "internalization." I made many efforts to hedge on these questions and to allow for wide variations. I also tried to allow for the emotionally loaded quality of the semantics, recognizing that the most technical formulations of all such questions, especially when analogy is being used, must necessarily partake of the metaphorical. Moreover, having convictions of my own as to the nucleus of irreducibility in the human spirit, I recognize that the very nature of the argument is such that it can never be finally settled. Or at least so I hope.

As for "infantilization," Fredrickson and Lasch categorically rule this out, calling such a hypothesis "quite untenable." They do refer—rather vaguely, I think—to "psychic damage," which could

---

[31] Sterling Stuckey, "Through the Prism of Folklore: The Black Ethos in Slavery," *Massachusetts Review,* IX (Summer 1968), 417–37; Wade, *Slavery in the Cities,* pp. 143–79; Harold Courlander, *Negro Folk Music, U.S.A.* (New York: Columbia University Press, 1963); Arna Bontemps and Langston Hughes, eds., *The Book of Negro Folklore* (New York: Dodd, Mead, 1958); and J. Mason Brewer, *American Negro Folklore* (Chicago: Quadrangle Books, 1968).

imply an alternative model, theoretical or at least descriptive, of psychic events. But they do not seem interested in pursuing this. As a result, they ignore a problem that to me was central. That problem concerned styles of behavior within a structure wherein the lines of authority are vastly more simplified than those which operate in the normal world of adult life. I assumed that these styles themselves fell short of the complexity one normally associates with full adult behavior. (And I am sure one may observe them to great advantage in the world of total institutions.) I should probably point out, resorting again to metaphor, the quite obvious fact that short of adulthood there are still infinite degrees of maturity, and that in such metaphors there are many choices. One need not be stuck with that of "infancy," or even of "childhood." My own experience in the army, for example, convinced me that whereas this particular "total institution" may have "made men of us," in other more pervasive respects it turned us into boys.[32] I venture to guess that prisons and asylums may produce much the same effects, without necessarily "zombiefying" their inmates.

On "internalization," Fredrickson and Lasch see a "curious contradiction between the difficulty of discipline and the slaves' professed devotion to their masters." This contradiction, in which "slaves could have accepted the legitimacy of their masters' authority without feeling any sense of obligation to obey it," is resolved in the theory of total institutions. I would quite agree (though I never thought of this as a contradiction), and would add that it might also be resolved in any of several theories of adolescent behavior as well. As for the pervasive effects of slavery upon personality, I note a deep reluctance—in Bryce-Laporte particularly—to face this problem fully, a very American unwillingness to believe that even slavery could really touch the "inner man." I can only suggest that it is still possible to romanticize the spaces in the system. There was a time when Ulrich Phillips was rightly censured for doing something not unlike this, and one might still unwittingly do much the same thing for purposes quite different from Phillips'.[33] It was, after all, a very hard system,

[32] There may be some ritual connection between this and the perennial behavior of aging "boys" at conventions of veterans' organizations.

[33] This is what Earl Thorpe tends to do in his "Chattel Slavery and Concentration Camps," *Negro History Bulletin,* XXV (May, 1962), 171–76.

and we would do well not to forget it. I would concede that there must have been room in it for the virtuosos, the master opportunists, the ones who "played it cool." But how much room? And how much of the system's infinite variety of coercions could the individual slave absorb without his finally internalizing the very role he was being forced to play? I remain uncertain, and can only repeat my willingness to settle for a "broad belt of indeterminacy between 'mere acting' and the 'true self.'"

Where does the argument go from here? Obviously it could go in any of several directions. I am struck by the possibilities for a new departure that are inherent in certain observations of Bryce-Laporte himself. Bryce-Laporte takes note of Goffman's statement that staffs of total institutions "tend to evolve what may be thought of as a theory of human nature," and to this he adds something very interesting of his own. "Such a theory," Bryce-Laporte says, "really is a composite ideological justification of the various interests and responsibilities of the total institution. . . ." What would we discover about these and analogous institutions by examining the ideological context in which they function? I would guess that a scrutiny of such ideologies on their own terms—their elaborateness, their complexity, the conviction and intensity with which they are held, their pervasiveness not only within the institution in question but in the larger society in which the institution operates—should tell us a very great deal, if done in comparative terms, about how coercive they might be upon *all* the individuals in any way concerned with such a system.

And yet, paradoxically and perhaps perversely, I fear that this would be the very point at which I would find prisons and asylums *least* satisfying as analogies to antebellum slavery. No doubt the employees of such institutions do operate, during their working day, upon something approximating an ideology, one that encompasses most of their relationships with the inmates and which they find generally serviceable for keeping the place running. Yet the degree of explicitness with which such an ideology is articulated and diffused throughout the environing society is another question, and a dubious one, while even the employees' own personal stake in either the ideology or the institution's survival is surely something less than total. It is under those circumstances, as well as all the others we have noted, that room is made for the "corruption of authority," for the seasoned inmate who becomes the master opportunist, "plays it cool," and exploits the system.

But then turn it around and consider the slaveholding ideology of the antebellum South. Consider its infinite permutations, and how thoroughly it dominated the entire political, social, economic, and psychological life of the Southern states. It left no realm of thought or feeling untouched. At its highest political reaches it generated a theory of state sovereignty at the root of which, as William Freehling has shown, lay the South's extravagant need to protect the institution of slavery against any and all federal encroachment, and in the end, with no sense of inconsistency, broke up the national party system with its insistence upon positive protection of slavery in the territories. It developed an elaborate "sociology"—the first Americans to use that term were the pro-slavery theorists—to expound the beneficent effects of a patriarchally organized society. Its economic rationale was "Cotton Is King," a theory which warned of the ruinous consequences of challenging either King Cotton or his legion of white and black retainers. And most pervasive of all, this ideology contained assumptions about race that governed every action, every attitude, every response, every relationship of white men to black. And the custodians of *this* institution were of all ages and of both sexes, and were located everywhere, all throughout white society and at all levels of it, and were on duty, as it were, at all hours. *Their* commitment was as close to total as anything could be. A full appreciation of this might give us yet another view of the system's resources for discouraging Sambo from becoming a Nat Turner, and of the limits the system placed on even its "master opportunists."

4

The final section of my book, concerning abolitionism and the intellectual and institutional context in which it functioned, was not as widely noticed as the others. The issues it raised were in certain ways quite different from those considered in the previous sections, and though it too has come in for some lively criticism, such criticism has been of rather a special sort. It has tended to come either from persons not inclined to challenge positions I have taken elsewhere on personality and on cross-cultural comparison, or else from those whose primary interests, being more or less exclusively tied to the American abolitionist movement rather than to slavery itself, lay outside such realms. Of this criticism the most prominent representatives are Nathan Glazer and Aileen Kraditor.[34]

Their basic objection is that I am unfair to the abolitionists and give them short shrift. I find both the abolitionists and their procedures distasteful; I blame them, as Glazer puts it, "for being moralistic, fanatical, uncompromising, vituperative," and deplore their refusal "to consider practical measures." "Elkins," according to Professor Kraditor, "regrets that slavery was not ended gradually, by piecemeal adjustments of the institutional arrangements that supported it." I "obviously" disapprove of "their alleged anti-institutional bias" (which she claims they did not really have), whereas, as Glazer insists, "because of the South's monolithic resistance to any change in the slavery system" the abolitionists in effect had no choice. It "was necessary for abolitionism to develop its own absolutism."

It appears that one of the things least controllable in one's writings is their overtones, and what they may betray about one's temperamental inclinations at the time they were set down. When I first encountered this line of criticism, I reflected with some irritation that it missed what I was really saying. Since then, the civil rights movement and the intransigence which it encountered have permitted me to empathize somewhat with the abolitionists of a century and more ago, and to experience in a vicarious way what they experienced directly. Consequently going back over what I wrote about them, I note with a certain discomfort a tone that would probably not be there if I were doing it now.

[34] Nathan Glazer, "The Differences among Slaves," *Commentary* XXIX (May, 1960), 454–58, reprinted as introduction to 1st paperback ed. of Elkins, *Slavery* (New York: Grosset and Dunlap, 1963), pp. ix–xvi; Aileen S. Kraditor, "A Note on Elkins and the Abolitionists," *Civil War History,* XIII (December, 1967), 330–39, and *Means and Ends in American Abolitionism: Garrison and His Critics on Strategy and Tactics, 1834–1850* (New York: Pantheon, 1969), esp. pp. 11–38. Another work in which similar criticism is made is Bertram Wyatt-Brown, *Lewis Tappan and the Evangelical War against Slavery* (Cleveland: Case Western Reserve University Press, 1969), pp. xii, xv, 355.

The rest of it, in all likelihood, still would be there. I do not believe the argument I made need depend in this case on the tone in which it was couched, or on whether I believed then, or believe now, that the abolitionists were my kind of people. Those things are essentially not debatable, but they can, I think, be separated from those that are. The two main problems now are the same two that concerned me then. One is that of locating the abolitionists in their culture, and the other is locating them in the general movement that led ultimately to emancipation. As to the latter, I would say now what I did not specifically say then, that the abolitionists and their activities were indispensable to that movement. Exactly how is, of course, another question and a very complex one. As to the former, I find myself quite willing to amplify my position, and less willing to shift ground on it than at any other point in the book.

Professor Kraditor accuses me of wrongly connecting the abolitionists with Transcendentalism in my effort to show the anti-institutional character of their crusade against slavery. I did indeed so connect them, though I think not wrongly. The connection was not intended as a "causal" one; it was intended to exhibit certain cultural attitudes characteristic of the age that were held in common by Transcendentalists, abolitionists, and a host of evangelists and reforming spirits of every sort in the America of the 1830's and '40s. "The perfectionism of Garrison and other reformers," as R. Jackson Wilson has put it, "was, like Transcendentalism, insistently antinomian; both implied a thorough, even ruthless, criticism and repudiation of existing social institutions."[35]

Professor Kraditor is herself ambivalent on the question of institutions, and is quite uncertain as to just where, and with what emphasis, she wishes to place the abolitionists generally in relation to it. On the one hand the Garrisonians, according to her, "insisted they were not anti-institutionalists," and she adds that "most abolitionists" were quite willing to "use institutions to destroy slavery." But on the other hand, "most radicals, including most Garrisonians and many other abolitionists . . . did not share the conservatives' reverence for institutions as such." She is not sure it is proper of me to imply that Garrison and his perfectionist

[35] R. Jackson Wilson, *In Quest of Community: Social Philosophy in the United States, 1860–1920* (New York: Wiley, 1968), p. 13.

cohorts represented more than a small and idiosyncratic group within the movement as a whole. But then in her own book she repeatedly puts Garrison forward as representative of all that was best and most effective in that movement.

Not that these various positions are necessarily incompatible. I would even, up to a point, support them myself. But I do not think they add up in quite the way she thinks they do. The abolitionists were, to be sure, quite willing to "use" institutions. But they and most other men of that age who were concerned in any sense with moral regeneration viewed institutions, as well as the individuals who "used" them, in a very special way. Their attitudes and assumptions were strikingly divergent from those with which men and women in European cultures had traditionally regarded institutions and their own relationships to them. Whether this was a good or a bad thing ought not to concern either of us; the important thing is to recognize that such a distinction existed. Professor Kraditor further pictures the abolitionists as calculating realists, concerned with tactics. As to this I have my reservations. But she also stresses their overriding concern with principle, upon which I am in full accord. Their objective, she says, was above all to combat racism. This, I think, is factually incorrect. The technique of action they put the most store by—whatever the varying degrees of concern for institutions or for racism, and regardless of other dissidences within the movement on doctrine and tactics—was the technique of conversion.

The anti-institutionalism that I and others found so impressive in the cultural attitudes of this period was in fact perennially inherent in American experience virtually from the first. John Winthrop and those who accompanied him to America in 1630, whatever they might subsequently do, had in their way been challenging institutions in the name of liberty for years before their voyage, which was itself a plenary repudiation of institutional continuities. A dynamic cycle was thus established then and there, one that would repeat itself over and over throughout the ensuing 200 years. It always began with an assertion of freedom, of freedom *from* something—from tyranny, from constriction, from stultification, and from the institutions that supported and perpetuated them. By the 1830's the other side of that coin—a transcendent individualism—was overwhelmingly evident in every mode of thought and feeling, be it economic, theological, political, philosophical, or literary. The "liberation" of the individual from the perennial constraints of institutions was a process—again using Wilson's words—that "comes as close as anything can to constituting the relative distinctiveness of men's experience in America."[36]

Behind the extraordinary impression made by America on Tocqueville in 1831 and 1832 was something that enabled him to perceive with great clarity any number of distinctive features in American society. This something was a set of gross cultural contrasts between what he was seeing and what he had left behind, involving a series of traditional European assumptions and understandings with regard to institutions. He found it hard at first to believe that America could even exist, much less survive, so little "reverence" did Americans have "for institutions as such." Much of his scheme of organization for *Democracy in America,* indeed, may be read as a systematic search for those social devices and mechanisms that Americans did respect, and for those principles of order that filled the place of institutions as he in his own society had known them. In his experience it was institutions that formed men; in America it was, if anything, the other way around.

In French society institutions provided a frame, a kind of given, within which a man pictured himself and the things he might legitimately do with his life. His family represented to him with some precision who he was, the kind of history he could claim, the connections he was entitled to form, and the responsibilities he would assume. His class position defined both his limits and his opportunities; from it might be projected his education, his career, his values, his very character. His school was not so much an institution where his "natural" potential might be released, as one that prescribed a certain form and order for his mind. Whatever might be the degree of his preoccupation with religion, the authority of the Church over various aspects of his life was taken for granted. (Nor did one innovate in the field of religion, at least not lightly.) In short, a man viewed himself and his actions and aspirations as moving through a series of institutions, and in the light of this it was far less easy to imagine the mark he might leave on his society than to understand the sort of impress his society

[36] *Ibid.,* 3.

would make on him. In America, on the other hand, a major cultural fact was the general inability to see any clear relationship, except perhaps a negative one, between institutions and individual character. The individual was what he was in spite of institutions; they stood in the way of his "real" self; "under all these screens," Emerson would say, "I have difficulty to detect the precise man you are."[37]

Institutions themselves, such as they were, thus assumed a very different character from that in which they had traditionally functioned. They were at best a convenience, something that men might deliberately bring into being and then "use," transform, or abandon as it suited them: the test was not the historic attachments such institutions generated, for they generated few, but rather the extent to which they released the creative energies of individuals for specific and immediate ends. They thereby became something different, almost requiring a different name, and the distinction might be called that between "institutions" and "organizations." Such devices—Tocqueville called them "associations" —were created for a bewildering variety of purposes. "In the United States associations are established to promote the public safety, commerce, industry, morality, and religion. There is no end which the human will despairs of attaining through the combined power of individuals united into a society." In sheer organizing energy, the Americans exceeded anything he had previously seen, and we do not need Tocqueville to remind us that this was the very age in which the promoter came fully into his own. James Willard Hurst has described the transforming of the entire idea of the "corporation" at this time from a body clothed in public interest to a device for facilitating the fullest sweep of individual enterprise. The churches themselves, as Sidney Mead has shown, owed their vitality not only to their evangelical zeal but also to their promotional activities. (The same thing, transposed, could be said of the new business ventures.) Even the family—judging from Catherine Beecher's treatise on that subject which went through innumerable editions—was not really a given, something that one inherited and in which one assumed a place; it was rather something one created anew with each generation as an act of free

---

[37] "Self-Reliance," in *Emerson's Complete Works* (Boston: Houghton Mifflin, 1883–93), II, 55.

choice, and subsequently maintained, as it were, through force of individual will.[38]

A major corollary of all this was the logic of evangelicalism, which suffused and permeated every notable reform movement in America from the 1830's to the Civil War. To effect moral transformation, it was necessary not simply to change institutions, but more fundamentally to change and reform individuals. This was done not through institutions, but directly: by liberating men's natural benevolence rather than by strengthening those institutions which might discipline men's natural selfishness. The instrument was conversion. Sin was no longer a matter of original depravity but of willful perversity, and could itself be cast out by an act of will if men could once be convinced, first of their perversity and then of their perfectibility. By manipulating individual guilt, by making the inspiration direct enough and powerful enough, the thing could be done: a man's eyes were opened, his heart was changed, he was converted. And the same logic applied to social evils, which were simply individual sins compounded. The primary object, therefore, was still conversion: to persuade enough people directly enough and powerfully enough, that the evil existed.[39]

[38] Alexis de Tocqueville, *Democracy in America,* ed. Phillips Bradley (New York: Knopf, 1945), I, 192; James Willard Hurst, *Law and the Conditions of Freedom in the Nineteenth-Century United States* (Madison: University of Wisconsin Press, 1956), pp. 15–29; Sidney E. Mead, *The Lively Experiment: The Shaping of Christianity in America* (New York: Harper & Row, 1963), esp. pp. 102–33; Catherine E. Beecher, *A Treatise on Domestic Economy for the Use of Young Ladies at Home and at School* (Boston: March, 1841). On the distinction between "institutions" and "organizations," see Eric L. McKitrick, "Goodbye to All That," *New York Review of Books,* June 9, 1966, pp. 6–7; on individualism, see John William Ward, "The Ideal of Individualism and the Reality of Organization," in *Red, White, and Blue: Men, Books, and Ideas in American Culture* (New York: Oxford, 1969), pp. 227–66.

[39] On this point see John L. Thomas, "Romantic Reform in America, 1815–1865," *American Quarterly,* XVII (Winter 1965), 656–81, and "Antislavery and Utopia," in Martin Duberman, ed., *The Antislavery Vanguard: New Essays on the Abolitionists* (Princeton: Princeton University Press, 1965), pp. 240–69. "The criticism and attack on institutions, which we have witnessed," Emerson asserted, "has made one thing plain, that society gains nothing whilst a man, not himself renovated, attempts to renovate things around him. . . ." ("New England Reformers," in *Works,* III, 248).

Such was the cultural context in which the abolitionist movement developed, and it is within such a context that its many ambiguities are to be understood. Whatever the doctrinal emphasis —immediate or gradual emancipation—and whatever the range of individual types, from the extravagantly abrasive Garrison to the extravagantly self-effacing Weld, the technique of the revival set the tone for the entire movement. Any purely intellectual rationale, any cold calculations on "tactics," were always subordinate to the basic effort to convert. "If your hearts ache and bleed," Weld urged, "we want you, you will help us; but if you merely adopt our principles as dry theories, do let us alone: we have millstones enough swinging at our necks already."[40] That the abolitionists effected many conversions is hardly to be denied; this was after all their primary object. But the dynamic of conversion was not the same as the dynamic of institutional change; when that occurred, it occurred in very different ways. Many of them might indeed "work within institutions," and just as readily abandon them. To those institutions that resisted their will, they were ruthless. One does less than justice to Garrison in suggesting that his position in this respect represented merely a "tactic." When Garrison insisted that a "Union with slaveholders" be torn in two, and that a Constitution sanctioning slavery be burned, he was acting on pure principle. True, they formed organizations of their own; those organizations were chronically unstable. The moral tensions *within* the movement, indeed, are as striking as any feature of it, in the light of which the logic of conversion, the manipulation of individual guilt to effect it, the anti-institutionalism, and the insistent primacy of individual will, all seem peculiarly of a piece. When Garrison called the churches "cages of unclean birds" despite the numbers of clergymen being daily converted to abolition, he was acting out the major fragmenting element of the movement. This was an unanticipated consequence, perhaps, but an inevitable one: an intense competition for moral purity among intensely dedicated men.

Only in such a context, moreover, is it possible to understand the bitter quarrel between the Garrisonians and Frederick Doug-

---

[40] *Emancipator,* July 28, 1836, quoted in Gilbert H. Barnes, *The Antislavery Impulse, 1830–1844* (Washington: American Historical Association, 1933), 79.

lass. It does not seem fair to accuse Garrison and the other abolitionists of "marked race prejudice," as some have done; in this
respect they come off better than any other group in a prejudice-
ridden society. But neither does it make much sense to represent
the eradication of racism as their overriding aim, and here the
Peases do have a point: "When immediate emancipation as a plan
of abolition was translated to mean only immediate repentance of
the sin of slavery," they observe, "the needs of the human beings
who were slaves were ignored."[41] In any case, for the Boston
group Frederick Douglass represented a major difficulty. Douglass'
independence, his decision to speak with his own voice rather
than theirs, his repudiation of their extreme anti-institutionalism,
his assumption of leadership for Negro aspirations, his efforts to
improve the condition of free Negroes in Rochester and elsewhere,
all added up to the profoundest challenge, and brought down their
full wrath upon him. At the beginning of their association, Douglass' principal value to the Garrisonians was as a symbolic abstraction rather than as a man who might have both group and personal
interests of his own to promote. As soon as he showed signs of
dissatisfaction with that role, he began getting into trouble. He
was told, in effect, that nobody would believe he had ever been
a slave unless he behaved and talked more like one when he lec-
tured: "Better have a little of the plantation speech than not; it
is not best that you seem too learned." They were piqued by his
successes in England. Their displeasure, when he decided to establish his own newspaper which would compete with theirs, was
such that they tried to persuade his English benefactors to cut off
his support. They were furious when Douglass was "not disposed to denounce as knaves those who believe that voting is a
duty," and when in 1851 Douglass announced his opposition to
Garrison's stand on the Constitution, Garrison exploded. "There
is roguery somewhere," he raged, and moved that Douglass' *North
Star* be stricken once and for all from the approved list of abolition
newspapers. This the convention of the American Anti-Slavery
Society promptly did. Douglass' plans for an industrial college at
Rochester, as well as his pleas for its support, were brushed aside

[41] William H. Pease and Jane H. Pease, "Antislavery Ambivalence: Immediatism, Expediency, Race," *American Quarterly*, XVII (Winter 1965),
695.

by the Bostonians. When he combined his paper with that of the Liberty Party, he was denounced for compromising his principles to gain the financial support of Gerrit Smith, and was ostracized at the Society's 1852 convention for consorting with political anti-slavery people. Eventually Garrison, after a preface that breathed more sorrow than anger, loosed a sweeping attack on Douglass' integrity, his motives, and his character, and even cast aspersions on the morality of his private life.[42]

One might regard all this as mere personal spite. But that would not be wholly fair either. The entire logic of reform placed enormous burdens on the individual and the individual conscience, and grossly magnified the personal aspect of everything. To be eligible for a meaningful role, a man had to have been converted and purged, which meant that he was convinced of both the enormity and the nature of the evil he was committed to fighting—and to challenge his definition of it was to challenge *him*. This self-righteousness, which in some sense was a necessity for psychological survival in such a movement, and this endless competition for individual moral purity were hardly better illustrated than in Garrison's ineffable public admonition to Douglass in the columns of the *Liberator:*

One thing should always be remembered in regard to the anti-slavery cause. . . . Unswerving fidelity to it, in this country, requires high moral attainments, the crucifixion of all personal considerations, a paramount regard for principle, absolute faith in the right. It does not follow, therefore, that because a man is or has been a slave, or because he is identified with a class meted out and trodden under foot, he will be the truest to the cause of human freedom. Already, that cause, both religiously and politically, has transcended the ability of the sufferers from American slavery and prejudice, as a class, to

[42] Accounts of this affair (which is strikingly reminiscent of Harold Cruse's recent complaints in *Crisis of the Negro Intellectual* about white radicals who presume to speak for black radicals without consulting them) are in Benjamin Quarles, "The Breach between Douglass and Garrison," *Journal of Negro History,* XXIII (April, 1938), 144–54; William H. Pease and Jane H. Pease, "Boston Garrisonians and the Problem of Frederick Douglass," *Canadian Journal of History,* II (September, 1967), 29–48; and Philip S. Foner, *The Life and Writings of Frederick Douglass* (New York: International Publishers, 1950), II, 48–66.

keep pace with it, or to perceive what are its demands, or to understand the philosophy of its operations.[43]

It is no wonder that Douglass, upon reading this, should have devoted a whole issue of his own paper to pointing out, among other things, that having been a slave did give a man some understanding of the institution of slavery.[44]

To return momentarily to my critics. Professor Kraditor says I "regret" that slavery was not ended gradually by piecemeal adjustments; Glazer believes that I "criticize" the abolitionists for failing to pursue institutional means of undermining the system prior to its eventual elimination. This is a misreading of something I intended neither as a "criticism" nor as an expression of "regret," but as a deliberate counterfactual projection. It was designed to exhibit those very choices which a culture so constituted as this one would *not* allow. As to why I should have bothered, there were at least two reasons. I was entitled, I thought, to ask questions about conceivable alternatives to the holocaust that did occur, before concluding—as I have—that such a holocaust was necessary. And with such a model, I hoped, one might be somewhat better sensitized to the limitations as well as the vitality of the abolitionist crusade.

Coming back to the main theme of this essay, I would predict that further progress on this subject, perhaps to a greater extent here than with the other aspects of it I have discussed in the foregoing pages, is most likely to come through studies in ideology. This would both impart a greater precision and supply an ampler framework than most of our work has so far done, and would do much toward releasing us from the closed cycle of debate in which we find ourselves. How did an ideology develop that could prepare the entire North psychologically to take up arms against the slaveholding South, and what exactly was its nature? And what relation did the abolitionist movement itself bear to that development? That there was, indeed, a relation is hardly to be questioned.

But what can and should be questioned is the extent to which the content of this ideology was a calculated logical extension of the abolitionists' work and doctrines. As the extremists of the

[43] *Liberator,* November 18, 1853.

[44] *Frederick Douglass' Paper,* December 9, 1853.

antislavery movement these men played a vital role. But the very conditions of the culture in which they had to function, and the very dynamic which those conditions imparted to their efforts, made it sociologically impossible that they should ever assume charge of the larger movement that did eventuate in the destruction of slavery, or that they could even contribute, other than indirectly, to the making of its ideology. With their own ranks in chronic fragmentation, institutionally and psychologically, they were in no position to do either.

The role of the extremist nonetheless was vital. It was not a political role he played, or even primarily an intellectual one; it was moral, and one of his functions was to establish the outer moral limits of the antislavery movement. In this he could hardly be "moderate," and his chief weapon, indeed his only weapon, was the manipulation of guilt. To play such a role at optimum did seem to require the insulation of a special kind of personality, and how "likeable" he was may remain an open question. But his other major function—the key one, I think—lay in his willingness to take risks.

The manner in which the abolitionists went forth to confront a hostile society has been set down as something of a "martyr complex." But it is hard not to admire the fortitude with which Weld, Garrison, and a host of others faced both potential and actual violence in locality after locality. Each occasion, considering the only thing they were armed with, was inherently unstable, and for the spectator, the experience on the one hand of coming to scoff and remaining to be converted, or, on the other, of mobbing the speaker, were seldom more than a hair's breadth apart. And with this process, one comes to the true functional link between the abolitionists and the growth of a sectional ideology—or, more accurately, of two sectional ideologies, one for the North and one for the South.

On one level, acts of martyrdom or graded equivalents of martyrdom (the killing of Lovejoy, the manhandling of Garrison, or the wrecking of Birney's press) served to engage a whole series of libertarian values not originally connected with slavery but shared by the entire Northern community. This is a process that has already been well described.[45] On another level, however, the

[45] By Barnes, *Antislavery Impulse,* and Russell B. Nye, *Fettered Free-*

impact of abolitionism on the South and the process of response and counter-response embracing ever widening clusters of emotional and intellectual commitments: it is this dynamic that must be followed out in all its complexity of detail in order to reconstruct the two massive ideological constellations that confronted one another by 1860.

By the decade of the 1830's, with the initial coming into prominence of abolitionism[46]—to which the South's own response contributed much—the process was fully launched. The South's immediate intransigence—the interference with the mails, the gag on petitions, the violence in Southern communities—was accompanied by a course of complicated political and social theorizing that began inexorably to set the South apart, and to make the South appear more and more in Northern eyes as a deviant and subversive cultural salient within the American Union. With this, the ideological cycle took on a life of its own, almost irrespective of what abolitionists might thereafter say or do. It came to involve everything from the nature of the Union, the Constitution, the Bible, majority rule, and democracy, to the very meaning of work.[47]

----

dom: Civil Liberties and the Slavery Controversy, 1830–1860 (East Lansing: Michigan State University Press, 1948). The terminology I myself used in dealing with this phenomenon was that of the "democratization" of antislavery feeling, in the course of which the movement was broadened and altered through—among other things—the "fellow-traveler" principle. And yet this need not be the only way to describe it. A more sophisticated and more inclusive approach might be in terms of ideology and its growth, a concept which has the advantage of containing its own dynamic.

[46] Though I have not as yet been challenged on this, one point in my book at which I now think I was mistaken was my implication (p. 207) that the proslavery movement did not require the appearance of abolitionism in the 1830's to set it on its way. Narrowly speaking, this may have been correct. But if one takes proslavery in its broadest ideological sense, it is apparent that its full development was in fact greatly stimulated by the sort of threat that abolitionism seemed to represent, and that the growth in scope and complexity of the two sectional ideologies was a product, from the 1830s on, of an oscillating process of challenge and counter-challenge.

[47] Two works which contribute greatly to an understanding of this process are Eugene D. Genovese, *The Political Economy of Slavery: Studies in the Economy and Society of the Slave South* (New York: Pantheon, 1965); and William W. Freehling, *Prelude to Civil War: The Nullification*

Most pervasively of all, it involved the entire meaning of the future. The previous experience of Americans had given them every reason to think of this in terms of land. "Territory" was above all else a moral metaphor for the future, and territorial expansion meant not simply physical but moral expansion. Thus the new cycle of ideological escalation that was touched off by the Texas question in the mid-1840's reflected a rising competition for nothing less than the country's moral future. Whether slavery should or should not be brought into the territories was more than an economic or even a political question. It was the question of whether those places would be dominated by one total ideological configuration or by the other.

By the middle and late 1850's the other side of the process, the mentality of imagined *conspiracy,* was fully evident. Neither the "Slave Power conspiracy" to fasten slavery on the entire North or the "Black Republican conspiracy" to destroy the South's domestic institutions may have drawn much reality from direct and immediate experience in either section. But with those "conspiracies" as part of an ideological dynamic, as elements of a struggle to control the entire country indirectly by controlling its future character, their power becomes very understandable and real.[48]

That a New England businessman, a New York lawyer, a Midwestern farmer—whatever their feelings about race—could feel just as threatened by 1860 as any Alabama planter, and that the ideology that sustained them had its own coherence and content, is apparent from a multitude of public and private writings. Such persons felt threatened, as Eric Foner has brilliantly shown, by a power that fostered what they saw as a whole set of deeply un-American values, subversive of majority rule, democracy, Union,

---

Controversy in South Carolina, 1816–1836 (New York: Harper & Row, 1966). Eric L. McKitrick ed., *Slavery Defended: The Views of the Old South* (Englewood Cliffs: Prentice-Hall, 1963), is a convenient compendium.

[48] See, e.g., "The Great Slave Power Conspiracy," Ch. VIII of Nye, *Fettered Freedom;* and Larry Gara, "Slavery and the Slave Power: A Crucial Distinction," *Civil War History,* XV (March, 1969), 5–18. Bernard Bailyn puts special emphasis on the "conspiracy" component of the Revolutionary ideology in *Ideological Origins of the American Revolution* (Cambridge: Harvard University Press, 1967), pp. 144–59.

and the dignity of free white labor.[49] Such an ideology constituted the fullest preparation for the North's response to the firing on Sumter. It had combined all the North's major convictions, including even its racism, into a party program. It had thus been placed in an institutional framework, the only one the culture really possessed, and fashioned into a powerful instrument for striking down slavery.

[49] Eric Foner, *Free Soil, Free Labor, Free Men: The Ideology of the Republican Party before the Civil War* (New York: Oxford, 1970). My reading of this work has been of great assistance in shaping the thoughts of the foregoing paragraphs.

VI

The Two Arguments on Slavery
(1975)

I

Beneath the debate that has been going on among English scholars over the state of the working classes during the Industrial Revolution lies a painful dilemma. One aspect of the question is all bound up with "immiseration": the demoralizing and brutalizing consequences of exploitation under the emerging industrial system. The other aspect is that of resistance to the exploitation, and *its* consequences: creative energy, the development of a distinctive cultural identity, a radical working-class literature and tradition. The dilemma, of course, is how you can emphasize vitality and achievement while you are also emphasizing decline and degradation. I mention this problem because of its resemblance to another that especially concerns me.[1] This is the debate that has proceeded for more than a decade over American black slavery.

In surveying the experience of any group subject to radical oppression and stress, and when your principal theme is damage, it is neither easy nor expedient to build in an alternative framework that provides adequately for resistance. On the other hand, there is bound to be resistance in *some* form, and this too needs to be recorded. And yet the more you make of it, the more you minimize the impact of brutality and exploitation upon powerlessness as a sociological, psychological, and moral fact. Although powerlessness corrupts, just as surely in its way as does power, our sympathy for the powerless puts limits on our tolerance of what their condition has done to them, and upon our willingness to survey the

[1] The resemblance has been pointed out by R. M. Hartwell in an unpublished paper, "Slave Labour and Factory Labour."

whole damage. Thus as resistance looms larger (both theirs and ours), the damage steadily shrinks; so, unavoidably, does the powerlessness; so, even, does the brutality itself. Indeed, it begins to look as though things generally were not so bad, after all, as they had been made out. Much of the strain in the current state of historical thinking on slavery is a reflection of this dilemma. Is there any resolution in sight? I have my doubts.

2

There has been a long tradition of writing about slavery that has put its primary stress upon brutality and damage. It goes at least as far back as Theodore Dwight Weld's *American Slavery as It Is: Testimony of a Thousand Witnesses* (1839), which is still being quoted from; it includes Frederic Bancroft's bleak *Slave Trading in the Old South,* published nearly a century later; and its spirit suffuses the authors of the Myrdal series on the Negro in America done in the 1930's and 40's, at all those points where their work refers back to slavery. Slavery was always hotly debated, but the debate that dominated the subject in antebellum times, and continued in modified form well into the twentieth century, was not at all the same debate I referred to above, the one that is in full swing now. Then, it was the evils of the system that preoccupied everyone, and the opposition's challenge was largely a matter of denying that the evils existed. Indeed, the Southerner Ulrich Phillips, whose work emphasized the benign aspects of the plantation regime and who thus managed to keep faith with his proslavery ancestors, was recognized for many years during the present century as the leading authority on the entire subject. That side of the debate, it goes without saying, was designed not to show how slaves resisted the system, but to mitigate and justify the practices of slaveholders.

But the abolitionists—we may as well call them that—were bound to win out, and the publication in 1956 of Kenneth Stampp's authoritative *The Peculiar Institution* signalled the final eclipse of Phillips' influence. My own book, *Slavery,* which came out three years later and which stressed the impact of an absolutist regime on slave personality, was actually part of that same tide, though I was hardly as willing to see it in such a way then as I am now. Stampp and I had our differences, but recent developments, as he wryly remarked to me not long ago, have retrospectively brought our positions a good deal closer together than they must have seemed then. I was a bit lofty about the need for value-free judgments, and I had some hard things to say about moralizing abolitionists. But for practical purposes I was one of them. I never once doubted, and certainly do not doubt now, that American chattel slavery was damaging to every man, woman, and child, white or black, who was in any way touched by it. I wanted to know what the damage was, and how it was done.

The tide has now turned once more, having begun to do so in the later 1960's. Interest is now focused almost wholly upon resistance, resistance to the degradations of the slave regime that took a variety of forms, and upon something that was of scant concern to white scholars of a generation ago, the growth under slavery of a black culture. The two have become inseparable, culture itself functioning as a form of resistance. The new work examines slavery at many points and in considerable depth, but whatever else it does, the best of this work—indeed, most of the current output—involves a search for culture, and by now there is very little in any of it about damage.

Something should probably be said about the ideological climate in which both these arguments have functioned, the argument on damage that reached its peak in the mid-60's, and the one on culture that has come for the time being to supersede it in the attention of scholars and public.

The crest of the "damage" cycle in the early 1960's coincided almost perfectly with a state of mind regarding race relations whose dominant concern was integration and civil rights. Most of the writing done up to this time could function as both theoretical and ideological underpinning for the movement, and the writers themselves—historians, psychologists, sociologists, or whatever—were well aware of this. Each had contributed details to the catalogue of abuses that white society had heaped upon American blacks beginning with slavery, and of the damage for which, it was now earnestly felt, restitution must at last be made.

The spirit that animated the civil rights movement was the hope of brotherhood, the conviction that the time had come when lines of separation on grounds of race should be resolutely swept away. The ideal had about it a certain grandeur, and one may still feel this in reading, say, the writings of Howard Zinn on SNCC activities in the deep South. But there was another aspect of it that is clearer now than it seemed then. It was still very much—certainly in the work that had served to form the intellectual background—a matter of whites talking to whites. To be sure, there stood in that same background such black scholars as W.E.B. DuBois, E. Franklin Frazier, Carter Woodson, and John Hope Franklin. But their work did not seem in the least inharmonious (Frazier's in particular was frequently referred to) with the perceptions of massive damage that permeated the writing of white intellectuals, and for which whites were guiltily considering remedies.

We may now see that such a situation—one in which whites told each other what was good for blacks, or at least took their own leadership in the interracial movement for granted—had its drawbacks. Still, it was not lacking in good will, and one can make too much of its condescensions. Moreover, there was one small advantage, for what it may have been worth. White intellectuals had not yet reached the point at which they would feel the need to weigh everything they said for its effect on an emergently aggressive black audience. The "civil rights" phase, together with all the attitudes that had fashioned it, may be said to have reached a kind of benign meridian with President Lyndon Johnson's remarkable address at Howard University in June 1965. "Much of the Negro community," the President said, "is buried under a blanket of history and circumstance." Positive action, he declared, must be taken to repair the damage done by "ancient brutality, past injustice, and present prejudice."

Few could then have known how transitory this phase would prove to be, how swiftly the emphasis upon civil rights and integration (and "ancient brutality") would evaporate, and how suddenly black spokesmen would emerge everywhere insisting that what was good for blacks would henceforth be defined by them, and not by whites. It was all to leave white intellectuals in rather a state of shock. In 1969 Marcus Cunliffe, observing the academic scene with the wicked detachment of an uninvolved Englishman, reported a deep sense of strain: "white facial muscles ache with nervous smiling, black ones with intimidating scowls."[2] What could possibly have happened?

[2] Marcus Cunliffe, "Black Culture and White America," *Encounter*, XXXIV (January, 1970), 22–35.

In reviewing the precipitous change that occurred in the intellectual weather of the mid-1960's, one must see the famous Moynihan Report, together with what happened to it, as a truly critical event. Both the report and the program Moynihan hoped to initiate with it were smothered in a landslide of recrimination. The main details are familiar enough. As Assistant Secretary of Labor, Daniel P. Moynihan had given considerable thought to what he saw as the perilously demoralized state of the black family in Northern city ghettoes, and the report he prepared on this subject was to open the way—or so he hoped—for a kind of sweeping domestic "Marshall Plan" of Federal assistance to the black community. "Three centuries of injustice," he wrote, "have brought about deep-seated structural distortions in the life of the Negro American." He advanced a synthesis of historical findings, sociological diagnoses, and current statistics to show the various forms of destruction this "injustice" had brought about and which should now be remedied through programs in the realms of employment, education, housing, and welfare reform. Moynihan's report, which defined the problem but deferred discussion of the remedies for subsequent planning, was completed by the spring of 1965. Moynihan had meanwhile persuaded President Johnson to give his own blessing to its spirit and principles, and this was what the President did in his Howard University address that June, of which Moynihan himself was the chief draftsman.[3]

For the subsequent failure of the Report, so prodigious in view of such promising beginnings, a variety of reasons could be assigned. These would certainly include covert resistance within the welfare bureaucracy, the piecemeal and somewhat lackadaisical way in which the Report's contents were leaked to the public, inadequate briefing of the press, insufficient consultation with civil rights leaders, and the draining away of official energy during the fall of 1965 amid the Administration's mounting preoccupation with the war in Vietnam. But the deepest reason of all, the one that underlay all the others, was that without anyone's quite realizing it the entire "damage" argument, as applied to any aspect of Negro life in America, had become ideologically untenable.

[3] Lee Rainwater and William Yancey, *The Moynihan Report and the Politics of Controversy* (Cambridge: MIT Press, 1967), is both a history of the Report and a useful collection of documents pertaining to it.

Simply as policy, Moynihan's conception had much to be said for it. Given its general Catholic working-class welfare perspective, there should have been nothing grossly unreasonable about assuming that the morale and well-being of any community depend in some way on the stability of the families that make it up, that exploitation and economic adversity place the family life of any community under severe strain, and that the primary object of any program of social welfare should lie in assisting hard-pressed fathers to support their families decently and provide a stable setting for their children to grow up in. (Needless to say, this was not the only theory on which social policy might have been based, but it had at least a rough consistency, and in any case theories are not everything.) And there was a potentially logical transition from this to the remedies Moynihan had had in mind all along: jobs, job training, education, public housing, and a welfare structure that did not put a premium on disrupted families or penalize families that had men present—in short, a massive Federal commitment to rebuilding the economic life of black communities everywhere. Moreover, there is plenty of evidence that neither the generality of black spokesmen nor of white intellectuals had any real quarrel with the actual prescriptions Moynihan envisioned.

The uproar came not over the remedies, but over the argument for them. The Report itself was a relentless, insistent, dreary picture of unrelieved damage, designed to prove beyond any doubt that the condition of the urban black family in America had deteriorated to the point of disaster. Beginning with claims made by me regarding the stultifications of individual personality experienced under slavery, adding material of a similar kind from the psychologist Thomas F. Pettigrew, and bringing in E. Franklin Frazier's account of the disruptive consequences of slavery upon the black family as a persistent legacy, Moynihan then produced a series of very depressing contemporary statistics. They dealt with differential rates (between whites and blacks) of unemployment, illegitimacy, crime, low educational performance, women with absent husbands, children with absent fathers, and families headed by women. "It was by destroying the Negro family under slavery," Moynihan balefully warned, "that white America broke the will of the Negro people. Although that will has reasserted itself in our time, it is a resurgence doomed to frustration unless the viability of the Negro family is restored." The report was not originally intended for public release, and Moynihan did not write under the constraints that might have been imposed by touchy persons watching over his shoulder. It was written to persuade inside policy-makers that the problem was so serious in scale that nothing short of a total commitment was thinkable. He wanted his paper to be "shocking enough that they would say, 'Well, we can't let this sort of thing go on. We've got to do something about it' "[4]

Shocking it was, but to all the wrong people, and, in the end, with the very opposite results from those he had so fervently hoped for. What they saw, based on incomplete newspaper accounts, was a vast slur on the whole American black population, past and present. James Farmer ("I'm angry . . . really angry") exploded in the *Amsterdam News* upon learning "that we've caught 'matriarchy,' and 'the tangle of Negro pathology' . . . a social plague recently diagnosed by Daniel Moynihan. . . ." Roy Wilkins, who himself supported the report, explained somewhat apologetically that the black community resented the emphasis on the black family, "as if it were a moral criticism of themselves." They were egged on, moreover, by prehensile white liberals who were beginning to try on "radical" attitudes. William Ryan, a mental health consultant, wrote a widely circulated paper which was printed both in the *Nation* and in NAACP's *Crisis,* in which he heaped scorn upon "this smug document." "The theme is: 'The Negro was not initially born inferior, he was made inferior by generations of harsh treatment.' Thus we continue to assert that the Negro is inferior while chastely maintaining that all men are equal." There is "no escape," Ryan declared, "in the world of sociological fakery." And the *Christian Century* loftily announced, after a discussion of the report's many fallacies, that the real agenda ought to be "jobs, housing, and education"—the very matters Moynihan had had closest to heart.[5]

Still, for all the fumbled handling of the report, one may wonder how much sustained intellectual support Moynihan could have had for his message in the years immediately ahead, no mat-

[4] *Ibid.,* pp. 25, 30.

[5] *Ibid.,* pp. 273, 409–10, 457–66; *Christian Century,* LXXXII (December 15, 1965), 1531–32.

ter what tactics had been used to promote it. The entire climate in which white intellectuals had hitherto functioned was changing. Charles Silberman, who had himself made a major contribution to what I have been calling the literature of "damage," said as much in November 1965. The civil rights phase, whose goals had been relatively simple and to a surprising degree successful, was over. The history of Negro-white relations, Silberman wrote,

has entered a new and radically different stage—a stage so different from the recent or distant past as to make the familiar approaches and solutions obsolete, irrelevant, and sometimes even harmful. . . . What is new is that Negroes have begun to reveal and express—indeed, to act out—the anger and hatred they have always felt, but had always been obliged to hide and suppress behind a mask of sweet docility.[6]

True, and white intellectuals would find the adjustment troublesome, especially with the rumblings of Black Power that arose shortly thereafter. The campus uprisings of 1968 and 1969 would leave many of them reeling. One of the by-products of that period was demands everywhere for elaborate Black Studies programs, to which professors and administrators alike agreed with an almost benumbed alacrity. The new insistence now was upon "black culture"—an expression which, at least in the common currency, had been all but unknown in 1965.

Daniel P. Moynihan knew that for his purpose, as one observer put it, "he needed to point to what poor Negroes were deprived of, not to how they managed to make out despite their deprivations."[7] And yet it was precisely the latter point, not the former, that had now come to seem all-important: "how they managed to make out." In short, it was no longer damage they wanted to hear about and talk about, but resistance.

3

Such, then, was the ideological bridge from "damage" to "resistance"—or, to put it more comprehensively, to "culture." But there was another kind of bridge as well, one of intellect and sensibility. And it was this, I think, that gave the search for black culture the

[6] Rainwater and Yancey, *Moynihan Report,* pp. 428–29.

[7] *Ibid.,* p. 32.

authenticity and legitimacy to which it was entitled, and still is entitled. The most impressive example of this point that I know of is that provided by Ralph Ellison.

The demand for a new vision of the American black experience that emerged in the later 1960's was, for Ellison, far more than a fashionable novelty. Early in his career Ellison saw "social science" for the standing menace that it is for any truly literary mind under any circumstances. But a more particular menace lay in social science categories as applied indiscriminately to the aggregate experience of American blacks. Efforts in the realm of psychology and sociology could, undertaken in good faith as most of them now were, appeal to the white conscience. By exhibiting, as they were bound to do, the injustice and degradation visited upon blacks from time out of mind, they could conceivably move white society to sweep away the barriers that had hitherto prevented blacks from taking their rightful place as full participants in the common current of American life.

So far so good; Ellison had no quarrel with that. But social science cannot possibly stop there, and well before it does stop, it has already taken away something that for Ellison was life itself. In every such undertaking there are two deadening implications. One is that the collectivity of blacks must be seen as essentially inert; the other, that when all this prejudice and discrimination is removed, blacks would somehow become undifferentiated Americans. Their past—by definition an ugly pathological blot—would be wiped out; their distinctive character, experience, contributions, and culture would in effect be denied, would really no longer exist. Brotherhood: splendid. The races cannot function separately, and in fact never have. But this was not it. This, for Ralph Ellison, was merely a new device of stultification.

Thus Ellison's responses to such material as it appeared were always measured (since he knew what he wanted) with a special nicety. He also retained a remarkable consistency over time, as two or three examples may show.

As early as 1944 Ellison wrote a review of Gunnar Myrdal's *American Dilemma,* a book widely acclaimed by whites (whose consciences were powerfully stirred) as well as by blacks (who saw white society as beginning at last to wake up). He praised Myrdal's book for its many insights, some of them "brilliant," and for offering the key "to a more democratic and fruitful usage of the South's natural and human resources." But when Myrdal asserted in effect that the Negro's life, his thoughts—and presumably his personality and his culture—"are, in the main, to be considered as secondary reactions to more primary pressures from the side of the dominant white majority," the young Ralph Ellison's hand came sharply down on the table. Can a people, he demanded,

live and develop for over three hundred years simply by *reacting*? Are American Negroes simply the creation of white men, or have they at least helped to create themselves out of what they found around them? Men have made a way of life in caves and upon cliffs, why cannot Negroes have made a life upon the horns of the white man's dilemma? ...

It does not occur to Myrdal that many of the Negro cultural manifestations which he considers merely reflective might also embody a *rejection* of what he considers "higher values." ... It is only partially true that Negroes turn away from white patterns because they are refused participation. There is nothing like distance to create objectivity, and exclusion gives rise to counter values.

This was written for *Antioch Review;* the editor—for whatever reasons—did not print it.[8] But twenty years later Ralph Ellison, now famous as the author of *The Invisible Man,* made another statement. The occasion this time was a lead review, for a national audience, of Howard Zinn's *Southern Mystique* in 1964. Again he made discriminations. He praised Zinn for his good will, his expenditures in deeds as well as words in the cause of civil rights, and his desire for massive contacts between blacks and whites. But when Zinn came to insist that history no longer mattered in the face of the Negro's new self-assertion, and of the white South's new willingness to make unwanted adjustments, Ellison once more drew the line.

Zinn had been impressed by my book, *Slavery,* and its discussion of the "Sambo" personality, which he thought explained much about the history that no longer mattered. ("That personality also becomes, Elkins suggests, reversible.") Ellison would have none of this. Zinn had let himself be taken in, "both by Elkins and by his own need to recreate man, or at least Negro man, in terms of

8 Ralph Ellison, *Shadow and Act* (New York: Random House, 1964), pp. 303–17.

the expediencies of the historical moment." The black American is something more than "a physical fact and a social artifice."

He is the product of the synthesis of his blood mixture, his social experience, and what he has made of his predicament, i.e., his *culture*. And his quality of wonder and his heroism alike spring no less from his brutalization than from that culture.[9]

Three years later Ellison was at it again, this time in an extended interview with three young black writers which appeared in *Harper's Magazine*. He condemned the Moynihan report; at the same time he praised President Johnson's Howard University speech (which was simple, direct, and unargumentative), though both had come from the same pen. Once again he warned the young men against Elkins.[10] We depend, he said, "upon outsiders—mainly sociologists—to interpret our lives for us." What all their abstractions left out—once again—was culture.[11]

In the years immediately ahead, Ellison's message would make a deep impression upon black intellectuals, though not upon all, precluding as it did the extreme positions of black nationalism. But to chastened whites the appeal was irresistible, especially to those writing about slavery.

4

The literature on American slavery that has appeared in the past four or five years, and continues to appear, is impressive in both depth and bulk. Among the many themes in it that will strike the casual reader is the strong belief of nearly every writer in the cultural bias of all who came before. Each also believes he has uncovered new material, which in a number of cases is true, and that the more familiar material, hitherto misinterpreted, is being properly read for the first time. None is primarily concerned with damage; all are absorbed with resistance and culture.[12]

[9] "If the Twain Shall Meet," *Book Week*, November 8, 1964.

[10] Note from the beleaguered Elkins: I am here conceding the full validity of Ellison's case. Naturally I will be taking some of it back later on.

[11] "'A Very Stern Discipline': An Interview with Ralph Ellison," *Harper's Magazine*, CCXXXIV (March 1967), 76–95.

[12] I have concerned myself in the following discussion with works that

John W. Blassingame's *The Slave Community: Plantation Life in the Ante-Bellum South* (1972), for instance (according to its author), "breaks sharply with American historiographic tradition." It rests on "new kinds of sources, viewed from different angles," which previous historians have "deliberately ignored." The typical pattern of plantation life was sufficiently open that the slave's individuality was in fact not crushed, and the picture most historians have drawn (using only planters' records and material from the white side of things) "of an all-powerful, monolithic institution which strip[ped] the slave of any meaningful and distinct culture, family life, religion, or manhood," is simply false. A far more accurate one would show a rich, diverse, and variegated community life in which family (the slave family was not destroyed either), religion, and a body of lore served as mechanisms of resistance against the debilitating effects the slave system was formerly supposed to have had. The slave's own contribution to the total picture—with the music, folk-tales, religion, and surviving autobiographies as evidence—must be brought to the foreground if this culture is to be fully seen for what it was.

As it happened, Blassingame's book was not received with much enthusiasm, though not because of its basic argument, which was already familiar and had by this time come to be widely accepted

---

deal directly with plantation life. A number of distinguished studies on slavery, or bearing on slavery, have appeared in the past decade which fall outside this category, and my omission of them here is in no way a judgment on their importance. Among them are David Brion Davis, *The Problem of Slavery in Western Culture* (Ithaca: Cornell University Press, 1966) and *The Problem of Slavery in the Age of Revolution* (Ithaca: Cornell University Press, 1975); Winthrop D. Jordan, *White Over Black: American Attitudes Toward the Negro, 1550–1812* (Chapel Hill: University of North Carolina Press, 1968) and *The White Man's Burden: Historical Origins of Racism in the United States* (New York: Oxford, 1974); George M. Fredrickson, *The Black Image in the White Mind: The Debate on Afro-American Character and Destiny, 1817–1914* (New York: Harper-Row, 1971); and Edmund S. Morgan, *American Slavery, American Freedom: The Ordeal of Colonial Virginia* (New York: Norton, 1975). Carl N. Degler's *Neither Black nor White: Slavery and Race Relations in Brazil and the United States* (New York: Macmillan, 1971) I have written about at length elsewhere (*Journal of Negro History*, LVIII [January, 1973], 86–90). Ira Berlin's fine *Slaves without Masters: The Free Negro in the Antebellum South* (New York: Pantheon, 1974) gives considerable support to my concluding point in the present essay.

in principle. It was rather that reviewers thought his conclusions not as original as he claimed them to be, and that he had neglected to exploit a large mass of readily available evidence—the WPA interviews with former slaves—of the very sort that should have been most pertinent to his case.[13] But a more serious difficulty lay in Blassingame's being so locked in combat with a previous version of slave personality, and so repeatedly denying its legitimacy, that he never quite got around to explaining what *did* go into the making of this culture, or what its distinctive character was, or how it got that way. It seems to have been entirely a culture of resistance, but there is surprisingly little interest shown in the nature of what it was that was being resisted. As Eugene Genovese[14] points out, one cannot begin to understand slave society—personality, culture, or anything else—without seeing the mutuality of the master-slave relationship as an indispensable key to it. In a society where men are enslaved by other men, human relationships must at least be taken as something special, and its human products—on both sides—as special too. Whereas the slave, at the end of Blassingame's book, "was no different in most ways from most men. The same range of personality types existed in the quarters as in the mansion." If slavery in practice made no more difference that that, perhaps the entire subject of slavery is less important than we thought.

George P. Rawick offered an argument the same year, 1972, which was in many respects similar. *From Sundown to Sunup: The Making of the Black Community* was the introductory volume to a nineteen-volume edition of slave narrative materials, hitherto mostly unpublished, the bulk of which represented the work originally done by the WPA Writers' Project in the 1930's.

---

[13] E.g., Marion deB. Kilson, *American Historical Review*, LXXVIII (October, 1973), 1132–33; John White, *Times Literary Supplement*, March 2, 1973, and *Reviews in American History*, I (December, 1973), 514–19; Orville W. Taylor, *Journal of Negro History*, LVIII (October, 1973), 1476–77; Willie Lee Rose, *Journal of American History*, LX (June, 1973), 131–33; Kenneth W. Porter, *Journal of Southern History*, XXXIX (May, 1973), 293–94; F. N. Boney, *Georgia Review*, XXVIII (Spring, 1974), 147–50; Gerald W. Mullin, *William and Mary Quarterly*, 3rd Ser., XXX (July, 1973), 513–16; and Stanley L. Engerman, *Journal of Political Economy*, LXXXI (November, 1973), 470–71.

[14] In *Roll, Jordan, Roll*, to be discussed below.

Rawick's preparation and publication of these materials, making them readily accessible for the first time, was an enormously valuable contribution. *From Sundown to Sunup,* presented as an interpretive study to accompany them, may thus be seen in two capacities—as a separate entity and as part of a larger undertaking.

In addition to the themes noted earlier, another that permeates all the new literature is a strong emphasis on "community." Rawick puts the word in his title (as does Blassingame); he even extends its meaning at many points to embrace blacks all over America, slave and free alike. As for slavery, "almost all historians have presented the black slaves as dehumanized victims, without culture, history, community, change, or development." Rawick, like Blassingame, believes this view of plantation slavery should be exchanged for one which recognizes the "social space" allowed by the system for both survival and resistance. He, too, insists on the positive functions of the slave family, slave religion, and slave folklore for tightening the internal bonds of community. And he, too, is convinced that the slave personality was certainly "not one that should be described . . . as 'infantile.' " A perpetual state of rebellion, among other things, kept it from becoming so.

Whatever the merits of Rawick's essay, one is perplexed about the kind of relationship that was intended between it and the eighteen volumes of source materials that follow it, materials being presented as a major new body of evidence for the study of American slavery. The ambiguity may be suggested by two examples. One is incidental to Rawick's assumptions about a nation-wide antebellum black "community." "The abolitionist movement," he writes,

was essentially a product of the black community, although whites played a role in it. Abolitionism was at all times dominated by Afro-American freedmen, not by whites, although the inherent racism of American ideology has obscured that fact[,] not only for present-day Americans but for most whites—with the notable exceptions of such men as James [*sic*] Wentworth Higginson and Wendell Phillips—who participated in the movement.

There is nothing in Rawick's evidence—eighteen volumes of it—to support such an extraordinary assertion, nor, so far as I know, in anyone else's evidence either.[15] The other example concerns per-

[15] William Lloyd Garrison had substantial support for his *Liberator*

sonality. "The slave narratives are the richest source we have ever had for a description of slave personality." Rawick is surely right there, except that the only systematic analysis that has been made of the narratives for this purpose (by the sociologist Norman R. Yetman, who inferred from them that plantation life, on the large holdings in particular, did in fact create a dependent personality type) offers conclusions very different from his own.[16] Evidence, it seems, does not always speak for itself. On what sort of authority, in such cases, do we decide what it *ought* to say?

Two new books on specific areas of slave culture will very shortly appear, one on songs and folk-tales by Lawrence Levine, and the other on the family by Herbert Gutman; unlike the works just referred to, these are not likely to have any aspersions cast on their scholarly thoroughness. Gutman's I can discuss with confidence, having the manuscript before me; with Levine's I shall have to be more tentative, limting myself to an observation or two based on three substantial published essays reflecting work in progress. The work of both is scrupulous, accurate, and authoritative, and should prove to be influential. Let me say something about Levine's first.

Levine, like other recent writers, is gravely concerned—no doubt justifiably—over the errors of his predecessors and the undependability of their work. Their research has been "narrow and culture-bound," and they have treated the distinctive features of black history "not as cultural forms but as disorganization and pathology." Even those who first collected the primary materials he is working with are not to be trusted. They "had little under-

---

from free blacks, and there were, of course, some notable black abolitionists. But these men came nowhere close to being a majority, and the highhanded manner in which the whites relegated them to a subordinate role in the movement was notorious. (On this, the work of Jane H. Pease and William H. Pease provides chapter and verse.) Moreover, though there was a significant class of reform-minded black leaders and publicists in the antebellum North, Frederick Cooper argues that they gave a relatively minor share of their attention to abolition. See "Elevating the Race: The Social Thought of Black Leaders, 1827–50," *American Quarterly*, XXIV (December, 1972), 604–25.

[16] "The Slave Personality: A Test of the 'Sambo' Hypothesis" (Ph.D. dissertation, University of Pennsylvania, 1969). Yetman made no attempt at the time to publish this work, though he may yet do so in some form.

standing of the culture from which [the songs and folk-tales] sprang, and little scruple about altering or suppressing them." Historians up to now "have rendered an articulate people historically inarticulate." Levine would like to render them articulate again, and so far he has done a very good job of it. Moreover, he has taken to heart Ralph Ellison's admonition that "if you would tell me who I am, at least take the trouble to discover what I have been."[17]

Examining slave songs as a key to slave consciousness, Levine makes two points that are both convincing and enlightening. One is that they represented "a distinctive cultural form," owing less to either white influence or African origins than to the circumstances of American slave life. The other concerns the extraordinarily fluid, improvisational character of this music. (When James McKim during the Civil War asked where the slaves got their songs, he was told, "Dey make em, sah.") It is wrong, Levine feels, to "conceive of slavery as a closed system which destroyed the vitality of the Negro and left him a dependent child," since it "never prevented the slaves from carving out independent cultural forms." And he argues throughout that these forms were a product of community, created out of a "communal consciousness."

The case for "community" holds up very well throughout the entire discussion of music, and is especially persuasive with regard to the spirituals. But with the folk-tales the claim is dropped; there, with entirely different forces at work, it somehow does not apply at all. This disjunction creates some puzzles. The Brer Rabbit trickster stories were certainly not the only kind, though they seem to have been the most popular. They were "didactic"; they gave instruction on how the weak must make their way in a world of hypocrisy and superior power—by tricking not only the strong but also each other. Many of Brer Rabbit's tricks are responses to the requirements of self-defense and survival. But many others

[17] The essays I am referring to and quoting from are: "Slave Songs and Slave Consciousness: An Exploration of Neglected Sources," in Tamara K. Hareven, ed., *Anonymous Americans: Explorations in Nineteenth-Century History* (Englewood Cliffs: Prentice-Hall, 1971), pp. 99–130; "The Concept of the New Negro and the Realities of Black Culture," in Nathan I. Huggins et al., eds., *Key Issues in the Afro-American Experience* (New York: Harcourt, Brace Jovanovich, 1971), II, 125–49; and " 'Some Go Up and Some Go Down': The Meaning of the Slave Trickster," in Stanley Elkins and Eric McKitrick, eds., *The Hofstadter Aegis: A Memorial* (New York: Knopf, 1974), pp. 94–124.

seem gratuitous and purposeless. He steals or cheats the other animals out of more of their food than he needs; he not only persuades them to help him out of traps but tricks them into taking his place; a lady who resists his wooing he kills, skins, and smokes over hickory chips. He assembles his neighbors to help him build a spring house, and when this act of community is accomplished he has them all drowned. Brer Wolf seeks revenge upon Brer Rabbit (for having boiled Wolf's grandmother and tricked Wolf into eating her), whereupon Rabbit callously sacrifices his own wife and children to save himself. There may be much "complexity and ambiguity" in the tales, as Levine insists, and "levels of meaning," but one thing about them is clear and simple enough: their "hero" is at best one nasty little hustler. The world he confronts and in which he survives, he also helps to perpetuate. He certainly does nothing to improve it. In that world of lying, stealing, duplicity, and murder there is no friendship, no affection, and no mutual trust; "family" counts for nothing, and of "community" there is not a shred. If this particular body of lore represents a form of psychic adjustment to slavery, as Levine seems to have proved, one is reluctant to take it as a very positive one. There were undoubtedly others, as we shall see when the rest of his evidence is in.

Herbert Gutman's *The Invisible Fact: Afro-Americans and their Families, 1750–1925* has an excellent chance of being received, along with Eugene Genovese's *Roll, Jordan, Roll,* as one of the two most important works of the 1970's on American plantation slavery. Its comprehensive scholarship and its technical skill as a work of social history will give it considerable effectiveness. It breathes with polemical passion, which raises problems, but its argument will be listened to, and I think with respect.

The particular vehicle for the growth and transmission of culture that concerns Gutman is the slave family. Using techniques of family reconstitution originally developed by historical demographers, and working with extraordinary persistence and imagination, he pieces out a picture of a widespread, complex family and kinship structure that evolved over a long period of time, in some cases extending back as far as the early eighteenth century.[18] The

[18] The claim is plausibly supported by Philip Curtin's demonstration that American slavery, which depended no more than nominally on fresh im-

members of that network could thus draw on a rich fund of accumulated experience. Gutman makes very ingenious use of the records of several large plantation units, one set of which had been kept over four generations and (in this particular case) without any slave's having been sold. Certain striking patterns emerge. One is a clear continuity of family groupings, some of whose earliest members were African-born. Another is a configuration of sexual behavior which varied from the norms of white society but was nonetheless coherent and subject to the group's own rules. (A girl might have intercourse fairly early and bear a child, but then she was generally expected to settle down with one man and have the rest of her children by him.) Another clear pattern involved the giving and taking of names. Boys were frequently named after their fathers, but girls seldom after their mothers (fatherhood did count for something), and when surnames were assumed, they were —perhaps oftener than not—taken from former owners rather than from current ones. Among the devices for absorbing the shocks of sale and separation, and for socializing newcomers, was that of adoption and "fictive kin." All told, the slave family system had a dynamic of its own which Gutman believes was largely independent of planter control.

It is evident, on the other hand, that the polemical requirements of Gutman's argument have affected not simply the argument's tone (which is often hot and fierce) but its very shape, structure, and even outcome. It would have been one thing to say that the black family, exposed to the debilitating rigors of slavery, in reality had access to a series of stabilizing mechanisms. Such a formulation would allow for its own reversibility, a margin essential to any experimental proposition. But it is quite another simply to make, as he does, the untestable claim that he has shown the black family emerging from slavery with a very high degree of stability, far greater than his predecessors have been willing to grant. The slave family, so the logic goes, was much more stable than we

---

ports, was—unlike slavery elsewhere—demographically successful. Curtin estimates that only about 4.5 per cent of slave imports from Africa to the New World were brought to the present United States, and concludes that the maintenance of the American slave population depended primarily on natural increase. *The Atlantic Slave Trade: A Census* (Madison: University of Wisconsin Press, 1969).

thought. But what if we had not thought anything? How in that case might a study on this subject have begun, and how might it have turned out?

Gutman, reasonably enough in principle, criticizes everyone else for using a static model which does not provide for development over time. But his own model is equally static in a lateral way; it makes no operative provision for stress, disintegration, or damage of any kind, at any point in time. He makes verbal gestures toward the severities of the system, but no serious analytical ones. Of course nobody expects him to stress the severities, his concerns being elsewhere, but he has not even left spaces in his scheme for how they might have worked. Might he not try to predict a new study (the older ones are all obsolete; he says so himself) which would be just as thorough, just as learned, just as sophisticated as his own, but which examined the other side, the "damage" side of slave life for the slave family, just as he himself has done for the "resistance" side? We are not even sure now whether such a side existed.

Put in another way, the slave family is given no credible setting in which to function. Gutman is rightly enthusiastic about Charles A. Valentine's "bicultural model" for explaining the socialization of ethnic minorities, a process of interacting "mainstream" and "ethnic" influences. Well and good, but here the "mainstream" hardly appears, much less *does* anything, whereas Gutman's greatest fury is aroused by the most coherent "mainstream" argument now going—Eugene Genovese's assertions about the paternalistic ethos of the master class and the ways in which it influenced the slaves' own culture. He flatly declares—probably wrongly and certainly unnecessarily—that there is no evidence for any such claims.

An analogy that comes to mind is the peculiar impression I once had in reading Irving Brant's version of James Madison's role in the nation's drift toward war in 1812. The biographer was determined to show Madison as far less the indecisive vacillator, tossed by events, "than we once thought," whereupon poor Madison begins to grow ever bigger and more resolute until all the powers of Europe, the entire setting—Napoleon, the Grand Army, Wellington, and the fleets and admirals of England—shrink into specks. In Gutman's pages the proportions of things—in themselves very good things—appear similarly warped. The family flourishes in slavery, and for all we know may even have been strengthened by it; the vitality of slave culture grows and grows; life under slavery looks better and better. And farther and farther into the distance recedes the planter class with its array of coercive powers—physical, psychological, and moral—as does a whole environing society with its vicious racism, determined in a thousand ways to render impotent and dependent the black presence in its midst. Gutman respectfully quotes me: "It was, after all, a very hard system, and we would do well not to forget it." But I fear he does forget it. His work is impressive; his case is potentially an excellent one. But it is made without a context.

There now seems to be a fair measure of agreement on the importance of the time dimension; others besides Gutman have recognized that slavery had a history, and that its development and growth began a long time before the immediate antebellum era upon which our focus normally rests. Gerald W. Mullin's *Flight and Rebellion: Slave Resistance in Eighteenth Century Virginia* (1972) and Peter H. Wood's *Black Majority: Negroes in Colonial South Carolina from 1670 through the Stono Rebellion* (1974) are two notable efforts to extend this historical perspective by examining the conditions of slavery in the eighteenth century. Resistance, as is implied in the titles, looms large in each. Each is admirable as a monographic undertaking; both have most of the merits of care, detail, and circumstance that such work at its disciplined best can embody. What they give us as building blocks for a general theory of American slavery, however, is somewhat less evident.

Wood shows that in early colonial South Carolina the combination of a numerical majority of blacks (two to one by 1740), special skills (Africans apparently knew more about rice culture than Europeans), great demand for labor of all kinds, and especially the loose and unsettled character of a frontier-plantation society, had by 1720 or 1730 provided the makings of a distinct Afro-American sub-culture, with Gullah as a kind of lingua franca. But growing signs of self-sufficiency among these lowland slaves became intolerable to the white minority. Efforts to hedge and limit the slave population generated tension and resistance, culminating in the Stono Rebellion of 1739 in which a band of fifty or more slaves killed about two dozen whites. The rebellion was brutally suppressed. The most rigorous legal features of the South Carolina slave system date from the comprehensive Negro Act of 1740—a direct consequence of the rebellion—which formed the core of the South Carolina slave code for the next hundred years.

The path to rebellion in Mullin's study, which ends with the Gabriel uprising of 1800, was different. In Virginia, it seems, it was not a climate of repression that produced rebellion, but something like its opposite: the setting of post-Revolutionary Virginia was permissive and ideologically rather open. The largest number of runaways during that period came not from the plantations but from a relatively mobile and highly valued class of slaves who had mastered a craft of some kind, spoke English fluently, and had become acclimated to European ways. It was from this group, moreover, that the leadership for Gabriel's Rebellion was drawn. Actually the uprising never took place, the conspirators having been detected before it could be carried into action. Here too the punishment was summary and swift.

These studies, terminating in the way each does, leave unresolved some important questions about culture. Is the passage of time bound to be "progressive," and are its effects in the way of cultural change always of a positive character? A rebellion and its consequences should present a potentially useful test of this—of the power of "ethnic" and "mainstream" cultures to assert themselves under stress—but if your examination *ends* with a rebellion, you cannot very well run such a test, and your historical slice remains in its way as truncated as any other "static" model.

As for rebellions in themselves, there is the oft-mooted question of which kinds of slaves were likely to rebel more effectively, the African-born or the fully acculturated American-born. Mullin says the latter; Wood implies the former. Perhaps the question itself is misleading. The key variable in each instance seems to have been a certain modicum of social space, provided in the South Carolina case by a "critical mass" of shared African behavior, speech, and myth, and in Virginia by a situation that allowed a privileged group to evade the full coercions of plantation slavery. Did they, for whatever reasons, have as much space afterwards? It seems not. Actually the entire problem of rebellion, not only in these works but in others as well, has become analytically rather blurred. I will come back to this point shortly.

The most impressive of the new books that has yet appeared is Eugene Genovese's *Roll, Jordan, Roll: The World the Slaves Made* (1974). This comprehensive survey of all elements of the plantation system is a work of obvious distinction, fully entitled to the honors so far accorded it. To be sure, the theme that continually recurs in the critical commentary (for reasons not as clear as they might be) is that of the "flawed masterpiece." The flaws must be duly examined. But it is only fair to consider first why it should have been regarded as a masterpiece, and for this one finds a variety of grounds.

Genovese's book represents a prodigious effort to see slavery whole. "No aspect of the lives of the slaves escapes his scrutiny," as one reviewer has written; "nothing his lively intellect touches remains obscure." Great learning has been combined with meticulous research in the widest range of sources, and unlike any other recent writer, Genovese has an inclusive theory which tries to account in a humane way for both the planter's side and the slave's side of the system. For him the key concept is "paternalism." With this he reaffirms, as in his previous work, the power of the master class—but with a difference. The ethos of paternalism was accepted, each in its own way, by both sides. For the master, it was the moral sanction for the exploitation and ownership of other men's labor, as well as for defining them as socially inferior, in return for his assuming their care and protection. But for the slave it meant a recognition of his humanity and a set of strong claims upon the master, claims he was able to manipulate for the preservation of his own dignity. The slave accepted paternalism, but reluctantly and not without extracting terms. Though we may think what we please of the theory, the work as a whole is massively documented, and we can examine the evidence for ourselves.

Genovese takes up a variety of problems, often in a challenging and original way. There was, for instance, the difficult position of the black driver, which required a constant balancing of diametrically opposed interests. Or the role of the "mammy," one of great authority and even more complex, which he treats with a fine subtlety. As for resistance, there is careful discrimination between individual acts (sabotage, thievery, petty insubordination, and so on, which did not imply non-acceptance of the system itself) and concerted measures of rebellion, which were admittedly few. The consciousness of the slave community, Genovese believes, must be regarded as generally "pre-political," even though he also thinks the idea of a "black nation" was already present. And finally, the very fullest attention is given to slave culture. There are appreciative discussions of speech patterns, folk-tales, conjuring, music, craftsmanship, and cooking. Many of Herbert Gutman's conclusions about slave family life, courtship, and sex mores have been anticipated—though of course in less depth—by Genovese. But that aspect of slave culture which receives the most extended and novel treatment is religion. Slave religion had neither a messianic tradition nor a concept of original sin, but its "life-affirming" quality served as "a weapon for personal and community survival." Christianity, as the slaves redefined it,

lacked that terrible inner tension between the sense of guilt and the sense of mission which once provided the ideological dynamism for Western civilization's march to world power. But in return for this loss of revolutionary dynamism, the slaves developed an Afro-American and Christian humanism that affirmed joy in life in the face of every trial.

Roll, Jordan, Roll, with its magisterial proportions, may well come to occupy the authoritative position once held by Ulrich Phillips' *American Negro Slavery* and later by Kenneth Stampp's *The Peculiar Institution.* Nonetheless, virtually everyone commenting upon the book has had some fault to find with it.

It has been objected, for instance, that Genovese does not know as much about the South as he ought to, that black religion was never really very different from lower-class white fundamentalism, and that if Genovese had had to eat more of that greasy cooking himself he would not have rhapsodized so much about it. But more serious and puzzling difficulties have been raised by his solemn claims for the makings of black nationalism under slavery, and—in view of Genovese's own earlier writings—by his having gone overboard for black culture. David Donald finds this explainable only "as a consequence of the immense pressure, both direct and indirect, exerted these days upon white scholars who write about Afro-American history," and suggests that the language of *Roll, Jordan, Roll* was so fashioned "as to appease the most ardent black militant." Blacks, on the other hand, have not been "appeased" at all. They appear to have little use for Genovese's central concept, paternalism, and judging from the doings at the recent conference of black scholars at Queens College, this has put them off from everything else in the book. At best it seems that Genovese has written a book that nearly everyone can praise, but mostly for somebody else's purposes. It should be of great interest, according to one black reviewer, to those who "sit and theorize about somebody else's oppression and humanity."[19]

But the most provocative of all the critiques has been that of the West Indian–born sociologist Orlando Patterson. Conceding the work to be "brilliant" and "indispensable," Patterson nonetheless sees it as an "analytically disappointing study." He thinks Genovese has abandoned much of his early Marxism, keeping its memory alive only through a few "redundant" quotations from the Italian theoretician Antonio Gramsci. (Donald found the Gramsci references similarly "pretentious.") Unlike American blacks, Patterson agrees with Genovese that antebellum paternalism as "a mechanism of social control . . . succeeded astonishingly well in welding together all the elements of the system, especially masters and slaves." But he will have none of Genovese's insistence that the accommodation made by the slaves was one that preserved their dignity, and he too sees no basis in slave culture for the talk of black nationalism. Despite the expressive component of that culture, it was "singularly lacking in range, flexibility, and dynamic adaptability," and represented "a total adjustment to the demands of plantation life." The slaves who pass through Genovese's pages Patterson finds, "as a class, morally degraded and utterly wanting in their capacity to resist, even when the system was crumbling around them." In other words Patterson, rather like a young Israeli tank sergeant of a decade ago commenting on the Holocaust, is demanding to know why they capitulated, why they were not more heroic.[20]

[19] David Herbert Donald, "Writing about Slavery," *Commentary*, LIX (January, 1975), 86–90; New York *Times*, April 13, 1975 (on the Queens College conference); Sterling Plumpp in *Black Books Bulletin*, III (Spring, 1975), 58–60.

[20] *New Republic*, CLXXI (November 9, 1974), 37–38. Other criticism which contributes to the "flawed masterpiece" pattern I have described above includes David Brion Davis, *New York Times Book Review*, Septem-

What does one make of all this? For one thing, I believe the abused Gramsci is more central to Genovese's overall scheme than he is generally given credit for being. Gramsci's thought provides Genovese with a way of bringing the slave fully into the equation without repudiating his earlier convictions either about the planter class's hegemony over Southern society at large or about the master's patriarchal role vis-à-vis his black dependents. Genovese theoretically had two choices as he prepared to write this book. He might have emphasized the deadening effects of paternalism on the slave population, which Patterson thinks he should have done. He chose instead, like a number of others, to put his emphasis on the positive aspects of slave life and culture. Moreover, Gramsci's thesis on the "man of the masses" whose struggle to transform the future is also a struggle for understanding between two opposing modes of consciousness within himself—one urging him forward, the other binding him to the past and inducing political passivity—allows Genovese both to keep his paternalism and to postulate a "pre-political" slave community that retains its moral integrity. Gramsci the gradualist insists on seeing things over the very long run, and will have no wasteful revolutionary posturing before the mass consciousness—morally, intellectually, politically—is good and ready for it. Under the Gramscian rubric even a "black nation" may be projected, however little the contemporary evidence might seem to warrant it.

But does it all make for a real balance? Has Genovese achieved a convincing synthesis of masters' and slaves' world-views—do the two sides of the model have a true organic relation, can they really be made to fit? I fear that Gramsci is, after all, just a bit too good to be true. Gramscian theory, not needed at all in Genovese's *Political Economy of Slavery*, functions here principally to justify

ber 29, 1974; Bertram Wyatt-Brown, *Journal of Southern History*, XLI (May, 1975), 240–42; George M. Fredrickson, *Journal of American History*, LXII (June, 1975), 130–33; C. Vann Woodward, *New York Review of Books*, October 3, 1974; F. N. Boney, *Georgia Review*, XXIX (Summer, 1975), 501–506; Grady McWhiney, *Book World*, April 6, 1975, pp. 1, 4 ("Southern Fried History"); Herbert Mitgang, New York *Times*, January 25, 1975; Joseph E. Illick, *New Leader*, LVIII (March 17, 1975), 18–21; Jack Chatfield, *National Review*, XXVII (February 14, 1975), 170–73; and Daniel Calhoun, *Agricultural History*, XLIX (April, 1975), 448–54.

the integrity of slave culture. But whereas it may apply admirably to the depressed classes of post-1918 southern Italy, it makes little allowance for immediate damage in a setting where some men not only exploit other men but deprive them of liberty itself, and keep them so deprived by force.

For Genovese, the workings of the American slave system somehow avoid corrupting either side. There is little room in his paternalism for *contempt*—self-contempt, or contempt for the other—as any built-in aspect of the total equation. He continues to deny, for example, that the planters as a class were afflicted with guilt, that there was ever a real failure of self-assurance, or that a hateful corrosive racism was ever a primary element of their mentality. They may have been genuinely shocked at the slaves' "ingratitude" in wartime, but that need hardly be inconsistent with either chronic self-deception or a basic sense of insecurity, or with guilt. Nor is there much room for self-contempt on the slave's part either, be it over his color or over his own powerlessness. Genovese claims, with no proof at all, that color envy was a product not of slavery but of post-emancipation times; and of the "slavish personality" he once made so much of, there remains scarcely a trace. Thus there is a strong sense here of having it both ways: paternalism, for all the qualifications and disclaimers, comes out on both sides as essentially positive in character. Few other aspects of it are allowed to show anywhere in *Roll, Jordan, Roll*.

A final problem concerns resistance. It is the question of just how much Genovese has done—any more than Mullin or Wood—either to advance a theory of rebellion or to predict one.[21] On the one hand, I think Orlando Patterson's demands for a heroic tradition—or rather his implication that the lack of one is a sign of moral failure—are inhumane and unreasonable. But on the other, Genovese's long-view Gramscian conjurations take less than serious account of immediate circumstances: the immense coercive powers at the master's command, the savage vengeance wreaked for the few insurrectionary gestures that were made, or the fact that those who did make such attempts were men who had escaped the full dead weight of plantation paternalism. Genovese is to be taxed not for a failure to recognize these factors (he does in his way recognize them), nor even for extenuating the thinness

[21] He says he plans to go into this in a subsequent book.

of the slaves' revolutionary tradition (which he does at some length), but simply for his supposing that such a "tradition" (long-term or short-term) was even thinkable.

Indeed, viewing the slaves' own culture with greater discrimination, and being less seduced by the idea of a "black nation," might have disclosed how essentially conservative it was. ("Pre-political" is surely the understatement of the century.) It might have shown some of that culture's most positive mechanisms—religion probably, the family almost certainly—functioning in a profoundly moderating way. One does not need to multiply entities—say, with pre-political contradictory consciousnesses—to see, for example, that men with families close at hand are those least likely to go on revolutionary rampages, especially under a standing threat of sale and separation. As for Patterson's wondering why there were no revolts even when the system was crumbling, for thousands there was no reason why they should want to revolt. They could simply pick up and leave. And the potential leadership, if any, for such revolts would have been the first to go. In short, every major force in the system—positive *and* negative—worked to discourage rebellion, and assumptions to the contrary by any modern writer will make heavy—even cruel—demands on the evidence.

6

For the slavery audience, the sensation of the 1974 publishing season was, of course, *Time on the Cross: The Economics of American Negro Slavery,* by Robert W. Fogel and Stanley L. Engerman. There has since been some speculation as to why such an extraordinary amount of attention was bestowed upon the authors' novel message of a thriving dynamic institution from which everyone benefited. Pure incredulity may well have been the main explanation for it. But in any case the glow did not last very long. Few books on slavery or any other historical subject have made more sweeping claims. Few have shot so high and fallen so far, so fast.

The message *was* sensational, supported as it seemed to be by the full resources of "cliometrics" or quantitative history—computers, statistical formulas, an army of research assistants, and a third of a million dollars in foundation money—all being brought to bear on the subject for the first time. Southern slave agriculture,

Fogel and Engerman announced, was "35 percent more efficient than the northern system of family farming," and the typical slave field hand was by and large "harder working and more efficient than his white counterpart." Most slaveowners encouraged stable families, seldom sold slaves, provided food and housing as good as what was available to the average Northern white worker, and probably better. Whippings were not as frequent as zealots have claimed; slaves tended not to be sexually promiscuous—like the whites, they were "Victorian" and even "prudish," the women especially; at least 25 per cent of the male slaves occupied "managerial" positions or were skilled workers; and the average slave in effect retained about 90 per cent of the earnings of his labor.

The masters thus emerge not as cruel exploiters but as shrewd entrepreneurs who used a variety of incentives to fashion a crack labor force, achievement-oriented, with a snug family life and a set of positive attitudes—a sort of "Protestant ethic"—toward work. It is a grievous libel, Fogel and Engerman sternly explained, to picture the blacks as having been so victimized and repressed by slavery that they could do nothing constructive with their lives. The authors' desire was "to strike down the view that black Americans were without culture, without achievement, and without development for their first two hundred and fifty years on American soil."

Fogel was not at all unwilling to talk about his and Engerman's work. (It will be more convenient henceforth to refer mainly to Fogel, since he has given more than the usual indications of his role as senior author, having made the key tactical decisions, given all the interviews, and posed for all the pictures.) He and his coadjutor had not at first dreamed of writing such a book, or suspected such results. But his duty as a disinterested scientist required him to follow the evidence wherever it led, come what might.

The scene opens in 1967. The two, as Fogel tells it, had just completed a modest little paper about what the cliometricians (themselves included) had contributed and might further contribute to such marginal questions as growth of per-capita income in the antebellum South and the profitability of investment in slaves. They had not presumed to encroach upon the concerns of such "mainstream historians" as Stampp, Elkins, and Genovese by involving themselves in issues like the black family or the psychological impact of slavery upon the slaves. This was because they "did not want to mire quantitative work in the marshlands of ideological dispute."[22] But the following year—still content to pursue their self-effacing researches unmired in ideology or other qualitative encumbrances—they ran an experiment on agricultural efficiency. It took them aback: "southern agriculture was 9 per cent more efficient than free northern agriculture—an absurd result."

Something was wrong. They must adjust their procedures, "recalibrate their inputs," and try again. "To our surprise, the adjustments went in the wrong direction: the relative advantage of slave agriculture *rose* from 9 to 39 per cent." Now they were really jolted. How could slavery, "deeply immoral and politically backward," produce such an outcome? "How could a system so impoverished in labor skills be efficient?" That would mean Stampp, Elkins, and Genovese would all have to be mistaken. The result "did not sit well with us." "Our instincts continued to resist the implications of our findings." But after much struggle with their resisting instincts, they simply had to recognize that "the time was at hand for a fundamental reinterpretation of the nature of the slave economy."

Farewell to the quiet life. They would wind up the other study they were doing (on the American iron industry), put safe and harmless things behind them, and square away. One startling discovery led to another, and this created a new crisis. By early 1971 it was obvious that their emerging reinterpretation was becoming so fundamental that they could no longer think of confining it to a scholarly monograph. It must be given to the general public, and it could not wait for the completion of all phases of their exhaustive research. To be sure, there were professional risks in undertaking a popular work. But what might happen if they left the interpretation of their discoveries to others? Though the work was technically sound, it might be "twisted into an

[22] R. W. Fogel, "From the Marxists to the Mormons," *Times Literary Supplement,* June 13, 1975. The date is misleading; the article was written roughly a year before, and the expansive mood reflects the period immediately following the book's publication. See also the interview by François Furet and Emmanuel LeRoy Ladurie, "A qui profitait l'esclavage?" in *Le Nouvel Observateur,* September 9, 1974, pp. 72–80. Fogel's sayings read particularly well in French.

apologia for slavery rather than used to demolish the myth of black incompentence." No, said Fogel; whatever the consequences, this must not happen. And besides: "How often are scholars presented with an opportunity to cut a gordian knot as massive, as urgent, and as deeply intertwined in the moral trauma of a nation as the racial issues that have tormented America for most of its history?" How often, indeed? They had no choice; they must grasp the opportunity. They must press on.

They did, and *Time on the Cross* duly made its appearance in the spring of 1974 amid a blaze of publicity arranged by Little, Brown ("with Professor Fogel's acquiescence," according to the New York *Times*).[23] For several months all seemed to go splendidly. The book was written up in all the leading periodicals, and it stirred up no end of excitement. Fogel himself attracted much interest in his transatlantic comings and goings that summer. Special sessions on the book were scheduled for historical meetings in the forthcoming season.

And yet by fall, the horizon was already beginning to darken. The thunderclouds were very noticeable by late October. By the end of the year, the deluge.

The blacks, from the beginning, never appreciated the special Fogel-Engerman version of their ancestors' "achievement," implying as it did a willing acceptance of slavery and the entire system of white values. "What's the use of discussing all the alleged benefits," demanded Kenneth Clark. "Would the authors recommend a return to slavery?" After this benign account of slavery, according to a reviewer in *Phylon*, whites would be able to claim that "the best explanation for the [subsequent] failure of blacks to 'progress' in American society is not . . . racism and its consequences, but their own ineptitude." "Fogel and Engerman," jeered Brenda Jones in *Freedomways*, "would cut the last rope restraining the racist hordes: *Come out, come out, wherever you are! You have no reason to denounce your slaveholding ancestors—they did nothing wrong. You have spent too much time on the cross!*"[24]

Meanwhile, scholars everywhere were beginning to sniff with

[23] New York *Times*, May 2, 1974.

[24] Kenneth Clark on "Today" show, April 30, 1974; Milfred C. Fierce in *Phylon*, XXXVI (March, 1975), 89–93; Brenda L. Jones in *Freedomways*, XV (1st Qtr., 1975), 26–33.

suspicion. There were no clear lines among them; it was not a matter of resistance to cliometrics, or of "conservatives" versus "radicals," or of "humanists" against quantifiers. If anything, the vanguard was led by Fogel's fellow-cliometricians challenging him on his own grounds. But perhaps the most accurate picture would be that of historians and economists of all persuasions descending on Fogel at once. By the time they were through, they had rendered doubtful the procedures by which every one of the book's major assertions had been reached. A few examples may suggest the extent of the wreckage.

For the superior "efficiency" of Southern agriculture, the index the authors used was based not on volume of cotton per slave hand but on prices received for the product, which meant it could measure little more than profitability, a very different thing from efficiency. It gave no warrant for qualitative conclusions about "diligent and efficient workers," "imbued like their masters with a Protestant ethic"; the worldwide demand for cotton, and returns on investment under near-monopoly conditions, were such that southern cotton growth could have looked "efficient" even with slovenly work habits, a refractory labor force, and an irrational mode of production. Then there was Fogel's claim that "the houses of slaves compared well with the housing of free workers." A check on his and Engerman's own sources for the typical size of slave cabins revealed they had exaggerated it by about 50 per cent, while the "comparison" was with tenements of the poor in the most wretched slums of New York, Chicago, and Baltimore at the depth of the 1893 depression—and at that, they had only counted the bedrooms. As for the slaves' sexual habits, "not promiscuous but prudish," all that this rested upon was an inference from the probate records that the average age of slave mothers at the birth of a first child was 22.5. But this was not what the records showed at all. They showed date of birth of the first *surviving* child; in a period of high infant mortality and separation of mothers from children, the true age would have been closer to 18. Perhaps the most remarkable assertion of all was that 70 percent of all overseers were slaves. (This was part of the authors' general contention that 25 per cent of the slaves were either "managers" or skilled artisans.) Though they could not give a single real-life example, they reasoned that if a white overseer was not listed in the census for a given plantation, there must still have been an overseer, and he must have been black. They seem not to have known that a resident overseer was not listed in the returns at all unless he lived in the master's house (an irregular arrangement), or that innumerable plantations were managed by the owner himself or one of his sons, or that thousands of whites who gave their occupation as "overseer" would according to the Fogel-Engerman logic have been unemployed. The fact was that a slave overseer in the antebellum South was almost as rare as a black slaveowner.[25]

There were any number of lesser items as well. The only source for the authors' contention about infrequent punishments was the published diary of the Louisiana planter Bennet Barrow, and from it they calculated that the average was "0.7 whippings per hand per year." But they inflated the numbers of slaves on the plantation, which brought down the average; other information in the diary on frequency of whipping was not counted, which brought it down still more; Barrow was in fact a brutal master, and some of his punishments were monstrous. None of this was mentioned. Even by their own figures, somebody was whipped every four and a half days on the Barrow plantation, which undoubtedly served as a strong incentive to hard work, a Protestant ethic, and so forth. Another misrepresentation was in the number of slaves sold, "only" 1.92 per cent of them each year. The same figures meant that any slave over a 35-year lifetime had a 50-50 chance of being sold himself and witnessing the sale of at least 11

[25] The body of criticism is already prodigious, and I have drawn only upon its highlights for these paragraphs. The principal items are Thomas L. Haskell, "Were Slaves More Efficient? Some Doubts About 'Time on the Cross,'" *New York Review of Books,* September 19, 1974, and "The True & Tragical History of 'Time on the Cross,'" *ibid.,* October 2, 1975 (Haskell was the first to throw doubts on the "efficiency" thesis); Herbert G. Gutman, *Slavery and the Numbers Game: A Critique of 'Time on the Cross'* (Urbana: University of Illinois Press, 1975), especially on punishments, sales, the family, etc.; Gary M. Walton, ed., "A Symposium on Time on the Cross," *Explorations in Economic History,* XII (October, 1975), especially the paper by Richard Sutch, who discovered the fallacy on housing; Eric Foner, "Redefining the Past," *Labor History,* XVI (Winter 1975), 127–138, which makes the striking point about the extent to which Fogel and Engerman have relied on non-quantitative sources; and Paul David and Peter Temin, "Slavery: The Progressive Institution?" *Journal of Economic History,* XXXIV (September, 1974), 739–83, and "Capitalist Masters, Bourgeois Slaves," *Journal of Interdisciplinary History,* V (Winter, 1975), 445–57.

members of his immediate family. Or the claim that "more than 84% of all sales over the age of fourteen involved unmarried individuals." They got this by taking a limited sample from the New Orleans slave market, assuming that all women not sold with children were unmarried, then assuming that the traders "strongly preferred unmarried women," then further assuming that such a "preference" carried over to men. And finally, a surprisingly large proportion of the "evidence" was not quantitative at all but came from traditional narrative sources. These too were garbled, otherwise they could not have yielded such strange assertions as that abolitionists and proslavery apologists were equally "racist," or that Southern planters on the eve of the Civil War were "optimistic" about the future of slavery, or that the planter class after emancipation "no longer existed."

How could it all have happened? It is certainly a fascinating phenomenon in the psychology of desire—in seeing most sharply those aspects of "the truth" that one most wants to see, and managing somehow to overlook the rest. Many have mused over this, and wondered how Fogel could have so hypnotized himself, or not have anticipated the consequences. However that may be, there are at least two elements of the case that seem worth noting. The primary thing seems to have been a total commitment to the "efficiency" thesis: this *had* to be correct, no matter what objections other econometricians might make, and Fogel as much as said so after three days of bombardment at Rochester.[26] Why? Because the superior efficiency of antebellum plantation agriculture had been his and Engerman's great discovery: this was the magic formula that promised to transform an essentially peripheral question—that of profitability—into one involving the entire character of slavery itself. It was from this that all the rest followed, and this was what made the other difficulty.

Fogel, it seems, was at some point seized with an imperial vision. The "culture" argument had come to dominate the discourse by the time his book was being planned; the impulse to absorb it into a grand synthesis which would in effect preempt the entire field was irresistible. He would simply reshape the argument in

[26] I am referring here to the conference of scholars convened at Rochester, October 24–26, 1974, for the sole purpose of discussing *Time on the Cross*. See Haskell, "True & Tragical History."

accordance with his primary claim, even though he presented no evidence whatever as to what this "culture" amounted to—values, beliefs, lore, or anything else. He would somehow redefine culture as a kind of occupational "achievement," no matter how grotesque the result might look. As for his predecessors, he would lump them all together into one indiscriminate category—"traditional historians"—and dismiss their work as having been mostly built on "racist" premises. He was determined, it appears, to have the argument all to himself.

So the convergence of everyone—scholars of every type—upon *Time on the Cross* was, after all, logical enough. They moved as they did not only because their own findings and procedures were threatened with disrepute (those of other cliometricians most of all), but also because they thought they saw the whole grand subject being brought into ridicule. The episode may nevertheless have had some salutary by-products. It may have brought us to a fruitful turning-point, and furnished a precipitant of sorts for rethinking the entire argument over American black slavery.

7

Ralph Ellison, judging from what others have published over the past few years, has clearly carried his point on black culture. But it seems equally clear that the culture argument is itself at something of a crossroads. Much of what Ellison once called for still eludes those pursuing it, especially that aspect which concerns blacks under slavery. Slavery is not the most typical context in which one explores such an entity as culture; the initial search for "resistance" may have propelled us farther into that area than we bargained for. The pursuit of culture is important but, as we have already seen, it is full of logical traps.

Any group that has been dispossessed of liberty by another group and subjected to daily assaults on its dignity, on the personalities of its members, and on their very physical being, is by the primal laws of life going to do something to protect itself. It brings to bear whatever individual and communal resources it has in order to make its condition tolerable; it develops patterns of response; it fashions a body of lore and a picture of itself that makes its own existence in some way comprehensible, predictable, and bearable.

The product—as with any other people seeking collectively to make sense out of the world—is "culture."

But it does not follow that simply in locating culture we have automatically found something ipso facto positive, in and of itself. No theory of culture I know of claims that much, though the point is by no means clear in much of the recent discussion of American black slavery. Culture, under such conditions as those of slavery, is not acquired without a price; the social and individual experience of any group with so little power, and enduring such insistent assaults (of cruelty, contempt, and, not least, uncertainty), is bound to contain more than the normal residue of pathology. Any theory that is worth anything must allow for this. It must allow, that is, for damage.

So there are two distinct arguments, equally worth pursuing, one on damage, the other on resistance and culture. This ought to have been obvious all along. But it has never been entirely obvious, either in the 1950's and early 60's when damage was the dominant concern, or later when the culture argument came to eclipse the one on damage. This state of things will surely no longer do. Each argument is in fact relatively undeveloped; there is much to be done on both.

One way to proceed would be simply to acknowledge this distinctness, and to pursue the two lines separately. It may be the same street, but the traffic goes in opposite directions, and in the present case it would seem exceedingly difficult for anyone to work both sides at once. Just to recognize this would in itself be an advance of sorts, though in practice it would go further than that. Though a useful discussion of culture need not devote inordinate attention to damage, it must still leave *spaces* in its theoretical structure—not mere verbal concessions and "exceptions," but a formal allowance— for damage and its workings, and the same would hold in reverse for those on the other side of the street.

And yet in the last analysis the two arguments on slavery cannot really be separate, and when ideological tensions eventually loosen, the two must and will meet. But how will we know when the time is at hand? We will know this when, for one thing, it can be shown without inhibitions just how the "mainstream" and "ethnic" cultures did interact, bearing in mind where the power lay, and exactly how it was exerted and responded to. And for another, we will know it when we are able to make discriminations *within* culture, and to see some cultural responses as more positive and creative than others.[27]

Then there is a final point, when it is a question of exploring the depth and variety of American black culture. Too much of the culture argument has been confined so far—artificially, it seems to me—to the era of slavery. Only by breaking out of such confinement, and carrying the argument forward, will we find it possible to test the development of culture over time and under varying conditions. Only thus, moreover, can we re-test a proposition which until recently nobody thought needed demonstrating. It is the conviction that freedom is better, after all, than slavery—however much "freedom" may have been hedged about in the century after emancipation—for the growth of culture, or of anything else that humankind most values.

[27] One of a number of possible examples of such discrimination comes to mind. It is now some time since I made my own initial statement on this subject. I have been told by well-wishers and critics alike that I really ought to have done something with Erik Erikson and his work on ego-psychology. This is a very sound point, and if I were writing *Slavery* over again I probably would. My argument on personality, thus enriched and modified, might then go somewhat as follows. The natural tendency of human beings anywhere, according to Erikson, is to move toward adulthood tentatively, even reluctantly. One of the normal functions of culture (through rites of passage and so on) is to encourage the process, to quicken and even to force it. Some cultural contexts are more efficient in doing this than others; some, conceivably, might even hold the process back. The cultural setting of the antebellum slave plantation might well be examined with this problem in mind.

Appendix

Essay on Materials and Method

There are certain aspects of procedure in the present work which I hope have fulfilled most of the functions normally performed by either a listed bibliography or a bibliographical essay. I have included a great deal of bibliographical as well as other kinds of commentary in the footnotes. Part I, moreover, is itself an essay on the literature of slavery.

I have decided that in place of a formal bibliography another sort of addendum would be somewhat more useful. I have had the benefit of an unusual amount of exceedingly helpful critical comment from the variety of audiences and readers upon whom the book, in various stages of its completion, has been "tried out." Particularly outstanding in this connection was the Ninth Newberry Library Conference on American Studies held in Chicago on May 3, 1958, under the chairmanship of Stanley Pargellis (see "The Question of Sambo," *Newberry Library Bulletin,* V [December, 1958], 14–40). When such criticism was of a substantive kind, immediately manageable, I promptly incorporated it into the main body of the text, and in some cases this resulted in extensive revisions and additions. But the bulk of it was concerned with matters of strategy and method, and the very fundamental nature of such criticism faced me with a special problem. No amount of qualification and hedging in the text would have done more than palliate the difficulties which it raised; for that matter, I finally realized that there comes a point beyond which such qualification becomes merely tedious. I still felt, however, that there were aspects of this critical commentary which might well be of interest to the general reader. These Appendixes, therefore, consisting of notes organized around the principal points raised by such commentary, is my solution to that dilemma.

1. *Scope of the work.*—Many of the reservations which were expressed to me (such as those on my neglect of certain kinds of source material, or my reluctance to discuss regional variations in the plantation system) were based, I believe, on the supposition that the work

was designed as a "history" of slavery. It does not pretend to be a history, in either the extended or limited sense. Other scholars have produced historical studies far more thorough in compass than anything I could hope to do. The present study is more properly a "proposal." It proposes that certain kinds of questions be asked in future studies of the subject that have not been asked in previous ones. This must necessarily be a highly selective business, since, on the one hand, there are a good many questions whose thoroughness of treatment in the past renders them less urgent now; on the other hand, my own study has been limited, perhaps seriously, by those questions which have seemed particularly pressing to me. I do feel, as is probably obvious, that in the very effort which goes into the formulation of any question one is implicitly programming the sort of effort that would be required for a full and satisfactory answer to it. Yet I also recognize that even with my own questions I have done no more than sketch in a beginning.

2. *The question of what constitutes "evidence."*—To agree, as most scholars apparently do in theory, that the legitimacy of any form of "evidence" depends very much on the sort of thing one wants to demonstrate with it, is deceptively easy. But on this same general point my own experience leads me to think that, when it comes to practice, a working consensus is very hard to come by. For instance, my decision here not to consult manuscript sources has raised questions which apparently assume that this sort of evidence is indispensable for *all* work having a historical dimension. Yet the truism that each subject has its special requirements is relevant to no subject more than to that of American Negro slavery. The available manuscript materials, the great bulk of which consists of plantation records, are useful principally on questions of health and maintenance, and they have already been worked over with great care and thoroughness by eminent scholars. If historical scholarship is to be at all cumulative, I should think that, within limits, a willingness to accept and use the work of one's predecessors would be indispensable. But in any case health and maintenance were not among the questions to which I felt I could make any original contribution. As for the special problem of "profitability," it appears that the very failure to agree on which kinds of evidence were pertinent, of those that did exist, has until quite recently blocked any satisfactory solution. The state of thinking on that particular question is the subject of Appendix B below.

Another problem in this line has to do with the use of laws as evidence for generalizing about the state of American slavery. The difficulty involves the wide gulf which is known to have existed between theory and practice in the administration of the ante-bellum slave codes. Ulrich Phillips, on the assumption that the codes did not accurately reflect daily practice, paid very little attention to them. But I do not think it wise to continue Phillips' procedure in this respect. Since his time, a very substantial compilation of court cases has been made by Helen Catterall, which enables one to use each kind of material—jurisprudence and laws—as a check on the other. Several things may be said here. With or without the jurisprudence, codes of law can be extremely useful in telling us what a society has *thought* about a subject over time, especially when in this case there is a pattern of consistency extending over two hundred years. As for daily practice, we may be certain that a fairly dependable relationship is discernible between laws and court cases. How the principle of presumption operated (the law presumes thus and so, other things being equal) in any given area becomes quite clear in examining the court cases. And finally, in answering any number of questions about recourse, we need only know what was, and what was not, in the lawbooks. Aside from the many privileges which the Negro slave may have enjoyed in practice, what rights were specifically guaranteed him by the law and what sort of protection might he look for in the courts?

3. *Analogy as evidence.*—My use of the German concentration camp as an analogy to illuminate certain aspects of Negro slavery encountered more comment than did anything else in the book. That portion of the comment which was hostile took fairly direct form; I was simply told that the analogy, being both repellent and misleading, did not fit. But although the approval probably overbalanced the disapproval, even the friendly reader sometimes tended to take the analogy too literally. I suspect that one major cause of such difficulties lay not necessarily in *this* analogy but rather in the fact that the technique itself is not a very familiar one for formal use. Any analogy, it seems to me, is a kind of extended metaphor. It brings together two situations, each of which—however dissimilar they may be otherwise—contains mechanisms that are metaphorically comparable and analytically interchangeable. In the analogy which I used, the mechanism was the infantilizing tendencies of absolute power.

One way of characterizing the principle of metaphor would be to say that a process enacted in one area might be more perfectly understood when an analogous one is enacted in another area and when the two are momentarily brought together in the same field of vision. Certain things then flash; the process of recognition, if it occurs, can be almost chemical. Abraham Lincoln, for instance, would depict the military problems of the Civil War in terms of skinning a mule, and then order those who were not skinning to hold the legs. He appears to have been generally understood. Metaphor is a mode of communication and demonstration which cannot occur on a literal plane, but it can be both effective and legitimate.

Metaphor and analogy do have, however, a serious point of vulnerability. Their very vividness and particularity are coercive: they are almost too concrete. One's impulse is thus to reach for extremes. The thing is either taken whole hog, as the Freudians tended to do with the Oedipus metaphor; or it is rejected out of hand on the ground that not all of the parts fit. This has happened on occasion with my concentration-camp analogy. Of slave system and concentration camp it may be, and has been, said that the basis of one was property, of the other, terror; that one was purposeful, the other purposeless. Morally the two existed on entirely different planes. The slaveholder boasted of "responsibility"; the SS took pride in brutality. Consequently, it might appear that the analogy, "collapsing" at all such points, was worthless.

Most of this criticism seems based, as I have said, on an unwillingness to let analogy be used for limited and controlled purposes, even when the purposes are made explicit and the limits defined with great care, as I have tried to do in Part III of this book. The basic variables were captivity, absolute power and their effects on personality. I was not comparing intentions, motives, or style; even "cruelty" was not indispensable as an item in my equation. There could be a tremendous amount of variation between these two situations without undermining the analogy for my purposes.

4. *Comparative studies.*—Comparison is a technique related to analogy; the two might even occasionally overlap, but they are not exactly the same. Comparison, like analogy, remains relatively unexploited. Comparative analysis, however, seems most useful in pointing up the contrasts between the things compared rather than—as is the case with analogy—the similarities. It is essentially a highlighting device. Without the contrasts, there could be items in the one setting unduly taken for granted and thus lost sight of; whereas if those same items turned out to be missing from the other setting, one's whole view of their significance might be very sharply refocused. Such considerations underlay the comparison of the North American and Latin American slave systems undertaken in Part II.

The principal objection to this strategy was that it blurred the differences *within* the two systems and tended to lose the "unique" in any given area where slavery existed. Here I am inclined to invoke the "one-thing-at-a-time" principle and protest that all is not lost; should the "unique" be wanted once more, there are still ways of getting it back again. In general, I should think that one cannot really make this sort of objection without claiming that comparison as a technique is useless; there is no single conceptual strategy known to the life of reason that does not operate at the expense of some other. In sum, it is not necessary to deny internal variations in order to allow that for certain purposes it may be permissible to lump together slavery in all of North America on the one side, and slavery in all of Latin America on the other, and then make some meaningful generalizations about two very different slave systems. You might then, for other purposes, make all the internal discriminations you wish. Indeed, there is no reason why comparisons cannot be made on a much closer and finer basis than the one I have used. Herbert Klein, in a recently completed study of Cuba and Virginia in the seventeenth century, has made a superb one.

5. *The use of cross-disciplinary "gimmicks."*—Back of this is a much larger controversy, one which for the time being I should like to stay clear of. But more than once I have heard historians express concern—prompted by other studies besides my own—over possible indiscriminateness in the use of techniques from other social sciences in historical investigation. I myself share these misgivings, to the extent that one may be tempted, after running across such a technique, to go looking about for some problem in history to "use" it on. In practice, however, it seems to work the other way around. Temporarily baffled by some historical problem, one tends to reach out for any tool in sight with which to attack it. The more familiar ones may not always be adequate, though I think that more often than not they are. Still, if a less orthodox tool should happen to work, that in itself should do something to establish its legitimacy.

6. *Implications about "human nature."*—Part III, the section on personality, raises profound questions of human value. They appear in general to fall under three related categories.

a) On the face of it, this section may seem not to account sufficiently for variations in personality, either on the plantation or in the concentration camp. The strategy of presentation, however, was planned in full awareness of this liability. I have tried to indicate my convictions about the irreducible uniqueness of each human "self" and the infinite variations which exist between one human personality and another. Yet there are certain problems in social psychology which require that this "uniqueness" aspect be for the moment taken for granted and set to one side, so that under specified conditions one may deal with whatever patterns and continuities are observable in group behavior. Plantation slavery, I felt, presented just such a problem. If there were no purposes for which this strategy were permissible, then I see no extent to which social psychology can actually be "social." Nor need such an approach in any way infringe upon the legitimacy of individual psychology; to say that the two are parallel, not mutually exclusive, disciplines, is to belabor the obvious.

b) What, then, of the "reality" of Sambo? Did the Sambo role really become part of the slave's "true" personality? Here I shrink from generalizing dogmatically one way or the other. The main thing I would settle for would be the existence of a broad belt of indeterminacy between "mere acting" and the "true self." I do not share the assurance, expressed by some who have debated this question with me, that a sharp line can be drawn between these two areas. I feel rather that the ways in which they may grade into one another are many and subtle. To the extent that they do, to that extent does it seem permissible to speak of Sambo as a personality "type." I might add that if certain patterns of social behavior can in fact be "internalized," or graded into the self under certain conditions, it ought to follow that under other conditions they could be graded back out again. How soon is of course an open question.

We could, if we wished, propose a theory of personality in which the self is divided into two parts, a "true" part and a "false" part, and then say that the false part is mutable and adaptable, and the true part rigid and unchanging. But that would be rather cumbersome. It would be better to postulate a great deal of flexibility for the whole self, without necessarily having to pass on the question of just how much. A corollary, moreover, could be added. Given the stresses which produce these features of group behavior, might there not be conditions under which those stresses could be resisted? I have tried to give some attention in the text to this and similar possibilities.

To recapitulate: If any generalizing about group behavior can be done at all, and if connections may be made between such behavior and personality itself, then to such an extent is one warranted in considering group personality "types." This need hardly implicate the total realm of the individual's behavior and character. Those things are sufficiently complex as to leave a great deal of room for uniqueness and idiosyncrasy and still to leave a little room for patterned behavior and even for "stereotyped" personality traits. It is primarily a question of how a given social or even cultural setting can put premiums on some kinds of behavior and discourage others. It is on just such a basis, for instance, that anthropologists have even been able to say a few general things about national character.

c) How legitimate is it to speak of the "infantilization" of adults? This difficulty may actually be no more than one of semantics. The term "infantilization" need not be taken altogether literally. I was concerned with features of behavior characteristic of relatively powerless individuals under a species of authority which was all but total and from which, generally speaking, there was no appeal. Let us say that the largest representative groups in which such behavior may be observed consist of children. In special circumstances, however, it may also be seen in adults. It is thus to some extent simply metaphorical convenience that leads me to refer to such behavior as "childlike"

—convenience plus the fact that a good many observers, both of life on slave plantations and of life in the concentration camps, have referred to it in the same terms.

I have put less stress on the "father" role in that relationship, since my concern does not specifically extend to the behavior appropriate to such a role—behavior in which a good deal more variety and "individuality" is possible than in that of the child. Nor does it matter for my purposes how "consciously" the SS (for example) may have played such a role. More important was the point that for the prisoners (according to observers who were themselves prisoners) the SS did in fact assume some of the attributes of a father-figure, however cruel.

7. *The sequence of "shock and detachment."*—One of my greatest conceptual difficulties, commented on by a number of readers, was the problem of what relative significance should be assigned to this shock sequence in the process of infantilization. It seemed fairly clear and plausible in the case of the concentration-camp prisoner, but rather less so in that of the Negro slave. The difficulty might be stated as follows: (*a*) The shock of enslavement must have been experienced with equal acuteness by Negroes going to Latin America and by those going to North America; why then should a "Sambo" type emerge in the latter and not in the former? (*b*) How in any case is this infantilization to be accounted for in later generations of slaves who did not experience such a shock? (*c*) For that matter, how much do we really know about the incidence of "Sambo" in the first generation?

The answer to these questions is certainly not simple. I have tried in the text to anticipate it, but I am not sure how successfully. Its very involved quality seems to require a summarization here.

The "shock" itself did not necessarily "produce" anything in particular, except perhaps a certain effect of "detachment" from prior standards—a kind of *tabula rasa* upon which subsequent experience could write. Far more critical was the subsequent experience itself—that of meeting the requirements of a "closed system" of absolute authority. This, not the experience of shock in itself, would produce the results described. Indeed, a much smoother adjustment ought to be possible if an individual were born into such a system. That would be a real *tabula rasa,* alongside of which the "erasing" or "detaching" effect of shock might be viewed as relatively inefficient.

Why discuss the shock at all then? The problem is one of emphasis and balance. It does seem that the shock, when combined (though only when combined) with what followed, made an immense difference for adults at the point of introduction. It seems to have served both as a mechanism of detachment from the old life and as a violent push in the direction of a new adjustment. The concentration-camp writers make quite a point of this, reporting personality changes in the survivors within a remarkably short time after the shock. (As for the Latin American slave, the same shock might conceivably serve as preparation for adjustment to a very different kind of system from that of North America.)

We know very little about the first generations of slaves in North America (or, for that matter, in Latin America), but this shock sequence does give us some handle for making projections. It offers clues to what we might find if we did know more. The infantilization process may or may not have been as effective among the first generations of slaves as it was for the inmates of the concentration camps. But it certainly was effective over time. The shock sequence may be more pertinent for explaining one of these experiences than it is for the other, but of this I cannot be sure. At any rate, it was present in both, and the concentration-camp accounts put great stress on it. The losses of omitting it from the equation, therefore, seemed greater than did those of leaving it in.

8. *Making the analogy with material other than that of the German camps.*—On several occasions it has been suggested to me that material on the Russian "slave labor" camps might have been useful for my purposes. It was also thought that the techniques of "brainwashing" employed by the Chinese and Russians might also have been relevant. I did at one time consider supplementing my analogy with such material, until I discovered how very little of it is actually available. Even were it otherwise, however, I now believe that the digression which it would have required might have carried me even farther away from my primary subject than I did in fact get. I suspect that the overuse of such "extended metaphor" can easily run into diminishing returns; if the main point in this case had not been made with the relatively complete data on the Nazi camps, then no amount of additional material would have helped much to shore it up. The interested reader may still wish, however, to consult David J. Dallin and Boris L. Nicolaevsky, *Forced Labor in Soviet Russia* (New Haven: Yale University Press, 1947) on the Russian camps; on brainwashing, see Joost A. M. Meerloo, *The Rape of the Mind: The Physiology of Thought Control, Menticide, and Brainwashing* (Cleveland: World Publishing Co., 1956); William Sargant, *Battle for the Mind: A Physiology of Conversion and Brainwashing* (New York: Doubleday, 1957); and Alexander Weissberg, *The Accused,* translated by Edward Fitzgerald (New York: Simon & Schuster, 1951).

Acknowledgments

I have been unusually fortunate in the assistance, advice, and criticism which I have received in the writing of this book. A Rockefeller Foundation fellowship enabled me to devote a full year to the initial research. A grant from the Ford Foundation, and another from the Walgreen Foundation, provided the necessary funds for typing and clerical assistance. The manuscript has been read in whole or in part by Bruno Bettelheim, K. Onwuka Dike, Charles Frankel, Marvin Harris, Bert Kaplan, Dumas Malone, Marvin Meyers, Dwight Miner, John Phelan, George Rawick, David Riesman, Peter Rossi, Frank Tannenbaum, Lionel Trilling, and Hans Zetterberg. Their advice and suggestions made available to me a wonderful range of skill, wisdom, and information. Without this, I hesitate to think how much more difficult my task would have been. I am especially obliged to Richard Hofstadter and C. Vann Woodward, who gave most generously of their time and energy in detailed and searching criticism of the entire manuscript. I am deeply grateful to Eric McKitrick for his unstinted assistance at every stage of the book's evolution.

A further set of acknowledgments is due certain friends and colleagues who have been particularly helpful in reading and criticizing the newer portions that have been added to the original edition. They are Eric Foner, Herbert S. Klein, Allen Weinstein, and R. Jackson Wilson.

Index

Berlin, Ira, 278n

Bernhardt, Sarah, 123n

Bettelheim, Bruno, 106, 109, 111, 112, 129n, 135n

Birney, James G., 179, 180n, 182, 189n, 212, 263

Black culture, emphasis on, in recent writings on slavery, 269, 274, 277, 299–302

Blackmur, R. P., 143–44

Blassingame, John W., 278–79, 280

Bledsoe, Albert Taylor, 220

Boas, Franz, 19

Botts, John Minor, 188n

Bourne, George, 36

Brackett, Jeffrey R., 9

"Brain-washing," 128n, 310

Brazil: African cultural survivals in, 103; high rate of manumission in, 229–31, 233, 236; influence of Church in, 66, 67, 69, 72, 73, 79, 227, 228, 232–34, 240; law and enforcement in, 230–31; race relations in, 236–41; racial stereotypes in, 84n, 244 and n; slavery in, 227–36

Bremer, Frederika, 154n

Brer Rabbit, 249, 282–83

Brigham, Carl, 17

Brook Farm, 153

Brotherhoods, lay, in Brazil, 228, 232, 239

Brougham, Henry, 204

Brownson, Orestes, 148

Bryce-Laporte, Roy, 243, 246–51

Buckmaster, Henrietta, 17

Bunche, Ralph, 19

Burke, Edmund, 144–45, 203, 207n

Buxton, Thomas Fowell, 197, 203–4

Calhoun, John C., 206, 214, 215n, 242

Canning, George, 203

Cardoso, Fernando Henrique, 237n

Carlton, Frank Tracy, 166n

Carlyle, Thomas, 216–17

Castlereagh, Viscount, 203

Catterall, Helen T., 305

Channing, Edward, 8n

Channing, William Ellery, 149, 150, 152, 153n, 167, 171–73, 178–79, 186, 197

Channing, William Henry, 142, 149, 153, 155, 156, 168, 173

Charles V, orders freeing of slaves in Spanish America, 67

Child, Lydia Maria, 191

Christianity, conversion to, as factor in slave status, 50

Christie, W. D., 237n

Church: Anglican, in America, 28, 50–51; Congregational, 28, 186; lay brotherhoods in Brazil, 228, 234, 239; of England, and abolition movement, 204; Roman, influence of on slavery in Latin America, 68–79 *passim*, 227–28, 232–34, 239–40; Unitarian, 148, 149. *See also* Brazil

Churches (Baptist, Methodist, Presbyterian): attacked by abolitionists, 175–76, 259; split over slavery, 184 and n

Civil rights, of slaves. *See* Property and other civil rights

Civil rights movement, 253, 269–70, 274

Clark, Kenneth, 296

Clarke, James Freeman, 149, 168, 169, 170, 174

Clarkson, Thomas, 27n, 204

Clay, Henry, 178

Cobb, Thomas R. R., 3, 54, 57, 196n, 231n

Codman, John, 236

Cohen, Elie, 110, 111, 112, 113, 117

Colonization. *See* American Colonization Society

Common-law tradition, influence of on slave codes, 37, 42n

"Community," emphasis on, in recent literature on slavery, 280, 282

Comparison, as analytical device, 225–26, 229, 306–7

Concentration camp: adjustment to, 108–11; analogy criticized, 242,